the knit stitch pattern HANDBOOK

AN ESSENTIAL COLLECTION OF 300 DESIGNER STITCHES AND TECHNIQUES

melissa leapman

POTTER CRAFT
NEW YORK

to **Jocelyn** (100%)

Published in the United States by Potter Craft, an imprint of the Crown Publishing Group, a division of Random House, Inc., New York.

www.pottercraft.com
www.crownpublishing.com

POTTER CRAFT and colophon are registered trademarks of Random House, Inc.

Library of Congress Cataloging-in-Publication Data

Leapman, Melissa.

the knit stitch pattern handbook: an essential collection of 300 designer stitches and techniques / by Melissa Leapman.—First Edition.
pages cm
Includes bibliographical references and index.

ISBN 978-0-449-81990-6 (print edition : alk. paper)—
ISBN 978-0-449-81991-3 (ebook edition : alk. paper)

1. Knitting—Patterns. I. Title.

TT825.L38815 2013
746.43'2—dc23

2012049411

ISBN 978-0-449-81990-6
eISBN 978-0-449-81991-3

Printed in China

design by Karla Baker
photographs by Marcus Tullis
technical editor: Debbie Radtke
technical illustrations: Joni Coniglio
all charts and schematic illustrations: Melissa Leapman
cover design by Laura Palese
cover photographs by Marcus Tullis
author photograph by Heather Weston

10 9 8 7 6 5 4 3 2 1
First Edition

Acknowledgments

I owe much gratitude to the following knitters for making literally hundreds of sample swatches—and testing all the patterns!—for this book: Patty Asher, Mink Barrett, Lee Gant, Cindy Grosch, Susan Hope, Cheryl Keeley, Cheryl McCray, Joan Murphy, Jen Owens, Debbie Radtke, Catherine Schiesz, Heather Start, Lauren Voeltz, and Renae Woolsey.

Once again, thanks go to Jean, Shannon, Bob, Rob, Bob, and everyone at Cascade Yarn Company for sending me furniture-sized boxes of yarn for all the swatches. (Trust me, there is photo documentation!) Cascade 220 wool yarn offers great stitch definition, making it the perfect choice for this book. My heart-felt thanks to all of you for your generosity!

Thank you Debbie Radtke for tech editing this book. I cannot begin to imagine how you managed to wrangle all the loose ends of this ginormous project. With so many moving parts, I could not have done this without you! I will definitely miss you around the office now. Mahna Mahna. . . .

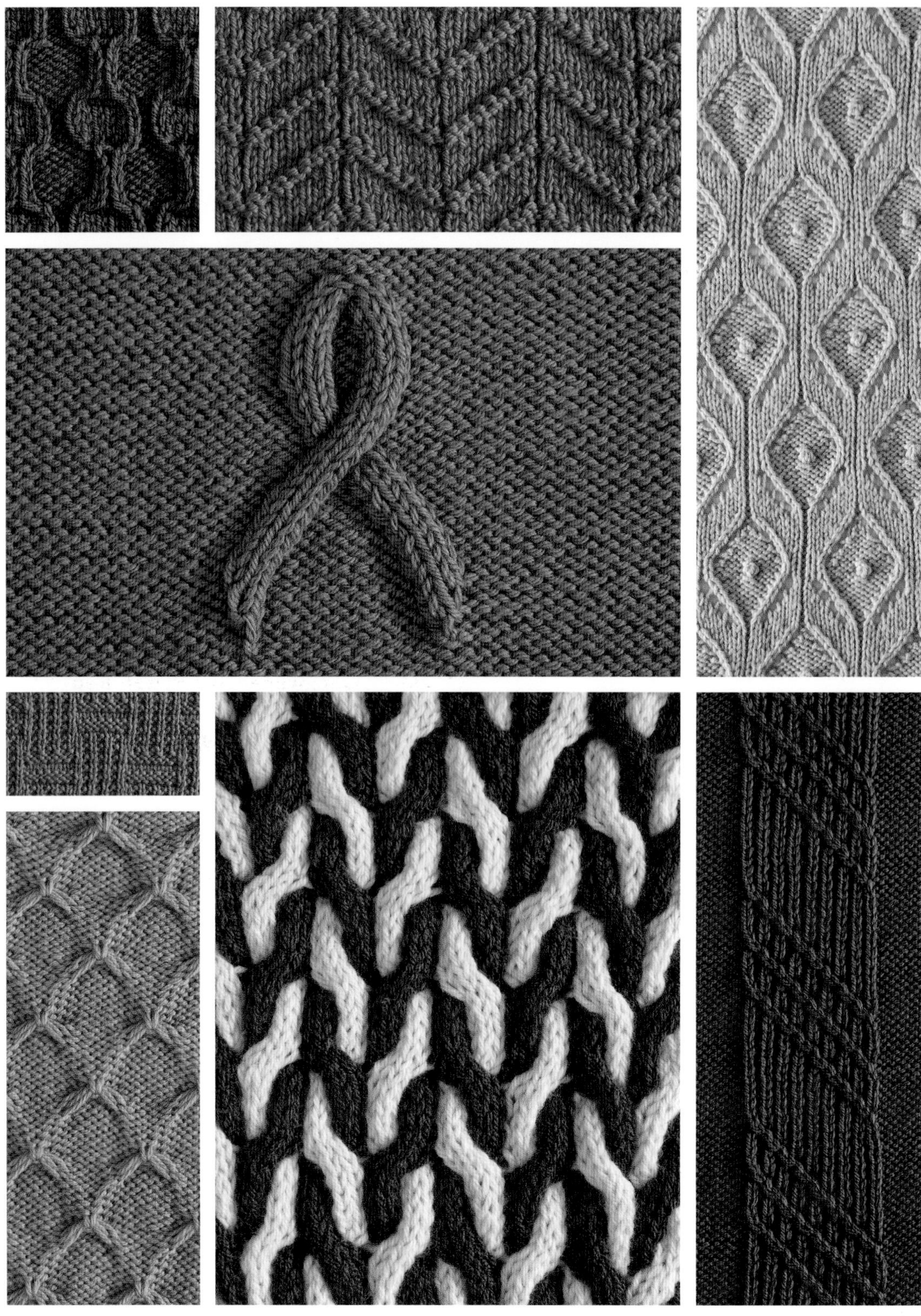

contents

introduction

Just as every knitter creates each and every project, no matter how simple or intricate, from basic knit and purl stitches, I have built an exhilarating career as a freelance knit and crochet designer and author using stitch patterns made from just knit and purl stitches. Stitch patterns are one of the basic building blocks that I use when I begin to design and are essential in much of my work.

One of my first jobs was working as a stitch designer for major fashion houses on Seventh Avenue in the garment district of New York City. I was handed giant cones of different yarns and sent off to create original swatches reflecting upcoming trends. I remember being told to "Think seashore" one season, and I designed textured fabrics that looked like sand and surf, like Sand Ripples (page 36), Surf Pattern (page 73), Ocean Lace (page 61) and Shifting Sand (page 109). An emerging cable trend another season inspired intricate patterns like O'Briensbridge Cables (page 128) and Caedmon Celtic Knot (page 184). It was a great opportunity for me to develop the design (and knitting!) skills I use every day.

Some of the stitch patterns in this book are long-standing favorites I created during my many years working in the yarn industry; some are variations on stitch patterns you may recognize; a few are the results of experimentation (swapping cable crossings, for example), and still others are the product of fortunate "errors" done while knitting. Inspiration, for me, comes from lots of different places—from fashion trends to art, architecture to nature.

You will find textured knit and purl patterns, lace and openwork, cables and crossed stitch patterns, slip stitch patterns, and novelty combinations. Most are accessible to any of you who are aspiring knitters while still being interesting enough for a knitting pro.

Writing this book has been an absolute dream come true. Just picture my happy design studio: giant commercial-sized boxes of wool in a kaleidoscope of colors, piles and piles of literally hundreds of knitted swatches, pads of graph paper with scribbled patterns and charts all over the place (in my knitting bag, travel carry-on, briefcase—even on the nightstand)!

Of course, as a knitter, you have many stitch dictionaries to choose from, but each collection opens a new world of creative possibilities by offering you a window into a designer's imagination and their innovations on our favorite craft. I am excited to share this collection of stitch designs with you and can hardly wait to see all the beautiful things you make!

What Is a Stitch Dictionary?

Most knitters know that, no matter the complexity, all knitted fabrics are made using just two basic stitches—knit and purl. Lucky for us, these simple stitches can be combined in an infinite number of ways to create designs that are beautiful, exciting, and unique. A stitch dictionary is a collection of such patterns and can become the basis for anything your imagination can create, from a romantic openwork shawl to a warm Aran pullover or a cozy sampler throw.

How to Use This Book

Choosing a Stitch

This stitch collection is divided into five chapters according to knitting technique: knit/purl combinations, lace patterns, cables and crossed-stitch patterns, slip stitch designs, and novelty stitch patterns.

Each section is arranged according to skill level, from the more straightforward to more complex patterns. That said, no matter your knitting experience, if you are intrigued by a more advanced stitch, give it a try. I encourage you to try them all! You'll find resources on pages 268–285 to help you gain new skills. After all, the best way to learn and grow is to challenge yourself.

Reading the Patterns

You'll notice that each pattern has both written and charted instructions. I have provided both versions to be complete and also because many knitters strongly prefer one over the other. If you've never tried reading a knitting chart, take a look at pages 257–261 for a complete demystification of the chart-reading process and symbols. Of course, please choose the format you prefer—or use both. You might find having the text nearby makes using the charts easier to follow.

Each individual design includes a *stitch multiple*, which indicates the number of stitches needed to repeat the pattern. Ribbed Squares (page 26), for example, is a multiple of 16 stitches. This means you should cast on a number of stitches that is divisible by 16, such as 32 or 48 or 112 or 160.

Some patterns require extra stitches on one or both sides in order to center the design, such as Buckeye Cables (page 126). This design is a multiple of 24 stitches plus 12 stitches, so 84 stitches would work nicely (24 × 3 + 12), as would 252 stitches (24 × 10 + 12).

In the charts, the stitch multiple, also known as the stitch repeat, is outlined by a bold black box; in the written-out instructions, it begins with an asterisk and ends with a semicolon.

You'll notice that some stitch designs, such as Moss Stitch Diamonds (page 31) and Lace Ribbons (page 63) have a special icon indicating that they look great on both sides, making them especially perfect for scarves, blankets, and other projects where the wrong side is frequently visible. In cases where the fabric is not exactly reversible, photographs show both sides of the fabric. You might even find you sometimes prefer the wrong side over the right side!

And, because wanting to knit unique fabrics doesn't mean we always want to count every little stitch and concentrate on every single row, look for the icon easy on some patterns. These marked designs, such as Daisy Stitch (page 234) and Chain Links (page 155), have what my students lovingly refer to as "rest rows." The wrong-side rows are just "purl across" or "knit the knit stitches and purl the purl stitches"—perfect for television or soccer-practice knitting!

Using the Patterns

One of the best parts of my job as a designer is experimenting with interesting stitches and finding new ways to use them. I hope you'll enjoy playing with the patterns, too.

Stand-Alone Designs

If you make your swatches approximately 6"/[15cm] square, you'll have handy dishcloths or spa cloths to use or to give as gifts. Of course, an afghan is really only a supersized swatch, with finished measurements of approximately 50" × 68"/[127cm × 172.5cm] for a full-sized version, or approximately 36" × 42"/[91.5cm × 106.5cm] for a baby version. Or, for a fun challenge, sew several squares together to create a one-of-a-kind sampler throw.

Substituting Stitches within Existing Patterns

It's easy to replace one stitch pattern for another within an existing pattern. Just knit a large swatch *in the stitch pattern you'd like to use*, at least 6"/[15cm] square, and count the number of stitches and rows over 4"/[10cm]. Divide those numbers by 4 to get the stitch and row gauge over 1"/[2.5cm].

If you can't see the stitches because of the patterning (because of the twisting of cables, for example), measure the width of one pattern repeat and divide by the number of stitches involved to find the gauge.

If you plan to wash and block your project pieces, it's important to take the time to treat your gauge swatch in the same manner *before* measuring it. Yarn often behaves differently after washing. Some fibers become limp while others bloom; some will contract lengthwise or widthwise. Not that you need another reason to knit swatches, but consider your gauge swatch the perfect opportunity to preview a tiny piece of your completed project and get a look at how the yarn behaves. Make your laundering mistakes here rather than on your final piece. (Been there, done that!)

That stitch pattern can now be used in any commercial pattern that calls for the same gauge! Of course, you might have to tweak the final width measurement a little in order to accommodate the stitch multiple for your particular stitch pattern. After all, knitwear design and pattern drafting are more an art form than an exact science.

Creating Original Designs

To design a project from scratch, start by making a large gauge swatch as described earlier. If you're like me, one swatch is never enough—you'll want to try different needle sizes to see which one gives the desired drape and feel.

If you're using several panels or stitch patterns within a single project, knit a separate gauge swatch for each of the panels or stitch patterns. This will give you a true gauge for each, unaffected by the pattern on either side.

Carefully measure your stitch and row gauges, being sure not to fudge. A difference of a half stitch means very little in an inch or two's worth of fabric, but that half stitch, multiplied over an entire sweater width, could result in a finished garment that is much larger or smaller than planned. (Don't ask me how I know. . . .)

Draw the shape of your project, keeping in mind that many projects will be assembled from several pieces. And don't worry, you don't have to have an art degree to be successful here. Just make a quick line drawing of the silhouette. A plain rectangle would suffice for an afghan or throw rug; a rectangle with cutouts for the neck opening and armholes will work perfectly for a pullover.

For the next step, add desired finished measurements to your sketch (see below). Be sure to include length and width measurements. You can look at schematic drawings in published patterns or else measure pieces you already own and love as guidelines for size and shape.

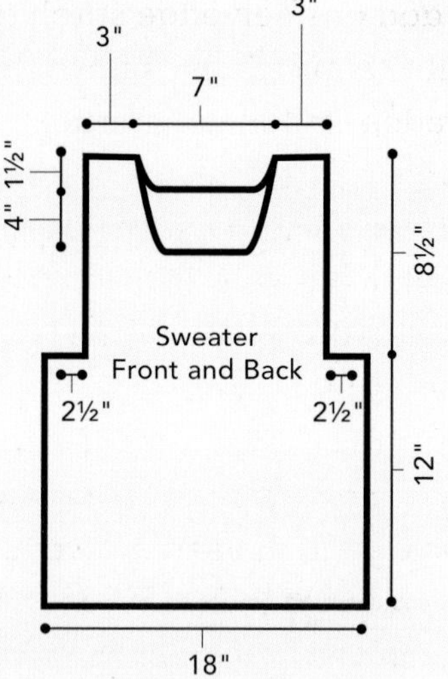

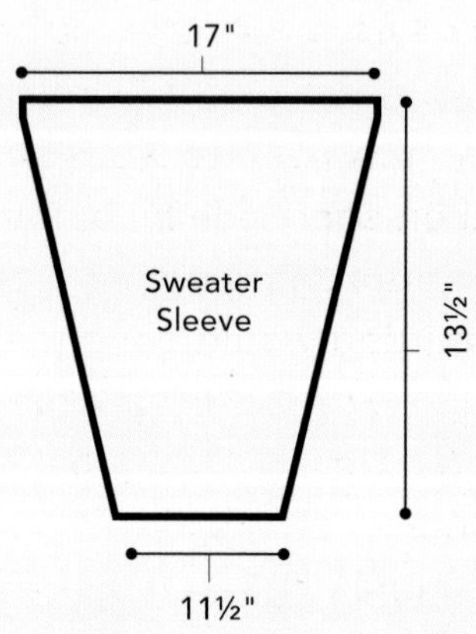

Multiply your gauge by your width measurements to determine the number of stitches to be cast on. Write the numbers onto your drawings. In my sweater example, the gauge is 4 stitches and 6 rows to the inch. To get a sweater piece that is 18"/[45.5cm] wide, we would have to cast on 72 stitches. Depending on the type of seam you plan to use, you might need to add one selvedge stitch to each side. Flat whipstitch seams require no selvedge stitches; mattress stitch seams do.

If this total number of stitches is not divisible by the stitch multiple in the pattern, the numbers will have to be fudged a bit. We can adjust the size of our finished garment or add filler stitches on each side in a plain pattern (like stockinette or seed stitch) to make the numbers work. Take a look at page 17 to see how.

Just by looking at the drawing, our knitter knows to cast on 72 stitches for the lower edge. Then, the fabric will be worked straight until it measures 12"/[30.5cm] from the beginning. For the armholes, 2½"/[6.5cm] would be removed on each side by binding off 10 stitches at the beginning of two rows.

The knitting would continue straight until the neck shaping for each piece, after 4½"/[11.5cm] for the front and after 7"/[18cm] for the back. To shape the neck, a number of stitches would be removed at the center all at once, and the remaining stitches would be decreased away until all 28 neck stitches are gone.

For the sleeves, 46 stitches would be cast on for the cuff. Then stitches would be gradually added until the stitch count becomes 68 in total—that's 11 increases (2 stitches each time) within 13½"/[34.5cm] worth of sleeve length.

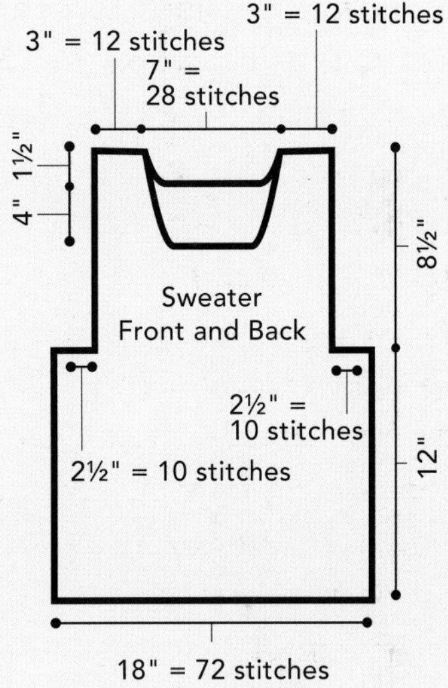

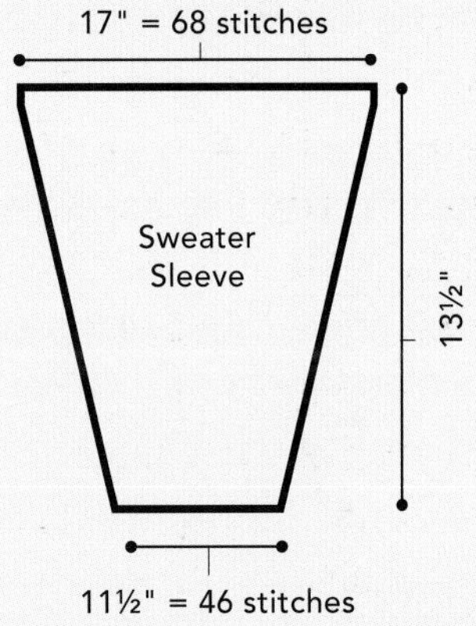

Simple algebra using the row gauge will determine the rate of increasing. If we keep 2½"/[6.5cm] straight at the top of the sleeve so that it fits neatly into the square indented armhole, then we have 11 × 6 = 66 rows available to us to increase all the stitches. To achieve a nice, gradual slope to our sleeve, we'd increase 1 stitch each side every 6 rows eleven times, and then continue straight until the piece measures 13½"/[34.5cm] from the beginning before binding off.

Designing Projects Knitted in the Round

Projects that are made in the round are designed in a similar way: multiply the stitch gauge by the total width of the fabric to determine the number of stitches to be cast on. The difference here is that the total number of stitches must be an exact multiple of the stitch repeat; those extra side stitches (outside the bold black stitch repeat box in the chart) are left off in order to get a continuous pattern.

Here's how to design a simple hat from scratch:

First, knit a piece of your fabric *in the round* so you can accurately measure gauge. If you don't want to swatch in the round on double-pointed needles, it is fine to work a flat piece of sample knitting as long as all rows are worked with the right side facing you. In others words, use a circular knitting needle and, at the end of each row, slide the stitches back to the beginning of the row and knit the next row.

Next, draw the shape of the project, including the finished dimensions.

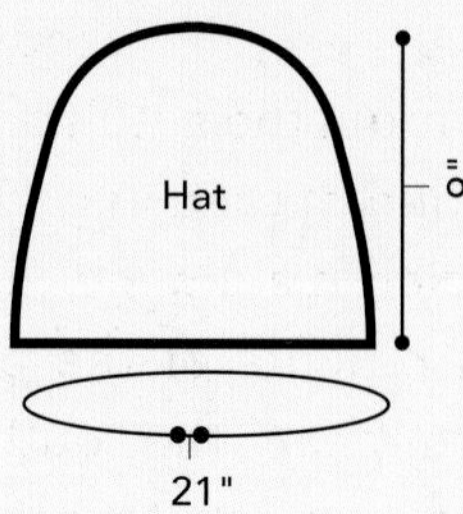

Then convert the dimensions to stitches using the knitting gauge.

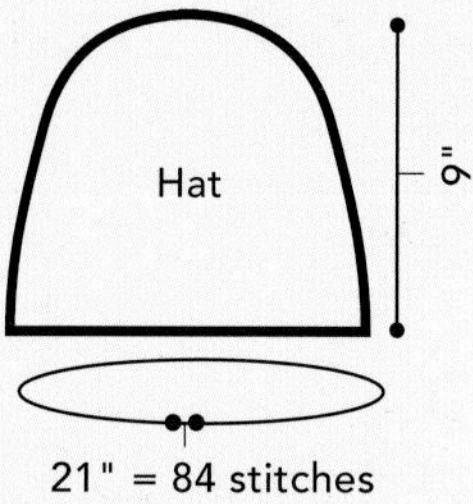

In our example hat, the number of stitches is 84. Ideally, we'd like to choose a stitch pattern that is a number that will divide evenly into 84, such as 2, 3, 7, 12, 28, or 42. Or, we could take advantage of the stretchy nature of knitted fabrics and round our main number down to 80, making it possible to incorporate a stitch pattern that's a multiple of 5, 8, 10, or 20.

Once the stitches are cast on for the hat, we'd knit even in the pattern until the piece measures an inch or two less than 9"/[23cm] from the beginning. Then a number of stitches would be decreased every round or two until only enough stitches remain to be gathered together for the crown.

Shaping Within Pattern Stitches

If your project requires shaping, you'll want to maintain the stitch pattern while increasing and decreasing. To make the process easier, it's a good idea to chart out several repeats of the pattern and then superimpose the outline of the shaped piece on top to see the stitch pattern. Knit-specific software such as Intwined Studio or Softbyte's Design-a-Knit can be used, but even general programs like Excel or Adobe Illustrator can be helpful for charting.

Increasing While Maintaining Pattern

Here, for example, is a chart showing how the allover textured pattern Embossed Blocks (page 26) could be incorporated into sleeve increases. Note how the design is symmetrical on both sides.

Some stitch patterns, such as cables and lace, are trickier than basic knit/purl combinations when shaping fabrics. For these designs, it is smart to wait until enough new stitches have been added (or taken away) so that a whole or half repeat can be incorporated into the pattern. A cable turned on only half the normal number of stitches is unsightly. Use a filler pattern such as stockinette or reverse stockinette on the stitches in the meantime.

The top chart on page 14 is an example of how increases might be incorporated in a cabled sleeve using

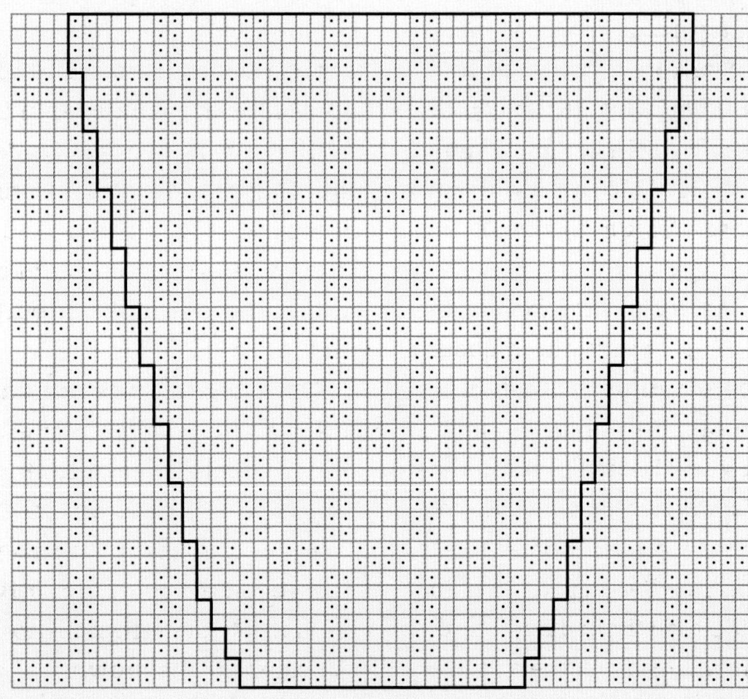

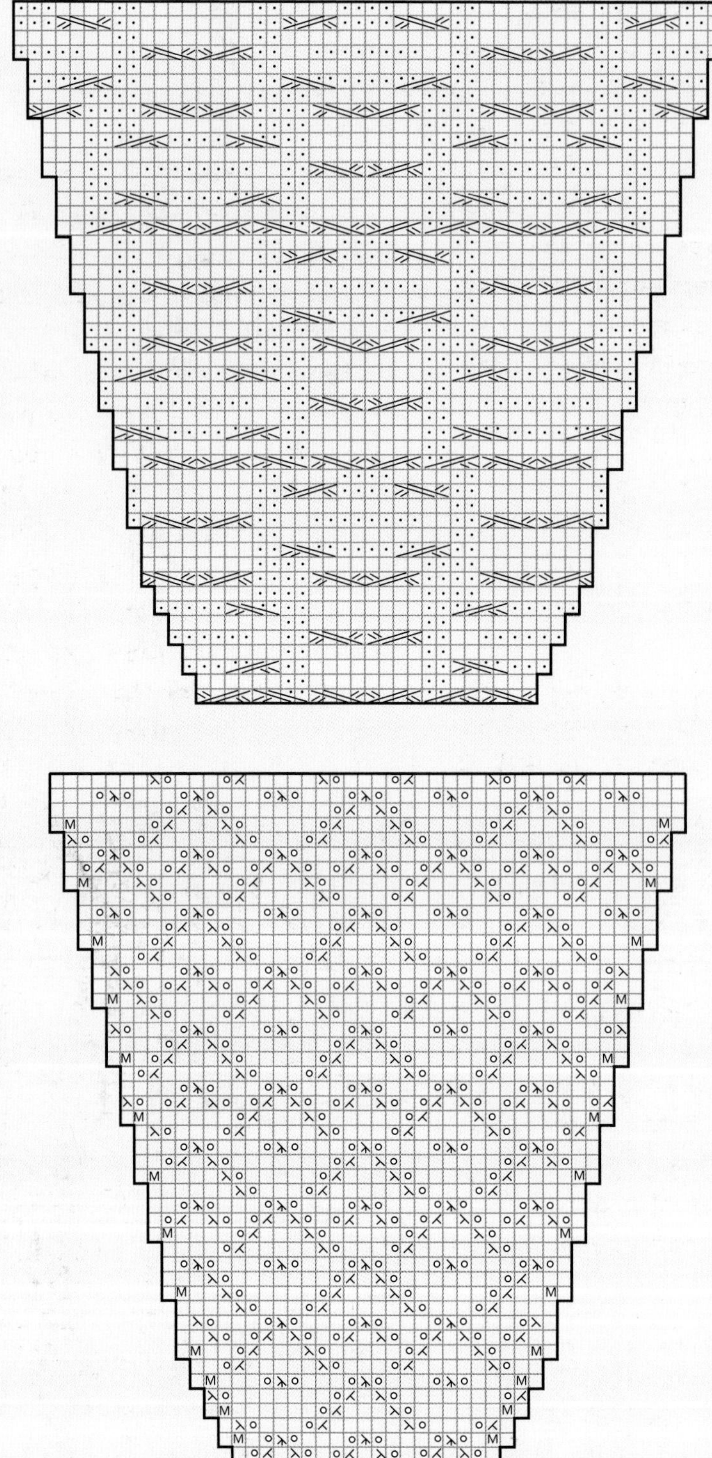

Buckeye Cables (page 126). Notice how the stitches on the sides are not cabled until enough new stitches are added to make a whole 4-stitch cable crossing.

Lace presents a whole different set of issues when shaping, since the stitch patterns themselves already have increases (yarn overs) and decreases (k2tog and ssk) when worked even. For every increase, there is a corresponding decrease, keeping the stitch count constant.

To actually shape a piece of lace fabric, an extra yarn over or decrease must be worked. Here, too, savvy knitters chart the patterns to make the knitting easier.

The bottom chart shows how sleeve increases might be worked when knitting Faceted Diamonds (page 92). In this example, the knitter is using the M1 technique (page 277), working the increases one stitch in from each edge. Note that sometimes the double decrease has been changed to a single decrease near the side edge, since a corresponding yarn over increase isn't available yet. Notice, too, yarn overs are never worked right on the edge, since they'd be difficult to work into a seam; in these cases, if a yarn over is omitted, the corresponding decrease is left off as well.

Decreasing While Maintaining Pattern

It is easier to decrease than increase while working in pattern, since the design is already set up. Stitches are simply worked together, allowing the innermost stitch to determine whether a knit decrease or purl decrease is appropriate.

Here is how one side of a neckline might be shaped while working Embossed Blocks. Bind off stitches whenever more than one stitch is being decreased at a time; use k2tog or ssk decreases whenever a single stitch is being removed. For this side of the neck, use the right-leaning k2tog decrease, and for the other side, use the left-leaning ssk decrease.

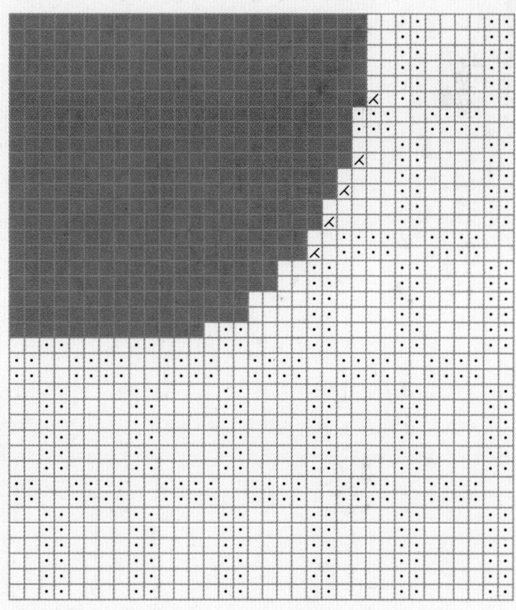

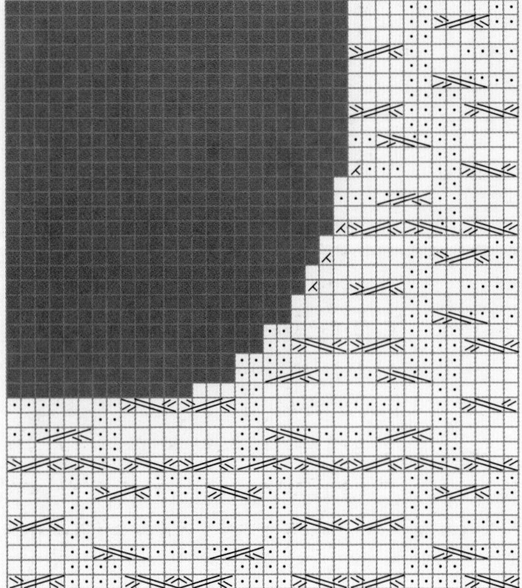

To continue cable patterns while decreasing, omit any cable crossings that would be comprised of fewer stitches than normal. In Buckeye Cables, for example, work cables only when 4 stitches are present, as seen above. Here, too, use the bind-off technique to decrease more than one adjacent stitch; choose the appropriate slanting single decrease (k2tog or ssk) for later decreases.

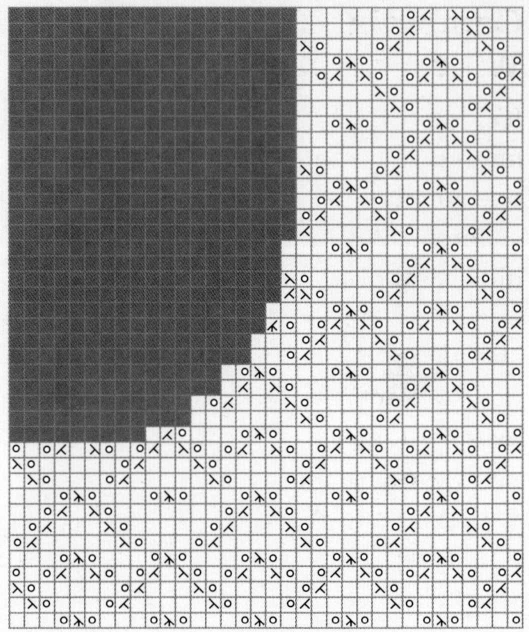

As with increasing, special care must be taken when decreasing in lace patterns. Sometimes, if a stitch used to perform a neckline decrease is already a decrease, for example, that single decrease will become a double decrease in order to maintain the lace while shaping the piece, as seen in this example worked in Faceted Diamonds.

Combining Patterns Within a Design

It's interesting to design—and fun to knit—a project that includes more than one stitch pattern. Here's how to do it.

First, knit individual swatches of all the stitch patterns you are considering for the project. Obviously, you should use the yarn you plan to use in your project for these swatches. Since every stitch pattern may have a different gauge, make your swatches large enough that you can also use them as gauge swatches later. (You might as well kill two birds with one stone!)

Experiment with possible arrangements of the stitch patterns by placing your swatches on a flat surface and shifting their positions until you find a combination you like.

Then make a sketch of your design, noting the arrangement of patterns. Here, for example, is a possible design idea combining a cable panel with a simple textured background pattern.

To draft the pattern for your project, measure the gauge for each stitch pattern separately, and then add the measurements to your sketch. In our example, let's use the Irish Panel (page 147) and Rice Stitch (page 20) for a sleeveless sweater.

Let's say that by carefully measuring the swatches, we determine that the 24 stitches of the Irish Panel measure 3"/[7.5cm] across, and that 5 stitches equal one inch in the Rice Stitch pattern.

If our sweater front and back were each going to be 18"/[45.5cm] across (to give us a 36"/[91.5cm] finished bust), then three panels of the cable will make up 9"/[23cm] of the sweater front, leaving 9"/[23cm] to be filled with the textured pattern, 3"/[7.5cm] on either side of the center cable and 1½"/[4cm] near the side seams. Use your stitch gauge to convert the measurements to stitch counts, and add them to your drawing. If you plan to knit the project in pieces and seam them later, be sure to add one stitch to each side for seam selvedge stitches.

Finally, to knit the pieces, cast on 120 stitches (or 122 stitches if you're knitting the project in pieces) and use stitch markers to separate the different patterns on your knitting needles.

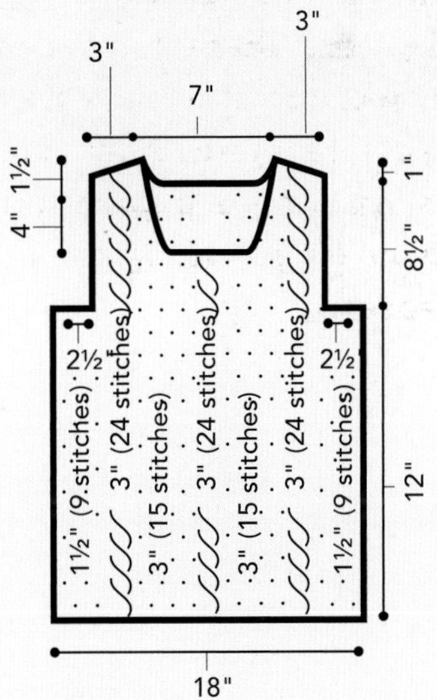

You'll find that it is easier to keep track of the patterns if they have compatible row repeats. For instance, it is better to combine a pattern that has an 8-row repeat with one that has a similar multiple, such as 4, 8, or 16.

Together, let's explore some of the exciting ways simple knitting techniques can be combined to create interesting—and useful!—fabrics.

Using Stitch Patterns in a Design

Here's a quick recap of the process for using any of these stitch patterns in a design.

1 Swatch, swatch, swatch! Knit up samples of several patterns using different yarns and needle sizes to find fabric you love.

2 Measure the stitch and row gauge before and after blocking your final swatch.

3 Sketch the shape of the project you want to knit.

4 Add final desired measurements to your project sketch or schematic.

5 Multiply your stitch gauge by the width of the project piece you want to knit to find the required number of stitches to be cast on.

6 If necessary, round the cast-on number up or down slightly to the desired multiple of stitches.

7 Using your stitch gauge, add shaping details such as armhole indentations and neck openings.

8 Cast on and happy knitting (and designing)!

chapter **one**

textured **knit and purl patterns**

Simple knit and purl stitches can be combined in nearly infinite ways to create beautifully textured fabrics, from stretchy ribbings to traditional Guernseys to various basketweave patterns and more. Many of these designs look great on both sides, making them perfect for use in reversible projects like scarves and blankets. Look for the icon to find them.

rice stitch

(multiple of 2 stitches plus 1 stitch)

Row 1 (RS): *P1, k1; repeat from the * across, ending with p1.

Row 2: Knit across.

Repeat Rows 1 and 2 for the pattern.

(WS) 2 1 (RS)

hurdle pattern

(multiple of 2 stitches plus 1 stitch)

Row 1 (RS): *K1, p1; repeat from the * across, ending with k1.

Row 2: P1, *k1, p1; repeat from the * across

Rows 3 and 4: Knit across.

Repeat Rows 1–4 for the pattern.

4 3 (WS) 2 1 (RS)

garter rib

(multiple of 2 stitches plus 1 stitch)

Row 1 (RS): *K1, p1; repeat from the * across, ending with k1.

Row 2: Purl across.

Repeat Rows 1 and 2 for the pattern.

(WS) 2 1 (RS)

double garter rib

(multiple of 4 stitches plus 2 stitches)

Row 1 (RS): *K2, p2; repeat from the * across, ending with k2.

Row 2: Purl across.

Repeat Rows 1 and 2 for the pattern.

(WS) 2 1 (RS)

dashes

(multiple of 6 stitches plus 3 stitches)

Row 1 (RS): *K3, p3; repeat from the * across, ending with k3.

Row 2: Purl across.

Row 3: *P3, k3; repeat from the * across, ending with p3.

Row 4: As Row 2.

Repeat Rows 1–4 for the pattern.

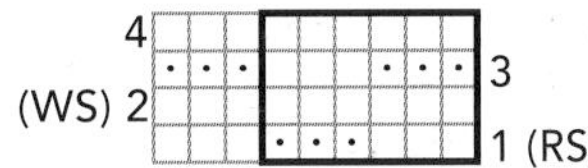

thermal stitch

(multiple of 4 stitches plus 2 stitches)

Row 1 (RS): *K2, p2; repeat from the * across, ending with k2.

Row 2: P2, *k2, p2; repeat from the * across.

Row 3: Knit across.

Row 4: Purl across.

Repeat Rows 1–4 for the pattern.

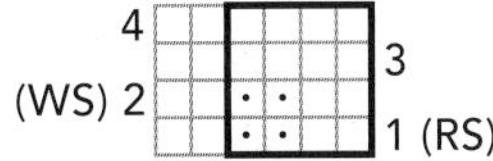

textured rib

(multiple of 4 stitches plus 1 stitch)

Row 1 (RS): *K1, p3; repeat from the * across, ending with k1.

Row 2: P1, *k1, p1; repeat from the * across.

Repeat Rows 1 and 2 for the pattern.

(WS) 2
1 (RS)

horizontal welts

(any number of stitches)

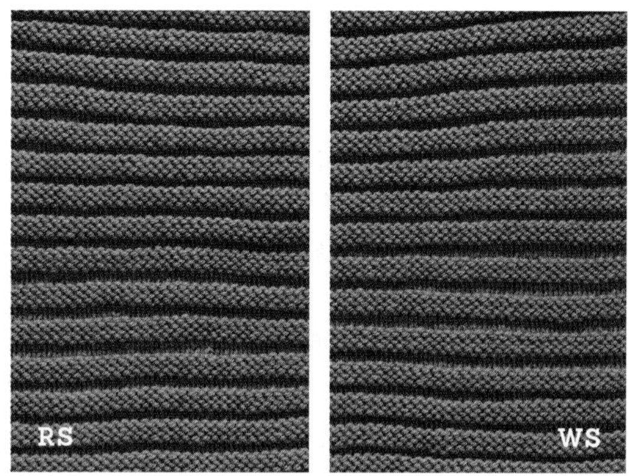

Rows 1 and 3 (RS): Knit across.

Rows 2 and 5: Purl across.

Rows 4 and 6: Knit across.

Repeat Rows 1–6 for the pattern.

6 5
4 3
(WS) 2 1 (RS)

stacked bricks

(multiple of 7 stitches plus 2 stitches)

Rows 1 and 3 (RS): Knit across.

Rows 2 and 4: Purl across.

Row 5: *K2, p5; repeat from the * across, ending with k2.

Row 6: P2, *k5, p2; repeat from the * across.

Repeat Rows 1–6 for the pattern.

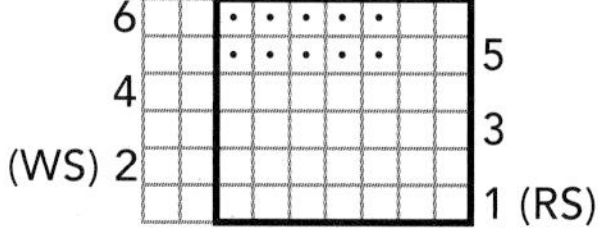

reversible columns rib 

(multiple of 6 stitches)

RS

WS

Rows 1 and 3 (RS): *P2, k2, p2; repeat from the * across.

Rows 2 and 4: *K2, p2, k2; repeat from the * across.

Rows 5 and 7: *P1, k4, p1; repeat from the * across.

Rows 6 and 8: *K1, p4, k1; repeat from the * across.

Repeat Rows 1–8 for the pattern.

Row							Row
8	•					•	
	•					•	7
6	•					•	
	•					•	5
4	•	•			•	•	
	•	•			•	•	3
(WS) 2	•	•			•	•	
	•	•			•	•	1 (RS)

ribs and bands  

(multiple of 4 stitches plus 2 stitches)

RS

WS

Rows 1, 3, 5, 7, and 9 (RS): *K2, p2; repeat from the * across ending with k2.

Row 2 and all WS rows: Knit the knit sts and purl the purl sts.

Rows 11, 14, and 15: Knit across.

Rows 12, 13, and 16: Purl across.

Repeat Rows 1–16 for the pattern.

Row							Row
16							
							15
14	•	•	•	•	•	•	
	•	•	•	•	•	•	13
12							
							11
10			•	•			
			•	•			9
8			•	•			
			•	•			7
6			•	•			
			•	•			5
4			•	•			
			•	•			3
(WS) 2			•	•			
			•	•			1 (RS)

boxes

(multiple of 11 stitches plus 2 stitches)

Row 1 (RS): Knit across.

Row 2 and all WS rows: Knit the knit sts and purl the purl sts.

Row 3: Purl across.

Row 5: *P2, k9; repeat from the * across, ending with p2.

Rows 7, 9, 11, and 13: *P2, k2, p5, k2; repeat from the * across, ending with p2.

Row 14: As Row 2.

Repeat Rows 1–14 for the pattern.

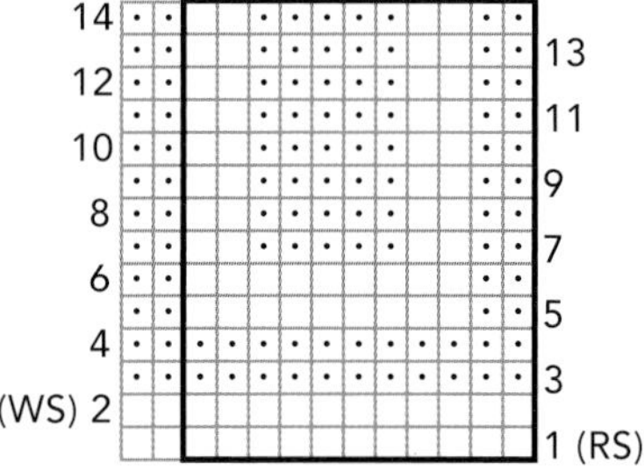

picket fences

(multiple of 5 stitches plus 4 stitches)

Rows 1, 3, and 5 (RS): *K4, p1; repeat from the * across, ending with k4.

Row 2 and all WS rows: Knit the knit sts and purl the purl sts.

Rows 7, 9, and 11: *P4, k1; repeat from the * across, ending with p4.

Row 12: As Row 2.

Repeat Rows 1–12 for the pattern.

12	•	•	•	•		•	•	•	•	
	•	•	•	•		•	•	•	•	11
10	•	•	•	•		•	•	•	•	
	•	•	•	•		•	•	•	•	9
8	•	•	•	•		•	•	•	•	
	•	•	•	•		•	•	•	•	7
6					•					
					•					5
4					•					
					•					3
(WS) 2					•					
					•					1 (RS)

pennants

(multiple of 14 stitches plus 2 stitches)

Rows 1 and 9 (RS): *K2, p1, k4, p2, k4, p1; repeat from the * across, ending with k2.

Rows 2 and 8: P2, *[k2, p3] twice, k2, p2; repeat from the * across.

Rows 3 and 7: *K2, p3, k2, p2, k2, p3; repeat from the * across, ending with k2.

Rows 4 and 6: P2, *k4, p1, k2, p1, k4, p2; repeat from the * across.

Row 5: *K2, p12; repeat from the * across, ending with k2.

Row 10: P2, *p5, k2, p7; repeat from the * across.

Repeat Rows 1–10 for the pattern.

10								•	•								
			•					•	•					•			9
8			•	•				•	•				•	•			
			•	•	•			•	•			•	•	•			7
6			•	•	•	•		•	•		•	•	•	•			
			•	•	•	•	•	•	•	•	•	•	•	•			5
4			•	•	•	•		•	•		•	•	•	•			
			•	•	•			•	•			•	•	•			3
(WS) 2			•	•				•	•				•	•			
			•					•	•					•			1 (RS)

little boxes

(multiple of 3 stitches plus 2 stitches)

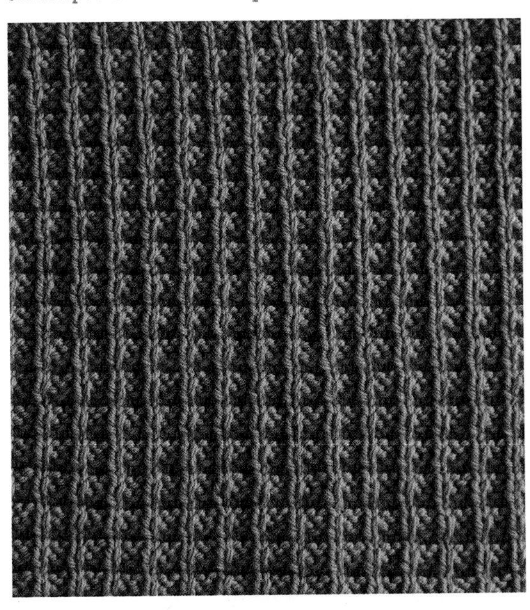

Row 1 (RS): Knit across.

Row 2: Purl across.

Row 3: *P2, k1; repeat from the * across, ending with p2.

Row 4: K2, *p1, k2; repeat from the * across.

Repeat Rows 1–4 for the pattern.

4	•	•		•	•	
	•	•		•	•	3
(WS) 2						
						1 (RS)

ribbed squares

(multiple of 16 stitches)

16	•	•			•	•			•	•			•	•			
	•	•			•	•			•	•			•	•			15
14	•	•			•	•			•	•			•	•	•	•	
	•	•			•	•			•	•			•	•	•	•	13
12	•	•			•	•			•	•							
	•	•			•	•			•	•							11
10	•	•			•	•			•	•	•	•	•	•	•	•	
	•	•			•	•			•	•	•	•	•	•	•	•	9
8	•	•			•	•											
	•	•			•	•											7
6	•	•			•	•	•	•	•	•	•	•	•	•	•	•	
	•	•			•	•	•	•	•	•	•	•	•	•	•	•	5
4	•	•															
	•	•															3
(WS) 2	•	•	•	•	•	•	•	•	•	•	•	•	•	•	•	•	
	•	•	•	•	•	•	•	•	•	•	•	•	•	•	•	•	1 (RS)

Row 1 (RS): Purl across.

Row 2 and all WS rows: Knit the knit sts and purl the purl sts.

Row 3: *K14, p2; repeat from the * across.

Row 5: *P12, k2, p2; repeat from the * across.

Row 7: *K10, p2, k2, p2; repeat from the * across.

Row 9: *P8, [k2, p2] twice; repeat from the * across.

Row 11: *K6, [p2, k2] twice, p2; repeat from the * across.

Row 13: *P4, [k2, p2] 3 times; repeat from the * across.

Row 15: *K2, p2; repeat from the * across.

Row 16: As Row 2.

Repeat Rows 1–16 for the pattern.

embossed blocks

(multiple of 6 stitches plus 2 stitches)

Row 1 (RS): *K2, p4; repeat from the * across, ending with k2.

Row 2 and all WS rows: Knit the knit sts and purl the purl sts.

Rows 3, 5, and 7: *P2, k4; repeat from the * across, ending with p2.

Row 8: As Row 2.

Repeat Rows 1–8 for the pattern.

8	•	•					•	•	
	•	•					•	•	7
6	•	•					•	•	
	•	•					•	•	5
4	•	•					•	•	
	•	•					•	•	3
(WS) 2			•	•	•	•			
			•	•	•	•			1 (RS)

vertical zigs and zags 

(multiple of 8 stitches)

32				•	•	•	•		
				•	•	•	•		31
30			•	•	•	•			
			•	•	•	•			29
28		•	•	•	•				
		•	•	•	•				27
26	•	•	•	•					
	•	•	•	•					25
24	•	•	•					•	
	•	•	•					•	23
22	•	•					•	•	
	•	•					•	•	21
20	•					•	•	•	
	•					•	•	•	19
18					•	•	•	•	
					•	•	•	•	17
16	•					•	•	•	
	•					•	•	•	15
14	•	•					•	•	
	•	•					•	•	13
12	•	•	•					•	
	•	•	•					•	11
10	•	•	•	•					
	•	•	•	•					9
8		•	•	•	•				
		•	•	•	•				7
6			•	•	•	•			
			•	•	•	•			5
4				•	•	•	•		
				•	•	•	•		3
(WS) 2					•	•	•	•	
					•	•	•	•	1 (RS)

Row 1 (RS): *P4, k4; repeat from the * across.

Row 2 and all WS rows: Knit the knit sts and purl the purl sts.

Rows 3 and 31: *K1, p4, k3; repeat from the * across.

Rows 5 and 29: *K2, p4, k2; repeat from the * across.

Rows 7 and 27: *K3, p4, k1; repeat from the * across.

Rows 9 and 25: *K4, p4; repeat from the * across.

Rows 11 and 23: *P1, k4, p3; repeat from the * across.

Rows 13 and 21: *P2, k4, p2; repeat from the * across.

Rows 15 and 19: *P3, k4, p1; repeat from the * across.

Row 17: *P4, k4; repeat from the * across.

Row 32: As Row 2.

Repeat Rows 1–32 for the pattern.

stairsteps

(multiple of 12 stitches)

24	•	•	•	•	•	•	•	•			•	•	
	•	•	•	•	•	•	•	•			•	•	23
22	•	•	•	•	•	•	•	•			•	•	
	•	•	•	•	•	•	•	•			•	•	21
20							•	•					
							•	•					19
18							•	•					
							•	•					17
16	•	•	•	•			•	•	•	•	•	•	
	•	•	•	•			•	•	•	•	•	•	15
14	•	•	•	•			•	•	•	•	•	•	
	•	•	•	•			•	•	•	•	•	•	13
12			•	•									
			•	•									11
10			•	•									
			•	•									9
8			•	•	•	•	•	•	•	•	•	•	
			•	•	•	•	•	•	•	•	•	•	7
6			•	•	•	•	•	•	•	•	•	•	
			•	•	•	•	•	•	•	•	•	•	5
4											•	•	
											•	•	3
(WS) 2											•	•	
											•	•	1 (RS)

Rows 1 and 3 (RS): *P2, k10; repeat from the * across.

Row 2 and all WS rows: Knit the knit sts and purl the purl sts.

Rows 5 and 7: *P10, k2; repeat from the * across.

Rows 9 and 11: *K8, p2, k2; repeat from the * across.

Rows 13 and 15: *P6, k2, p4; repeat from the * across.

Rows 17 and 19: *K4, p2, k6; repeat from the * across.

Rows 21 and 23: *P2, k2, p8; repeat from the * across.

Row 24: As Row 2.

Repeat Rows 1–24 for the pattern.

harlequin

(multiple of 8 stitches plus 1 stitch)

Row 1 (RS): Knit across.

Row 2 and all WS rows: Knit the knit sts and purl the purl sts.

Rows 3 and 19: *K4, p1, k3; repeat from the * across, ending with k1.

Rows 5 and 17: *K3, p3, k2; repeat from the * across, ending with k1.

Rows 7 and 15: *K2, p5, k1; repeat from the * across, ending with k1.

Rows 9 and 13: *K1, p7; repeat from the * across, ending with k1.

Row 11: Purl across.

Row 20: As Row 2.

Repeat Rows 1–20 for the pattern.

brocade

(multiple of 16 stitches plus 1 stitch)

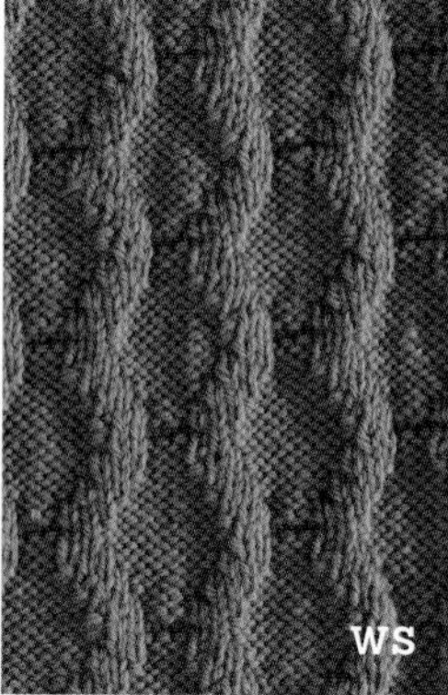

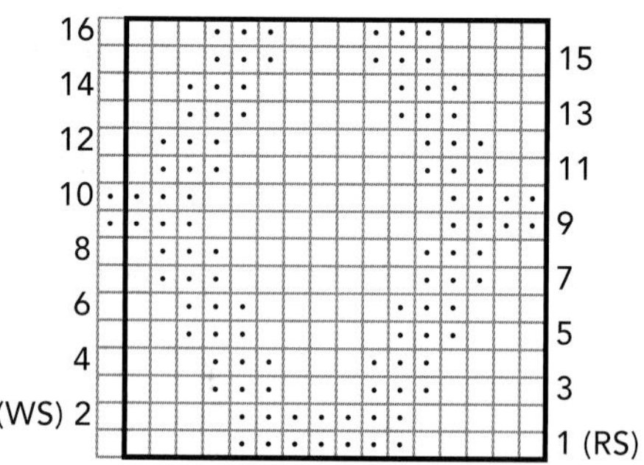

Row 1 (RS): *K5, p7, k4; repeat from the * across, ending with k1.

Row 2 and all WS rows: Knit the knit sts and purl the purl sts.

Rows 3 and 15: *K4, [p3, k3] twice; repeat from the * across, ending with k1.

Rows 5 and 13: *K3, p3, k5, p3, k2; repeat from the * across, ending with k1.

Rows 7 and 11: *K2, p3, k7, p3, k1; repeat from the * across, ending with k1.

Row 9: *P4, k9, p3; repeat from the * across, ending with p1.

Row 16: As Row 2.

Repeat Rows 1–16 for the pattern.

ribbed chevrons

(multiple of 20 stitches plus 1 stitch)

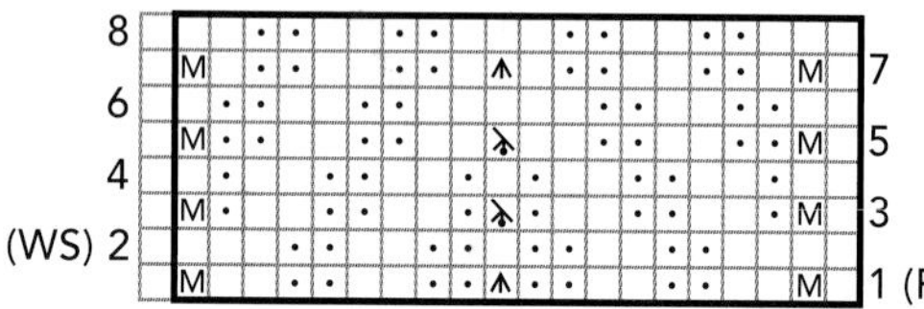

Row 1 (RS): *K1, M1 (page 277), [k2, p2] twice, s2kp2 (page 272), [p2, k2] twice, M1; repeat from the * across, ending with k1.

Row 2 and all WS rows: Knit the knit sts and purl the purl sts.

Row 3: *K1, M1, p1, k2, p2, k2, p1, p3tog, p1, k2, p2, k2, p1, M1; repeat from the * across, ending with k1.

Row 5: *K1, M1, [p2, k2] twice, p3tog, [k2, p2] twice, M1; repeat from the * across, ending with k1.

Row 7: *K1, M1, k1, p2, k2, p2, k1, s2kp2, k1, p2, k2, p2, k1, M1; repeat from the * across, ending with k1.

Row 8: As Row 2.

Repeat Rows 1–8 for the pattern.

moss stitch diamonds 

(multiple of 14 stitches)

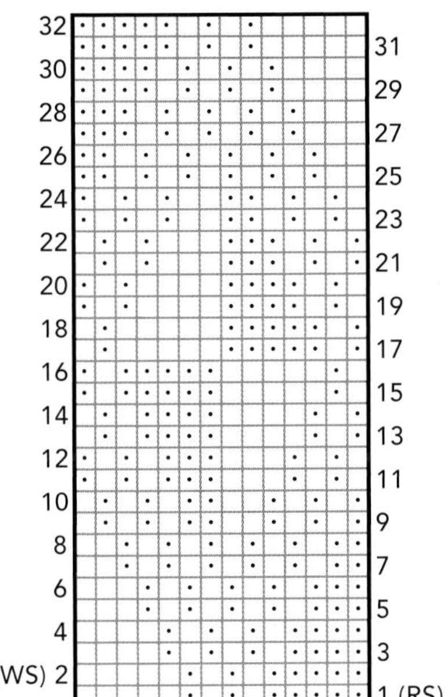

Row 1 (RS): *P5, [k1, p1] twice, k5; repeat from the * across.

Row 2 and all WS rows: Knit the knit sts and purl the purl sts.

Row 3: *P4, [k1, p1] 3 times, k4; repeat from the * across.

Row 5: *P3, [k1, p1] 4 times, k3; repeat from the * across.

Row 7: *P2, [k1, p1] 5 times, k2; repeat from the * across.

Row 9: *[P1, k1] twice, p1, k2, p2, [k1, p1] twice, k1; repeat from the * across.

Row 11: *[K1, p1] twice, k3, p3, [k1, p1] twice; repeat from the * across.

Row 13: *P1, k1, p1, k4, p4, k1, p1, k1; repeat from the * across.

Row 15: *K1, p1, k5, p5, k1, p1; repeat from the * across.

Row 17: *P1, k1, p5, k5, p1, k1; repeat from the * across.

Row 19: *K1, p1, k1, p4, k4, p1, k1, p1; repeat from the * across.

Row 21: *[P1, k1] twice, p3, k3, [p1, k1] twice; repeat from the * across.

Row 23: *[K1, p1] twice, k1, p2, k2, [p1, k1] twice, p1; repeat from the * across.

Row 25: *K2, [p1, k1] 5 times, p2; repeat from the * across.

Row 27: *K3, [p1, k1] 4 times, p3; repeat from the * across.

Row 29: *K4, [p1, k1] 3 times, p4; repeat from the * across.

Row 31: *K5, [p1, k1] twice, p5; repeat from the * across.

Row 32: As Row 2.

Repeat Rows 1–32 for the pattern.

almond clusters

(multiple of 4 stitches plus 5 stitches, increases to multiple of 6 stitches plus 7 stitches)

NOTE

- Stitch count varies from row to row.

Row										Row
20										
										19
18										
	·	·	·	·	Λ	·	·	·	·	17
16										
	·	·	·	·	III	·	·	·	·	15
14										
	·	·	·	·	III	·	·	·	·	13
12										
	·	·	·	·	V	·	·	·	·	11
10										
										9
8										
	·	·	Λ	·	·	·	Λ	·	·	7
6										
	·	·	III	·	·	·	III	·	·	5
4										
	·	·	III	·	·	·	III	·	·	3
(WS) 2										
	·	·	V	·	·	·	V	·	·	1 (RS)

Row 1 (RS): P2, *[k1, yarn over, k1] into the next st (page 268), p3; repeat from the * across, ending with [k1, yarn over, k1] into the next st, p2.

Row 2 and all WS rows: Purl across.

Rows 3 and 5: P2, *k3, p3; repeat from the * across, ending with k3, p2.

Row 7: P2, *s2kp2 (page 272), p3; repeat from the * across, ending with s2kp2, p2.

Rows 9 and 19: Knit across.

Row 11: P2, *p2, [k1, yarn over, k1] into the next st, p1; repeat from the * across, ending with p3.

Rows 13 and 15: P2, *p2, k3, p1; repeat from the * across, ending with p3.

Row 17: P2, *p2, s2kp2, p1; repeat from the * across, ending with p3.

Row 20: As Row 2.

Repeat Rows 1–20 for the pattern.

subtle stripes

(multiple of 6 stitches plus 3 stitches)

Row 1 (RS): *P3, k3; repeat from the * across, ending with p3.

Row 2: As Row 1.

Repeat Rows 1 and 2 for the pattern.

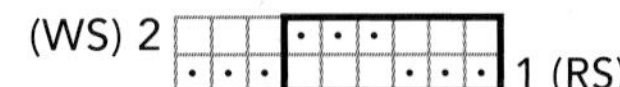

nubby pattern

(multiple of 2 stitches plus 1 stitch)

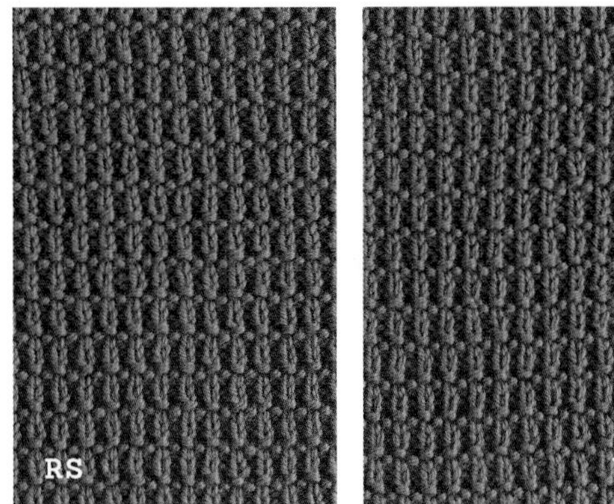

Rows 1 and 3 (RS): *P1, k1; repeat from the * across, ending with p1.

Row 2: K1, *p1, k1; repeat from the * across.

Row 4: P1, *k1, p1; repeat from the * across.

Repeat Rows 1–4 for the pattern.

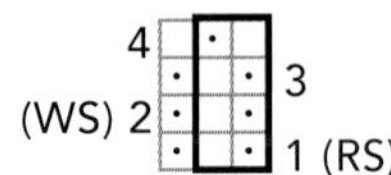

farrow rib

(multiple of 3 stitches)

Row 1 (RS): *K2, p1; repeat from the * across.

Row 2: As Row 1.

Repeat Rows 1 and 2 for the pattern.

(WS) 2 1 (RS)

ridged rib

(multiple of 4 stitches plus 2 stitches)

Row 1 (RS): *K2, p2; repeat from the * across, ending with k2.

Row 2: P2, *k2, p2; repeat from the * across.

Rows 3 and 4: Knit across.

Repeat Rows 1–4 for the pattern.

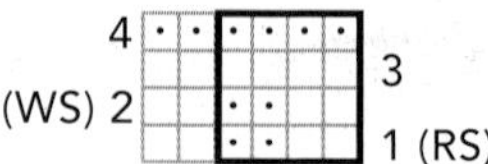

bales

(multiple of 12 stitches plus 6 stitches)

Rows 1, 3, 5, 7, 9, and 11 (RS): *K8, p2, k2; repeat from the * across, ending with k6.

Rows 2, 4, 6, 8, 10, and 12: K6, *p2, k2, p2, k6; repeat from the * across.

Rows 13, 15, 17, 19, 21, and 23: *K2, p2, k8; repeat from the * across, ending with k2, p2, k2.

Rows 14, 16, 18, 20, 22, and 24: P2, k2, p2, *k6, p2, k2, p2; repeat from the * across.

Repeat Rows 1–24 for the pattern.

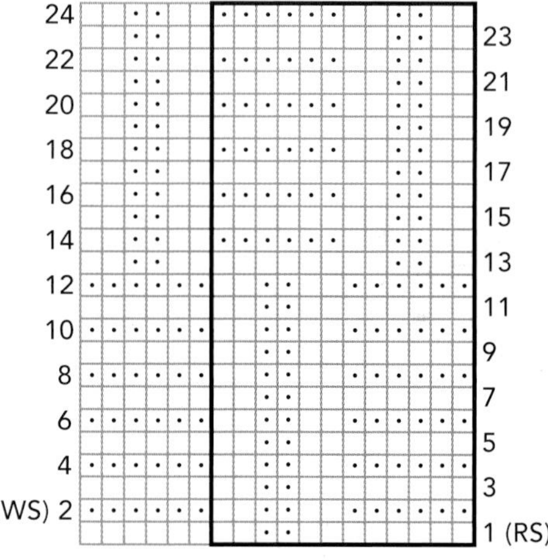

textured cubes

(multiple of 5 stitches plus 1 stitch)

Rows 1, 3, 5, and 7 (RS): Knit across.

Rows 2, 4, and 6: K1, *p4, k1; repeat from the * across.

Row 8: Knit across.

Repeat Rows 1–8 for the pattern.

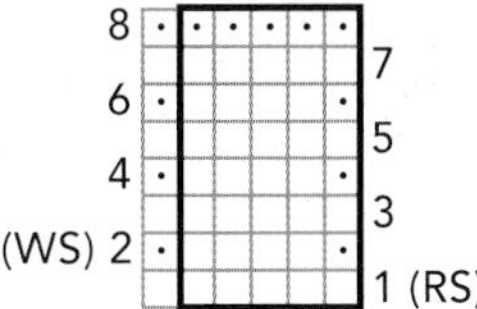

emerald-cut ribs

(multiple of 4 stitches plus 2 stitches)

Rows 1 and 3 (RS): *K2, p2; repeat from the * across, ending with k2.

Rows 2 and 4: P2, *k2, p2; repeat from the * across.

Rows 5–8: Knit across.

Repeat Rows 1–8 for the pattern.

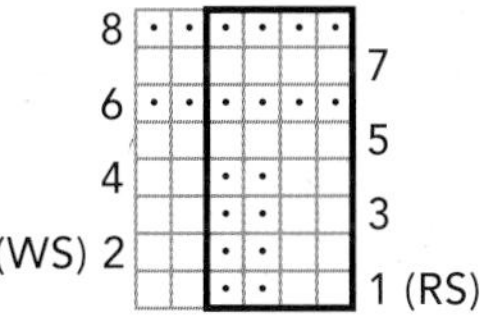

textured stripes

(multiple of 15 stitches)

Row 1 (RS): *[K3, p1, k1, p1] twice, k3; repeat from the * across.

Row 2: *P3, k4, p1, k4, p3; repeat from the * across.

Repeat Rows 1 and 2 for the pattern.

(WS) 2 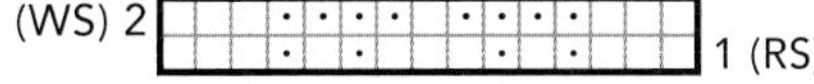 1 (RS)

mock cables

(multiple of 12 stitches)

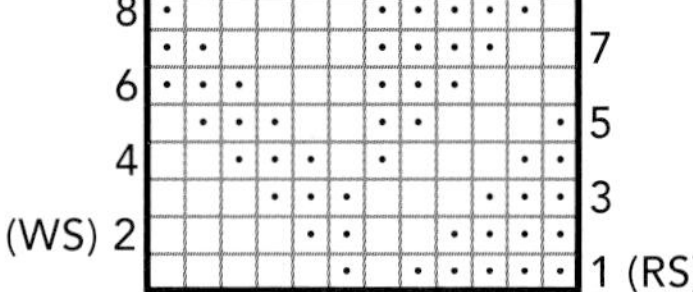

Row 1 (RS): *P5, k1, p1, k5; repeat from the * across.

Row 2: *P4, k2, p2, k4; repeat from the * across.

Row 3: *P3, k3; repeat from the * across.

Row 4: *P2, k3, p1, k1, p3, k2; repeat from the * across.

Row 5: *P1, k3, p2, k2, p3, k1; repeat from the * across.

Row 6: *K3, p3; repeat from the * across.

Row 7: *K2, p4, k4, p2; repeat from the * across.

Row 8: *K1, p5, k5, p1; repeat from the * across.

Repeat Rows 1–8 for the pattern.

sand ripples

(multiple of 14 stitches)

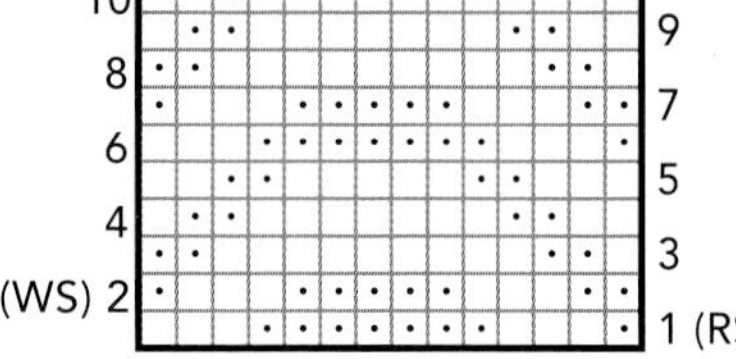

Row 1 (RS): *P1, k3, p7, k3; repeat from the * across.

Row 2: *K1, p3, k5, p3, k2; repeat from the * across.

Row 3: *K1, p2, k9, p2; repeat from the * across.

Row 4: *P1, k2, p7, k2, p2; repeat from the * across.

Row 5: *K3, p2, k5, p2, k2; repeat from the * across.

Row 6: *P3, k7, p3, k1; repeat from the * across.

Row 7: *P2, k3, p5, k3, p1; repeat from the * across.

Row 8: *K2, p9, k2, p1; repeat from the * across.

Row 9: *K2, p2, k7, p2, k1; repeat from the * across.

Row 10: *P2, k2, p5, k2, p3; repeat from the * across.

Repeat Rows 1–10 for the pattern.

gansey chevrons

(multiple of 16 stitches plus 1 stitch)

8	•	•							•							•	•	
	•	•	•						•						•	•	•	7
6	•		•	•					•					•	•		•	
	•			•	•				•				•	•			•	5
4	•				•	•			•			•	•				•	
	•					•	•		•		•	•					•	3
(WS) 2	•						•	•	•	•	•						•	
	•							•	•	•							•	1 (RS)

Row 1 (RS): *P1, k6, p3, k6; repeat from the * across, ending with p1.

Row 2: K1, *p5, k5, p5, k1; repeat from the * across.

Row 3: *P1, k4, p2, k1, p1, k1, p2, k4; repeat from the * across, ending with p1.

Row 4: K1, *p3, k2, p2, k1, p2, k2, p3, k1; repeat from the * across.

Row 5: *P1, k2, p2, k3, p1, k3, p2, k2; repeat from the * across, ending with p1.

Row 6: K1, *p1, k2, p4, k1, p4, k2, p1, k1; repeat from the * across.

Row 7: *P3, k5, p1, k5, p2; repeat from the * across, ending with p1.

Row 8: K1, *k1, p6, k1, p6, k2; repeat from the * across.

Repeat Rows 1–8 for the pattern.

fences

(multiple of 4 stitches)

Rows 1 and 3 (RS): *P2, k2; repeat from the * across.

Rows 2 and 4: *P2, k2; repeat from the * across.

Rows 5 and 11: Purl across.

Row 6: Purl across.

Rows 7 and 9: *K2, p2; repeat from the * across.

Rows 8 and 10: *K2, p2; repeat from the * across.

Row 12: Purl across.

Repeat Rows 1–12 for the pattern.

12					
	•	•	•	•	11
10	•	•			
	•	•			9
8	•	•			
	•	•			7
6					
	•	•	•	•	5
4			•	•	
			•	•	3
(WS) 2			•	•	
			•	•	1 (RS)

textured knit and purl patterns

1

textured check

(multiple of 5 stitches plus 2 stitches)

Rows 1 and 3 (RS): *P2, k3; repeat from the * across, ending with p2.

Row 2: K2, *p3, k2; repeat from the * across.

Row 4: Knit across.

Repeat Rows 1–4 for the pattern.

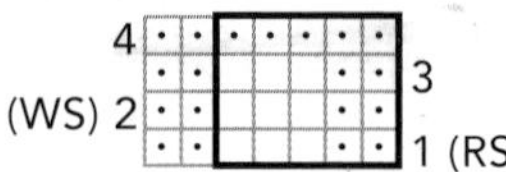

flags

(multiple of 9 stitches)

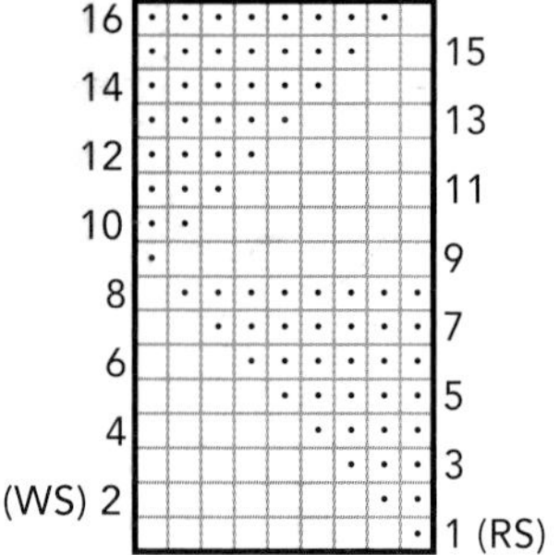

Row 1 (RS): *P1, k8; repeat from the * across.

Row 2: *P7, k2; repeat from the * across.

Row 3: *P3, k6; repeat from the * across.

Rows 4 and 5: *P5, k4; repeat from the * across.

Row 6: *P3, k6; repeat from the * across.

Row 7: *P7, k2; repeat from the * across.

Row 8: *P1, k8; repeat from the * across.

Row 9: *K8, p1; repeat from the * across.

Row 10: *K2, p7; repeat from the * across.

Row 11: *K6, p3; repeat from the * across.

Rows 12 and 13: *K4, p5; repeat from the * across.

Row 14: *K6, p3; repeat from the * across.

Row 15: *K2, p7; repeat from the * across.

Row 16: *K8, p1; repeat from the * across.

Repeat Rows 1–16 for the pattern.

framed ovals

(multiple of 6 stitches plus 3 stitches)

Row 1 (RS): *K3, p3; repeat from the * across, ending with k3.

Rows 2 and 8: P3, *k1, p1, k1, p3; repeat from the * across.

Rows 3, 5, and 7: *P1, k1, p1, k3; repeat from the * across, ending with p1, k1, p1.

Rows 4 and 6: K3, *p3, k3; repeat from the * across.

Row 9: As Row 1.

Row 10: As Row 2.

Repeat Rows 1–10 for the pattern.

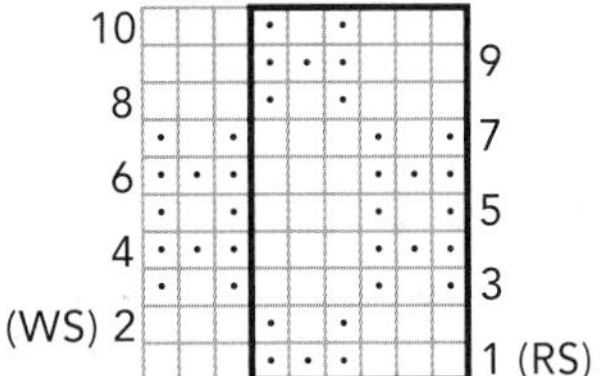

lightning

(multiple of 5 stitches)

Row 1 (RS): *P1, k4; repeat from the * across.

Row 2: *P3, k1, p1; repeat from the * across.

Rows 3 and 9: *K2, p1, k2; repeat from the * across.

Rows 4 and 8: *P1, k1, p3; repeat from the * across.

Rows 5 and 7: *K4, p1; repeat from the * across.

Row 6: *P4, k1; repeat from the * across.

Row 10: As Row 2.

Repeat Rows 1–10 for the pattern.

10
9
8
7
6
5
4
3
(WS) 2
1 (RS)

diamonds and ridges 

(multiple of 22 stitches)

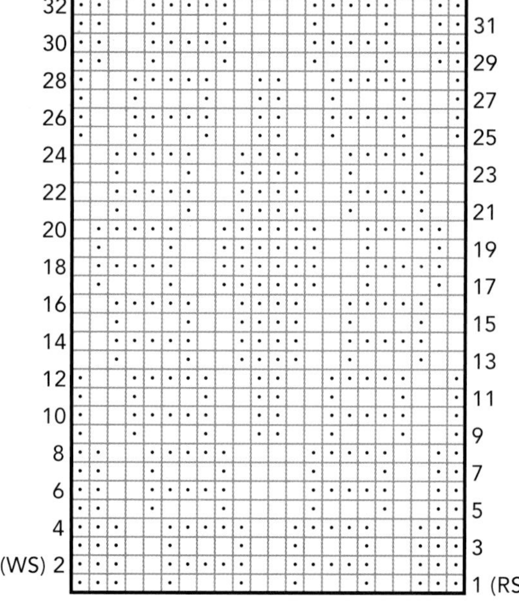

Rows 1 and 3 (RS): *P3, [k2, p1, k3, p1] twice, k2, p3; repeat from the * across.

Rows 2 and 4: *K3, [p2, k5] twice, p2, k3; repeat from the * across.

Rows 5, 7, 29, and 31: *P2, k2, p1, k3, p1, k4, p1, k3, p1, k2, p2; repeat from the * across.

Rows 6, 8, and 30: *K2, p2, k5, p4, k5, p2, k2; repeat from the * across.

Rows 9, 11, 25, and 27: *P1, k2, p1, k3, p1, k2, p2, k2, p1, k3, p1, k2, p1; repeat from the * across.

Rows 10, 12, 26, and 28: *K1, p2, k5, p2, k2, p2, k5, p2, k1; repeat from the * across.

Rows 13, 15, 21, and 23: *K2, p1, k3, p1, k2, p4, k2, p1, k3, p1, k2; repeat from the * across.

Rows 14, 16, 22, and 24: *P2, k5, p2, k4, p2, k5, p2; repeat from the * across.

Rows 17 and 19: *K1, p1, k3, p1, k2, p6, k2, p1, k3, p1, k1; repeat from the * across.

Rows 18 and 20: *P1, k5, p2, k6, p2, k5, p1; repeat from the * across.

Row 32: As Row 6.

Repeat Rows 1–32 for the pattern.

textured chains

(multiple of 12 stitches plus 1 stitch)

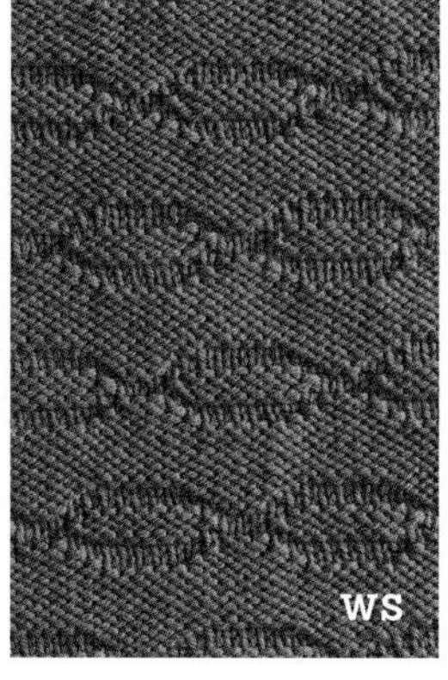

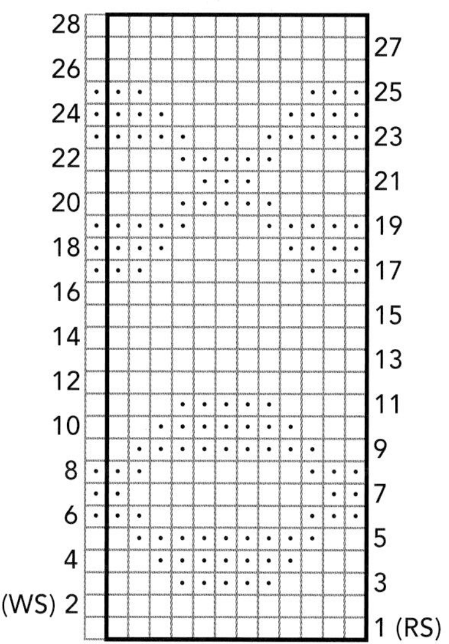

Rows 1, 13, 15, and 27 (RS): Knit across.

Rows 2, 12, 14, 16, and 26: Purl across.

Rows 3, 11, 18, and 24: *K4, p5, k3; repeat from the * across, ending with k1.

Rows 4, 10, 17, and 25: P1, *p2, k7, p3; repeat from the * across.

Rows 5 and 9: *K2, p9, k1; repeat from the * across, ending with k1.

Rows 6 and 8: K1, *k2, p7, k3; repeat from the * across.

Row 7: *P2, k9, p1; repeat from the * across, ending with p1.

Rows 19 and 23: *P5, k3, p4; repeat from the * across, ending with p1.

Rows 20 and 22: P1, *p3, k5, p4; repeat from the * across.

Row 21: *K5, p3, k4; repeat from the * across, ending with k1.

Row 28: Purl across.

Repeat Rows 1–28 for the pattern.

seed stitch trellis

(multiple of 10 stitches plus 1 stitch)

Row 1 (RS): *K1, p1, k7, p1; repeat from the * across, ending with k1.

Row 2: K1, *p1, k1, p5, k1, p1, k1; repeat from the * across.

Rows 3 and 9: *[K1, p1] twice, k3, p1, k1, p1; repeat from the * across, ending with k1.

Rows 4 and 8: P1, *[p1, k1] 4 times, p2; repeat from the * across.

Rows 5 and 7: *K3, [p1, k1] twice, p1, k2; repeat from the * across, ending with k1.

Row 6: P1, *p3, k1, p1, k1, p4; repeat from the * across.

Row 10: As Row 2.

Repeat Rows 1–10 for the pattern.

triangles in relief

(multiple of 8 stitches)

Row 1 (RS): *K4, p4; repeat from the * across.

Row 2: *P1, k3, p4; repeat from the * across.

Row 3: *K4, p2, k2; repeat from the * across.

Row 4: *P3, k1, p4; repeat from the * across.

Row 5: *P4, k4; repeat from the * across.

Row 6: *P5, k3; repeat from the * across.

Row 7: *P2, k6; repeat from the * across.

Row 8: *P7, k1; repeat from the * across.

Repeat Rows 1–8 for the pattern.

circles and squares

(multiple of 12 stitches plus 1 stitch)

Rows 1, 3, and 15 (RS): *K3, [p1, k1] 3 times, p1, k2; repeat from the * across, ending with k1.

Rows 2, 4, and 14: P1, *p3, [k1, p1] twice, k1, p4; repeat from the * across.

Row 5: *K1, p1, k3, p1, k1, p1, k3, p1; repeat from the * across, ending with k1.

Rows, 6, 8, 10, and 12: K1, *p1, k1, p7, k1, p1, k1; repeat from the * across.

Rows 7, 9, and 11: *[K1, p1] twice, k5, p1, k1, p1; repeat from the * across, ending with k1.

Row 13: *K1, p1, k3, p1, k1, p1, k3, p1; repeat from the * across, ending with k1.

Row 16: P1, *p3, [k1, p1] twice, k1, p4; repeat from the * across.

Repeat Rows 1–16 for the pattern.

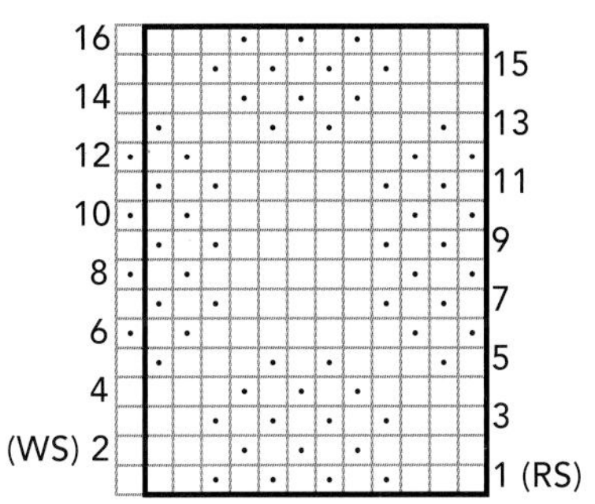

anchor

(over 15 stitches on stockinette background)

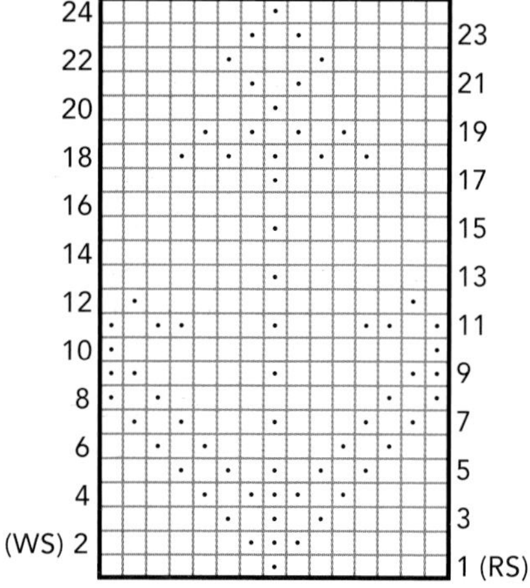

Row 1 (RS): K7, p1, k7.

Row 2: P6, k3, p6.

Row 3: K5, [p1, k1] twice, p1, k5.

Row 4: P4, k1, p1, k3, p1, k1, p4.

Row 5: K3, [p1, k1] 4 times, p1, k3.

Row 6: P2, k1, p1, k1, p5, k1, p1, k1, p2.

Row 7: [K1, p1] twice, k3, p1, k3, [p1, k1] twice.

Row 8: K1, p1, k1, p9, k1, p1, k1.

Row 9: P2, k5, p1, k5, p2.

Row 10: K1, p13, k1.

Row 11: P1, k1, p2, k3, p1, k3, p2, k1, p1.

Row 12: P1, k1, p11, k1, p1.

Rows 13, 15, and 17: K7, p1, k7.

Rows 14 and 16: Purl across.

Row 18: P3, [k1, p1] 4 times, k1, p3.

Row 19: K4, [p1, k1] 3 times, p1, k4.

Row 20: P7, k1, p7.

Rows 21 and 23: K6, p1, k1, p1, k6.

Row 22: P5, k1, p3, k1, p5.

Row 24: P7, k1, p7.

snowflake

(over 33 stitches on stockinette background)

Rows 1 (RS): K16, p1, k16.

Rows 2 and 34: P15, k1, p1, k1, p15.

Rows 3 and 33: K14, [p1, k1] twice, p1, k14.

Rows 4 and 32: P3, k1, p1, k1, p9, k1, p1, k1, p9, k1, p1, k1, p3.

Rows 5 and 31: K4, p1, k11, p1, k11, p1, k4.

Rows 6 and 30: P3, k1, p1, k1, p4, k1, p11, k1, p4, k1, p1, k1, p3.

Rows 7 and 29: K6, p1, k4, p1, k9, p1, k4, p1, k6.

Rows 8 and 28: P7, k1, p2, k1, p1, k1, p7, k1, p1, k1, p2, k1, p7.

Rows 9 and 27: K11, p1, k1, p1, k5, p1, k1, p1, k11.

Rows 10 and 26: P10, [k1, p1] twice, k1, p3, [k1, p1] twice, k1, p10.

Rows 11 and 25: K11, [p1, k1] 5 times, p1, k11.

Rows 12 and 24: P3, [k1, p1] twice, k1, p2, [k1, p1] twice, k1, p3, [k1, p1] twice, k1, p2, [k1, p1] twice, k1, p3.

Rows 13 and 23: K4, [p1, k1] twice, p1, k2, [p1, k1] 5 times, p1, k2, [p1, k1] twice, p1, k4.

Rows 14 and 22: P5, [k1, p1] twice, k1, p2, k1, p1, k1, p3, k1, p1, k1, p2, [k1, p1] twice, k1, p5.

Rows 15 and 21: K6, [p1, k1] twice, p1, k2, [p1, k1] 3 times, p1, k2, [p1, k1] twice, p1, k6.

Rows 16 and 20: P2, k1, p4, [k1, p1] twice, k1, p2, k1, p3, k1, p2, [k1, p1] twice, k1, p4, k1, p2.

Rows 17 and 19: [K1, p1] twice, k4, [p1, k1] twice, p1, k2, p1, k1, p1, k2, [p1, k1] twice, p1, k4, [p1, k1] twice.

Row 18: [K1, p1] twice, k1, p23, [k1, p1] twice, k1.

Row 35: As Row 1.

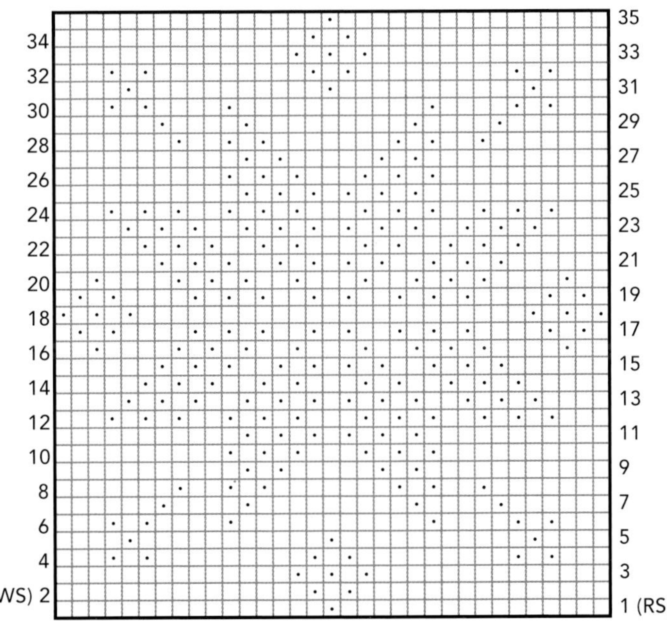

tumbling blocks

(multiple of 14 stitches)

Rows 1 and 13 (RS): *P1, k1; repeat from the * across.

Row 2: *P2, [k1, p1] 5 times, k2; repeat from the * across.

Row 3: *P3, [k1, p1] 4 times, k3; repeat from the * across.

Row 4: *P4, [k1, p1] 3 times, k4; repeat from the * across.

Row 5: *P5, [k1, p1] twice, k5; repeat from the * across.

Row 6: *P6, k1, p1, k6; repeat from the * across.

Row 7: *P7, k7; repeat from the * across.

Row 8: *K1, p6, k6, p1; repeat from the * across.

Row 9: *P1, k1, p5, k5, p1, k1; repeat from the * across.

Row 10: *K1, p1, k1, p4, k4, p1, k1, p1; repeat from the * across.

Row 11: *[P1, k1] twice, p3, k3, [p1, k1] twice; repeat from the * across.

Row 12: *[K1, p1] twice, k1, p2, k2, [p1, k1] twice, p1; repeat from the * across.

Row 14: *K1, p1; repeat from the * across.

Row 15: *[P1, k1] twice, p1, k2, p2, [k1, p1] twice, k1; repeat from the * across.

Row 16: *[K1, p1] twice, k3, p3, [k1, p1] twice; repeat from the * across.

Row 17: *P1, k1, p1, k4, p4, k1, p1, k1; repeat from the * across.

Row 18: *K1, p1, k5, p5, k1, p1; repeat from the * across.

Row 19: *P1, k6, p6, k1; repeat from the * across.

Row 20: *K7, p7; repeat from the * across.

Row 21: *K6, p1, k1, p6; repeat from the * across.

Row 22: *K5, [p1, k1] twice, p5; repeat from the * across.

Row 23: *K4, [p1, k1] 3 times, p4; repeat from the * across.

Row 24: *K3, [p1, k1] 4 times, p3; repeat from the * across.

Row 25: *K2, [p1, k1] 5 times, p2; repeat from the * across.

Row 26: *K1, p1; repeat from the * across.

Repeat Rows 1–26 for the pattern.

pretty bow

(over 20 stitches on a reverse stockinette background)

Row 1 (RS): P2, k1, p14, k1, p2.

Row 2: K1, p2, k14, p2, k1.

Row 3: K3, p14, k3.

Row 4: P3, k14, p3.

Row 5: P1, k3, p12, k3, p1.

Row 6: K1, p3, k12, p3, k1.

Row 7: P2, k3, p10, k3, p2.

Row 8: K2, p3, k10, p3, k2.

Row 9: P3, k3, p8, k3, p3.

Row 10: K3, p3, k8, p3, k3.

Row 11: P4, k3, p6, k3, p4.

Row 12: K4, p3, k6, p3, k4.

Row 13: P5, k3, p4, k3, p5.

Row 14: K5, p3, k4, p3, k5.

Row 15: P3, k2, p1, k3, p2, k3, p1, k2, p3.

Row 16: K2, p4, k1, p3, k1, p2, k1, p4, k2.

Row 17: P1, k6, p1, k1, p1, k2, p1, k7.

Row 18: P8, k1, p1, k2, p8.

Row 19: K9, p2, k9.

Row 20: P8, k1, p2, k1, p8.

Row 21: K7, p1, k4, p1, k7.

Row 22: P7, k1, p4, k1, p7.

Row 23: K8, p1, k2, p1, k8.

Row 24: P9, k2, p9.

Row 25: K8, p4, k8.

Row 26: K1, p6, k6, p6, k1.

Row 27: P2, k4, p8, k4, p2.

Row 28: K3, p2, k10, p2, k3.

basket stitch

(multiple of 18 stitches)

18		•	•			•	•												
		•	•			•	•			•	•	•	•	•	•	•	•		17
16		•	•			•	•			•	•	•	•	•	•	•	•		
		•	•			•	•												15
14		•	•			•	•												
		•	•			•	•			•	•	•	•	•	•	•	•		13
12		•	•			•	•			•	•	•	•	•	•	•	•		
		•	•			•	•												11
10																			
											•	•			•	•			9
8	•	•	•	•	•	•	•	•			•	•			•	•			
	•	•	•	•	•	•	•	•			•	•			•	•			7
6											•	•			•	•			
											•	•			•	•			5
4	•	•	•	•	•	•	•	•			•	•			•	•			
	•	•	•	•	•	•	•	•			•	•			•	•			3
(WS) 2											•	•			•	•			
																			1 (RS)

Row 1 (RS): Knit across.

Rows 2 and 6: *P10, [k2, p2] twice; repeat from the * across.

Rows 3 and 7: *[K2, p2] twice, k2, p8; repeat from the * across.

Rows 4 and 8: *K8, [p2, k2] twice, p2; repeat from the * across.

Rows 5 and 9: *[K2, p2] twice, k10; repeat from the * across.

Row 10: Purl across.

Rows 11 and 15: *K11, p2, k2, p2, k1; repeat from the * across.

Rows 12 and 16: *P1, [k2, p2] twice, k8, p1; repeat from the * across.

Rows 13 and 17: *K1, p8, [k2, p2] twice, k1; repeat from the * across.

Row 14: *P1, k2, p2, k2, p11; repeat from the * across.

Row 18: As Row 14.

Repeat Rows 1–18 for the pattern.

undulating ribs

(multiple of 24 stitches plus 15 stitches)

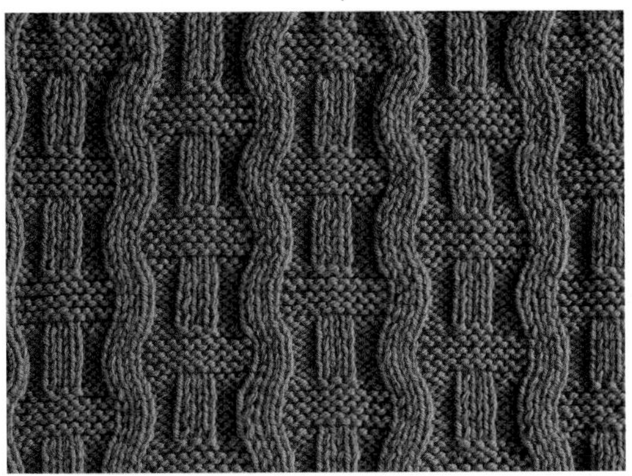

Rows 1, 3, 5, and 7 (RS): *[K3, p3] twice, k12; repeat from the * across, ending with [k3, p3] twice, k3.

Rows 2, 4, 6, and 8: [P3, k3] twice, p3, *k9, [p3, k3] twice, p3; repeat from the * across.

Rows 9, 11, 13, and 15: *K15, p3, k3, p3; repeat from the * across, ending with k15.

Rows 10, 12, 14, and 16: P3, k9, p3, *[k3, p3] twice, k9, p3; repeat from the * across.

Repeat Rows 1–16 for the pattern.

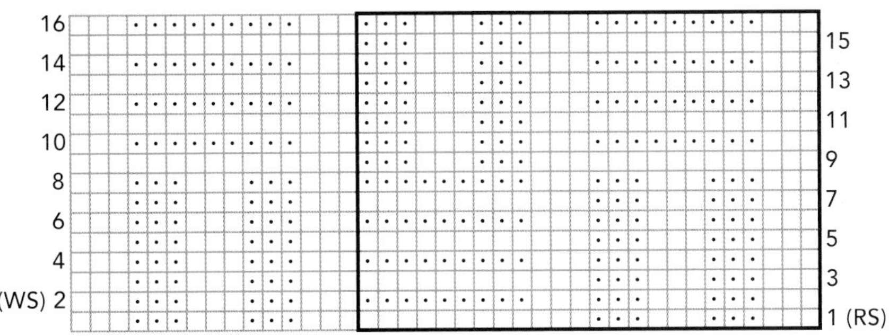

jute stitch

(multiple of 2 stitches)

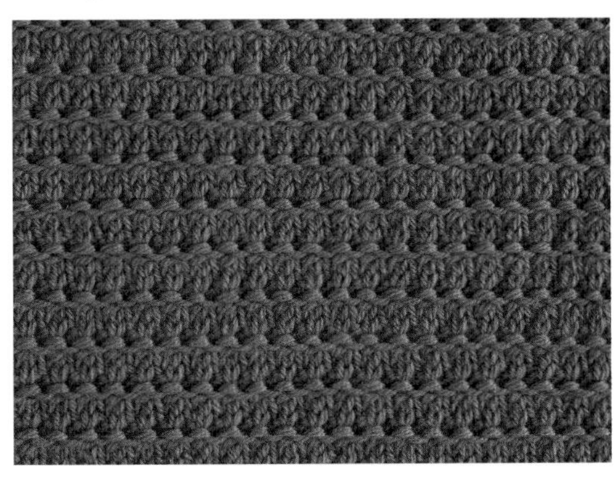

Row 1 (RS): Knit across.

Row 2: *K2tog; repeat from the * across.

Row 3: *K1f&b (page 274); repeat from the * across.

Row 4: Purl across.

Repeat Rows 1–4 for the pattern.

4
(WS) 2
3
1 (RS)

NOTE

- Stitch count varies from row to row.

textured sampler

(multiple of 18 stitches plus 11 stitches)

Row 1 (RS): Knit across.

Rows 2, 3, 4, 17, 18, 19, 20, 21, 31, 32, 33, 34, 47, 48, 49, 50, and 51: As Row 1.

Rows 5, 9, 13, 35, 39, and 43: *P2, k7; repeat from the * across, ending with p2.

Row 6, 8, 10, 12, 14, 16, 36, 38, 40, 42, 44, and 46: K2, p7, k2, *p7, k2; repeat from the * across.

Rows 7, 11, and 15: *P2, slip the next 2 sts onto cn and hold in back, k1, k2 from cn, k1, slip the next st onto cn and hold in front, k2, k1 from cn, p2, k3, bobble (page 270), k3 bobble; repeat from the * across, ending with p2, slip the next 2 sts onto cn and hold in back, k1, k2 from cn, k1, slip the next st onto cn and hold in front, k2, k1 from cn, p2.

Rows 22, 30, and 52: Purl across.

Rows 23 and 59: *K7, p2; repeat from the * across, ending with k2.

Rows 24 and 58: P3, k2, p6,*p1, k2, p6; repeat from the * across.

Rows 25 and 57: *K5, p2, k2; repeat from the * across, ending with k5, p2, k4.

Rows 26 and 56: P5, k2, p4,*p3, k2, p4; repeat from the * across, ending with p4.

Rows 27 and 55: *K3, p2, k4; repeat from the * across, ending with k3, p2, k6.

Rows 28 and 54: P7, k2, p2, *p5, k2, p7, k2, p2; repeat from the * across.

Rows 29 and 53: *K1, p2, k7, p2, k6; repeat from the * across, ending with k1, p2, k8.

Rows 37, 41, and 45: *P2, k3, bobble (see page 270), k3, p2, slip the next 2 sts onto cn and hold in back, k1, k2 from cn, k1, slip the next st onto cn and hold in front, k2, k1 from cn; repeat from the * across, ending with p2, k3, bobble, k3, p2.

Row 60: Purl across.

Repeat Rows 1–60 for the pattern.

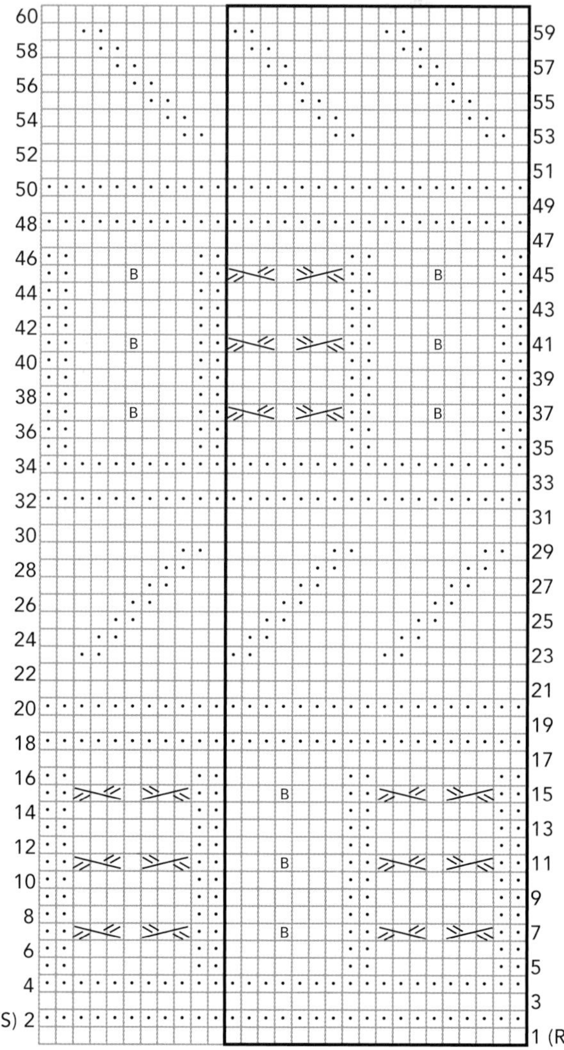

roman columns

(multiple of 14 stitches plus 7 stitches)

20	•	•	•	•	•	•	•	•	•	•	•	•	•	•	•	•	•	•	•	•	•	
	•		•		•		•	•		•		•		•	•		•		•		•	19
18	•	•	•	•	•	•	•	•	•	•	•	•	•	•	•	•	•	•	•	•	•	
	•		•		•		•	•		•		•		•	•		•		•		•	17
16	•	•	•	•	•	•	•								•	•	•	•	•	•	•	
	•		•		•		•								•		•		•		•	15
14	•	•	•	•	•	•	•	•	•	•	•	•	•	•	•	•	•	•	•	•	•	
	•		•		•		•	•	•	•	•	•	•	•	•		•		•		•	13
12	•	•	•	•	•	•	•								•	•	•	•	•	•	•	
	•		•		•		•								•		•		•		•	11
10	•	•	•	•	•	•	•	•	•	•	•	•	•	•	•	•	•	•	•	•	•	
	•		•		•		•	•		•		•		•	•		•		•		•	9
8	•	•	•	•	•	•	•	•	•	•	•	•	•	•	•	•	•	•	•	•	•	
	•		•		•		•	•		•		•		•	•		•		•		•	7
6								•	•	•	•	•	•	•								
								•		•		•		•								5
4	•	•	•	•	•	•	•	•	•	•	•	•	•	•	•	•	•	•	•	•	•	
	•	•	•	•	•	•	•	•		•		•		•	•	•	•	•	•	•	•	3
(WS) 2								•	•	•	•	•	•	•								
								•		•		•		•								1 (RS)

Rows 1 and 5 (RS): *K7, [p1, k1] 3 times, p1; repeat from the * across, ending with k7.

Rows 2 and 6: P7, *k7, p7; repeat from the * across.

Row 3: *P8, [k1, p1] 3 times; repeat from the * across, ending with p7.

Rows 4, 8, 10, 14, and 18: Knit across.

Rows 7, 9, 17, and 19: *[P1, k1] 3 times, p2, [k1, p1] 3 times; repeat from the * across, ending with [p1, k1] 3 times, p1.

Rows 11 and 15: *[P1, k1] 3 times, p1, k7; repeat from the * across, ending with [p1, k1] 3 times, p1.

Rows 12 and 16: K7, *p7, k7; repeat from the * across.

Row 13: *[P1, k1] 3 times, p8; repeat from the * across, ending with [p1, k1] 3 times, p1.

Row 20: Knit across.

Repeat Rows 1–20 for the pattern.

oscillating texture

(multiple of 6 stitches plus 2 stitches)

Row 1 (RS): K1, *k4, k2tog, M1 (page 277); repeat from the * across, ending with k1.

Rows 2, 12 and 14: Purl across.

Row 3: K1, *k3, k2tog, M1, k1; repeat from the * across, ending with k1.

Row 4: K1, *k1, p5; repeat from the * across, ending with p1.

Row 5: K1, *k2, k2tog, M1, k2; repeat from the * across, ending with k1.

Row 6: K1, *k2, p4; repeat from the * across, ending with p1.

Row 7: K1, *k1, k2tog, M1, k3; repeat from the * across, ending with k1.

Row 8: K1, *k3, p3; repeat from the * across, ending with p1.

Row 9: K1, *k2tog, M1, k4; repeat from the * across, ending with k1.

Row 10: K1, *k4, p2; repeat from the * across, ending with p1.

Rows 11 and 23: Knit across.

Row 13: K1, *M1, ssk (page 280), k4; repeat from the * across, ending with k1.

Row 15: K1, *k1, M1, ssk, k3; repeat from the * across, ending with k1.

Row 16: P1, *p5, k1; repeat from the * across, ending with k1.

Row 17: K1, *k2, M1, ssk, k2; repeat from the * across, ending with k1.

Row 18: P1, *p4, k2; repeat from the * across, ending with k1.

Row 19: K1, *k3, M1, ssk, k1; repeat from the * across, ending with k1.

Row 20: P1, *p3, k3; repeat from the * across, ending with k1.

Row 21: K1, *k4, M1, ssk; repeat from the * across, ending with k1.

Row 22: P1, *p2, k4; repeat from the * across, ending with k1.

Row 24: As Row 2.

Repeat Rows 1–24 for the pattern.

24									
									23
22				•	•	•	•	•	
		⋋	M						21
20					•	•	•	•	
			⋋	M					19
18						•	•	•	
				⋋	M				17
16							•	•	
					⋋	M			15
14									
						⋋	M		13
12									
									11
10	•	•	•	•	•				
						M	⋌		9
8	•	•	•	•					
					M	⋌			7
6	•	•	•						
				M	⋌				5
4	•	•							
			M	⋌					3
(WS) 2									
		M	⋌						1 (RS)

slate

(multiple of 3 stitches plus 1 stitch)

Rows 1 and 3 (RS): *P2, k1-tbl (page XX); repeat from the * across, ending with p1.

Row 2 and all WS rows: Knit the knit sts and purl the purl sts, working sts that were worked in the back loop on the last row *through their back loops* again.

Row 5: *P1, [k1-tbl] twice; repeat from the * across, ending with p1.

Rows 7 and 9: *P1, k1-tbl, p1; repeat from the * across, ending with p1.

Row 10: As Row 2.

Repeat Rows 1–10 for the pattern.

10	·	·	ℓ	·	
	·	·	ℓ	·	9
8	·	·	ℓ	·	
	·	·	ℓ	·	7
6	·	ℓ	ℓ	·	
	·	ℓ	ℓ	·	5
4	·	ℓ	·	·	
	·	ℓ	·	·	3
(WS) 2	·	ℓ	·	·	
	·	ℓ	·	·	1 (RS)

woven blocks

(multiple of 16 stitches plus 9 stitches)

Rows 1, 3, 5, 7, and 9 (RS): *P9, [k1-tbl (page 275), p1] 3 times, k1-tbl; repeat from the * across, ending with p9.

Rows 2, 4, 6, and 8: K1, p7, k1, *[p1-tbl (page 279), k1] 4 times, p7, k1; repeat from the * across.

Rows 10, 12, 14, and 16: [K1, p1-tbl] 4 times, k1, *k8, [p1-tbl, k1] 4 times; repeat from the * across.

Rows 11, 13, 15, and 17: *[P1, k1-tbl] 4 times, p1, k7; repeat from the * across, ending with [p1, k1-tbl] 4 times, p1.

Row 18: As row 10.

Repeat Rows 1–18 for the pattern.

18	·	ℓ	·	ℓ	·	ℓ	·	ℓ	·	·	·	·	·	·	·	·	·	ℓ	·	ℓ	·	ℓ	·	ℓ	·	
	·	ℓ	·	ℓ	·	ℓ	·	ℓ	·								·	ℓ	·	ℓ	·	ℓ	·	ℓ	·	17
16	·	ℓ	·	ℓ	·	ℓ	·	ℓ	·	·	·	·	·	·	·	·	·	ℓ	·	ℓ	·	ℓ	·	ℓ	·	
	·	ℓ	·	ℓ	·	ℓ	·	ℓ	·								·	ℓ	·	ℓ	·	ℓ	·	ℓ	·	15
14	·	ℓ	·	ℓ	·	ℓ	·	ℓ	·	·	·	·	·	·	·	·	·	ℓ	·	ℓ	·	ℓ	·	ℓ	·	
	·	ℓ	·	ℓ	·	ℓ	·	ℓ	·								·	ℓ	·	ℓ	·	ℓ	·	ℓ	·	13
12	·	ℓ	·	ℓ	·	ℓ	·	ℓ	·	·	·	·	·	·	·	·	·	ℓ	·	ℓ	·	ℓ	·	ℓ	·	
	·	ℓ	·	ℓ	·	ℓ	·	ℓ	·								·	ℓ	·	ℓ	·	ℓ	·	ℓ	·	11
10	·	ℓ	·	ℓ	·	ℓ	·	ℓ	·	·	·	·	·	·	·	·	·	ℓ	·	ℓ	·	ℓ	·	ℓ	·	
	·	·	·	·	·	·	·	·	·	ℓ	·	ℓ	·	ℓ	·	ℓ	·	·	·	·	·	·	·	·	·	9
8	·								·	ℓ	·	ℓ	·	ℓ	·	ℓ	·								·	
	·	·	·	·	·	·	·	·	·	ℓ	·	ℓ	·	ℓ	·	ℓ	·	·	·	·	·	·	·	·	·	7
6	·								·	ℓ	·	ℓ	·	ℓ	·	ℓ	·								·	
	·	·	·	·	·	·	·	·	·	ℓ	·	ℓ	·	ℓ	·	ℓ	·	·	·	·	·	·	·	·	·	5
4	·								·	ℓ	·	ℓ	·	ℓ	·	ℓ	·								·	
	·	·	·	·	·	·	·	·	·	ℓ	·	ℓ	·	ℓ	·	ℓ	·	·	·	·	·	·	·	·	·	3
(WS) 2	·								·	ℓ	·	ℓ	·	ℓ	·	ℓ	·								·	
	·	·	·	·	·	·	·	·	·	ℓ	·	ℓ	·	ℓ	·	ℓ	·	·	·	·	·	·	·	·	·	1 (RS)

guernsey bands

(multiple of 6 stitches plus 1 stitch)

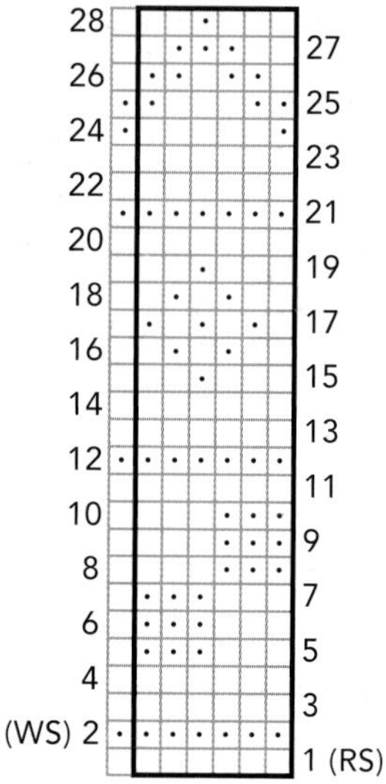

Row 1 (RS): Knit across.

Rows 2, 3, 11, 12, 13, and 23: As Row 1.

Rows 4, 14, 20, 21, and 22: Purl across.

Rows 5 and 7: *K3, p3; repeat from the * across, ending with kl.

Row 6: P1, *k3, p3; repeat from the * across.

Rows 8 and 10: P1, *p3, k3; repeat from the * across.

Row 9: *P3, k3; repeat from the * across, ending with k1.

Rows 15 and 19: *K3, p1, k2; repeat from the * across, ending with k1.

Rows 16 and 18: P1, *[p1, k1] twice, p2; repeat from the * across.

Row 17: *K1, p1; repeat from the * across, ending with k1.

Row 24: K1, *p5, k1; repeat from the * across.

Row 25: *P2, k3, p1; repeat from the * across, ending with p1.

Row 26: P1, *k2, p1; repeat from the * across.

Row 27: *K2, p3, k1; repeat from the * across, ending with k1.

Row 28: P1, *p2, k1, p3; repeat from the * across.

Repeat Rows 1–28 for the pattern.

chapter **two**

lace and openwork patterns

One of the reasons lace is fascinating to design—and to knit!—is because the patterns are created from the negative space between the stitches. Increases and decreases are balanced every row to ensure a consistent stitch count; for every yarn over increase, there's a matching k2tog or ssk decrease.

True lace requires a bit of concentration, but simple openwork patterns are glorious in their own right. The mirrored decreases are the key to beautiful patterns. If any of the techniques seem unfamiliar to you, refer to Knitting Techniques (page 268), for technical resources.

elongated garter stitch

(any number of stitches)

Row 1 (RS): Knit across.

Rows 2, 3 and 4: Knit across.

Row 5: Knit, *wrapping yarn twice as you make each st* (page 274).

Row 6: Knit, *allowing the extra loops to drop.*

Repeat Rows 1–6 for the pattern.

simple dropped stitch cables

(multiple of 6 stitches plus 2 stitches)

Row 1 (RS): K1, *knit the next st *wrapping the yarn twice around the needle* (page 274); repeat from the * across, ending with k1.

Row 2: P1, *slip the next 3 sts onto cn, *allowing the extra loops to drop*, and hold in front, p3, *allowing the extra loops to drop*, p3 from cn; repeat from the * across, ending with p1.

Rows 3 and 5: Knit across.

Rows 4 and 6: Purl across.

Repeat Rows 1–6 for the pattern.

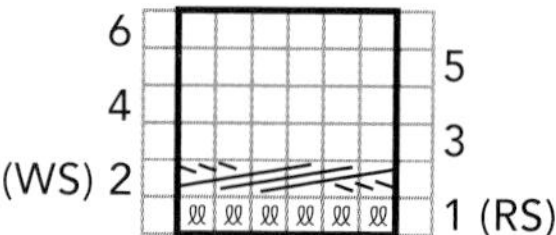

tip

- Many knitters like to use a "lifeline" when knitting lace patterns. They insert a length of super fine yarn (or even dental floss) along one row to make it easier to find all the stitches in case the knitting needs to be ripped out to fix an error. Better safe than sorry!

textured dropped stitch cables

(multiple of 6 stitches plus 2 stitches)

Row 1 (RS): P1, *purl the next st *wrapping the yarn twice around the needle* (page 274); repeat from the * across, ending with p1.

Row 2: P1, *slip the next 3 sts onto cn, *allowing the extra loops to drop*, and hold in front, p3, *allowing the extra loops to drop*, p3 from cn; repeat from the * across, ending with p1.

Rows 3 and 4: Purl across.

Repeat Rows 1–4 for the pattern.

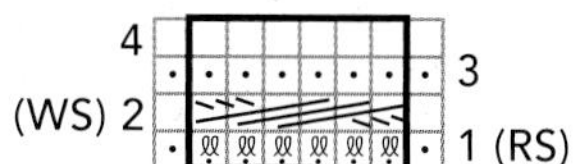

hyacinths

easy

(multiple of 12 stitches plus 11 stitches)

Rows 1 and 15 (RS): Knit across.

Row 2 and all WS rows: Purl across.

Rows 3, 9, 11, and 13: K3, k2tog, yarn over, k1, *yarn over, ssk, k7, k2tog, yarn over, k1; repeat from the * across, ending with yarn over, ssk, k3.

Row 5: K2, k2tog, yarn over, k2, *k1, yarn over, ssk, k5, k2tog, yarn over, k2; repeat from the * across, ending with k1, yarn over, ssk, k2.

Row 7: K1, k2tog, yarn over, k3, *k2, yarn over, ssk, k3, k2tog, yarn over, k3; repeat from the * across, ending with k2, yarn over, ssk, k1.

Rows 17, 23, 25, and 27: K6, *k3, k2tog, yarn over, k1, yarn over, ssk, k4; repeat from the * across, ending with k5.

Row 19: K6, *k2, k2tog, yarn over, k3, yarn over, ssk, k3; repeat from the * across, ending with k5.

Row 21: K6, *k1, k2tog, yarn over, k5, yarn over, ssk, k2; repeat from the * across, ending with k5.

Row 28: As Row 2.

Repeat Rows 1–28 for the pattern.

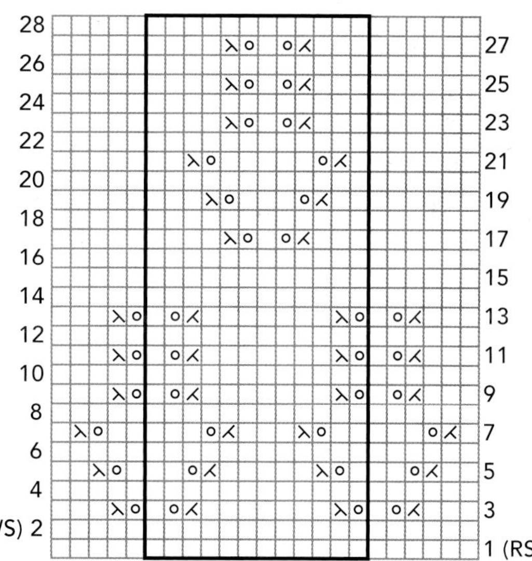

textured eyelets

easy

(multiple of 4 stitches plus 1 stitch)

Rows 1 and 3 (RS): *K1, p3; repeat from the * across, ending with k1.

Row 2 and all WS rows: Purl across.

Row 5: *K1, yarn over, s2kp2 (page 272), yarn over; repeat from the * across, ending with k1.

Row 6: As Row 2.

Repeat Rows 1–6 for the pattern.

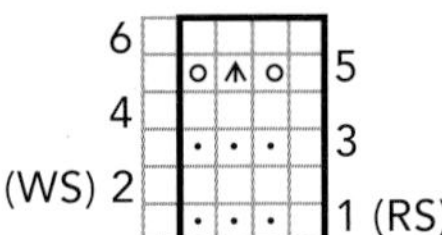

dotted diamonds

(multiple of 8 stitches plus 9 stitches)

12
11
10
9
8
7
6
5
4
3
(WS) 2
1 (RS)

Row 1 (RS): K1, yarn over, ssk, k1, *k2, k2tog, yarn over, k1, yarn over, ssk, k1; repeat from the * across, ending with k2, k2tog, yarn over, k1.

Row 2 and all WS rows: Purl across.

Row 3: K2, yarn over, ssk, *k1, k2tog, yarn over, k3, yarn over, ssk; repeat from the * across, ending with k1, k2tog, yarn over, k2.

Row 5: K3, yarn over, *sssk (page 281), yarn over, k2, yarn over, ssk, k1, yarn over; repeat from the * across, ending with sssk, yarn over, k3.

Row 7: K2, k2tog, yarn over, *k1, yarn over, ssk, k3, k2tog, yarn over; repeat from the * across, ending with k1, yarn over, ssk, k2.

Row 9: K1, k2tog, yarn over, k1, *k2, yarn over, ssk, k1, k2tog, yarn over, k1; repeat from the * across, ending with k2, yarn over, ssk, k1.

Row 11: K2tog, yarn over, k2, *yarn over, ssk, k1, yarn over, sssk, yarn over, k2; repeat from the * across, ending with yarn over, ssk, k1, yarn over, ssk.

Row 12: As Row 2.

Repeat Rows 1–12 for the pattern.

diamond shadows

easy

(multiple of 12 stitches plus 13 stitches)

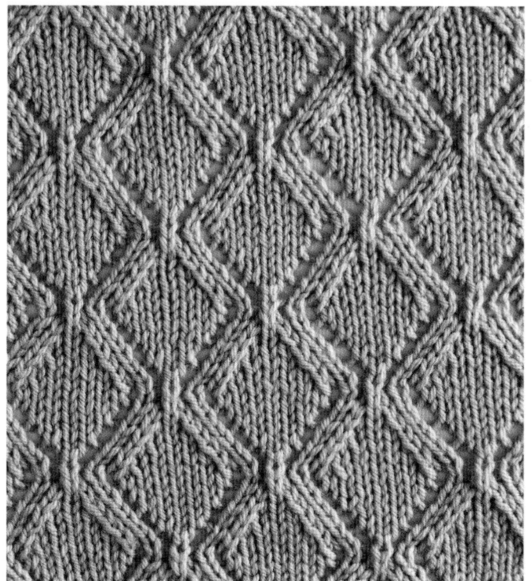

Row 1 (RS): K1, *yarn over, k1, ssk, k5, k2tog, k1, yarn over, k1; repeat from the * across.

Row 2 and all WS rows: Purl across.

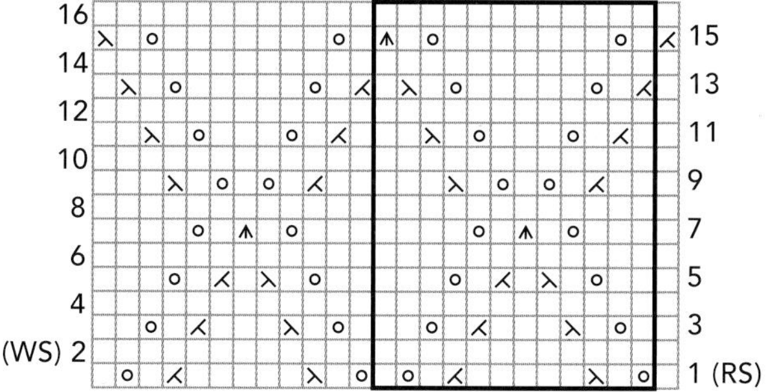

Row 3: K1, *k1, yarn over, k1, ssk, k3, k2tog, k1, yarn over, k2; repeat from the * across.

Row 5: K1, *k2, yarn over, k1, ssk, k1, k2tog, k1, yarn over, k3; repeat from the * across.

Row 7: K1, *k3, yarn over, k1, s2kp2 (page 272), k1, yarn over, k4; repeat from the * across.

Row 9: K1, *k2, k2tog, [k1, yarn over] twice, k1, ssk, k3; repeat from the * across.

Row 11: K1, *k1, k2tog, k1, yarn over, k3, yarn over, k1, ssk, k2; repeat from the * across.

Row 13: K1, *k2tog, k1, yarn over, k5, yarn over, k1, ssk, k1; repeat from the * across.

Row 15: K2tog, *k1, yarn over, k7, yarn over, k1, s2kp2; repeat from the * across, ending with k1, yarn over, k7, yarn over, k1, ssk.

Row 16: As Row 2.

Repeat Rows 1–16 for the pattern.

badminton shuttles

(multiple of 12 stitches plus 11 stitches)

Rows 1 and 13 (RS): Knit across.

Row 2 and all WS rows: Purl across.

Row 3: K5, * make a bobble (page 270), k11; repeat from the * across, ending with make a bobble, k5.

Row 5: K4, yarn over, *s2kp2 (page 272), yarn over, k9, yarn over; repeat from the * across, ending with s2kp2, yarn over, k4.

Row 7: K3, yarn over, k1, *s2kp2, k1, yarn over, k7, yarn over, k1; repeat from the * across, ending with s2kp2, k1, yarn over, k3.

Row 9: K2, yarn over, k2, *s2kp2, k2, yarn over, k5, yarn over, k2; repeat from the * across, ending with s2kp2, k2, yarn over, k2.

Row 11: K1, yarn over, k3, *s2kp2, k3, yarn over, k3, yarn over, k3; repeat from the * across, ending with s2kp2, k3, yarn over, k1.

Row 15: K5, *k6, make a bobble, k5; repeat from the * across, ending with k6.

Row 17: K5, *k5, yarn over, s2kp2, yarn over, k4; repeat from the * across, ending with k6.

Row 19: K5, *k4, yarn over, k1, s2kp2, k1, yarn over, k3; repeat from the * across, ending with k6.

Row 21: K5, *k3, yarn over, k2, s2kp2, k2, yarn over, k2; repeat from the * across, ending with k6.

Row 23: K5, *k2, yarn over, k3, s2kp2, k3, yarn over, k1; repeat from the * across, ending with k6.

Row 24: As Row 2.

Repeat Rows 1–24 for the pattern.

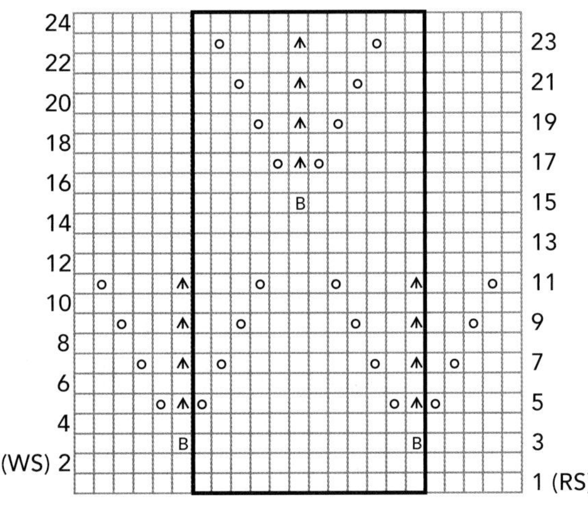

scattered wheat

 easy

(multiple of 12 stitches plus 1 stitch)

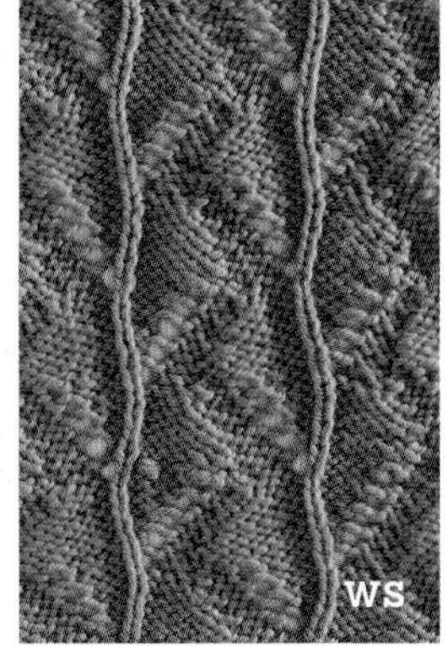

Row 1 (RS): *P1, k6, k2tog, k2, yarn over, k1; repeat from the * across, ending with p1.

Row 2 and all WS rows: Knit the knit sts and purl the purl sts and yarn over sts.

Row 3: *P1, k5, k2tog, k2, yarn over, k2; repeat from the * across, ending with p1.

Row 5: *P1, k4, k2tog, k2, yarn over, k3; repeat from the * across, ending with p1.

Row 7: *P1, yarn over, k2, k3tog, k2, yarn over, k4; repeat from the * across, ending with p1.

Row 9: *P1, k1, yarn over, k2, ssk, k6; repeat from the * across, ending with p1.

Row 11: *P1, k2, yarn over, k2, ssk, k5; repeat from the * across, ending with p1.

Row 13: *P1, k3, yarn over, k2, ssk, k4; repeat from the * across, ending with p1.

Row 15: *P1, k4, yarn over, k2, sssk (page 281), k2, yarn over; repeat from the * across, ending with p1.

Row 16: As Row 2.

Repeat Rows 1–16 for the pattern.

ocean lace

(multiple of 11 stitches plus 1 stitch)

Rows 1, 3, and 5 (RS): *K1, yarn over, k3, k2tog, ssk, k3, yarn over; repeat from the * across, ending with k1.

Rows 2, 4 and 6: Purl across.

Row 7: Purl across.

Row 8: Knit across.

Repeat Rows 1–8 for the pattern.

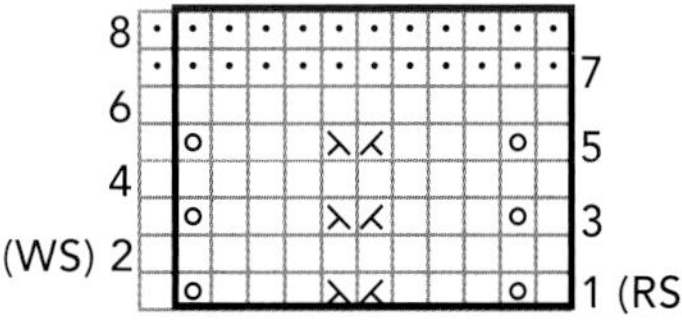

cables 'n' lace

(multiple of 15 stitches plus 1 stitch)

Row 1 (RS): *K1, yarn over, ssk, k1, slip the next 4 sts onto cn and hold in back, k4, k4 from cn, k1, k2tog, yarn over; repeat from the * across, ending with k1.

Row 2 and all WS rows: Purl across.

Row 3: *K2, yarn over, ssk, k8, k2tog, yarn over, k1; repeat from the * across, ending with k1.

Row 5: *K3, yarn over, ssk, k6, k2tog, yarn over, k2; repeat from the * across, ending with k1.

Row 7: *K4, yarn over, ssk, k4, k2tog, yarn over, k3; repeat from the * across, ending with k1.

Row 8: As Row 2.

Repeat Rows 1–8 for the pattern.

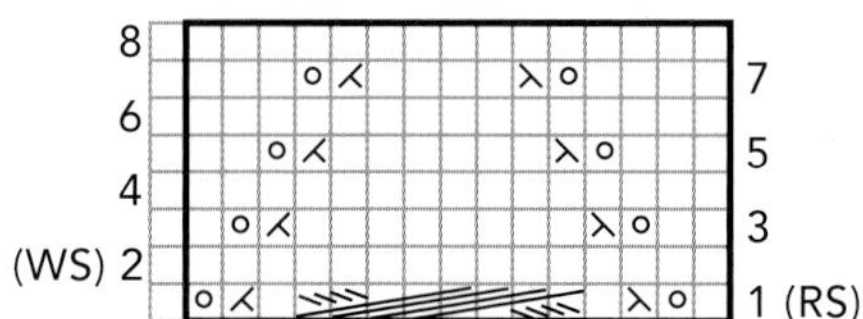

syncopated lace squares

easy

(multiple of 20 stitches plus 10 stitches)

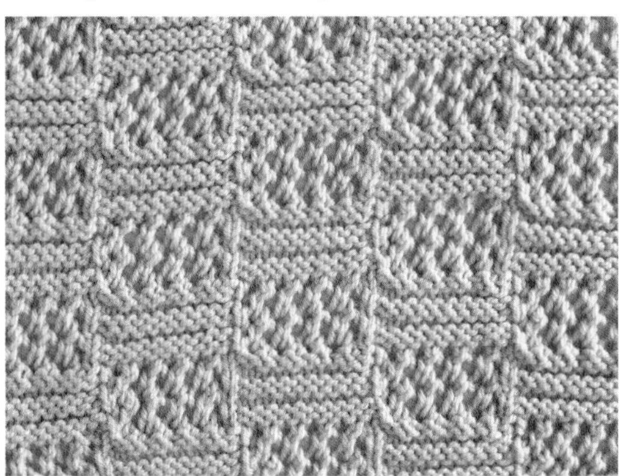

Rows 1, 5 and 9 (RS): *K1, [k2tog, yarn over] 4 times, k1, p10; repeat from the * across, ending with k1, [k2tog, yarn over] 4 times, k1.

Row 2 and all remaining WS rows: Knit the knit sts and purl the purl sts and yarn over sts.

Rows 3 and 7: *K1, [yarn over, k2tog] 4 times, k11; repeat from the * across, ending with k1, [yarn over, k2tog] 4 times, k1.

Rows 11, 15 and 19: *P10, k1, [k2tog, yarn over] 4 times, k1; repeat from the * across, ending with p10.

Rows 13 and 17: *K11, [yarn over, k2tog] 4 times, k1; repeat from the * across, ending with k10.

Row 20: As Row 2.

Repeat Rows 1–20 for the pattern.

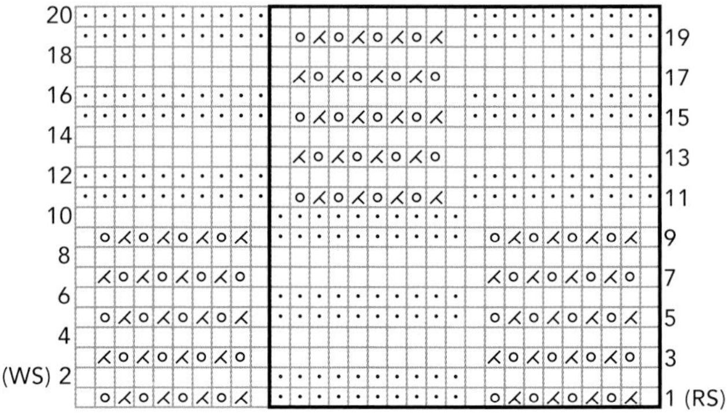

tilted tiles

easy

(multiple of 4 stitches plus 5 stitches)

Row 1 (RS): K1, *yarn over, k3tog, yarn over, k1; repeat from the * across.

Row 2 and all WS rows: Purl across.

Row 3: K1, *k2tog, yarn over, k2; repeat from the * across.

Row 5: K2tog, *yarn over, k1, yarn over, k3tog; repeat from the * across, ending with yarn over, k1, yarn over, k2tog.

Row 7: K1, *k2, k2tog, yarn over; repeat from the * across, ending with k4.

Row 8: As Row 2.

Repeat Rows 1–8 for the pattern.

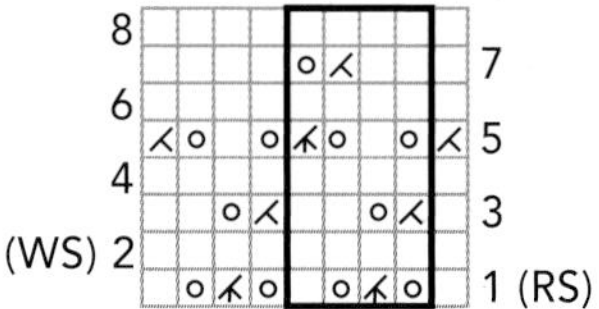

lace ribbons

(multiple of 13 stitches plus 3 stitches)

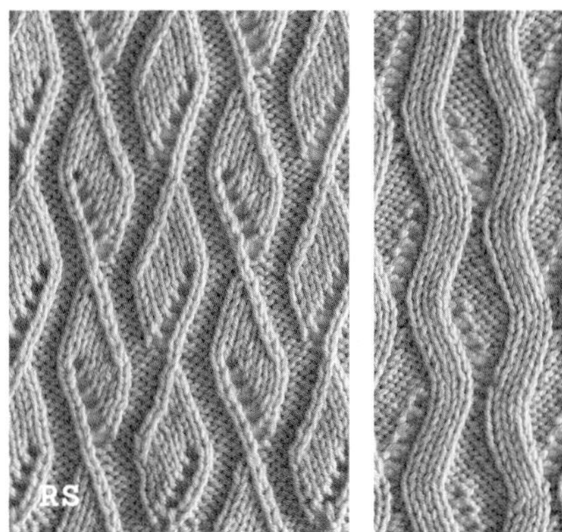

Row 1 (RS): *P3, ssk, k4, p3, k1, yarn over; repeat from the * across, ending with p3.

Row 2 and all WS rows: Knit the knit sts, purl the purl sts, and purl the yarn over sts.

Row 3: *P3, ssk, k3, p3, k1, yarn over, k1; repeat from the * across, ending with p3.

Row 5: *P3, ssk, k2, p3, k1, yarn over, k2; repeat from the * across, ending with p3.

Row 7: *P3, ssk, k1, p3, k1, yarn over, k3; repeat from the * across, ending with p3.

Row 9: *P3, ssk, p3, k1, yarn over, k4; repeat from the * across, ending with p3.

Row 11: *P3, yarn over, k1, p3, k4, k2tog; repeat from the * across, ending with p3.

Row 13: *P3, k1, yarn over, k1, p3, k3, k2tog; repeat from the * across, ending with p3.

Row 15: *P3, k2, yarn over, k1, p3, k2, k2tog; repeat from the * across, ending with p3.

Row 17: *P3, k3, yarn over, k1, p3, k1, k2tog; repeat from the * across, ending with p3.

Row 19: *P3, k4, yarn over, k1, p3, k2tog; repeat from the * across, ending with p3.

Row 20: As Row 2.

Repeat Rows 1–20 for the pattern.

allover floral

(multiple of 12 stitches plus 13 stitches)

Foundation Row 1 (RS): K4, *k2tog, yarn over, k1, yarn over, ssk, k7; repeat from the * across, ending with k2tog, yarn over, k1, yarn over, ssk, k4.

Foundation Row 2 and all WS rows: Purl across.

Row 1: K3, k2tog, yarn over, *k3, yarn over, ssk, k5, k2tog, yarn over; repeat from the * across, ending with k3, yarn over, ssk, k3.

Row 3: K2, k2tog, yarn over, k1, *k4, yarn over, ssk, k3, k2tog, yarn over, k1; repeat from the * across, ending with k4, yarn over, ssk, k2.

Row 5: K4, k2tog, *yarn over, k1, yarn over, ssk, k7, k2tog; repeat from the * across, ending with yarn over, k1, yarn over, ssk, k4.

Row 7: K3, k2tog, yarn over, *k1, yarn over, k2tog, yarn over, ssk, k5, k2tog, yarn over; repeat from the * across, ending with k1, yarn over, k2tog, yarn over, ssk, k3.

Row 9: K4, ssk, *yarn over, k1, yarn over, k2tog, k7, ssk; repeat from the * across, ending with yarn over, k1, yarn over, k2tog, k4.

Row 11: K1, yarn over, ssk, k2, *yarn over, s2kp2 (page 272), yarn over, k2, k2tog, yarn over, k1, yarn over, ssk, k2; repeat from the * across, ending with yarn over, s2kp2, yarn over, k2, k2tog, yarn over, k1.

Row 13: K2, yarn over, ssk, k1, *k4, k2tog, yarn over, k3, yarn over, ssk, k1; repeat from the * across, ending with k4, k2tog, yarn over, k2.

Row 15: K3, yarn over, ssk, *k3, k2tog, yarn over, k5, yarn over, ssk; repeat from the * across, ending with k3, k2tog, yarn over, k3.

Row 17: K1, yarn over, ssk, k2, *k5, k2tog, yarn over, k1, yarn over, ssk, k2; repeat from the * across, ending with k5, k2tog, yarn over, k1.

Row 19: K2, yarn over, ssk, k1, *k4, k2tog, yarn over, k1, yarn over, k2tog, yarn over, ssk, k1; repeat from the * across, ending with k4, k2tog, yarn over, k2.

Row 21: K1, yarn over, k2tog, k2, *k5, ssk, yarn over, k1, yarn over, k2tog, k2; repeat from the * across, ending with k5, ssk, yarn over, k1.

Row 23: K2tog, yarn over, k2, k2tog, *yarn over, k1, yarn over, ssk, k2, yarn over, s2kp2, yarn over, k2, k2tog; repeat from the * across, ending with yarn over, k1, yarn over, ssk, k2, yarn over, ssk.

Row 24: As Row 2.

Repeat Rows 1–24 for the pattern.

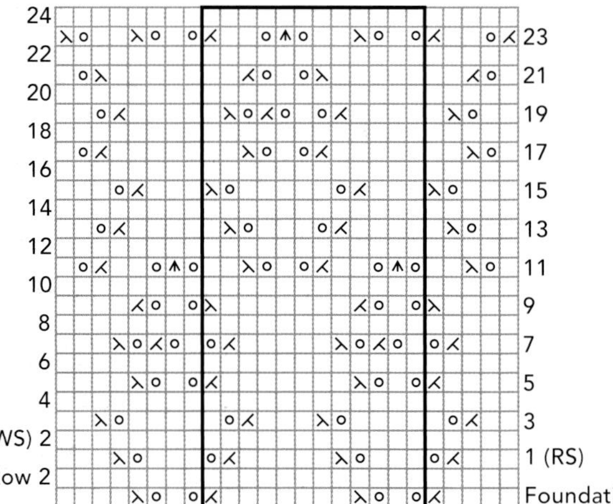

lucky wishbones

easy

(multiple of 16 stitches)

Rows 1 and 3 (RS): *K2tog, yarn over, k4, yarn over, ssk, k2tog, yarn over, k4, yarn over, ssk; repeat from the * across.

Row 2 and all WS rows: Purl across.

Row 5: *K6, yarn over, ssk, k2tog, yarn over, k6; repeat from the * across.

Row 7: *K4, k2tog, yarn over, k4, yarn over, ssk, k4; repeat from the * across.

Row 9: *K3, k2tog, yarn over, k6, yarn over, ssk, k3; repeat from the * across.

Row 11: *K2, k2tog, yarn over, k8, yarn over, ssk, k2; repeat from the * across.

Row 13: *K1, k2tog, yarn over, k10, yarn over, ssk, k1; repeat from the * across.

Row 15: *K2tog, yarn over, k12, yarn over, ssk; repeat from the * across.

Row 16: As Row 2.

Repeat Rows 1–16 for the pattern.

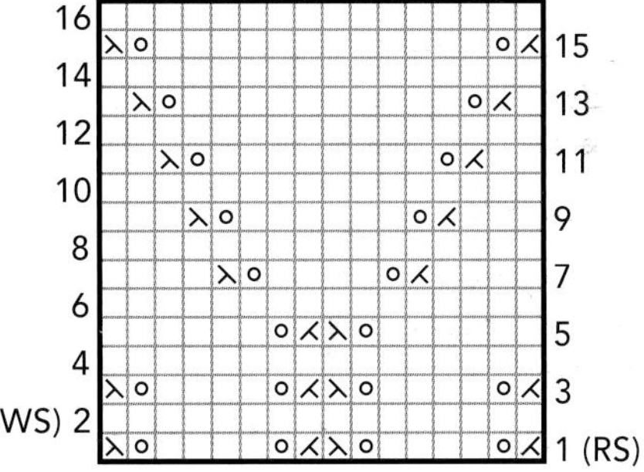

hoof prints

(multiple of 14 stitches plus 8 stitches)

Row 1 (RS): *P1, k1, p4, k1, p1, yarn over, ssk, p2, k2tog, yarn over; repeat from the * across, ending with p1, k1, p4, k1, p1.

Rows 2 and 6: Knit the knit sts, purl the purl sts, and purl the yarn overs.

Row 3: *P1, k1, p4, k1, p2, yarn over, ssk, k2tog, yarn over, p1; repeat from the * across, ending with p1, k1, p4, k1, p1.

Row 4: K1, p1, k4, p1, *k8, p1, k4, p1; repeat from the * across, ending with k1.

Row 5: *P1, yarn over, ssk, p2, k2tog, yarn over, p1, k1, p4, k1; repeat from the * across, ending with p1, yarn over, ssk, p2, k2tog, yarn over, p1.

Row 7: *P2, yarn over, ssk, k2tog, yarn over, p2, k1, p4, k1; repeat from the * across, ending with p2, yarn over, ssk, k2tog, yarn over, p2.

Row 8: K8, *p1, k4, p1, k8; repeat from the * across.

Repeat Rows 1–8 for the pattern.

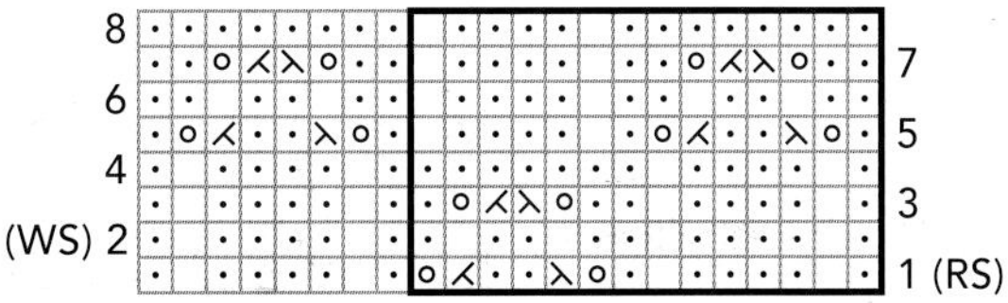

8
7
6
5
4
3
(WS) 2
1 (RS)

openwork bow cables

(multiple of 26 stitches plus 15 stitches)

Row 1 (RS): *P2, k4, yarn over, s2kp2 (page 272), yarn over, k4, p2, k1, yarn over, k3, s2kp2, k3, yarn over, k1; repeat from the * across, ending with p2, k4, yarn over, s2kp2, yarn over, k4, p2.

Row 2 and all WS rows: Knit the knit sts, purl the purl sts, and purl the yarn over sts.

Row 3: *P2, slip the next 2 sts onto cn and hold in back, k2, k2 from cn, yarn over, s2kp2, yarn over, slip the next 2 sts onto cn and hold in front, k2, k2 from cn, p2, k2, yarn over, k2, s2kp2, k2, yarn over, k2; repeat from the * across, ending with p2, slip the next 2 sts onto cn and hold in back, k2, k2 from cn, yarn over, s2kp2, yarn over, slip the next 2 sts onto cn and hold in front, k2, k2 from cn, p2.

Row 5: *P2, k3, yarn over, k1, s2kp2, k1, yarn over, k3; repeat from the * across, ending with p2.

Rows 7 and 11: *P2, k2, yarn over, k2, s2kp2, k2, yarn over, k2, p2, k4, yarn over, s2kp2, yarn over, k4; repeat from the * across, ending with p2, k2, yarn over, k2, s2kp2, k2, yarn over, k2, p2.

Row 9: *P2, k1, yarn over, k3, s2kp2, k3, yarn over, k1, p2, slip the next 2 sts onto cn and hold in front, k2, k2 from cn, yarn over, s2kp2, yarn over, slip the next 2 sts onto cn and hold in back, k2, k2 from cn; repeat from the * across, ending with p2, k1, yarn over, k3, s2kp2, k3, yarn over, k1, p2.

Row 13: *P2, k3, yarn over, k1, s2kp2, k1, yarn over, k3, p2, slip the next 2 sts onto cn and hold in back, k2, k2 from cn, yarn over, s2kp2, yarn over, slip the next 2 sts onto cn and hold in front, k2, k2 from cn; repeat from the * across, ending with p2, k3, yarn over, k1, s2kp2, k1, yarn over, k3, p2.

Row 15: *P2, k4, yarn over, s2kp2, yarn over, k4, p2, k3, yarn over, k1, s2kp2, k1, yarn over, k3; repeat from the * across, ending with p2, k4, yarn over, s2kp2, yarn over, k4, p2.

Row 17: *P2, slip the next 2 sts onto cn and hold in front, k2, k2 from cn, yarn over, s2kp2, yarn over, slip the next 2 sts onto cn and hold in back, k2, k2 from cn, p2, k2, yarn over, k2, s2kp2, k2, yarn over, k2; repeat from the * across, ending with p2, slip the next 2 sts onto cn and hold in front, k2, k2 from cn, yarn over, s2kp2, yarn over, slip the next 2 sts onto cn and hold in back, k2, k2 from cn, p2.

Row 18: As Row 2.

Repeat Rows 1–18 for the pattern.

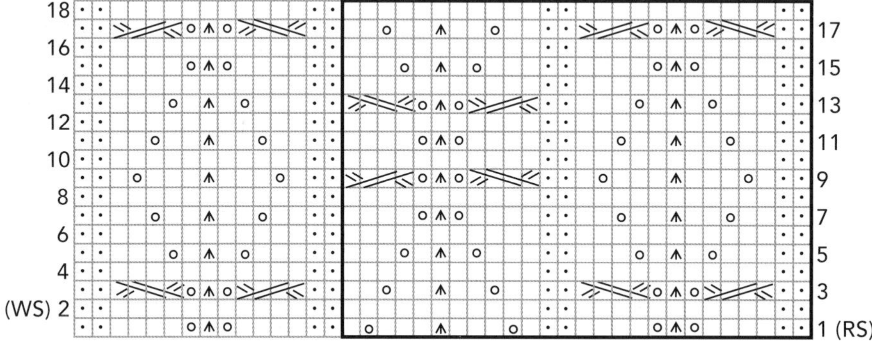

lacy triangles

easy

(multiple of 10 stitches plus 9 stitches)

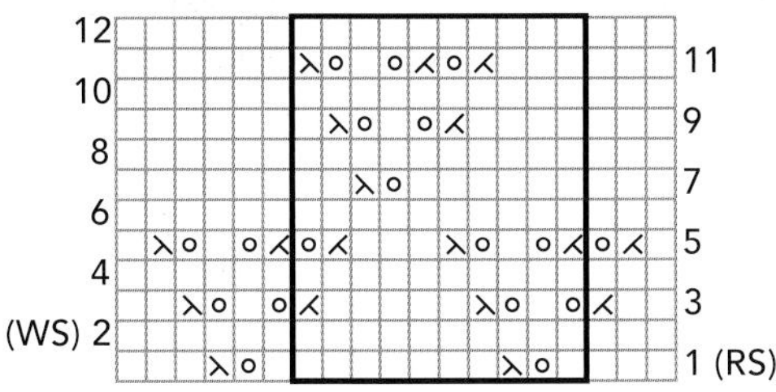

Row 1 (RS): K3, *k1, yarn over, ssk, k7; repeat from the * across, ending with k1, yarn over, ssk, k3.

Row 2 and all WS rows: Purl across.

Row 3: K2, k2tog, *yarn over, k1, yarn over, ssk, k5, k2tog; repeat from the * across, ending with yarn over, k1, yarn over, ssk, k2.

Row 5: K1, k2tog, yarn over, *k2tog, yarn over, k1, yarn over, ssk, k3, k2tog, yarn over; repeat from the * across, ending with k2tog, yarn over, k1, yarn over, ssk, k1.

Row 7: K3, *k6, yarn over, ssk, k2; repeat from the * across, ending with k6.

Row 9: K3, *k4, k2tog, yarn over, k1, yarn over, ssk, k1; repeat from the * across, ending with k6.

Row 11: K3, *k3, [k2tog, yarn over] twice, k1, yarn over, ssk; repeat from the * across, ending with k6.

Row 12: As Row 2.

Repeat Rows 1–12 for the pattern.

thistles

easy

(multiple of 8 stitches plus 1 stitch)

Row 1 (RS): *K1, ssk, [k1, yarn over] twice, k1, k2tog; repeat from the * across, ending with k1.

Row 2 and all WS rows: Purl across.

Row 3: *K1, ssk, yarn over, k3, yarn over, k2tog; repeat from the * across, ending with k1.

Row 5: *K1, yarn over, k1, k2tog, k1, ssk, k1, yarn over; repeat from the * across, ending with k1.

Row 7: *K2, yarn over, k2tog, k1, ssk, yarn over, k1; repeat from the * across, ending with k1.

Row 8: As Row 2.

Repeat Rows 1–8 for the pattern.

8 6 4 (WS) 2 — 7 5 3 1 (RS)

paper dolls

easy

(multiple of 6 stitches plus 7 stitches)

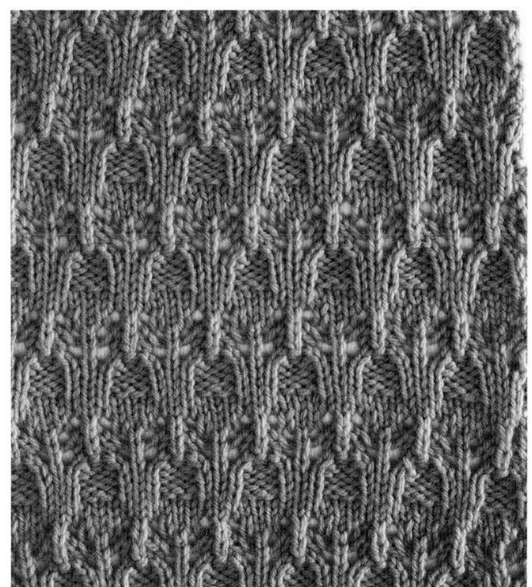

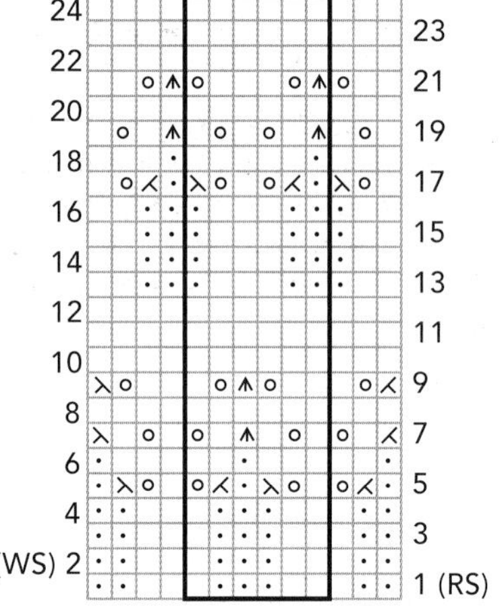

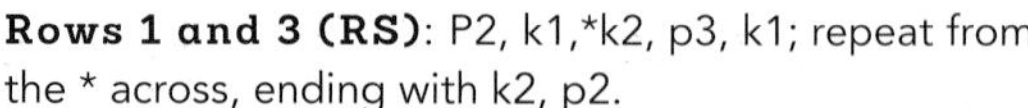

Rows 1 and 3 (RS): P2, k1,*k2, p3, k1; repeat from the * across, ending with k2, p2.

Row 2 and all WS rows: Knit the knit sts and purl the purl sts and the yarn over sts.

Row 5: P1, k2tog, yarn over, *k1, yarn over, ssk, p1, k2tog, yarn over; repeat from the * across, ending with k1, yarn over, ssk, p1.

Row 7: K2tog, k1, yarn over, *k1, yarn over, k1, s2kp2 (page 272), k1, yarn over; repeat from the * across, ending with k1, yarn over, k1, ssk.

Row 9: K2tog, yarn over, k1, *k2, yarn over, s2kp2, yarn over, k1; repeat from the * across, ending with k2, yarn over, ssk.

Rows 11 and 23: Knit across.

Rows 13 and 15: K2, p1, *p2, k3, p1; repeat from the * across, ending with p2, k2.

Row 17: K1, yarn over, ssk, *p1, k2tog, yarn over, k1, yarn over, ssk; repeat from the * across, ending with p1, k2tog, yarnover, k1.

Row 19: K1, yarn over, k1, *s2kp2, k1, [yarn over, k1] twice; repeat from the * across, ending with s2kp2, k1, yarn over, k1.

Row 21: K2, yarn over, *s2kp2, yarn over, k3, yarn over; repeat from the * across, ending with s2kp2, yarn over, k2.

Row 24: Purl across.

Repeat Rows 1–24 for the pattern.

hearts

easy

(multiple of 36 stitches plus 18 stitches)

Row 1 (RS): *K1, ssk, yarn over, k3, k2tog, [k1, yarn over] twice, k1, ssk, k3, yarn over, k2tog, [k1, ssk, yarn over] twice, k7, yarn over, k2tog, k1, yarn over, k2tog; repeat from the * across, ending with k1, ssk, yarn over, k3, k2tog, [k1, yarn over] twice, k1, ssk, k3, yarn over, k2tog.

Row 2 and all WS rows: Knit the knit sts, purl the purl sts, and purl the yarn over sts.

Row 3: *K1, ssk, yarn over, k2, k2tog, k1, yarn over, k3, yarn over, k1, ssk, k2, yarn over, k2tog, [k1, ssk, yarn over] 3 times, [k1, yarn over, k2tog] 3 times; repeat from the * across, ending with k1, ssk, yarn over, k2, k2tog, k1, yarn over, k3, yarn over, k1, ssk, k2, yarn over, k2tog.

Row 5: *K1, ssk, yarn over, k1, k2tog, k1, yarn over, k5, yarn over, k1, ssk, k1, yarn over, k2tog, [k1, ssk, yarn over] twice, ssk, yarn over, k3, [yarn over, k2tog] twice, k1, yarn over, k2tog; repeat from the * across, ending with k1, ssk, yarn over, k1, k2tog, k1, yarn over, k5, yarn over, k1, ssk, k1, yarn over, k2tog.

Row 7: *K1, ssk, yarn over, k2tog, k1, yarn over, k7, yarn over, k1, ssk, yarn over, k2tog, k1, ssk, yarn over, k2, k2tog, yarn over, k5, yarn over, ssk, k2, yarn over, k2tog; repeat from the * across, ending with k1, ssk, yarn over, k2tog, k1, yarn over, k7, yarn over, k1, ssk, yarn over, k2tog.

Row 9: *[K1, ssk, yarn over] twice, k7, [yarn over, k2tog, k1] twice, ssk, yarn over, k3, k2tog, [k1, yarn over] twice, k1, ssk, k3, yarn over, k2tog; repeat from the * across, ending with [k1, ssk, yarn over] twice, k7, yarn over, k2tog, k1, yarn over, k2tog.

Row 11: *[K1, ssk, yarn over] 3 times, [k1, yarn over, k2tog] 3 times, k1, ssk, yarn over, k2, k2tog, k1, yarn over, k3, yarn over, k1, ssk, k2, yarn over, k2tog; repeat from the * across, ending with [k1, ssk, yarn over] 3 times, [k1, yarn over, k2tog] 3 times.

Row 13: *[K1, ssk, yarn over] twice, ssk, yarn over, k3, [yarn over, k2tog] twice, k1, yarn over, k2tog, k1, ssk, yarn over, k1, k2tog, k1, yarn over, k5, yarn over, k1, ssk, k1, yarn over, k2tog; repeat from the * across, ending with [k1, ssk, yarn over] twice, ssk, yarn over, k3, [yarn over, k2tog] twice, k1, yarn over, k2tog.

Row 15: *K1, ssk, yarn over, k2, k2tog, yarn over, k5, yarn over, ssk, k2, yarn over, k2tog, k1, ssk, yarn over, k2tog, k1, yarn over, k7, yarn over, k1, ssk, yarn over, k2tog; repeat from the * across, ending with k1, ssk, yarn over, k2, k2tog, yarn over, k5, yarn over, ssk, k2, yarn over, k2tog.

Row 16: As Row 2.

Repeat Rows 1–16 for the pattern.

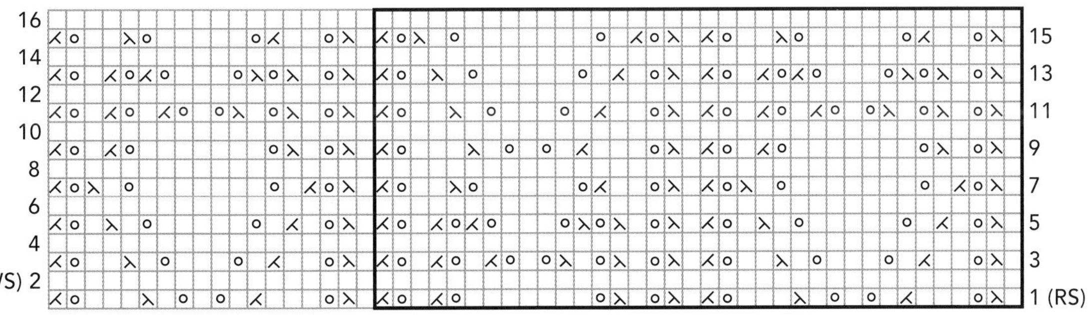

x marks the spot

(over 18 stitches, on a stockinette background)

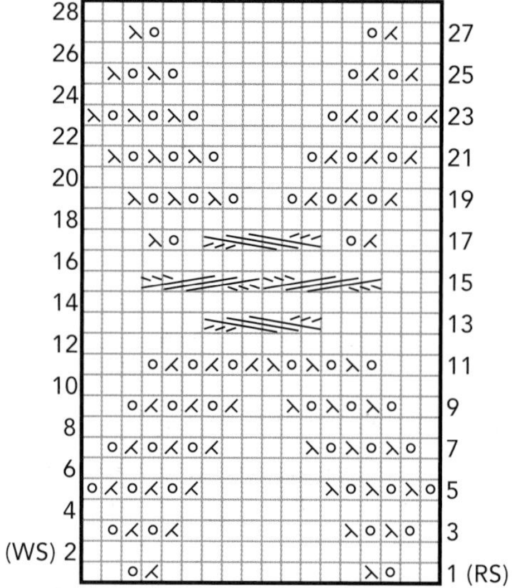

Row 1 (RS): K2, yarn over, ssk, k10, k2tog, yarn over, k2.

Row 2 and all WS rows: Purl across.

Row 3: K1, [yarn over, ssk] twice, k8, [k2tog, yarn over] twice, k1.

Row 5: [Yarn over, ssk] 3 times, k6, [k2tog, yarn over] 3 times.

Row 7: K1, [yarn over, ssk] 3 times, k4, [k2tog, yarn over] 3 times, k1.

Row 9: K2, [yarn over, ssk] 3 times, k2, [k2tog, yarn over] 3 times, k2.

Row 11: K3, [yarn over, ssk] 3 times, [k2tog, yarn over] 3 times, k3.

Row 13: K6, slip the next 3 sts onto cn and hold in front, k3, k3 from cn, k6.

Row 15: K3, [slip the next 3 sts onto cn and hold in back, k3, k3 from cn] twice, k3.

Row 17: K3, k2tog, yarn over, k1, slip the next 3 sts onto cn and hold in front, k3, k3 from cn, k1, yarn over, ssk, k3.

Row 19: K2, [k2tog, yarn over] 3 times, k2, [yarn over, ssk] 3 times, k2.

Row 21: K1, [k2tog, yarn over] 3 times, k4, [yarn over, ssk] 3 times, k1.

Row 23: [K2tog, yarn over] 3 times, k6, [yarn over, ssk] 3 times.

Row 25: K1, [k2tog, yarn over] twice, k8, [yarn over, ssk] twice, k1.

Row 27: K2, k2tog, yarn over, k10, yarn over, ssk, k2.

Row 28: As Row 2.

open basketweave

easy

(multiple of 10 stitches plus 3 stitches)

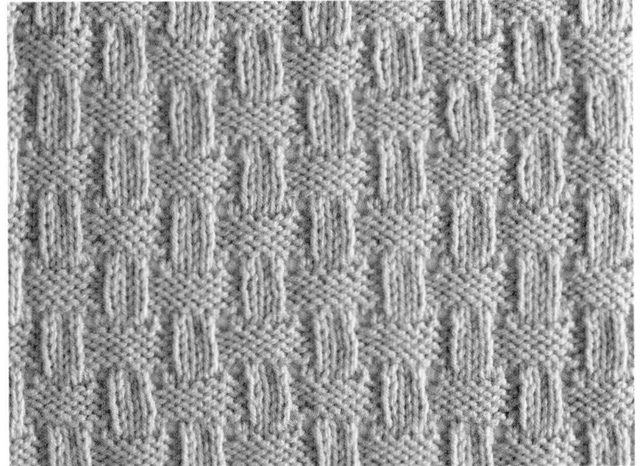

Rows 1 and 3 (RS): K1, *k2, p7, k1; repeat from the * across, ending with k2.

Row 2 and all WS rows: Knit the knit sts, purl the purl sts, and purl the yarn over sts.

Row 5: K1, *k1, ssk, yarn over, k5, yarn over, k2tog; repeat from the * across, ending with k2.

Rows 7 and 9: P1, *p4, k3, p3; repeat from the * across, ending with p2.

Row 11: K1, *k3, yarn over, k2tog, k1, ssk, yarn over, k2; repeat from the * across, ending with k2.

Row 12: As Row 2.

Repeat Rows 1–12 for the pattern.

12														
					o	⋋		⋌	o					11
10	•	•	•	•	•				•	•	•	•	•	
	•	•	•	•	•				•	•	•	•	•	9
8	•	•	•	•	•				•	•	•	•	•	
	•	•	•	•	•				•	•	•	•	•	7
6														
			⋌	o						o	⋋			5
4				•	•	•	•	•	•	•				
				•	•	•	•	•	•	•				3
(WS) 2				•	•	•	•	•	•	•				
				•	•	•	•	•	•	•				1 (RS)

lace peaks

(multiple of 8 stitches plus 9 stitches)

Row 1 (RS): K4, *yarn over, ssk, k6; repeat from the * across, ending with yarn over, ssk, k3.

Row 2 and all WS rows: Purl across.

Row 3: K2, k2tog, yarn over, *k1, yarn over, ssk, k3, k2tog, yarn over; repeat from the * across, ending with k1, yarn over, ssk, k2.

Row 5: K1, k2tog, yarn over, k1, *k2, yarn over, ssk, k1, k2tog, yarn over, k1; repeat from the * across, ending with k2, yarn over, ssk, k1.

Row 7: K2tog, yarn over, k2, *k3, yarn over, s2kp2 (page 272), yarn over, k2; repeat from the * across, ending with k3, yarn over, ssk.

Row 8: As Row 2.

Repeat Rows 1–8 for the pattern.

8																	
	⋋	o						o	ʌ	o						o	⋌	7
6																	
		⋋	o				o	⋌		⋋	o				o	⋌		5
4																	
			⋋	o		o	⋌					⋋	o	o	⋌			3
(WS) 2																	
				⋋	o							⋋	o					1 (RS)

fancy diamonds

(multiple of 12 stitches plus 13 stitches)

Rows 1 and 9 (RS): P1, k2, k2tog, k1, *yarn over, p1, yarn over, k1, ssk, k2, p1, k2, k2tog, k1; repeat from the * across, ending with yarn over, p1, yarn over, k1, ssk, k2, p1.

Row 2 and all WS rows: Knit the knit sts, purl the purl sts, and purl the yarn over sts.

Rows 3 and 11: P1, k1, k2tog, k1, yarn over, *k1, p1, k1, yarn over, k1, ssk, k1, p1, k1, k2tog, k1, yarn over; repeat from the * across, ending with k1, p1, k1, yarn over, k1, ssk, k1, p1.

Rows 5 and 13: P1, k2tog, k1, yarn over, k1, *k1, p1, k2, yarn over, k1, ssk, p1, k2tog, k1, yarn over, k1; repeat from the * across, ending with k1, p1, k2, yarn over, k1, ssk, p1.

Rows 7 and 15: K2tog, k1, yarn over, k2, *k1, p1, k3, yarn over, k1, s2kp2 (page 272), k1, yarn over, k2; repeat from the * across, ending with k1, p1, k3, yarn over, k1, ssk.

Rows 17 and 25: P1, yarn over, k1, ssk, k1, *k1, p1, k2, k2tog, k1, yarn over, p1, yarn over, k1, ssk, k1; repeat from the * across, ending with k1, p1, k2, k2tog, k1, yarn over, p1.

Rows 19 and 27: P1, k1, yarn over, k1, ssk, *k1, p1, k1, k2tog, k1, yarn over, k1, p1, k1, yarn over, k1, ssk; repeat from the * across, ending with k1, p1, k1, k2tog, k1, yarn over, k1, p1.

Rows 21 and 29: P1, k2, yarn over, k1, *ssk, p1, k2tog, k1, yarn over, k2, p1, k2, yarn over, k1; repeat from the * across, ending with ssk, p1, k2tog, k1, yarn over, k2, p1.

Rows 23 and 31: P1, k3, yarn over, *k1, s2kp2, k1, yarn over, k3, p1, k3, yarn over; repeat from the * across, ending with k1, s2kp2, k1, yarn over, k3, p1.

Row 32: As Row 2.

Repeat Rows 1–32 for the pattern.

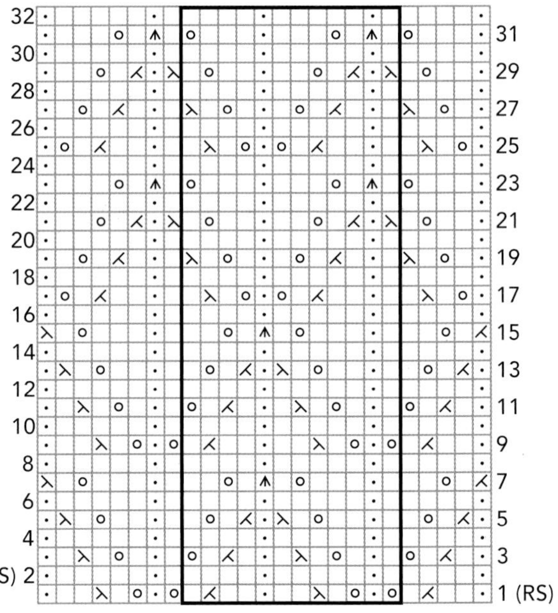

baby eyelet cables

(multiple of 6 stitches plus 3 stiches)

NOTE

- Always slip stitches purlwise (page 279) unless told otherwise.

Row 1 (RS): *P3, slip next 3 sts onto the right-hand needle, pass the third st on the right-hand needle over the first 2 sts as if you're binding it off, slip those 2 sts back onto the left-hand needle, k1, yarn over, k1; repeat from * across, ending with p3.

Row 2 and all WS rows: Knit the knit sts, purl the purl sts, and purl the yarn over sts.

Row 3: *P3, k3; repeat from * across, ending with p3.

Row 4: As Row 2.

Repeat Rows 1–4 for the pattern.

4
3
(WS) 2
1 (RS)

surf pattern

(multiple of 15 stitches plus 1 stitch, increases to multiple of 23 stitches plus 1 stitch)

NOTE

- Stitch count varies from row to row.

Row 1 (RS): *K1, yarn over, k14, yarn over; repeat from the * across, ending with k1.

Row 2 and all WS rows: Purl across.

Row 3: *K2, yarn over, k14, yarn over, k1; repeat from the * across, ending with k1.

Row 5: *K3, yarn over, k14, yarn over, k2; repeat from the * across, ending with k1.

Row 7: *K4, yarn over, k14, yarn over, k3; repeat from the * across, ending with k1.

Row 9: *K4, [p2tog] 8 times, k3; repeat from the * across, ending with k1.

Row 10: As Row 2.

Repeat Rows 1–10 for the pattern.

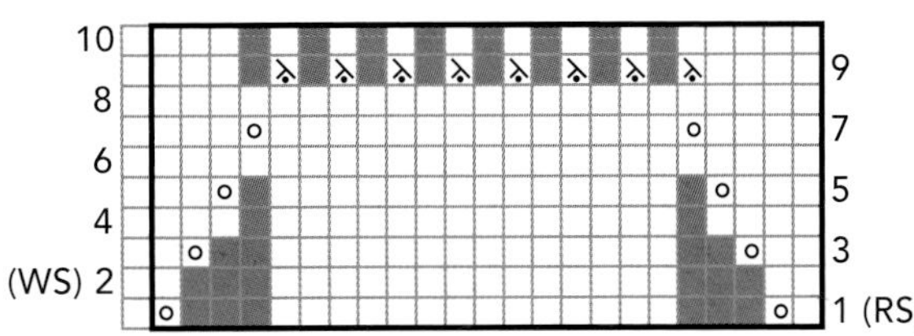

orchid panel

(over 29 stitches, on a stockinette background)

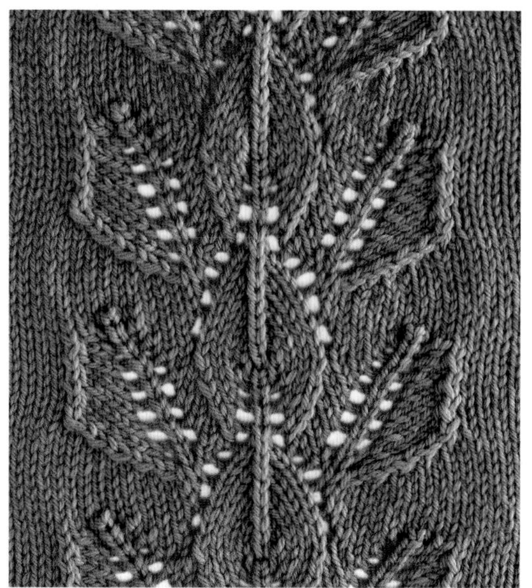

Row 1 (RS): K4, k3tog, k2, yarn over, k1, yarn over, k2, k2tog, yarn over, k1, yarn over, ssk, k2, yarn over, k1, yarn over, k2, sssk (page 281), k4.

Row 2 and all WS rows: Purl across.

Row 3: K2, k3tog, k3, yarn over, k1, yarn over, k2, k2tog, [k1, yarn over] twice, k1, ssk, k2, yarn over, k1, yarn over, k3, sssk, k2.

Row 5: K3tog, k4, yarn over, k1, yarn over, k2, k2tog, k2, yarn over, k1, yarn over, k2, ssk, k2, yarn over, k1, yarn over, k4, sssk.

Row 7: Sssk, k3, yarn over, k1, yarn over, k2, k2tog, k3, yarn over, k1, yarn over, k3, ssk, k2, yarn over, k1, yarn over, k3, k3tog.

Row 9: Sssk, k2, yarn over, k1, yarn over, k3, yarn over, k4, s2kp2 (page 272), k4, yarn over, k3, yarn over, k1, yarn over, k2, k3tog.

Row 11: Sssk, [k1, yarn over] twice, k5, yarn over, k3, s2kp2, k3, yarn over, k5, [yarn over, k1] twice, k3tog.

Row 13: K11, yarn over, k2, s2kp2, k2, yarn over, k11.

Row 15: K8, k2tog, yarn over, k2, yarn over, k1, s2kp2, k1, yarn over, k2, yarn over, ssk, k8.

Row 17: K6, k3tog, [k1, yarn over] twice, k2, yarn over, s2kp2, yarn over, k2, [yarn over, k1] twice, sssk, k6.

Row 18: As Row 2.

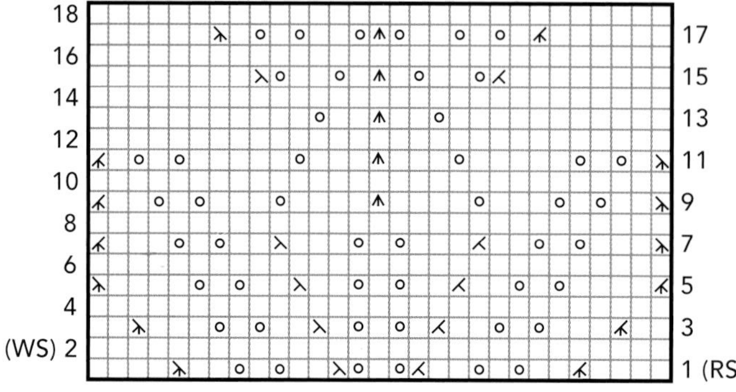

lace blossoms

easy

(multiple of 14 stitches plus 11 stitches)

Row 1 (RS): K3, k2tog, yarn over, *k1, yarn over, ssk, k9, k2tog, yarn over; repeat from the * across, ending with k1, yarn over, ssk, k3.

Row 2 and all WS rows: Purl across.

Row 3: K2, k2tog, yarn over, k1, *k2, yarn over, ssk, k7, k2tog, yarn over, k1; repeat from the * across, ending with k2, yarn over, ssk, k2.

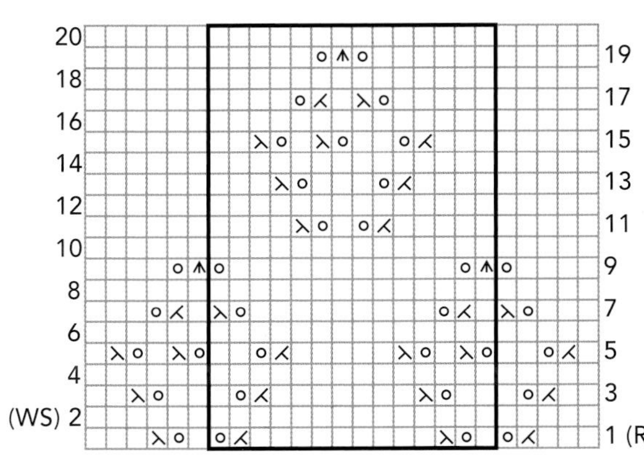

Row 5: K1, k2tog, yarn over, k2, *yarn over, ssk, k1, yarn over, ssk, k5, k2tog, yarn over, k2; repeat from the * across, ending with [yarn over, ssk, k1] twice.

Row 7: K3, yarn over, ssk, *k1, k2tog, yarn over, k9, yarn over, ssk; repeat from the * across, ending with k1, k2tog, yarn over, k3.

Row 9: K4, yarn over, *s2kp2 (page 272), yarn over, k11, yarn over; repeat from the * across, ending with s2kp2, yarn over, k4.

Row 11: K5, *k5, k2tog, yarn over, k1, yarn over, ssk, k4; repeat from the * across, ending with k6.

Row 13: K5, *k4, k2tog, yarn over, k3, yarn over, ssk, k3; repeat from the * across, ending with k6.

Row 15: K5, *k3, k2tog, yarn over, k2, yarn over, ssk, k1, yarn over, ssk, k2; repeat from the * across, ending with k6.

Row 17: K5, *k5, yarn over, ssk, k1, k2tog, yarn over, k4; repeat from the * across, ending with k6.

Row 19: K5, *k6, yarn over, s2kp2, yarn over, k5; repeat from the * across, ending with k6.

Row 20: As Row 2.

Repeat Rows 1–20 for the pattern.

birdhouses

easy

(multiple of 12 stitches)

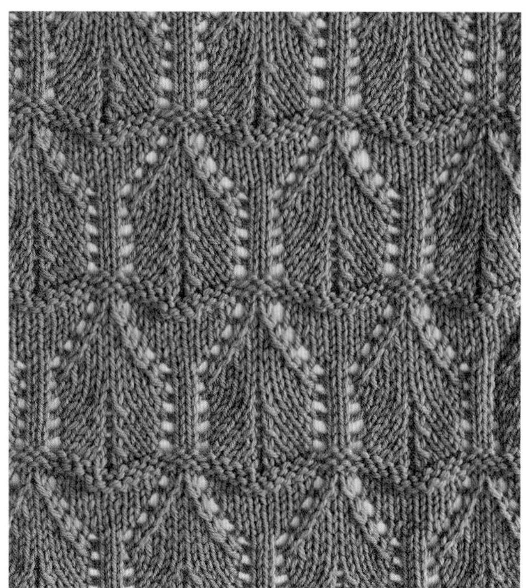

Rows 1 and 19 (RS): Purl across.

Row 2 and all WS rows: Knit the knit sts, purl the purl sts, and purl the yarn over sts.

Rows 3, 5, 7, and 9: *K2tog, k3, yarn over, k2, yarn over, k3, ssk; repeat from the * across.

Row 11: *K3, k2tog, yarn over, k2, yarn over, ssk, k3; repeat from the * across.

Row 13: *K2, k2tog, yarn over, k4, yarn over, ssk, k2; repeat from the * across.

Row 15: *K1, k2tog, yarn over, k6, yarn over, ssk, k1; repeat from the * across.

Row 17: *K2tog, yarn over, k8, yarn over, ssk; repeat from the * across.

Rows 21, 23, 25, and 27: *K1, yarn over, k3, ssk, k2tog, k3, yarn over, k1; repeat from the * across.

Row 29: *K1, yarn over, ssk, k6, k2tog, yarn over, k1; repeat from the * across.

Row 31: *K2, yarn over, ssk, k4, k2tog, yarn over, k2; repeat from the * across.

Row 33: *K3, yarn over, ssk, k2, k2tog, yarn over, k3; repeat from the * across.

Row 35: *K4, yarn over, ssk, k2tog, yarn over, k4; repeat from the * across.

Row 36: As Row 2.

Repeat Rows 1–36 for the pattern.

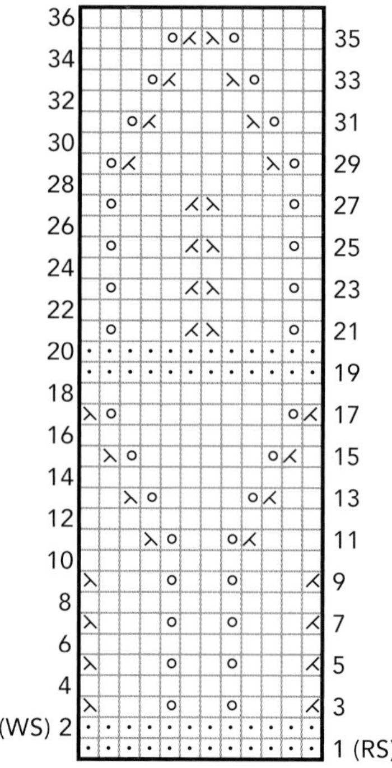

pinecones

easy

(multiple of 18 stitches plus 11 stitches)

Row 1 (RS): K1, *yarn over, p3, s2kp2 (page 272), p3, yarn over, k9; repeat from the * across, ending with yarn over, p3, s2kp2, p3, yarn over, k1.

Row 2 and all WS rows: Purl across.

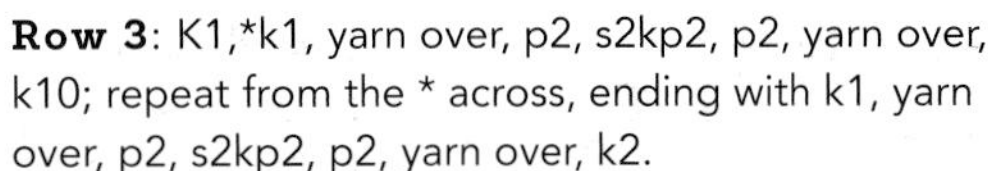

Row 3: K1,*k1, yarn over, p2, s2kp2, p2, yarn over, k10; repeat from the * across, ending with k1, yarn over, p2, s2kp2, p2, yarn over, k2.

Row 5: K1, *k2, yarn over, p1, s2kp2, p1, yarn over, k11; repeat from the * across, ending with k2, yarn over, p1, s2kp2, p1, yarn over, k3.

Row 7: K1,*k3, yarn over, s2kp2, yarn over, k12; repeat from the * across, ending with k3, yarn over, s2kp2, yarn over, k4.

Row 9: K1, *k9, yarn over, p3, s2kp2, p3, yarn over; repeat from the * across, ending with k10.

Row 11: K1, *k10, yarn over, p2, s2kp2, p2, yarn over, k1; repeat from the * across, ending with k10 .

Row 13: K1, *k11, yarn over, p1, s2kp2, p1, yarn over, k2; repeat from the * across, ending with k10.

Row 15: K1, *k12, yarn over, s2kp2, yarn over, k3; repeat from the * across, ending with k10.

Row 16: As Row 2.

Repeat Rows 1–16 for the pattern.

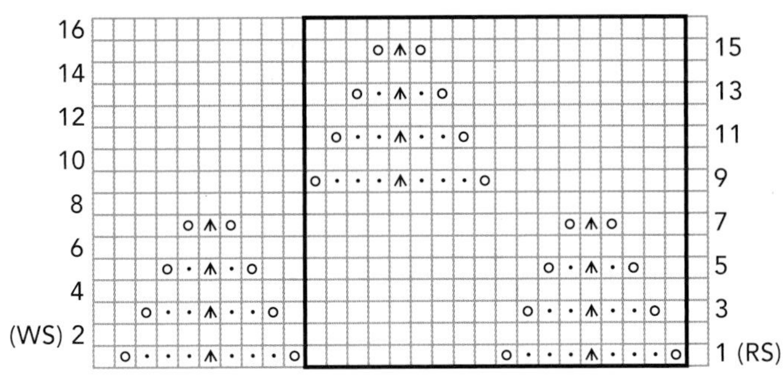

lace on the diagonal 

(multiple of 9 stitches plus 3 stitches)

Row 1 (RS): K1, *k5, [k2tog, yarn over] twice; repeat from the * across, ending with k2.

Row 2 and all WS rows: Purl across.

Row 3: K1, *k4, [k2tog, yarn over] twice, k1; repeat from the * across, ending with k2.

Row 5: K1, *k3, [k2tog, yarn over] twice, k2; repeat from the * across, ending with k2.

Row 7: K1, *k2, [k2tog, yarn over] twice, k3; repeat from the * across, ending with k2.

Row 9: K1, *k1, [k2tog, yarn over] twice, k4; repeat from the * across, ending with k2.

Row 11: K1, *[k2tog, yarn over] twice, k5; repeat from the * across, ending with k2.

Row 13: K2tog, *yarn over, k2tog, yarn over, k5, k2tog; repeat from the * across, ending with yarn over, k1.

Row 15: K1, *k2tog, yarn over, k5, k2tog, yarn over; repeat from the * across, ending with k2.

Row 17: K2tog, *yarn over, k5, k2tog, yarn over, k2tog; repeat from the * across, ending with yarn over, k1.

Row 18: As Row 2.

Repeat Rows 1–18 for the pattern.

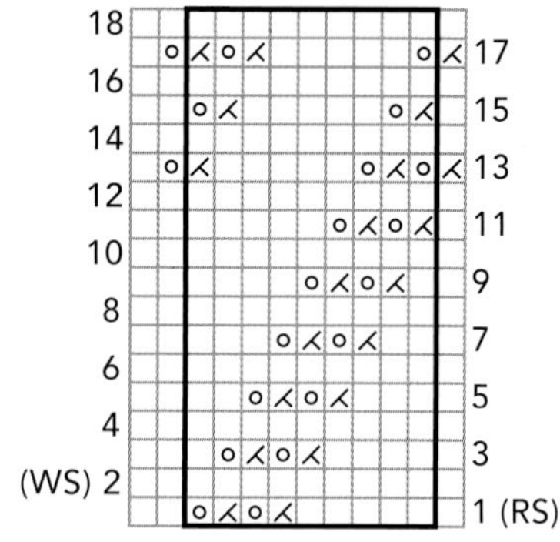

horizontal river stitch 

(any number of stitches)

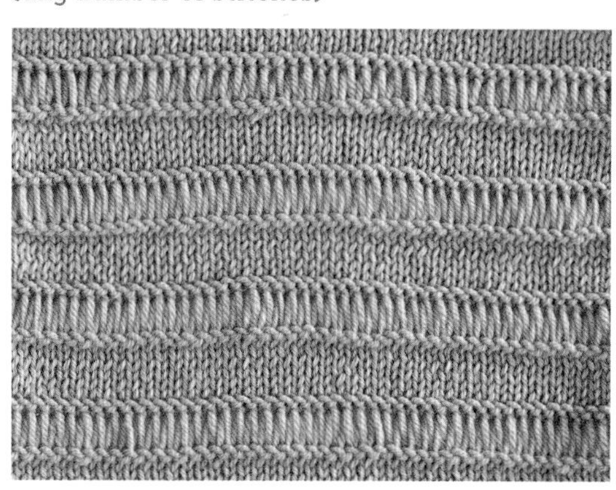

Row 1 (RS): Knit across.

Rows 2, 4, and 6: Purl across.

Rows 3, 5, 7, and 8: Knit across.

Row 9: Knit, *wrapping yarn 3 times as you make each st.*

Row 10: Knit, *allowing the extra loops to drop.*

Repeat Rows 1–10 for the pattern.

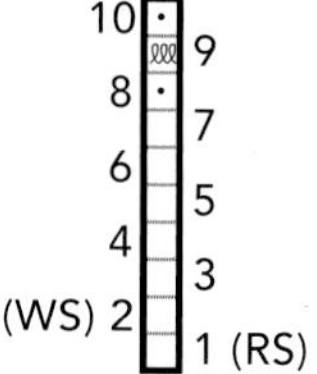

layette lace

easy

(multiple of 4 stitches plus 5 stitches)

Row 1 (RS): K1, yarn over, sssk (page 281), *yarn over, k1, yarn over, sssk; repeat from the * across, ending with yo, k1.

Row 2 and all WS rows: Purl across.

Rows 3 and 7: Knit across.

Row 5: K2tog, yarn over, k1, *yarn over, sssk, yarn over, k1; repeat from the * across, ending with yarn over, ssk.

Row 8: As Row 2.

Repeat Rows 1–8 for the pattern.

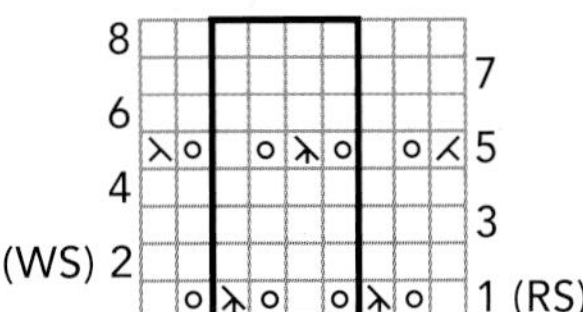

eyelet ripple

(multiple of 16 stitches plus 17 stitches)

Rows 1, 3, and 5 (RS): K2tog, k6, yarn over, k1, *yarn over, k6, s2kp2 (page 272), k6, yarn over, k1; repeat from the * across, ending with yarn over, k6, ssk.

Rows 2, 4, 6, and 10: Purl across.

Rows 7, 8, and 11: Knit across.

Row 9: *K2tog, yarn over; repeat from the * across, ending with k1.

Row 12: Knit across.

Repeat Rows 1–12 for the pattern.

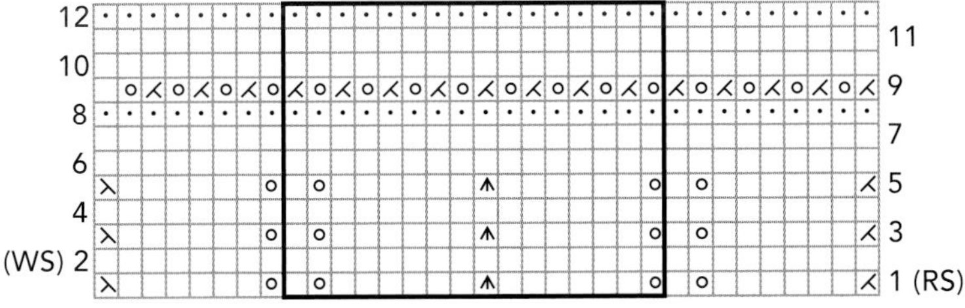

tulip motif

(over 15 stitches on a reverse stockinette background)

Rows 1 and 3 (RS): P7, k1, p7.

Rows 2, 4, 6, 8, 10, 12, 18, 20, 22, 24, and 26: Knit the knit sts, purl the purl sts, and purl the yarn over sts.

Row 5: P5, k2tog, yarn over, k1, yarn over, ssk, p5.

Row 7: P4, k2tog, yarn over, k3, yarn over, ssk, p4.

Row 9: P3, [k2tog, yarn over] twice, k1, [yarn over, ssk] twice, p3.

Row 11: P2, [k2tog, yarn over] twice, p1, k1, p1, [yarn over, ssk] twice, p2.

Row 13: P1, [k2tog, yarn over] twice, p2, k1, p2, [yarn over, ssk] twice, p1.

Row 14: K1, p2, k4, p1, k4, p2, k1.

Row 15: K2tog, yarn over, p4, yarn over, s2kp2 (page 272), yarn over, p4, yarn over, ssk.

Row 16: K6, p3, k6.

Row 17: P4, k2tog, yarn over, k3, yarn over, ssk, p4.

Row 19: P3, k2tog, yarn over, k1, yarn over, s2kp2, yarn over, k1, yarn over, ssk, p3.

Row 21: P3, M1 purlwise (page 278), ssk, yarn over, ssk, k1, k2tog, yarn over, k2tog, M1 purlwise, p3.

Row 23: P4, M1 purlwise, ssk, yarn over, s2kp2, yarn over, k2tog, M1 purlwise, p4.

Row 25: P5, M1 purlwise, ssk, k1, k2tog, M1 purlwise, p5.

Row 27: P6, M1 purlwise, s2kp2, M1 purlwise, p6.

Row 28: Knit across.

leaning doors

(multiple of 14 stitches)

Rows 1, 3, 5, 7, and 9 (RS): *K7, [k2tog, yarn over] 3 times, k1; repeat from the * across.

Rows 2, 4, 6, and 8: *P7, k7; repeat from the * across.

Row 10: Knit across.

Rows 11, 13, 15, 17, and 19: *K1, [yarn over, ssk] 3 times, k7; repeat from the * across.

Rows 12, 14, 16, and 18: *K7, p7; repeat from the * across.

Row 20: As Row 10.

Repeat Rows 1–20 for the pattern.

20	•	•	•	•	•	•	•	•	•	•	•	•	•	•	
								⋋	o	⋋	o	⋋	o		19
18	•	•	•	•	•	•	•								
								⋋	o	⋋	o	⋋	o		17
16	•	•	•	•	•	•	•								
								⋋	o	⋋	o	⋋	o		15
14	•	•	•	•	•	•	•								
								⋋	o	⋋	o	⋋	o		13
12	•	•	•	•	•	•	•								
								⋋	o	⋋	o	⋋	o		11
10	•	•	•	•	•	•	•	•	•	•	•	•	•	•	
		o	⋌	o	⋌	o	⋌								9
8								•	•	•	•	•	•	•	
		o	⋌	o	⋌	o	⋌								7
6								•	•	•	•	•	•	•	
		o	⋌	o	⋌	o	⋌								5
4								•	•	•	•	•	•	•	
		o	⋌	o	⋌	o	⋌								3
(WS) 2								•	•	•	•	•	•	•	
		o	⋌	o	⋌	o	⋌								1 (RS)

cross hatch

(multiple of 10 stitches plus 2 stitches)

Row 1 (RS): K1, *k7, k2tog, yarn over, k1; repeat from the * across, ending with k1.

Row 2: P1, *p2, yarn over, p2tog, p6; repeat from the * across, ending with p1.

Row 3: K1, *k5, k2tog, yarn over, k3; repeat from the * across, ending with k1.

Row 4: P1, *p4, yarn over, p2tog, p4; repeat from the * across, ending with p1.

Row 5: K1, *yarn over, ssk, k1, k2tog, yarn over, k5; repeat from the * across, ending with k1.

Row 6: P1, *p7, ssp (page 281), yarn over, p1; repeat from the * across, ending with p1.

Row 7: K1, *k2, yarn over, ssk, k6; repeat from the * across, ending with k1.

Row 8: P1, *p5, ssp, yarn over, p3; repeat from the * across, ending with p1.

Row 9: K1, *k4, yarn over, ssk, k4; repeat from the * across, ending with k1.

Row 10: P1, *yarn over, p2tog, p1, ssp, yarn over, p5; repeat from the * across, ending with p1.

Repeat Rows 1–10 for the pattern.

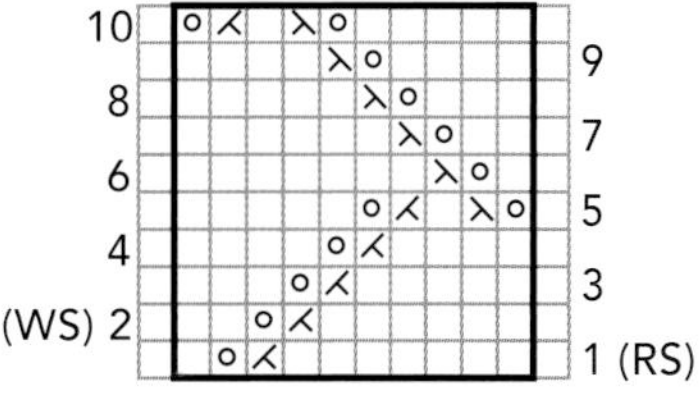

textured waves

(multiple of 7 stitches plus 4 stitches)

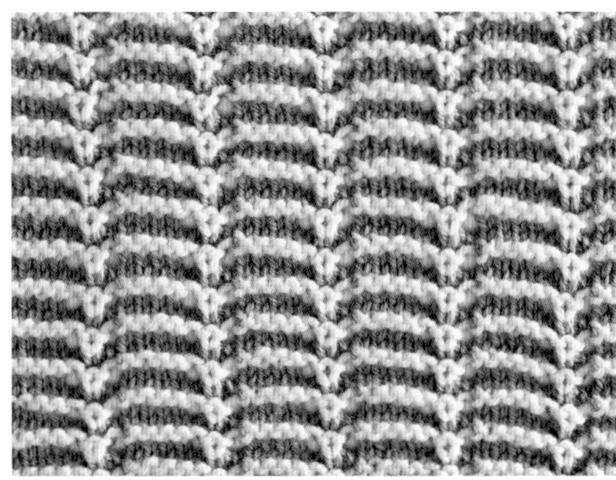

Row 1 (RS): With A, *k4, yarn over, s2kp2 (page 272), yarn over; repeat from the * across, ending with k4.

Row 2: With A, knit across.

Row 3: With B, knit across.

Row 4: With B, purl across.

Repeat Rows 1–4 for the pattern.

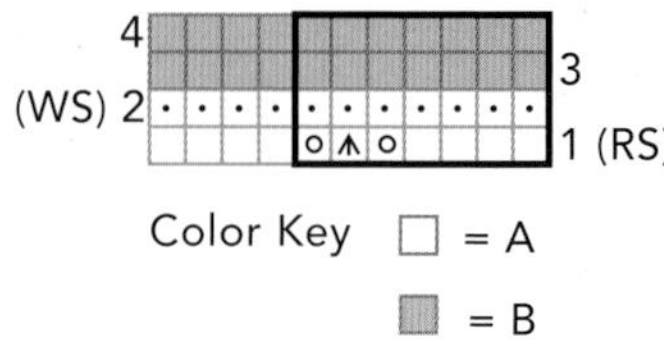

old danube lace

(multiple of 8 stitches plus 1 stitch)

Row 1 (RS): *P2, k2tog, yarn over, p1, yarn over, ssk, p1; repeat from the * across, ending with p1.

Rows 2, 4, 5, 6, 12, 13, and 14: Knit the knit sts, purl the purl sts, and purl the yarn over sts.

Row 3: *P1, k2tog, yarn over, k3, yarn over, ssk; repeat from the * across, ending with p1.

Row 7: *P1, k1, k2tog, yarn over, p1, yarn over, ssk, k1; repeat from the * across, ending with p1.

Row 8: K1, *p2, k3, p2, k1; repeat from the * across.

Row 9: *P1, yarn over, ssk, p3, k2tog, yarn over; repeat from the * across, ending with p1.

Row 10: P1, *p2, k3, p3; repeat from the * across.

Row 11: *K2, yarn over, ssk, p1, k2tog, yarn over, k1; repeat from the * across, ending with k1.

Row 15: *P1, yarn over, ssk, k1, p1, k1, k2tog, yarn over; repeat from the * across, ending with p1.

Row 16: K1, *k1, p2, k1, p2, k2; repeat from the * across.

Repeat Rows 1–16 for the pattern.

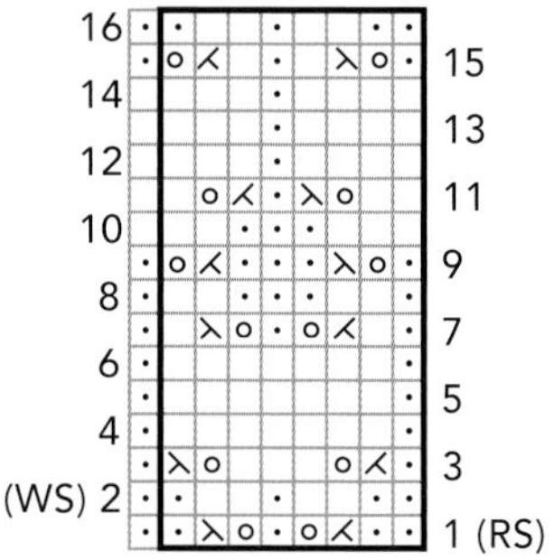

church windows

(multiple of 10 stitches plus 1 stitch)

Rows 1, 3, 5, and 7 (RS): *K3, k2tog, yarn over, k5; repeat from the * across, ending with k1.

Rows 2, 4, 6, and 8: P1, *p7, yarn over, ssp (page 281), p1; repeat from the * across.

Rows 9, 11, 13, and 15: *K8, k2tog, yarn over; repeat from the * across, ending with k1.

Rows 10, 12, 14, and 16: P1, *p2, yarn over, ssp, p6; repeat from the * across.

Repeat Rows 1–16 for the pattern.

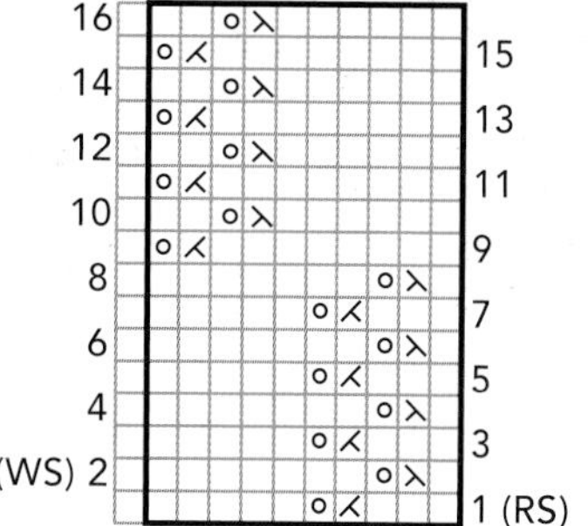

eyelet trellis

(multiple of 4 stitches plus 6 stitches)

Row 1 (RS): K1, p1, *left twist (page 276), p2; repeat from the * across, ending with left twist, p1, k1.

Rows 2 and 6: Knit the knit sts and purl the purl sts.

Row 3: K1, k2tog, *[yarn over] twice, ssk, k2tog; repeat from the * across, ending with [yarn over] twice, ssk, k1.

Row 4: P2, [k1, p1] into the double yarn over from the previous row, *p2, [k1, p1] into the double yarn over from the previous row; repeat from the * across, ending with p2.

Row 5: K2, *p2, right twist (page 279); repeat from the * across, ending with p2, k2.

Row 7: K1, yarn over, *ssk, k2tog, [yarn over] twice; repeat from the * across, ending with ssk, k2tog, yarn over, k1.

Row 8: P4, *[k1, p1] into the double yarn over from the previous row, p2; repeat from the * across, ending with k1, p1.

Repeat Rows 1–8 for the pattern.

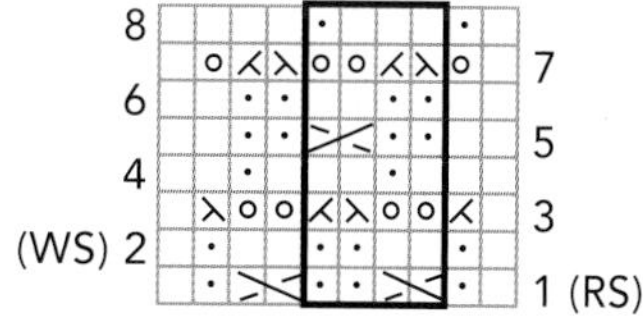

flickering lace

(multiple of 18 stitches plus 11 stitches)

Row 1 (RS): *P3, k2tog, yarn over, k1, yarn over, ssk, p3, yarn over, ssk, k3, k2tog, yarn over; repeat from the * across, ending with p3, k2tog, yarn over, k1, yarn over, ssk, p3.

Rows 2 and 8: K3, p5, k3, *k1, p5, k4, p5, k3; repeat from the * across.

Row 3: *P3, k2tog, yarn over, k1, yarn over, ssk, p4, yarn over, ssk, k1, k2tog, yarn over, p1; repeat from the * across, ending with p3, k2tog, yarn over, k1, yarn over, ssk, p3.

Row 4: K3, p5, k3, *k2, p3, k5, p5, k3; repeat from the * across.

Row 5: *P2, k2tog, yarn over, k3, yarn over, ssk, p4, yarn over, s2kp2 (page 272), yarn over, p2; repeat from the * across, ending with p2, k2tog, yarn over, k3, yarn over, ssk, p2.

Row 6: K2, p7, k2, *k3, p1, k5, p7, k2; repeat from the * across.

Row 7: *P2, yarn over, ssk, k3, k2tog, yarn over, p3, k2tog, yarn over, k1, yarn over, ssk, p1; repeat from the * across, ending with p2, yarn over, ssk, k3, k2tog, yarn over, p2.

Row 9: *P3, yarn over, ssk, k1, k2tog, yarn over, p4, k2tog, yarn over, k1, yarn over, ssk, p1; repeat from the * across, ending with p3, yarn over, ssk, k1, k2tog, yarn over, p3.

Row 10: K4, p3, k4, *k1, p5, k5, p3, k4; repeat from the * across.

Row 11: *P4, yarn over, s2kp2, yarn over, p4, k2tog, yarn over, k3, yarn over, ssk; repeat from the * across, ending with p4, yarn over, s2kp2, yarn over, p4.

Row 12: K5, p1, k5, *p7, k5, p1, k5; repeat from the * across.

Repeat Rows 1–12 for the pattern.

fern grotto lace

(multiple of 21 stitches plus 1 stitch)

Row 1 (RS): *K1, yarn over, k3, ssk, k10, k2tog, k3, yarn over; repeat from the * across, ending with k1.

Row 2: P1, *p1, yarn over, p3, p2tog, p8, ssp (page 281), p3, yarn over, p2; repeat from the * across.

Row 3: *K3, yarn over, k3, ssk, k6, k2tog, k3, yarn over, k2; repeat from the * across, ending with k1.

Row 4: P1, *p3, yarn over, p3, p2tog, p4, ssp, p3, yarn over, p4; repeat from the * across.

Row 5: *K5, yarn over, k3, ssk, k2, k2tog, k3, yarn over, k4; repeat from the * across, ending with k1.

Row 6: P1, *p5, yarn over, p3, p2tog, ssp, p3, yarn over, p6; repeat from the * across.

Repeat Rows 1–6 for the pattern.

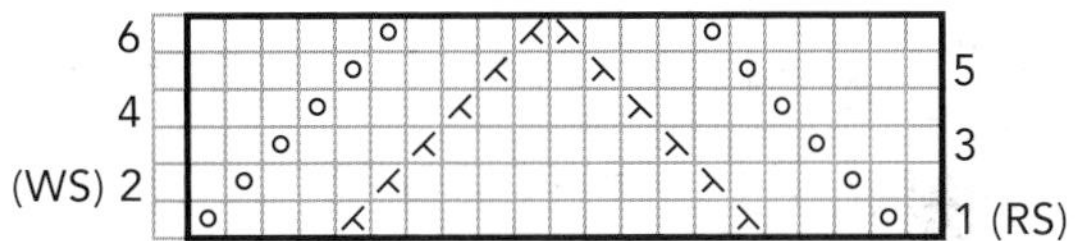

pyramid lace

(multiple of 12 stitches)

Row 1 (RS): *K1, yarn over, ssk, k6, k2tog, yarn over, k1; repeat from the * across.

Row 2: *P1, k1, p8, k1, p1; repeat from the * across.

Row 3: *K1, p1, yarn over, ssk, k4, k2tog, yarn over, p1, k1; repeat from the * across.

Row 4: *P1, k2, p6, k2, p1; repeat from the * across.

Row 5: *K1, p2, yarn over, ssk, k2, k2tog, yarn over, p2, k1; repeat from the * across.

Row 6: *P1, k3, p4, k3, p1; repeat from the * across.

Row 7: *K1, p3, yarn over, ssk, k2tog, yarn over, p3, k1; repeat from the * across.

Row 8: *P1, k4, p2, k4, p1; repeat from the * across.

Repeat Rows 1–8 for the pattern.

8
7
6
5
4
3
(WS) 2
1 (RS)

graceful leaves

(multiple of 17 stitches)

Row 1 (RS): *P1, k12, k2tog, yarn over, k1, p1; repeat from the * across.

Row 2: *K1, yarn over, p2, p2tog, p11, k1; repeat from the * across.

Row 3: *P1, k10, k2tog, k1, yarn over, k2, p1; repeat from the * across.

Row 4: *K1, p1, yarn over, p3, p2tog, p9, k1; repeat from the * across.

Row 5: *P1, k8, k2tog, k2, yarn over, k3, p1; repeat from the * across.

Row 6: *K1, p2, yarn over, p4, p2tog, p7, k1; repeat from the * across.

Row 7: *P1, k6, k2tog, k3, yarn over, k4, p1; repeat from the * across.

Row 8: *K1, p3, yarn over, p5, p2tog, p5, k1; repeat from the * across.

Row 9: *P1, k4, k2tog, k4, yarn over, k5, p1; repeat from the * across.

Row 10: *K1, p4, yarn over, p6, p2tog, p3, k1; repeat from the * across.

Row 11: *P1, k1, yarn over, ssk, k12, p1; repeat from the * across.

Row 12: *K1, p11, ssp (page 281), p2, yarn over, k1; repeat from the * across.

Row 13: *P1, k2, yarn over, k1, ssk, k10, p1; repeat from the * across.

Row 14: *K1, p9, ssp, p3, yarn over, p1, k1; repeat from the * across.

Row 15: *P1, k3, yarn over, k2, ssk, k8, p1; repeat from the * across.

Row 16: *K1, p7, ssp, p4, yarn over, p2, k1; repeat from the * across.

Row 17: *P1, k4, yarn over, k3, ssk, k6, p1; repeat from the * across.

Row 18: *K1, p5, ssp, p5, yarn over, p3, k1; repeat from the * across.

Row 19: *P1, k5, yarn over, k4, ssk, k4, p1; repeat from the * across.

Row 20: *K1, p3, ssp, p6, yarn over, p4, k1; repeat from the * across.

Repeat Rows 1–20 for the pattern.

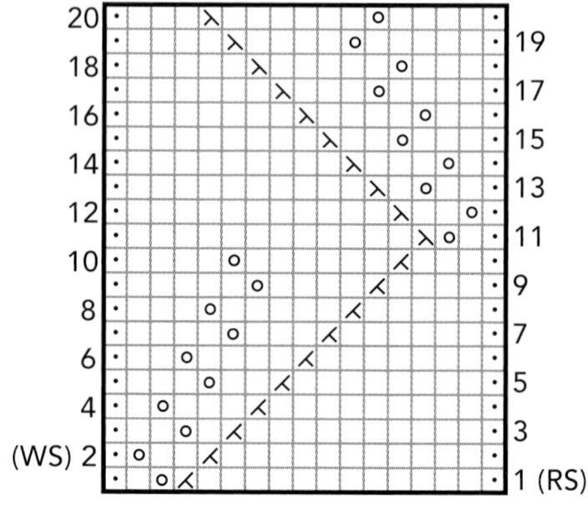

lace zigzag

(multiple of 7 stitches plus 2 stitches)

Row 1 (RS): K1, *k5, k2tog, yarn over; repeat from the * across, ending with k1.

Row 2: P1, *p1, yarn over, p2tog, p4; repeat from the * across, ending with p1.

Row 3: K1, *k3, k2tog, yarn over, k2; repeat from the * across, ending with k1.

Row 4: P1, *p3, yarn over, p2tog, p2; repeat from the * across, ending with p1.

Row 5: K1, *k1, k2tog, yarn over, k4; repeat from the * across, ending with k1.

Row 6: P1, *p5, yarn over, p2tog; repeat from the * across, ending p1.

Row 7: K1, *yarn over, ssk, k5; repeat from the * across, ending with k1.

Row 8: P1, *p4, ssp (page 281), yarn over, p1; repeat from the * across, ending with p1.

Row 9: K1, *k2, yarn over, ssk, k3; repeat from the * across, ending with k1.

Row 10: P1, *p2, ssp, yarn over, p3; repeat from the * across, ending with p1.

Row 11: K1, *k4, yarn over, ssk, k1; repeat from the * across, ending with k1.

Row 12: P1, *ssp, yarn over, p5; repeat from the * across, ending with p1.

Repeat Rows 1–12 for the pattern.

12 11
10 9
8 7
6 5
4 3
(WS) 2 1 (RS)

parquet

(multiple of 16 stitches plus 11 stitches)

Row 1 (RS): K4, k2tog, *yarn over, k4, k2tog, yarn over, k1, p1, k1, yarn over, ssk, k3, k2tog; repeat from the * across, ending with yarn over, k5.

Rows 2, 10, and 12: P6, *p6, k1, p1, k1, p7; repeat from the * across, ending with p5.

Row 3: K3, k2tog, yarn over, *k4, k2tog, yarn over, [p1, k1] twice, p1, yarn over, ssk, k1, k2tog, yarn over; repeat from the * across, ending with k6.

Rows 4, 6, and 8: K1, p5, *p4, [k1, p1] 3 times, k1, p5; repeat from the * across, ending with p4, k1.

Row 5: K1, yarn over, sssk (page 281), yarn over, k1, *k3, k2tog, yarn over, [k1, p1] 3 times, k1, yarn over, sssk, yarn over, k1; repeat from the * across, ending with k3, k2tog, yarn over, k1.

Row 7: K1, k2tog, yarn over, k2, *k2, k2tog, yarn over, [p1, k1] 4 times, k2tog, yarn over, k2; repeat from the * across, ending with k2, k2tog, yarn over, p1, k1.

Row 9: K2tog, yarn over, k3, *k1, k2tog, yarn over, k1, yarn over, ssk, [p1, k1] twice, p1, k2tog, yarn over, k3; repeat from the * across, ending with k1, k2tog, yarn over, k1, yarn over, ssk.

Row 11: K5, *k2tog, yarn over, k3, yarn over, ssk, k1, p1, k1, k2tog, yarn over, k4; repeat from the * across, ending with k2tog, yarn over, k4.

Row 13: K4, k2tog, *yarn over, k5, yarn over, ssk, p1, k2tog, yarn over, k4, k2tog; repeat from the * across, ending with yarn over, k5.

Rows 14 and 30: Purl across.

Row 15: K3, k2tog, yarn over, *p1, yarn over, ssk, k4, yarn over, sssk, yarn over, k4, k2tog, yarn over; repeat from the * across, ending with p1, yarn over, ssk, k3.

Rows 16, 18, 26, and 28: P4, k1, p1, *k1, p13, k1, p1; repeat from the * across, ending with k1, p4.

Row 17: K2, k2tog, yarn over, k1, *p1, k1, yarn over, ssk, k4, yarn over, ssk, k3, k2tog, yarn over, k1; repeat from the * across, ending with p1, k1, yarn over, ssk, k2.

Row 19: K1, k2tog, yarn over, p1, k1, *p1, k1, p1, yarn over, ssk, k4, yarn over, ssk, k1, k2tog, yarn over, p1, k1; repeat from the * across, ending with p1, k1, p1, yarn over, ssk, k1.

Rows 20, 22, and 24: P2, [k1, p1] twice, *k1, p1, k1, p9, [k1, p1] twice; repeat from the * across, ending with k1, p1, k1, p2.

Row 21: Ssk, yarn over, k1, p1, k1, *[p1, k1] twice, yarn over, ssk, k4, yarn over, sssk, yarn over, k1, p1, k1; repeat from the * across, ending with [p1, k1] twice, yarn over, ssk.

Row 23: [K1, p1] twice, k1, *[p1, k1] twice, p1, yarn over, ssk, k4, yarn over, ssk, k1, p1, k1; repeat from the * across, ending with [p1, k1] 3 times.

Row 25: K1, yarn over, ssk, p1, k1, *p1, k1, p1, k2tog, yarn over, k1, yarn over, ssk, k4, yarn over, ssk, p1, k1; repeat from the * across, ending with p1, k1, p1, k2tog, yarn over, k1.

Row 27: K2, yarn over, ssk, k1, *p1, k1, k2tog, yarn over, k3, yarn over, ssk, k4, yarn over, ssk, k1; repeat from the * across, ending with p1, k1, k2tog, yarn over, k2.

Row 29: K3, yarn over, ssk, *p1, k2tog, yarn over, k5, yarn over, ssk, k4, yarn over, ssk; repeat from the * across, ending with p1, k2tog, yarn over, k3.

Row 31: K4, *yarn over, sssk, yarn over, k4, k2tog, yarn over, p1, yarn over, ssk, k4, yarn over; repeat from the * across, ending with sssk, yarn over, k4.

Row 32: As Row 2.

Repeat Rows 1–32 for the pattern.

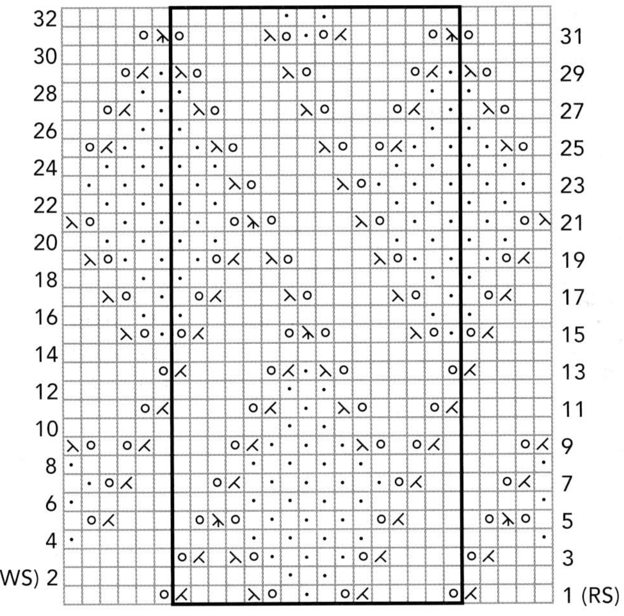

cobbled stripes

(multiple of 2 stitches plus 1 stitch)

Row 1 (RS): With A, knit across.

Row 2: With A, knit across.

Row 3: With B, knit across.

Row 4: With B, k1, *yarn over, k2tog; repeat from the * across.

Repeat Rows 1–4 for the pattern.

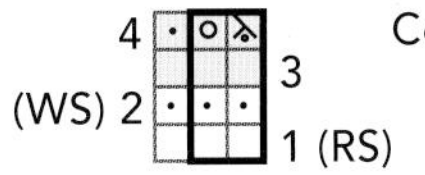

4
3
(WS) 2
1 (RS)

Color Key □ = A
□ = B

fairy-tale lace

(multiple of 10 stitches plus 1 stitch)

Rows 1, 3, and 5 (RS): *P1, yarn over, k2, k2tog, p1, ssk, k2, yarn over; repeat from the * across, ending with p1.

Rows 2, 4, 6, 14, 16, and 18: K1, *p4, k1; repeat from the * across.

Row 7: *P1, ssk, k2, yarn over, p1, yarn over, k2, k2tog; repeat from the * across, ending with p1.

Row 8: K1, *p3, k3, p3, k1; repeat from the * across.

Row 9: *P1, ssk, k1, yarn over, p3, yarn over, k1, k2tog; repeat from the * across, ending with p1.

Row 10: K1, *p2, k5, p2, k1; repeat from the * across.

Row 11: *P1, ssk, yarn over, p5, yarn over, k2tog; repeat from the * across, ending with p1.

Row 12: K1, *p1, k7, p1, k1; repeat from the * across.

Rows 13, 15, and 17: *P1, ssk, k2, yarn over, p1, yarn over, k2, k2tog; repeat from the * across, ending with p1.

Row 19: *P1, yarn over, k2, k2tog, p1, ssk, k2, yarn over; repeat from the * across, ending with p1.

Row 20: K1, *k1, p3, k1, p3, k2; repeat from the * across.

Row 21: *P2, yarn over, k1, k2tog, p1, ssk, k1, yarn over, p1; repeat from the * across, ending with p1.

Row 22: K1, *k2, p2, k1, p2, k3; repeat from the * across.

Row 23: *P3, yarn over, k2tog, p1, ssk, yarn over, p2; repeat from the * across, ending with p1.

Row 24: K1, *k3, p1, k1, p1, k4; repeat from the * across.

Repeat Rows 1–24 for the pattern.

24	•	•	•	•		•		•	•	•	•	
	•	•	•	o	⋋	•	⋌	o	•	•	•	23
22	•	•	•			•			•	•	•	
	•	•	o		⋋	•	⋌		o	•	•	21
20	•	•				•				•	•	
	•	o			⋋	•	⋌			o	•	19
18	•					•					•	
	•	⋌			o	•	o			⋋	•	17
16	•					•					•	
	•	⋌			o	•	o			⋋	•	15
14	•					•					•	
	•	⋌			o	•	o			⋋	•	13
12	•		•	•	•	•	•	•	•		•	
	•	⋌	o	•	•	•	•	•	o	⋋	•	11
10	•			•	•	•	•	•			•	
	•	⋌		o	•	•	•	o		⋋	•	9
8	•				•	•	•				•	
	•	⋌			o	•	o			⋋	•	7
6	•					•					•	
	•	o			⋋	•	⋌			o	•	5
4	•					•					•	
	•	o			⋋	•	⋌			o	•	3
(WS) 2	•					•					•	
	•	o			⋋	•	⋌			o	•	1 (RS)

cathedrals

(multiple of 12 stitches)

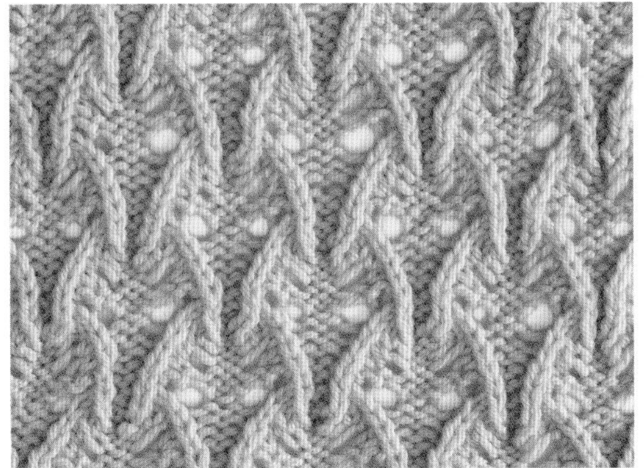

Rows 1 and 3 (RS): *P1, ssk, k2, yarn over, p2, yarn over, k2, k2tog, p1; repeat from the * across.

Rows 2 and 4: *K1, p2tog, p2, yarn over, k2, yarn over, p2, ssp (page 281), k1; repeat from the * across.

Row 5: *P1, yarn over, k2, k2tog, p2, ssk, k2, yarn over, p1; repeat from the * across.

Row 6: *K2, yarn over, p1, ssp, k2, p2tog, p1, yarn over, k2; repeat from the * across.

Row 7: *P3, yarn over, k2tog, p2, ssk, yarn over, p3; repeat from the * across.

Rows 8 and 10: *K1, yarn over, p2, ssp, k2, p2tog, p2, yarn over, k1; repeat from the * across.

Rows 9 and 11: *P1, yarn over, k2, k2tog, p2, ssk, k2, yarn over, p1; repeat from the * across.

Row 12: *K1, p2tog, p2, yarn over, k2, yarn over, p2, ssp, k1; repeat from the * across.

Row 13: *P1, ssk, k1, yarn over, p4, yarn over, k1, k2tog, p1; repeat from the * across.

Row 14: *K1, p2tog, yarn over, k6, yarn over, ssp, k1; repeat from the * across.

Repeat Rows 1–14 for the pattern.

14	•	⋌	o	•	•	•	•	•	•	o	⋋	•	
	•	⋌		o	•	•	•	•	o		⋋	•	13
12	•	⋌			o	•	•	o			⋋	•	
	•	o			⋋	•	•	⋌			o	•	11
10	•	o			⋋	•	•	⋌			o	•	
	•	o			⋋	•	•	⋌			o	•	9
8	•	o			⋋	•	•	⋌			o	•	
	•	•	•	o	⋋	•	•	⋌	o	•	•	•	7
6	•	•	o		⋋	•	•	⋌		o	•	•	
	•	o			⋋	•	•	⋌			o	•	5
4	•	⋌			o	•	•	o			⋋	•	
	•	⋌			o	•	•	o			⋋	•	3
(WS) 2	•	⋌			o	•	•	o			⋋	•	
	•	⋌			o	•	•	o			⋋	•	1 (RS)

herringbone lace

(multiple of 3 stitches)

Row 1 (RS): *K1, yarn over, k2tog; repeat from the * across.

Row 2: As Row 1.

Repeat Rows 1 and 2 for the pattern.

(WS) 2	•	o	⋋	
	⋌	o		1 (RS)

faceted diamonds

(multiple of 12 stitches plus 13 stitches)

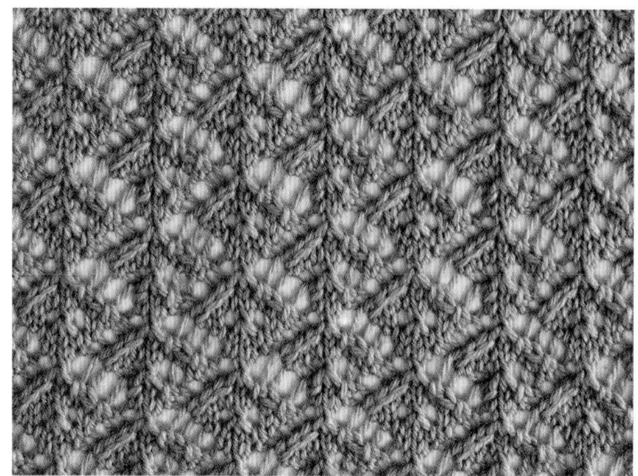

Row 1 (RS): Ssk, yarn over, k3, yarn over, *[sssk (page 281), yarn over, k3, yarn over] twice; repeat from the * across, ending with sssk, yarn over, k3, yarn over, ssk.

Row 2: P2, yarn over, p2tog, p3, *p2, ssp (page 281), yarn over, p3, yarn over, p2tog, p3; repeat from the * across, ending with p2, ssp, yarn over, p2.

Row 3: K3, yarn over, ssk, k1, *k2, k2tog, yarn over, k5, yarn over, ssk, k1; repeat from the * across, ending with k2, k2tog, yarn over, k3.

Row 4: P4, yarn over, p2tog, p1, *[ssp, yarn over, p1, yarn over, p2tog, p1] twice; repeat from the * across, ending with ssp, yarn over, p4.

Row 5: K5, yarn over, *[sssk, yarn over, k3, yarn over] twice; repeat from the * across, ending with sssk, yarn over, k5.

Row 6: P3, ssp, yarn over, p2, *p1, yarn over, p2tog, p5, ssp, yarn over, p2; repeat from the * across, ending with p1, yarn over, p2tog, p3.

Row 7: K2, k2tog, yarn over, k2, *k3, yarn over, ssk, k3, k2tog, yarn over, k2; repeat from the * across, ending with k3, yarn over, ssk, k2.

Row 8: P1, ssp, yarn over, p4, *p3, yarn over, p2tog, p1, ssp, yarn over, p4; repeat from the * across, ending with p3, yarn over, p2tog, p1.

Repeat Rows 1–8 for the pattern.

traditional feather and fan

(multiple of 17 stitches)

Row 1 (RS): Knit across.

Row 2: Purl across.

Row 3: *[K2tog] 3 times, [yarn over, k1] 5 times, yarn over, [ssk] 3 times; repeat from the * across.

Row 4: Knit across.

Repeat Rows 1–4 for the pattern.

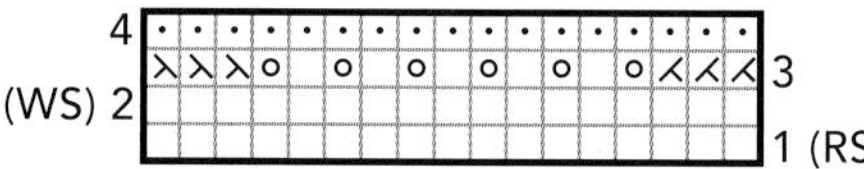

ridged waves

(multiple of 14 stitches plus 1 stitch)

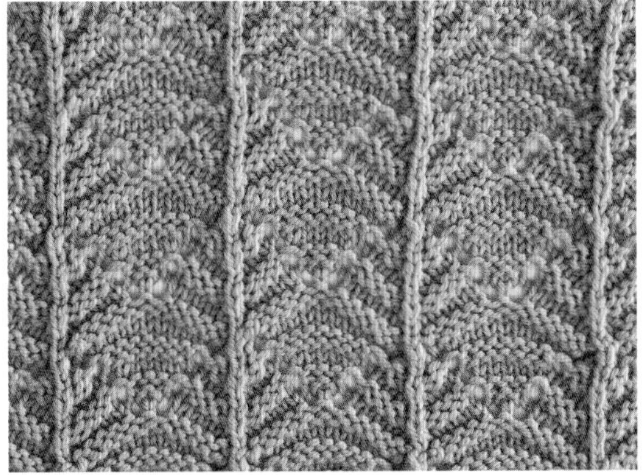

Row 1 (RS): *K1, yarn over, k5, s2kp2 (page 272), k5, yarn over; repeat from the * across, ending with k1.

Rows 2, 6, and 10: Purl across.

Row 3: *P2, yarn over, p4, s2kp2, p4, yarn over, p1; repeat from the * across, ending with p1.

Rows 4 and 8: K1, *k6, p1, k7; repeat from the * across.

Row 5: *K3, yarn over, k3, s2kp2, k3, yarn over, k2; repeat from the * across, ending with k1.

Row 7: *P4, yarn over, p2, s2kp2, p2, yarn over, p3; repeat from the * across, ending with p1.

Row 9: *K5, yarn over, k1, s2kp2, k1, yarn over, k4; repeat from the * across, ending with k1.

Row 11: *P6, yarn over, s2kp2, yarn over, p5; repeat from the * across, ending with p1.

Row 12: As Row 4.

Repeat Rows 1–12 for the pattern.

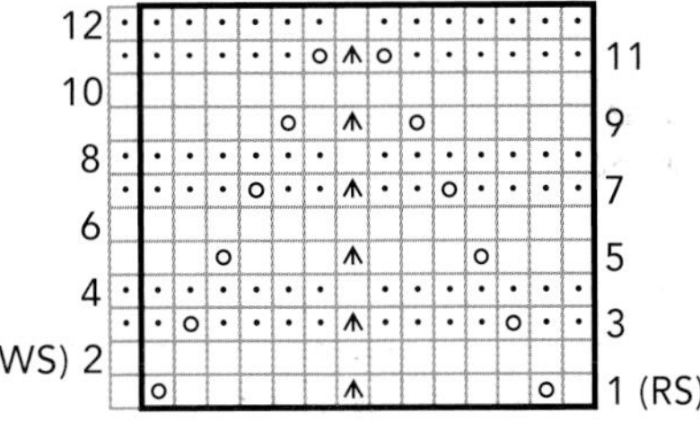

victorian wallpaper

(multiple of 15 stitches plus 4 stitches)

Rows 1, 3, and 13 (RS): K1, *yarn over, ssk, k13; repeat from the * across, ending with yarn over, ssk, k1.

Row 2 and all WS rows: P1, yarn over, ssk, *p13, yarn over, ssk; repeat from the * across, ending p1.

Row 5: K1, *yarn over, ssk, k4, k2tog, yarn over, k1, yarn over, ssk, k4; repeat from the * across, ending with yarn over, ssk, k1.

Row 7: K1, *yarn over, ssk, k3, k2tog, yarn over, k3, yarn over, ssk, k3; repeat from the * across, ending with yarn over, ssk, k1.

Row 9: K1, *yarn over, ssk, k4, yarn over, ssk, yarn over, k3tog, yarn over, k4; repeat from the * across, ending with yarn over, ssk, k1.

Row 11: K1, *yarn over, ssk, k5, yarn over, sssk (page 281), yarn over, k5; repeat from the * across, ending with yarn over, ssk, k1.

Row 14: As Row 2.

Repeat Rows 1–14 for the pattern.

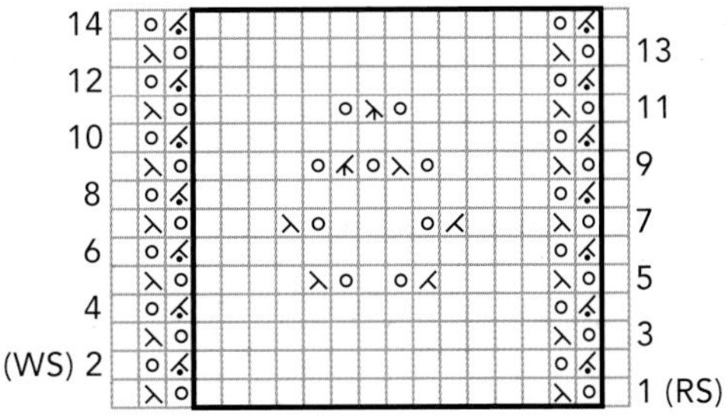

great bernera lace

(multiple of 14 stitches plus 15 stitches)

Row 1 (RS): P4, k2tog, yarn over, k1, *p1, k1, yarn over, ssk, p7, k2tog, yarn over, k1; repeat from the * across, ending with p1, k1, yarn over, ssk, p4.

Rows 2, 4, 6, 8, 20, 22, 24, and 26: Knit the knit sts, purl the purl sts, and purl the yarn over sts.

Row 3: P3, k2tog, yarn over, k2, *p1, k2, yarn over, ssk, p5, k2tog, yarn over, k2; repeat from the * across, ending with p1, k2, yarn over, ssk, p3.

Row 5: P2, k2tog, yarn over, k3, *p1, k3, yarn over, ssk, p3, k2tog, yarn over, k3; repeat from the * across, ending with p1, k3, yarn over, ssk, p2.

Row 7: P1, k2tog, yarn over, k4, *p1, k4, yarn over, ssk, p1, k2tog, yarn over, k4; repeat from the * across, ending with p1, k4, yarn over, ssk, p1.

Row 9: P1, k4, k2tog, yarn over, *p1, yarn over, ssk, k4, p1, k4, k2tog, yarn over; repeat from the * across, ending with p1, yarn over, ssk, k4, p1.

Rows 10, 12, 14, 16, 28, 30, 32, and 34: Knit the knit sts, knit the yarn over sts, and purl the purl sts.

Row 11: P1, k3, k2tog, yarn over, p1, *p2, yarn over, ssk, k3, p1, k3, k2tog, yarn over, p1; repeat from the * across, ending with p2, yarn over, ssk, k3, p1.

Row 13: P1, k2, k2tog, yarn over, p2, *p3, yarn over, ssk, k2, p1, k2, k2tog, yarn over, p2; repeat from the * across, ending with p3, yarn over, ssk, k2, p1.

Row 15: P1, k1, k2tog, yarn over, p3, *p4, yarn over, ssk, k1, p1, k1, k2tog, yarn over, p3; repeat from the * across, ending with p4, yarn over, ssk, k1, p1.

Row 17: P1, k2, p4, *make a knot (page 276), p4, k2, p1, k2, p4; repeat from the * across, ending with make a knot, p4, k2, p1.

Row 18: K1, p2, k5, *k4, p2, k1, p2, k5; repeat from the * across, ending with k4, p2, k1.

Row 19: P1, k1, yarn over, ssk, p3, *p4, k2tog, yarn over, k1, p1, k1, yarn over, ssk, p3; repeat from the * across, ending with p4, k2tog, yarn over, k1, p1.

Row 21: P1, k2, yarn over, ssk, p2, *p3, k2tog, yarn over, k2, p1, k2, yarn over, ssk, p2; repeat from the * across, ending with p3, k2tog, yarn over, k2, p1.

Row 23: P1, k3, yarn over, ssk, p1, *p2, k2tog, yarn over, k3, p1, k3, yarn over, ssk, p1; repeat from the * across, ending with p2, k2tog, yarn over, k3, p1.

Row 25: P1, k4, yarn over, ssk, *p1, k2tog, yarn over, k4, p1, k4, yarn over, ssk; repeat from the * across, ending with p1, k2tog, yarn over, k4, p1.

Row 27: P1, yarn over, ssk, k4, *p1, k4, k2tog, yarn over, p1, yarn over, ssk, k4; repeat from the * across, ending with p1, k4, k2tog, yarn over, p1.

Row 29: P2, yarn over, ssk, k3, *p1, k3, k2tog, yarn over, p3, yarn over, ssk, k3; repeat from the * across, ending with p1, k3, k2tog, yarn over, p2.

Row 31: P3, yarn over, ssk, k2, *p1, k2, k2tog, yarn over, p5, yarn over, ssk, k2; repeat from the * across, ending with p1, k2, k2tog, yarn over, p3.

Row 33: P4, yarn over, ssk, k1, *p1, k1, k2tog, yarn over, p7, yarn over, ssk, k1; repeat from the * across, ending with p1, k1, k2tog, yarn over, p4.

Row 35: P5, k2, *p1, k2, p4, make a knot, p4, k2; repeat from the * across, ending with p1, k2, p5.

Row 36: K5, p2, k1, *p2, k9, p2, k1; repeat from the * across, ending with p2, k5.

Repeat Rows 1–36 for the pattern.

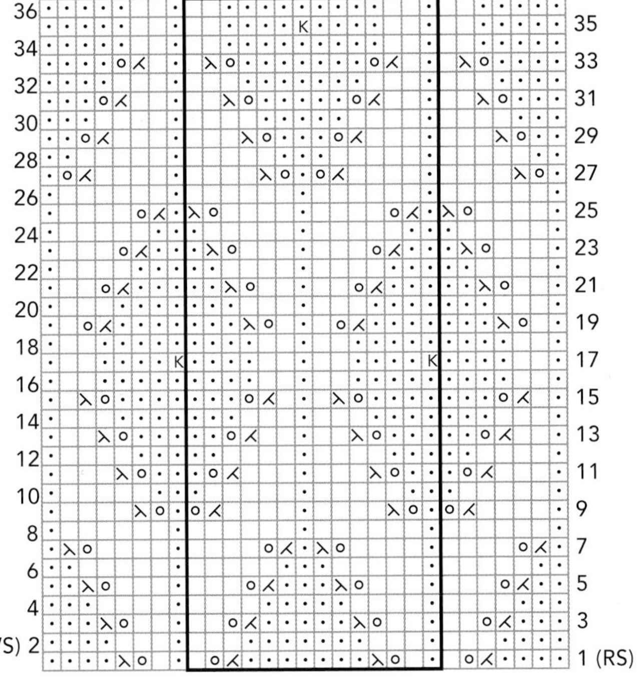

embossed flow 

(multiple of 12 stitches plus 7 stitches)

Row 1 (RS): K1, k2tog, yarn over, *p2, k3tog, [yarn over, k1] 3 times, yarn over, sssk (page 281), p1; repeat from the * across, ending with p1, yarn over, ssk, k1.

Rows 2 and 4: K2, p1, k1, *k1, p9, k2; repeat from the * across, ending with p1, k2.

Row 3: K1, k2tog, yarn over, *p2, k9, p1; repeat from the * across, ending with p1, yarn over, ssk, k1.

Row 5: K1, k2tog, yarn over, *[k1, yarn over] twice, sssk, p3, k3tog, yarn over, k1, yarn over; repeat from the * across, ending with k1, yarn over, ssk, k1.

Row 6: K2, p2, *p4, k3, p5; repeat from the * across, ending with p1, k2.

Row 7: K1, k2tog, yarn over, *k5, p3, k4; repeat from the * across, ending with k1, yarn over, ssk, k1.

Row 8: As Row 6.

Repeat Rows 1–8 for the pattern.

angel lace

(multiple of 14 stitches plus 1 stitch)

Row 1 (RS): *K1, yarn over, k4, ssk, k1, k2tog, k4, yarn over; repeat from the * across, ending with k1.

Row 2: P1, *p1, yarn over, p3, p2tog, p1, ssp (page 281), p3, yarn over, p2; repeat from the * across.

Row 3: *K3, yarn over, k2, ssk, k1, k2tog, k2, yarn over, k2; repeat from the * across, ending with k1.

Row 4: P1, *p3, yarn over, p1, p2tog, p1, ssp, p1, yarn over, p4; repeat from the * across.

Row 5: *K5, yarn over, ssk, k1, k2tog, yarn over, k4; repeat from the * across, ending with k1.

Row 6: P1, *ssp, p4, yarn over, p1, yarn over, p4, p2tog, p1; repeat from the * across.

Row 7: *K1, k2tog, [k3, yarn over] twice, k3, ssk; repeat from the * across, ending with k1.

Row 8: P1, *ssp, p2, yarn over, p5, yarn over, p2, p2tog, p1; repeat from the * across.

Row 9: *K1, k2tog, k1, yarn over, k7, yarn over, k1, ssk; repeat from the * across, ending with k1.

Row 10: P1, *ssp, yarn over, p9, yarn over, p2tog, p1; repeat from the * across.

Repeat Rows 1–10 for the pattern.

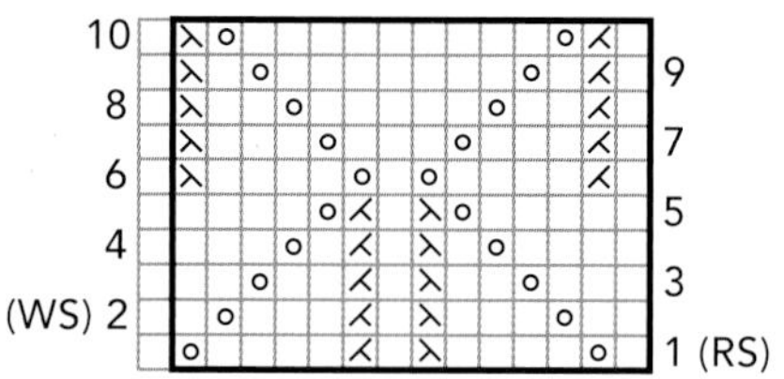

spring lace

(multiple of 12 stitches plus 1 stitch)

Row 1 (RS): *P1, yarn over, p4, p3tog, p4, yarn over; repeat from the * across, ending with p1.

Row 2 and all WS rows: Purl across.

Row 3: *P2, yarn over, p3, p3tog, p3, yarn over, p1; repeat from the * across, ending with p1.

Row 5: *P3, yarn over, p2, p3tog, p2, yarn over, p2; repeat from the * across, ending with p1.

Row 7: *P4, yarn over, p1, p3tog, p1, yarn over, p3; repeat from the * across, ending with p1.

Row 9: *P5, yarn over, p3tog, yarn over, p4; repeat from the * across, ending with p1.

Row 10: As Row 2.

Repeat Rows 1–10 for the pattern.

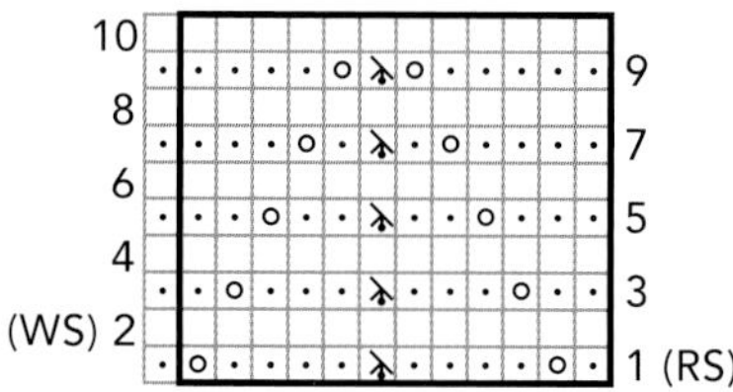

snakeskin

(multiple of 5 stitches plus 2 stitches)

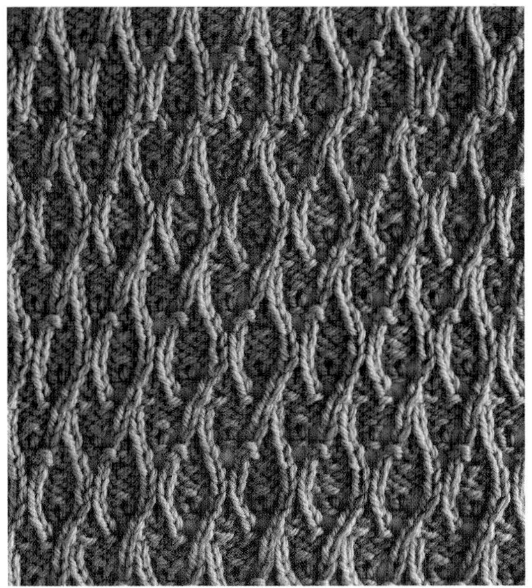

Row 1 (RS): K1, *k1, p3, k1; repeat from the * across, ending with p1.

Row 2: K1, *p1, k3, p1; repeat from the * across, ending with p1.

Row 3: K1, *k1, p1, p2tog, k1, yarn over; repeat from the * across, ending with p1.

Row 4: K1, *k4, p1; repeat from the * across, ending with p1.

Row 5: P1, *yarn over, ssk, k2tog, yarn over, p1; repeat from the * across, ending with p1.

Rows 6 and 8: K1, *k2, p2, k1; repeat from the * across, ending with k1.

Row 7: P1, *p1, k2, p2; repeat from the * across, ending with p1.

Row 9: P1, *p2tog, k1, yarn over, k1, p1; repeat from the * across, ending with p1.

Row 10: K1, *[k1, p1] twice, k1; repeat from the * across, ending with k1.

Row 11: P1, *k2tog, yarn over, p1, yarn over, ssk; repeat from the * across, ending with p1.

Row 12: K1, *p1, k3, p1; repeat from the * across, ending with k1.

Repeat Rows 1–12 for the pattern.

12	•		•	•	•		•	
	•	⋋	o	•	o	⋌	•	11
10	•	•		•		•	•	
	•	•		o		⋋•	•	9
8	•	•	•			•	•	
	•	•	•			•	•	7
6	•	•	•			•	•	
	•	•	o	⋌	⋋	o	•	5
4	•	•	•	•	•			
	•	o		⋋•	•			3
(WS) 2	•		•	•	•			
	•		•	•	•			1 (RS)

sevignac lace

(multiple of 10 stitches plus 11 stitches)

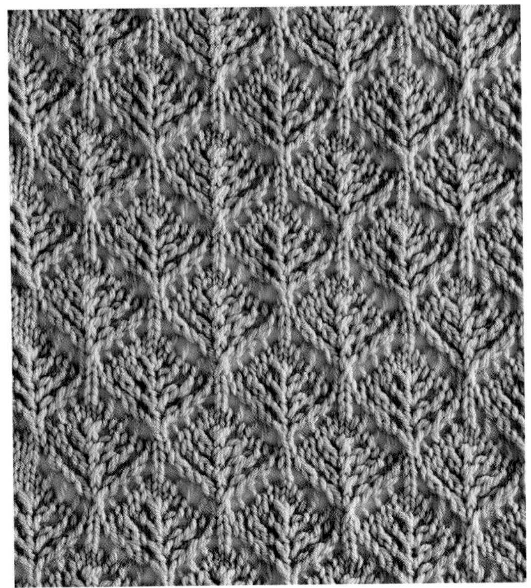

Rows 1 and 7 (RS): K4, yarn over, *sssk (page 281), yarn over, k7, yarn over; repeat from the * across, ending with sssk, yarn over, k4.

Rows 2 and 6: P3, yarn over, p2tog, p1, *ssp (page 281), yarn over, p5, yarn over, p2tog, p1; repeat from the * across, ending with ssp, yarn over, p3.

Rows 3 and 5: K2, yarn over, ssk, yarn over, *sssk, yarn over, k2tog, yarn over, k3, yarn over, ssk, yarn over; repeat from the * across, ending with sssk, yarn over, k2tog, yarn over, k2.

Row 4: P1, [yarn over, p2tog] twice, p1, *[ssp, yarn over] twice, p1; [yarn over, p2tog] twice, p1; repeat from the * across, ending with [ssp, yarn over] twice, p1.

Row 8: P6, *p3, yarn over, sssp (page 281), yarn over, p4; repeat from the * across, ending with p5.

Rows 9 and 13: K5, *k3, yarn over, ssk, k1, k2tog, yarn over, k2; repeat from the * across, ending with k6.

Rows 10 and 12: P6, *p1, yarn over, p2tog, yarn over, sssp, yarn over, ssp, yarn over, p2; repeat from the * across, ending with p5.

Row 11: K5, *k1, [yarn over, ssk] twice, k1, [k2tog, yarn over] twice; repeat from the * across, ending with k6.

Row 14: As Row 8.

Repeat Rows 1–14 for the pattern.

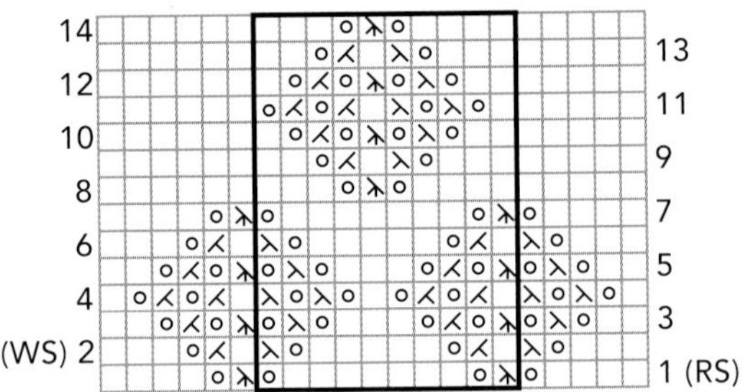

diamond openwork panel

(over 20 stitches on a stockinette background)

Row 1 (RS): Yarn over, ssk, k5, k2tog, yarn over, k2, yarn over, ssk, k5, yarn over, ssk.

Rows 2, 4, 8, 12, and 16: Yarn over, p2tog, p16, yarn over, p2tog.

Row 3: Yarn over, ssk, k4, k2tog, yarn over, k4, yarn over, ssk, k4, yarn over, ssk.

Row 5: Yarn over, ssk, k3, k2tog, yarn over, k1, k2tog, [yarn over] twice (page 284), ssk, k1, yarn over, ssk, k3, yarn over, ssk.

Row 6: Yarn over, p2tog, p7, [k1, p1] into the double yarn over from the previous row, p7, yarn over, p2tog.

Row 7: Yarn over, ssk, k2, k2tog, yarn over, k8, yarn over, ssk, k2, yarn over, ssk.

Row 9: Yarn over, ssk, k1, k2tog, yarn over, k1, [(k2tog, [yarn over] twice, ssk)] twice, k1, yarn over, ssk, k1, yarn over, ssk.

Row 10: Yarn over, p2tog, p5, [k1, p1] into double yarn over, p2, [k1, p1] into double yarn over, p5, yarn over, p2tog.

Row 11: Yarn over, ssk, k3, yarn over, ssk, k6, k2tog, yarn over, k3, yarn over, ssk.

Row 13: Yarn over, ssk, k4, yarn over, ssk, k2tog, [yarn over] twice, ssk, k2tog, yarn over, k4, yarn over, ssk.

Row 14: Yarn over, p2tog, p7, [k1, p1] into double yarn over, p7, yarn over, p2tog.

Row 15: Yarn over, ssk, k5, yarn over, ssk, k2, k2tog, yarn over, k5, yarn over, ssk.

Row 17: Yarn over, ssk, k6, yarn over, ssk, k2tog, yarn over, k6, yarn over, ssk.

Row 18: As Row 2.

Repeat Rows 1–18 for the pattern.

spring leaves

(multiple of 20 stitches plus 20 stitches)

Row 1 (RS): P10, *p8, slip the next st onto cn and hold in back, k1-tbl (page 275), p1 from cn, slip the next st onto cn and hold in front, p1, k1-tbl from cn, p8; repeat from the * across, ending with p10.

Rows 2, 4, 6, 8, 18, 20, 22, and 24: Knit the knit sts and purl the purl sts, and purl the yarn over sts, working sts that were worked in the back loop on the last row *through their back loops* again.

Row 3: P1, yarn over, k1, yarn over, sssk (page 281), p5, *p5, k3tog, yarn over, k1, yarn over, p2, yarn over, k1, yarn over, sssk, p5; repeat from the * across, ending with p5, k3tog, yarn over, k1, yarn over, p1.

Row 5: P1, [k1, yarn over] twice, k1, sssk, p3, *p3, k3tog, [k1, yarn over] twice, k1, p2, [k1, yarn over] twice, k1, sssk, p3; repeat from the * across, ending with p3, k3tog, [k1, yarn over] twice, k1, p1.

Row 7: P1, k2, yarn over, k1, yarn over, k2, sssk, p1, *p1, k3tog, k2, yarn over, k1, yarn over, k2, p2, k2, yarn over, k1, yarn over, k2, sssk, p1; repeat from the * across, ending with p1, k3tog, k2, yarn over, k1, yarn over, k2, p1.

Row 9: P1, k6, k2tog, yarn over, p1, *p1, yarn over, ssk, k6, p2, k6, k2tog, yarn over, p1; repeat from the * across, ending with p1, yarn over, ssk, k6, p1.

Row 10: K1, p7, k2, *[k2, p7] twice, k2; repeat from the * across, ending with k2, p7, k1.

Row 11: P1, yarn over, ssk, k3, k2tog, yarn over, k1-tbl, p1, *p1, k1-tbl, yarn over, ssk, k3, k2tog, yarn over, p2, yarn over, ssk, k3, k2tog, yarn over, k1-tbl, p1; repeat from the * across, ending with p1, k1-tbl, yarn over, ssk, k3, k2tog, yarn over, p1.

Row 12: K2, p5, k1, p1-tbl (page 279), k1, *k1, p1-tbl, k1, p5, k4, p5, k1, p1-tbl, k1; repeat from the * across, ending with k1, p1-tbl, k1, p5, k2.

Row 13: P2, yarn over, ssk, k1, k2tog, yarn over, p1, slip the next st onto cn and hold in front, p1, k1-tbl from cn, *slip the next st onto cn and hold in back, k1-tbl, p1 from cn, p1, yarn over, ssk, k1, k2tog, yarn over, p4, yarn over, ssk, k1, k2tog, yarn over, p1, slip the next st onto cn and hold in front, p1, k1-tbl from cn; repeat from the * across, ending with slip the next st onto cn and hold in back, k1-tbl, p1 from cn, p1, yarn over, ssk, k1, k2tog, yarn over, p2.

Row 14: K3, p3, k3, p1-tbl, *p1-tbl, k3, p3, k6, p3, k3, p1-tbl; repeat from the * across, ending with p1-tbl, k3, p3, k3.

Row 15: P3, yarn over, k3tog, yarn over, p3, *slip the next st onto cn and hold in front, k1-tbl, k1-tbl from cn, p3, yarn over, sssk, yarn over, p6, yarn over, k3tog, yarn over, p3; repeat from the * across, ending with slip the next st onto cn and hold in front, k1-tbl, k1-tbl from cn, p3, yarn over, k3tog, yarn over, p3.

Row 16: K9, p1-tbl, *p1-tbl, k18, p1-tbl; repeat from the * across, ending with p1-tbl, p9.

Row 17: P8, slip the next st onto cn and hold in back, k1-tbl, p1 from cn, *slip the next st onto cn and hold in front, p1, k1-tbl from cn, p16, slip the next st onto cn and hold in back, k1-tbl, p1 from cn; repeat from the * across, ending with slip the next st onto cn and hold in front, p1, k1-tbl from cn, p8.

Row 19: P5, k3tog, yarn over, k1, yarn over, p1, *p1, yarn over, k1, yarn over, sssk, p10, k3tog, yarn over, k1, yarn over, p1; repeat from the * across, ending with p1, yarn over, k1, yarn over, sssk, p5.

Row 21: P3, k3tog, [k1, yarn over] twice, k1, p1, *p1, [k1, yarn over] twice, k1, sssk, p6, k3tog, [k1, yarn over] twice, k1, p1; repeat from the * across, ending with p1, [k1, yarn over] twice, k1, sssk, p3.

Row 23: P1, k3tog, k2, yarn over, k1, yarn over, k2, p1, *p1, k2, yarn over, k1, yarn over, k2, sssk, p2, k3tog, k2, yarn over, k1, yarn over, k2, p1; repeat from the * across, ending with p1, k2, yarn over, k1, yarn over, k2, sssk, p1.

Row 25: P1, yarn over, ssk, k6, p1, *p1, k6, k2tog, yarn over, p2, yarn over, ssk, k6, p1; repeat from the * across, ending with p1, k6, k2tog, yarn over, p1.

Row 26: K2, p7, k1, *k1, p7, k4, p7, k1; repeat from the * across, ending with k1, p7, k2.

Row 27: P1, k1-tbl, yarn over, ssk, k3, k2tog, yarn over, p1, *p1, yarn over, ssk, k3, k2tog, yarn over, k1-tbl, p2, k1-tbl, yarn over, ssk, k3, k2tog, yarn over, p1; repeat from the * across, ending with p1, yarn over, ssk, k3, k2tog, yarn over, k1-tbl, p1.

Row 28: K1, p1-tbl, k1, p5, k2, *k2, p5, k1, p1-tbl, k2, p1-tbl, k1, p5, k2; repeat from the * across, ending with k2, p5, k1, p1-tbl, k1.

Row 29: P3, yarn over, ssk, k1, k2tog, yarn over, p2, *p2, yarn over, ssk, k1, k2tog, yarn over, p1, slip the next st onto cn and hold in front, p1, k1-tbl from cn, slip the next st onto cn and hold in back, k1-tbl, p1 from cn, p1, yarn over, ssk, k1, k2tog, yarn over, p2; repeat from the * across, ending with p2, yarn over, ssk, k1, k2tog, yarn over, p3.

Row 30: K4, p3, k3, *k3, p3, k3, [p1-tbl] twice, k3, p3, k3; repeat from the * across, ending with k3, p3, k4.

Row 31: P4, yarn over, sssk, yarn over, p3, *p3, yarn over, k3tog, yarn over, p3, slip the next st onto cn and hold in back, k1-tbl, k1-tbl from cn, p3, yarn over, sssk, yarn over, p3; repeat from the * across, ending with p3, yarn over, k3tog, yarn over, p4.

Row 32: K10, *k9, [p1-tbl] twice, k9; repeat from the * across, ending with k10.

Repeat Rows 1–32 for the pattern.

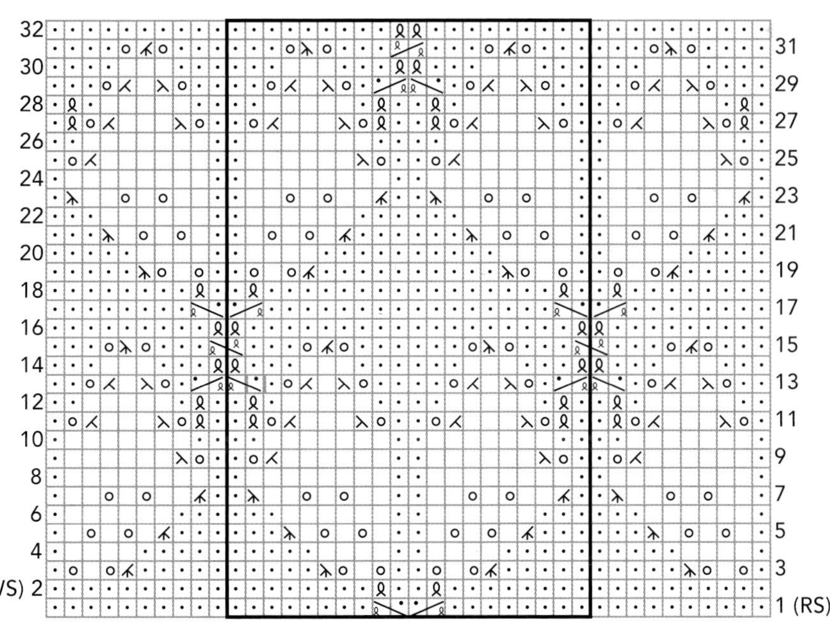

perforated pattern

(multiple of 4 stitches plus 6 stitches)

Row 1 (RS): K1, k2tog, *[yarn over] twice (page 284), ssk, k2tog; repeat from the * across, ending with [yarn over] twice, ssk, k1.

Row 2: P2, [k1, p1] into the double yarn over, *p2, [k1, p1] into the double yarn over; repeat from the * across, ending with p2.

Row 3: K1, yarn over, *ssk, k2tog, [yarn over] twice; repeat from the * across, ending with ssk, k2tog, yarn over, k1.

Row 4: P4, *[k1, p1] into the double yarn over, p2; repeat from the * across, ending with p2.

Repeat Rows 1–4 for the pattern.

4 3 (WS) 2 1 (RS)

flambé lace

(multiple of 13 stitches, increases to multiple of 18 stitches)

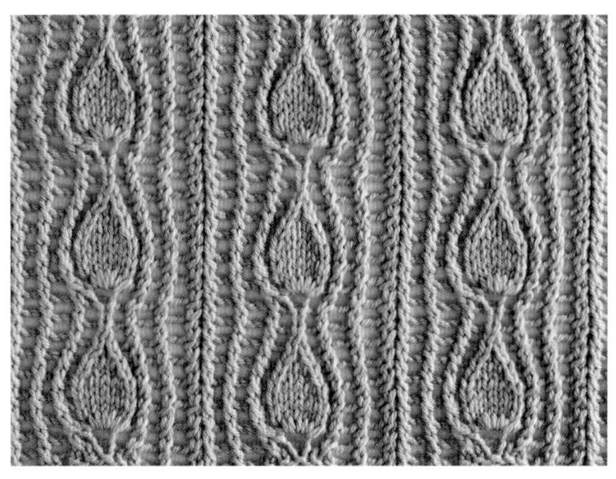

NOTE

- Stitch count varies from row to row.

Row 1 (RS): *[K2tog, yarn over] 3 times, [[k1, yarn over] 3 times, k1] all into the next st, [ssk, yarn over] twice, ssk; repeat from the * across.

Row 2 and all WS rows: Purl across.

Rows 3 and 5: *[K2tog, yarn over] 3 times, k6, [yarn over, ssk] 3 times; repeat from the * across.

Row 7: *[K2tog, yarn over] 3 times, ssk, k2, k2tog, [yarn over, ssk] 3 times; repeat from the * across.

Row 9: *[K2tog, yarn over] 3 times, ssk, k2tog, [yarn over, ssk] 3 times; repeat from the * across.

Row 11: *[K2tog, yarn over] 3 times, k2tog, [yarn over, ssk] 3 times; repeat from the * across.

Row 13: *[K2tog, yarn over] 3 times, k1, [yarn over, ssk] 3 times; repeat from the * across.

Row 14: As Row 2.

Repeat Rows 1–14 for the pattern.

14 13 12 11 10 9 8 7 6 5 4 3 (WS) 2 7 1 (RS)

peacock lace

(multiple of 4 stitches plus 6 stitches)

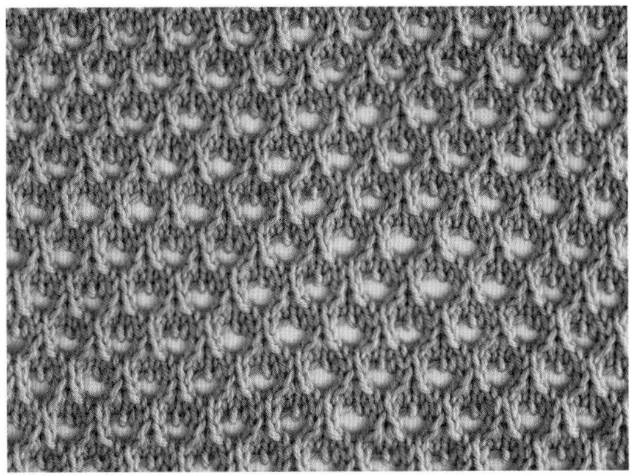

Row 1 (RS): K1, k2tog, *[yarn over] twice, ssk, k2tog; repeat from the * across, ending with [yarn over] twice, ssk, k1.

Row 2: P2, [k1, p1] into the double yarn over, *p2, [k1, p1] into the double yarn over; repeat from the * across, ending with p2.

Rows 3 and 7: Knit across.

Row 4: Purl across.

Row 5: K1, yarn over, *ssk, k2tog, [yarn over] twice; repeat from the * across, ending with ssk, k2tog, yarn over, k1.

Row 6: P4, *[k1, p1] into the double yarn over, p2; repeat from the * across, ending with p2.

Row 8: Purl across.

Repeat Rows 1–8 for the pattern.

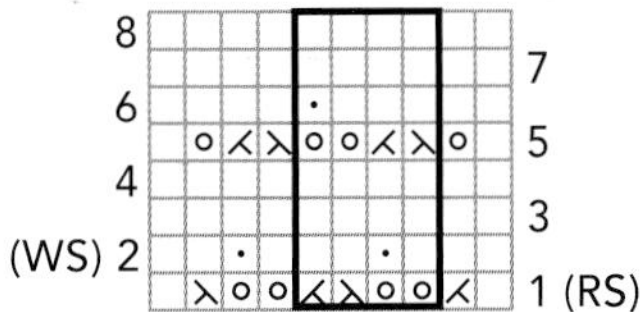

faux crochet

(multiple of 3 stitches plus 5 stitches)

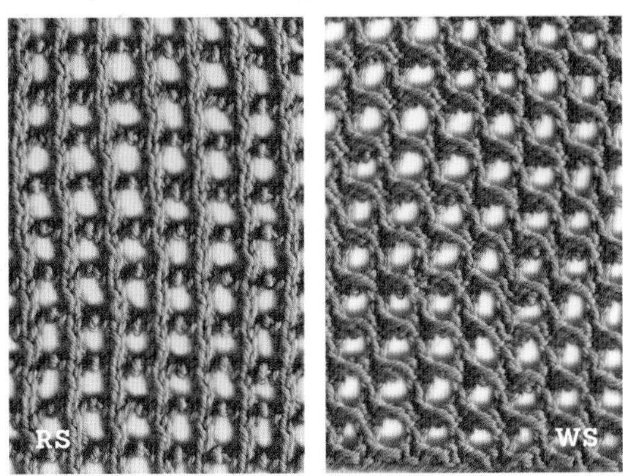

Row 1 (RS): Knit across.

Row 2: Purl across.

Row 3: K1, yarn over, *s2kp2 (page 272), [yarn over] twice (page 284); repeat from the * across, ending with s2kp2, yarn over, k1.

Row 4: P3, *[k1, p1] into the double yarn over, p1; repeat from the * across, ending with p2.

Repeat Rows 1–4 for the pattern.

4
(WS) 2
3
1 (RS)

lacy bubbles

(multiple of 10 stitches plus 11 stitches, increases to a multiple of 12 stitches plus 13 stitches)

NOTE

- Stitch count varies from row to row.

Row 1 (RS): P3, yarn over, ssk, *p1, k2tog, yarn over, p2, [k1, yarn over, k1] (page 268) all into the next st, p2, yarn over, ssk; repeat from the * across, ending with p1, k2tog, yarn over, p3.

Rows 2 and 4: K4, p2, *p1, k3, p3, k3, p2; repeat from the * across, ending with p1, k4.

Row 3: P4, k1, *k2, p3, k3, p3, k1; repeat from the * across, ending with k2, p4.

Row 5: P3, k2tog, yarn over, *p1, yarn over, ssk, p2, k3tog, p2, k2tog, yarn over; repeat from the * across, ending with p1, yarn over, ssk, p3.

Row 6: K3, p1, k2, *k1, p1, k5, p1, k2; repeat from the * across, ending with k1, p1, k3.

Row 7: P2, k2tog, yarn over, p1, *p2, yarn over, ssk, p3, k2tog, yarn over, p1; repeat from the * across ending with p2, yarn over, ssk, p2.

Rows 8 and 14: K2, p1, k3, *k2, [p1, k3] twice; repeat from the * across, ending with k2, p1, k2.

Row 9: P1, k2tog, yarn over, p2, *[k1, yarn over, k1] all into the next st, p2, yarn over, ssk, p1, k2tog, yarn over, p2; repeat from the * across, ending with [k1, yarn over, k1] all into the next st, p2, yarn over, ssk, p1.

Rows 10 and 12: P2, k3, p3, *[k3, p3] twice; repeat from the * across, ending with k3, p2.

Row 11: K2, p3, *[k3, p3] twice; repeat from the * across, ending with k3, p3, k2.

Row 13: P1, yarn over, ssk, p2, *k3tog, p2, k2tog, yarn over, p1, yarn over, ssk, p2; repeat from the * across, ending with k3tog, p2, k2tog, yarn over, p1.

Row 15: P2, yarn over, ssk, p1, *p2, k2tog, yarn over, p3, yarn over, ssk, p1; repeat from the * across, ending with p2, k2tog, yarn over, p2.

Row 16: As Row 6.

Repeat Rows 1–16 for the pattern.

16	•	•	•		•	•	•		•	•	•	•	•		•	•	•		•	•	•	
	•	•	o	/	•	•	•	\	o	•	•	•	o	/	•	•	•	\	o	•	•	15
14	•	•		•	•	•	•	•		•	•	•		•	•	•	•	•		•	•	
	•	o	/	•	•	ʌ	•	•	\	o	•	o	/	•	•	ʌ	•	•	\	o	•	13
12			•	•	•	|||	•	•	•				•	•	•	|||	•	•	•			
			•	•	•	|||	•	•	•				•	•	•	|||	•	•	•			11
10			•	•	•	|||	•	•	•				•	•	•	|||	•	•	•			
	•	\	o	•	•	V	•	•	o	/	•	\	o	•	•	V	•	•	o	/	•	9
8	•	•		•	•	•	•	•		•	•	•		•	•	•	•	•		•	•	
	•	•	\	o	•	•	•	o	/	•	•	•	\	o	•	•	•	o	/	•	•	7
6	•	•	•		•	•	•		•	•	•	•	•		•	•	•		•	•	•	
	•	•	•	\	o	•	o	/	•	•	ʌ	•	•	\	o	•	o	/	•	•	•	5
4	•	•	•	•				•	•	•	|||	•	•	•				•	•	•	•	
	•	•	•	•				•	•	•	|||	•	•	•				•	•	•	•	3
(WS) 2	•	•	•	•				•	•	•	|||	•	•	•				•	•	•	•	
	•	•	•	o	/	•	\	o	•	•	V	•	•	o	/	•	\	o	•	•	•	1 (RS)

lace lattice

(multiple of 4 stitches plus 6 stitches, increases to multiple of 6 stitches plus 8 stitches)

NOTE

- Stitch count varies from row to row.

Row 1 (RS): K1, yarn over, *slip the next 2 sts onto cn and hold in back, k2, k2 from cn, [yarn over] twice; repeat from the * across, ending with slip the next 2 sts onto cn and hold in back, k2, k2 from cn, yarn over, k1.

Row 2: P6, *[k1, p1] into the double yarn over of the previous row, p4; repeat from the * across, ending with p2.

Row 3: K1, *k2tog, k2, ssk; repeat from the * across, ending with k1.

Row 4: Purl across.

Row 5: K3, *[yarn over] twice, slip the next 2 sts onto cn and hold in front, k2, k2 from cn; repeat from the * across, ending with [yarn over] twice, k3.

Row 6: P3, *[k1, p1] into the double yarn over of the previous row, p4; repeat from the * across, ending with *[k1, p1] into the double yarn over of the previous row, p3.

Row 7: K2, *ssk, k2tog, k2; repeat from the * across.

Row 8: Purl across.

Repeat Rows 1–8 for the pattern.

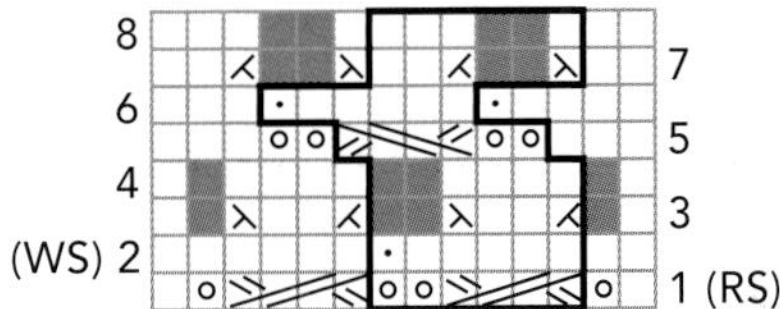

britney lace

(multiple of 8 stitches plus 11 stitches)

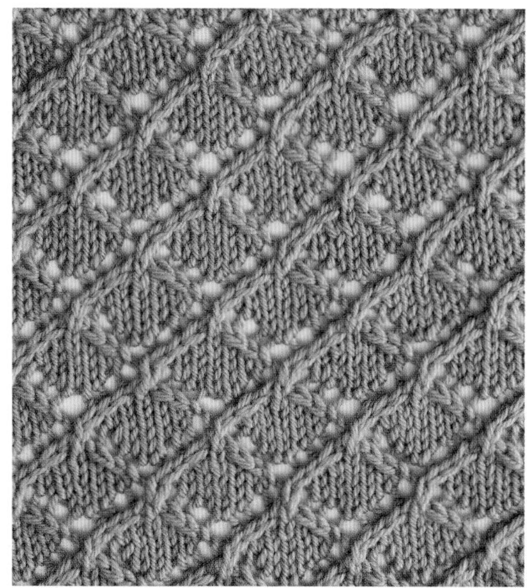

Row 1 (RS): K4, k2tog, *yarn over, k6, k2tog; repeat from the * across, ending with yarn over, k5.

Row 2: P3, ssp (page 281), yarn over, p1, *yarn over, p2tog, p3, ssp, yarn over, p1; repeat from the * across, ending with yarn over, p2tog, p3.

Row 3: K2, k2tog, yarn over, k1, *k2, yarn over, ssk, k1, k2tog, yarn over, k1; repeat from the * across, ending with k2, yarn over, ssk, k2.

Row 4: P1, ssp, yarn over, p3, *p2, yarn over, s2kp2 purlwise (page 272), yarn over, p3; repeat from the * across, ending with p2, yarn over, p2tog, p1.

Row 5: Knit across.

Row 6: P1, yarn over, p2tog, p3, *p3, yarn over, p2tog, p3; repeat from the * across, ending with p3, yarn over, p2tog.

Row 7: K2, yarn over, ssk, k1, *k2, k2tog, yarn over, k1, yarn over, ssk, k1; repeat from the * across, ending with k2, k2tog, yarn over, k2.

Row 8: P3, yarn over, p2tog, p1, *ssp, yarn over, p3, yarn over, p2tog, p1; repeat from the * across, ending with ssp, yarn over, p3.

Row 9: K4, yarn over, *s2kp2 (page 272), yarn over, k5, yarn over; repeat from the * across, ending with s2kp2, yarn over, k4.

Row 10: Purl across.

Repeat Rows 1–10 for the pattern.

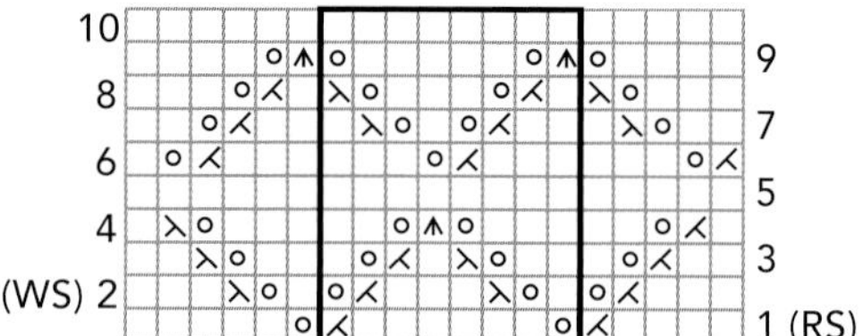

chapter **three**

cables and crossed stitch patterns

No matter how intricate they seem, cables are simply two or more sets of stitches changing places. Endless variations can be knitted by crossing cables in different directions at various spots in the fabric. Some use colorwork to great effect. Still others are completely reversible! I've written two books on cable designs, but I never tire of them. Here are some of my favorite cables for you to explore. Enjoy!

honeycombs

(multiple of 8 stitches)

Row 1 (RS): *Slip the next 2 sts onto cn and hold in back, k2, k2 from cn, slip the next 2 sts onto cn and hold in front, k2, k2 from cn; repeat from the * across.

Row 2 and all WS rows: Purl across.

Rows 3 and 7: Knit across.

Row 5: *Slip the next 2 sts onto cn and hold in front, k2, k2 from cn, slip the next 2 sts onto cn and hold in back, k2, k2 from cn; repeat from the * across.

Row 8: As Row 2.

Repeat Rows 1–8 for the pattern.

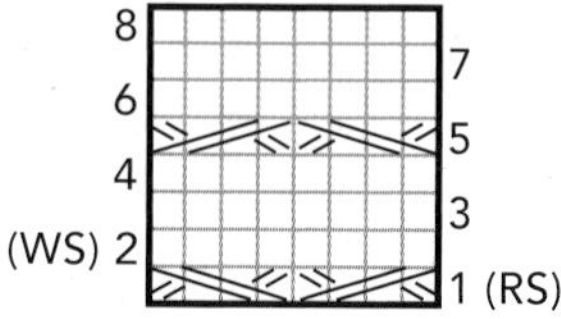

offset cables

(multiple of 9 stitches)

Row 1 (RS): *K3, slip the next 3 sts onto cn and hold in back, k3, k3 from cn; repeat from the * across.

Row 2 and all WS rows: Purl across.

Rows 3 and 7: Knit across.

Row 5: *Slip the next 3 sts onto cn and hold in front, k3, k3 from cn, k3; repeat from the * across.

Row 8: As Row 2.

Repeat Rows 1–8 for the pattern.

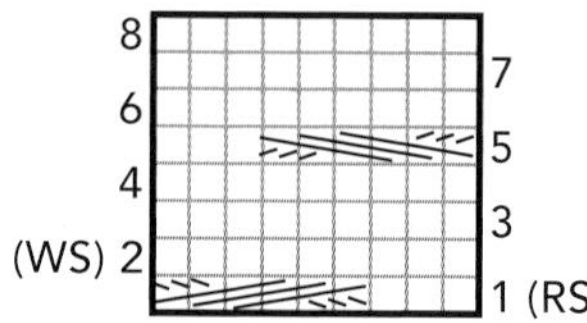

shifting sand

(multiple of 8 stitches)

Row 1 (RS): *Slip the next 2 sts onto cn and hold in back, k2, k2 from cn, k4; repeat from the * across.

Row 2: Purl across.

Rows 3 and 5: Knit across.

Row 4: *Slip the next 2 sts onto cn and hold in front, p2, p2 from cn, p4; repeat from the * across.

Row 6: As Row 2.

Repeat Rows 1–6 for the pattern.

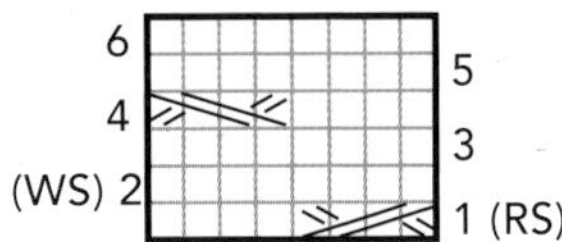

pinched cables

(multiple of 12 stitches plus 2 stitches)

Row 1 (RS): K1, *slip the next 2 sts onto cn and hold in back, k2, k2 from cn, k4, slip the next 2 sts onto cn and hold in front, k2, k2 from cn; repeat from the * across, ending with k1.

Row 2 and all WS rows: Purl across.

Rows 3 and 7: Knit across.

Row 5: K1, *k2, slip the next 2 sts onto cn and hold in front, k2, k2 from cn, slip the next 2 sts onto cn and hold in back, k2, k2 from cn, k2; repeat from the * across, ending with k1.

Row 8: As Row 2.

Repeat Rows 1–8 for the pattern.

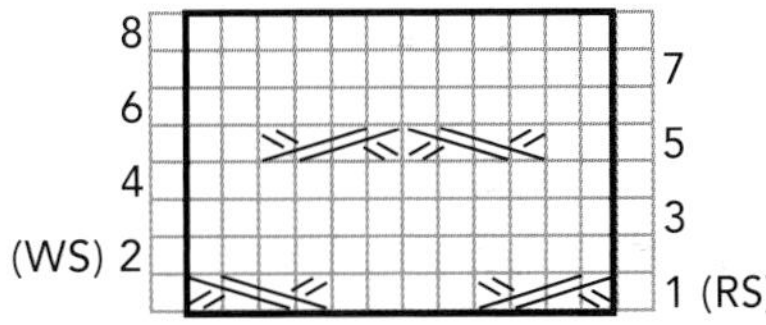

shuffling cables

(multiple of 5 stitches plus 1 stitch)

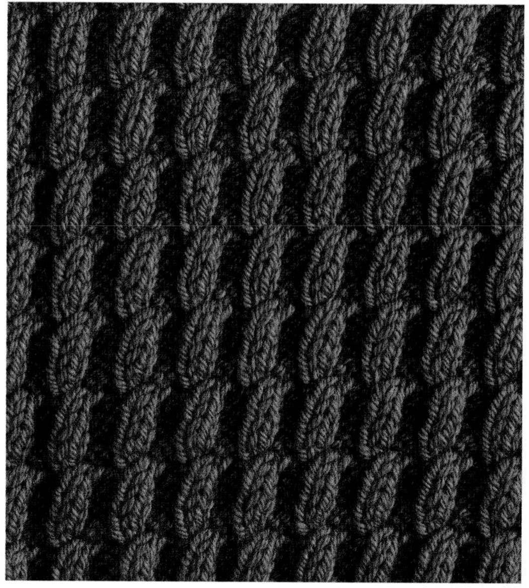

Row 1 (RS): *P1, slip the next 2 sts onto cn and hold in back, k2, k2 from cn; repeat from the * across, ending with p1.

Rows 2 and 4: K1, *p2, k3; repeat from the * across.

Rows 3 and 5: *P3, k2; repeat from the * across, ending with p1.

Row 6: As Row 2.

Repeat Rows 1–6 for the pattern.

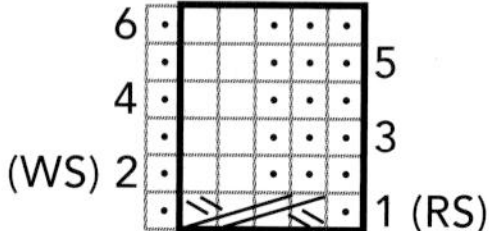

waterfall cables

(multiple of 18 stitches plus 3 stitches)

Row 1 (RS): *P9, slip the next 3 sts onto cn and hold in back, k3, k3 from cn, k3; repeat from the * across ending with p3.

Row 2 and all WS rows: Knit the knit sts and purl the purl sts.

Rows 3, 5, and 7: *P9, k9; repeat from the * across, ending with p3.

Row 9: *P3, k3, slip the next 3 sts onto cn and hold in front, k3, k3 from cn, p6; repeat from the * across, ending with p3.

Rows 11, 13, and 15: *P3, k9, p6; repeat from the * across, ending with p3.

Row 16: As Row 2.

Repeat Rows 1–16 for the pattern.

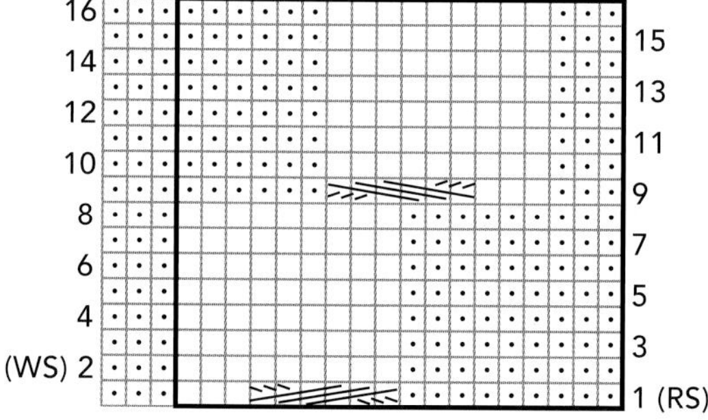

ukuleles

(multiple of 8 stitches)

Rows 1 and 3 (RS): *P3, k2, p3; repeat from the * across.

Row 2 and all WS rows: Knit the knit sts and purl the purl sts.

Row 5: *P1, slip the next 2 sts onto cn and hold in back, k1, k2 from cn, slip the next st onto cn and hold in front, k2, k1 from cn, p1; repeat from the * across.

Rows 7 and 9: *P1, k6, p1; repeat from the * across.

Row 11: *P1, slip the next st onto cn and hold in front, p2, k1 from cn, slip the next 2 sts onto cn and hold in back, k1, p2 from cn, p1; repeat from the * across.

Row 12: As Row 2.

Repeat Rows 1–12 for the pattern.

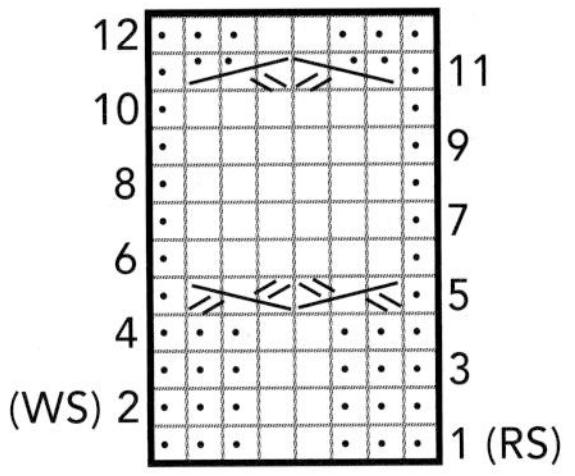

diagonal texture

(multiple of 6 stitches plus 2 stitches)

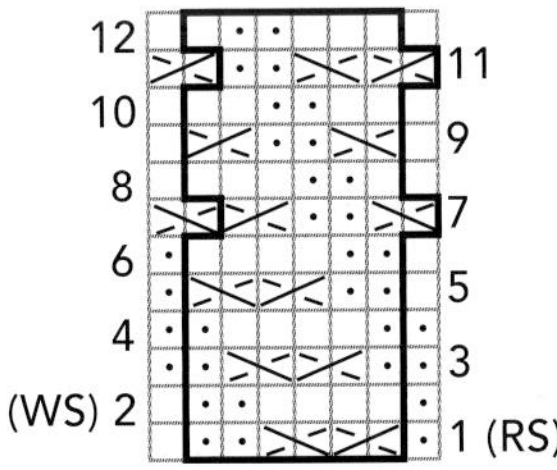

Row 1 (RS): P1, *right twist (page 279), left twist (page 276), p2; repeat from the * across, ending with k1.

Row 2 and all WS rows: Knit the knit sts and purl the purl sts.

Row 3: P1, *p1, right twist, left twist, p1; repeat from the * across, ending with p1.

Row 5: K1, *p2, right twist, left twist; repeat from the * across, ending with p1.

Row 7: *Left twist, p2, right twist; repeat from the * across, ending with left twist.

Row 9: K1, *left twist, p2, right twist; repeat from the * across, ending with k1.

Row 11: *Right Twist, left twist, p2; repeat from the * across, ending with right twist.

Row 12: As Row 2.

Repeat Rows 1–12 for the pattern.

inishmore cable

(over 20 stitches on a reverse stockinette background)

Row 1 (RS): P4, slip the next 2 sts onto cn and hold in back, k2, k2 from cn, [p4, k2] twice.

Row 2 and all WS rows: Knit the knit sts and purl the purl sts.

Row 3: P2, slip the next 2 sts onto cn and hold in back, k2, p2 from cn, slip the next 2 sts onto cn and hold in front, p2, k2 from cn, slip the next 2 sts onto cn and hold in back, k2, p2 from cn, p3, slip the next st onto cn and hold in back, k2, p1 from cn.

Row 5: P1, slip the next st onto cn and hold in back, k2, p1 from cn, p4, slip the next 2 sts onto cn and hold in front, k2, k2 from cn, p4, slip the next st onto cn and hold in back, k2, p1 from cn, p1.

Row 7: Slip the next st onto cn and hold in back, k2, p1 from cn, p3, slip the next 2 sts onto cn and hold in back, k2, p2 from cn, slip the next 2 sts onto cn and hold in front, p2, k2 from cn, slip the next 2 sts onto cn and hold in back, k2, p2 from cn, p2.

Row 9: [K2, p4] twice, slip the next 2 sts onto cn and hold in back, k2, k2 from cn, p4.

Row 11: Slip the next 2 sts onto cn and hold in front, p1, k2 from cn, p3, slip the next 2 sts onto cn and hold in front, p2, k2 from cn, slip the next 2 sts onto cn and hold in back, k2, p2 from cn, slip the next 2 sts onto cn and hold in front, p2, k2 from cn, p2.

Row 13: P1, slip the next 2 sts onto cn and hold in front, p1, k2 from cn, p4, slip the next 2 sts onto cn and hold in front, k2, k2 from cn, p4, slip the next 2 sts onto cn and hold in front, p1, k2 from cn, p1.

Row 15: P2, slip the next 2 sts onto cn and hold in front, p2, k2 from cn, slip the next 2 sts onto cn and hold in back, k2, p2 from cn, slip the next 2 sts onto cn and hold in front, p2, k2 from cn, p3, slip the next 2 sts onto cn and hold in front, p1, k2 from cn.

Row 16: As Row 2.

Repeat Rows 1–16 for the pattern.

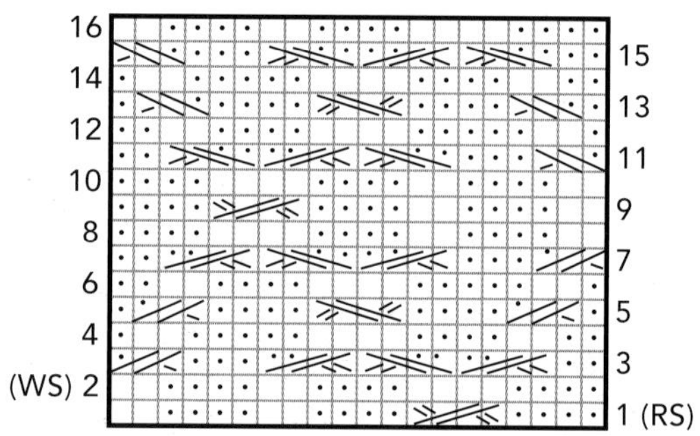

x's and o's

easy

(over 15 stitches on a reverse stockinette background)

Rows 1, 3, 5, 9, and 13 (RS): [K3, p1] 3 times, k3.

Row 2 and all WS rows: Knit the knit sts and purl the purl sts.

Row 7: Slip the next 3 sts onto cn #1 and hold in front, slip the next st onto cn #2 and hold in back, k3 from the left-hand needle, p1 from cn #2, k3 from cn #1, p1, slip the next 3 sts onto cn #1 and hold in back, slip the next st onto cn #2 and hold in back, k3 from left-hand needle, p1 from cn #2, k3 from cn #1.

Row 11: K3, p1, slip the next 3 sts onto cn #1 and hold in back, slip the next st onto cn #2 and hold in back, k3 from the left-hand needle, p1 from cn #2, k3 from cn #1, p1, k3.

Row 15: Slip the next 3 sts onto cn #1 and hold in back, slip the next st onto cn #2 and hold in back, k3 from the left-hand needle, p1 from cn #2, k3 from cn #1, p1, slip the next 3 sts onto cn #1 and hold in front, slip the next st onto cn #2 and hold in back, k3 from the left-hand needle, p1 from cn #2, k3 from cn #1.

Row 16: As Row 2.

Repeat Rows 1–16 for the pattern.

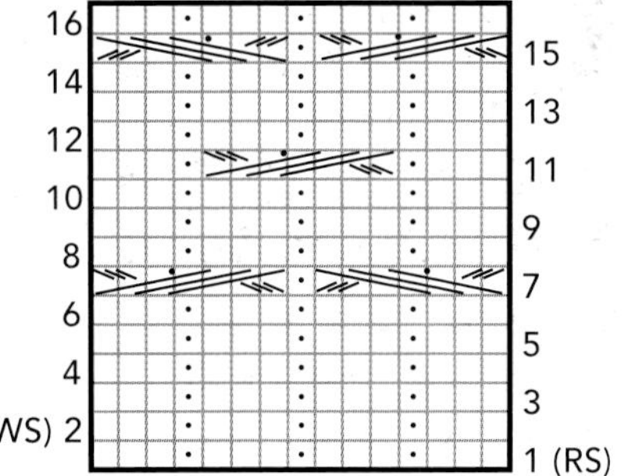

branches

(over 18 stitches on a reverse stockinette background)

Row 1 (RS): P3, slip the next 3 sts onto cn and hold in back, k3, k3 from cn, slip the next 3 sts onto cn and hold in front, k3, k3 from cn, p3.

Row 2 and all WS rows: Knit the knit sts and purl the purl sts.

Row 3: Slip the next 3 sts onto cn and hold in back, k3, k3 from cn, k6, slip the next 3 sts onto cn and hold in front, k3, k3 from cn.

Rows 5 and 7: P3, k12, p3.

Row 8: As Row 2.

Repeat Rows 1–8 for the pattern.

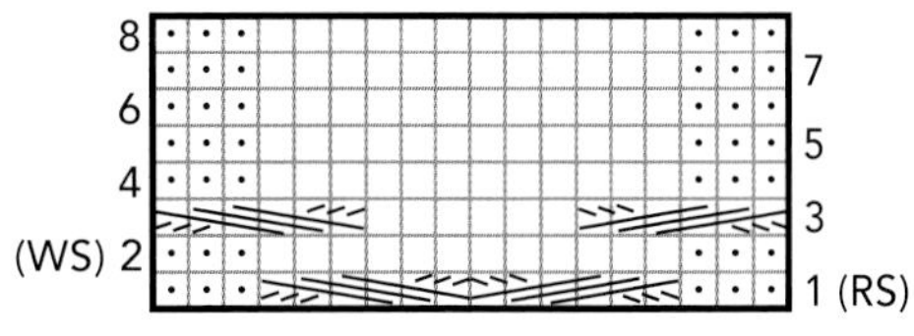

sculpted diamonds

(multiple of 10 stitches plus 2 stitches)

Row 1 (RS): K1, *k3, right twist (page 279), left twist (page 276), k3; repeat from the * across, ending with k1.

Row 2 and all WS rows: Purl across.

Row 3: K1, *k2, right twist, k2, left twist, k2; repeat from the * across, ending with k1.

Row 5: K1, *k1, right twist, k4, left twist, k1; repeat from the * across, ending with k1.

Row 7: K1, *right twist, k1, right twist, left twist, k1, left twist; repeat from the * across, ending with k1.

Row 9: K1, *left twist, k1, left twist, right twist, k1, right twist; repeat from the * across, ending with k1.

Row 11: K1, *k1, left twist, k4, right twist, k1; repeat from the * across, ending with k1.

Row 13: K1, *k2, left twist, k2, right twist, k2; repeat from the * across, ending with k1.

Row 15: K1, *k3, left twist, right twist, k3; repeat from the * across, ending with k1.

Row 16: As Row 2.

Repeat Rows 1–16 for the pattern.

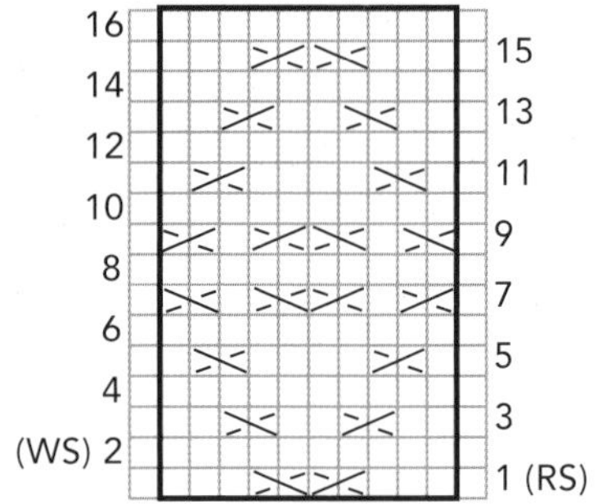

wishbone ribs

(multiple of 16 stitches)

Row 1 (RS): *Slip the next 4 sts onto cn and hold in front, [k1, p2, k1] from the left-hand needle, [k1, p2, k1] from the cn, slip the next 4 sts onto cn and hold in back, [k1, p2, k1] from the left-hand needle, [k1, p2, k1] from the cn; repeat from the * across.

Rows 2–10: Knit the knit sts and purl the purl sts.

Repeat Rows 1–10 for the pattern.

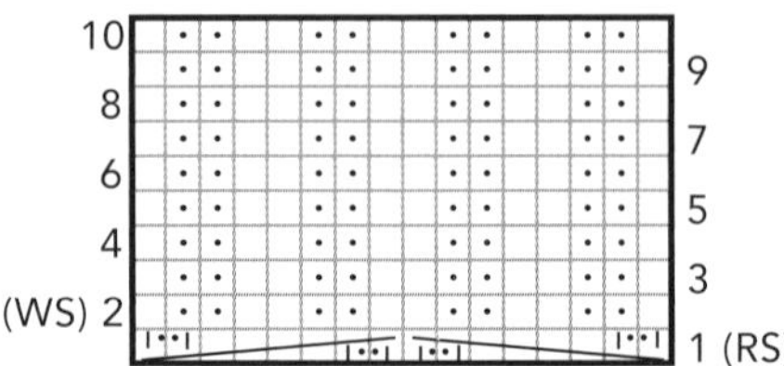

cables and plaits

(over 12 stitches on a reverse stockinette background)

Rows 1 and 5 (RS): P2, [slip the next 2 sts onto cn and hold in back, k2, k2 from cn] twice, p2.

Row 2 and all WS rows: Knit the knit sts and purl the purl sts.

Row 3: P2, k2, slip the next 2 sts onto cn and hold in front, k2, k2 from cn, k2, p2.

Row 7: Slip the next 2 sts onto cn and hold in back, k2, p2 from cn, slip the next 2 sts onto cn and hold in front, k2, k2 from cn, slip the next 2 sts onto cn and hold in front, p2, k2 from cn.

Row 9: K2, slip the next 2 sts onto cn and hold in back, k2, p2 from cn, slip the next 2 sts onto cn and hold in front, p2, k2 from cn, k2.

Rows 11 and 15: Slip the next 2 sts onto cn and hold in back, k2, k2 from cn, p4, slip the next 2 sts onto cn and hold in back, k2, k2 from cn.

Row 13: K4, p4, k4.

Row 17: K2, slip the next 2 sts onto cn and hold in front, p2, k2 from cn, slip the next 2 sts onto cn and hold in back, k2, p2 from cn, k2.

Row 19: Slip the next 2 sts onto cn and hold in front, p2, k2 from cn, slip the next 2 sts onto cn and hold in front, k2, k2 from cn, slip the next 2 sts onto cn and hold in back, k2, p2 from cn.

Row 20: As Row 2.

Repeat Rows 1–20 for the pattern.

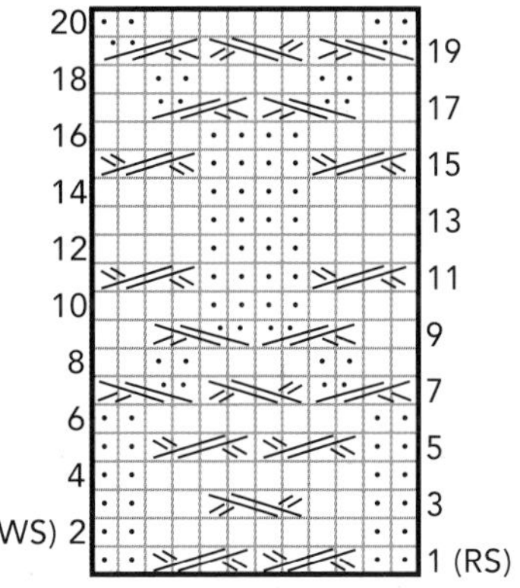

rag dolls

(multiple of 8 stitches plus 2 stitches)

Rows 1, 3, 13, and 15 (RS): P1, *p1, k2, p1; repeat from the * across, ending with p1.

Row 2 and all WS rows: Knit the knit sts and purl the purl sts.

Row 5: P1, *slip the next st onto cn and hold in back, k2, p1 from cn, p2, slip the next 2 sts onto cn and hold in front, p1, k2 from cn; repeat from the * across, ending with p1.

Row 7: P1, *left twist (page 276), p4, right twist (page 279); repeat from the * across, ending with p1.

Row 9: P1, *right twist, p4, left twist; repeat from the * across, ending with p1.

Row 11: P1, *slip the next 2 sts onto cn and hold in front, p1, k2 from cn, p2, slip the next st onto cn and hold in back, k2, p1 from cn; repeat from the * across, ending with p1.

Row 17: P1, *p1, slip the next 2 sts onto cn and hold in front, p1, k2 from cn, slip the next st onto cn and hold in back, k2, p1 from cn, p1; repeat from the * across, ending with p1.

Row 19: P1, *p2, right twist, left twist, p2; repeat from the * across, ending with p1.

Row 21: P1, *p2, left twist, right twist, p2; repeat from the * across, ending with p1.

Row 23: P1, *p1, slip the next st onto cn and hold in back, k2, p1 from cn, slip the next 2 sts onto cn and hold in front, p1, k2 from cn, p1; repeat from the * across, ending with p1.

Row 24: As Row 2.

Repeat Rows 1–24 for the pattern.

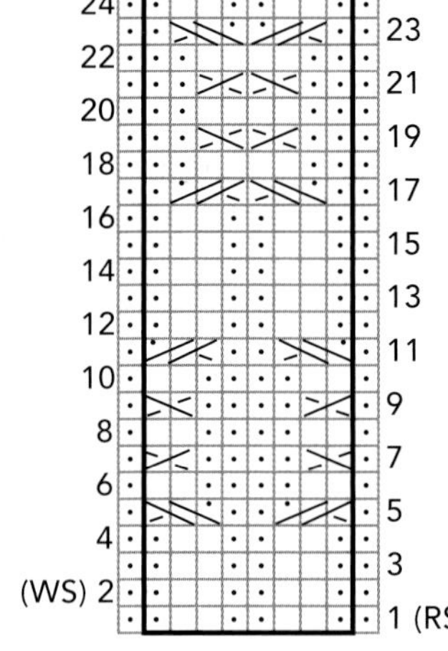

traveling garter ribs 

(multiple of 24 stitches plus 2 stitches)

Rows 1, 3, 5, 15, 17, and 19 (RS): *P2, k2; repeat from the * across, ending with p2.

Row 2 and all WS rows: Purl across.

Row 7: *[P2, k2] twice, slip the next 2 sts onto cn and hold in back, k2, k2 from cn, p2, slip the next 2 sts onto cn and hold in front, k2, k2 from cn, k2, p2, k2; repeat from the * across, ending with p2.

Row 9: *P2, k2, p2, slip the next 2 sts onto cn and hold in back, k2, p2 from cn, k2, p2, k2, slip the next 2 sts onto cn and hold in front, p2, k2 from cn, p2, k2; repeat from the * across, ending with p2.

Row 11: *P2, k2, slip the next 2 sts onto cn and hold in back, k2, k2 from cn, [p2, k2] twice, p2, slip the next 2 sts onto cn and hold in front, k2, k2 from cn, k2; repeat from the * across, ending with p2.

Row 13: *P2, slip the next 2 sts onto cn and hold in back, k2, p2 from cn, [k2, p2] 3 times, k2, slip the next 2 sts onto cn and hold in front, p2, k2 from cn; repeat from the * across, ending with p2.

Row 21: *P2, slip the next 2 sts onto cn and hold in front, k2, k2 from cn, [k2, p2] 3 times, k2, slip the next 2 sts onto cn and hold in back, k2, k2 from cn; repeat from the * across, ending with p2.

Row 23: *P2, k2, slip the next 2 sts onto cn and hold in front, p2, k2 from cn, [p2, k2] twice, p2, slip the next 2 sts onto cn and hold in back, k2, p2 from cn, k2; repeat from the * across, ending with p2.

Row 25: *P2, k2, p2, slip the next 2 sts onto cn and hold in front, k2, k2 from cn, k2, p2, k2, slip the next 2 sts onto cn and hold in back, k2, k2 from cn, p2, k2; repeat from the * across, ending with p2.

Row 27: *[P2, k2] twice, slip the next 2 sts onto cn and hold in front, p2, k2 from cn, p2, slip the next 2 sts onto cn and hold in back, k2, p2 from cn, k2, p2, k2; repeat from the * across, ending with p2.

Row 28: As Row 2.

Repeat Rows 1–28 for the pattern.

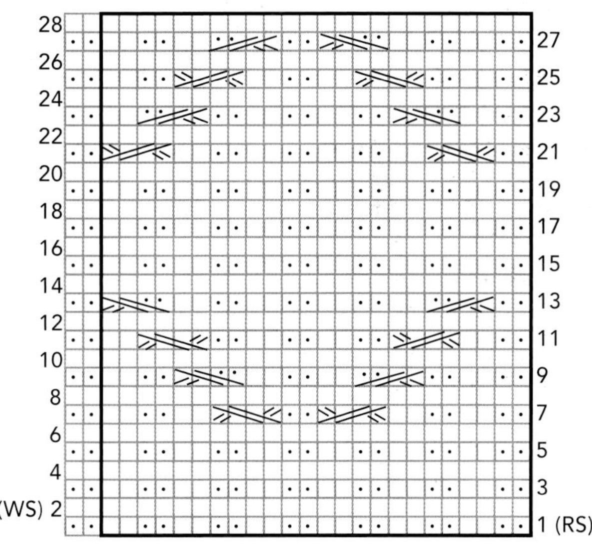

framed cable

(over 20 stitches on a reverse stockinette background)

Row 1 (RS): P8, k4, p8.

Row 2 and all WS rows: Knit the knit sts and purl the purl sts.

Rows 3 and 35: P8, slip the next 2 sts onto cn and hold in front, k2, k2 from cn, p8.

Row 5: P6, slip the next 2 sts onto cn and hold in back, k2, p2 from cn, slip the next 2 sts onto cn and hold in front, p2, k2 from cn, p6.

Row 7: P4, slip the next 2 sts onto cn and hold in back, k2, k2 from cn, p4, slip the next 2 sts onto cn and hold in front, k2, k2 from cn, p4.

Row 9: P4, k2, slip the next 2 sts onto cn and hold in front, p2, k2 from cn, slip the next 2 sts onto cn and hold in back, k2, p2 from cn, k2, p4.

Rows 11 and 27: P4, k2, p2, slip the next 2 sts onto cn and hold in front, k2, k2 from cn, p2, k2, p4.

Rows 13 and 25: P4, k2, p2, k4, p2, k2, p4.

Row 15: P2, slip the next 2 sts onto cn and hold in back, k2, p2 from cn, p2, slip the next 2 sts onto cn and hold in front, k2, k2 from cn, p2, slip the next 2 sts onto cn and hold in front, p2, k2 from cn, p2.

Row 17: Slip the next 2 sts onto cn and hold in back, k2, p2 from cn, p2, slip the next 2 sts onto cn and hold in back, k2, p2 from cn, slip the next 2 sts onto cn and hold in front p2, k2 from cn, p2, slip the next 2 sts onto cn and hold in front, p2, k2 from cn.

Row 19: [K2, p4] 3 times, k2.

Row 21: Slip the next 2 sts onto cn and hold in front, p2, k2 from cn, p2, slip the next 2 sts onto cn and hold in front, p2, k2 from cn, slip the next 2 sts onto cn and hold in back, k2, p2 from cn, p2, slip the next 2 sts onto cn and hold in back, k2, p2 from cn.

Row 23: P2, slip the next 2 sts onto cn and hold in front, p2, k2 from cn, p2, slip the next 2 sts onto cn and hold in front, k2, k2 from cn, p2, slip the next 2 sts onto cn and hold in back, k2, p2 from cn, p2.

Row 29: P4, k2, slip the next 2 sts onto cn and hold in back, k2, p2 from cn, slip the next 2 sts onto cn and hold in front, p2, k2 from cn, k2, p4.

Row 31: P4, slip the next 2 sts onto cn and hold in front, p2, k2 from cn, p4, slip the next 2 sts onto cn and hold in back, k2, p2 from cn, p4.

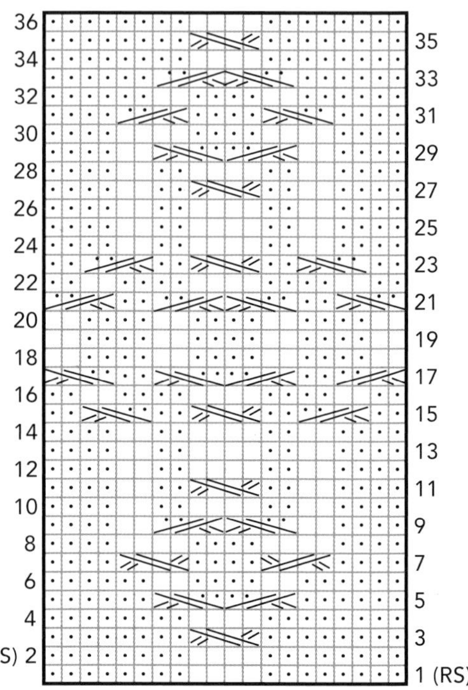

Row 33: P6, slip the next 2 sts onto cn and hold in front, p2, k2 from cn, slip the next 2 sts onto cn and hold in back, k2, p2 from cn, p6.

Row 36: As Row 2.

Repeat Rows 1–36 for the pattern.

dimpled diamonds 

(over 18 stitches on a reverse stockinette background)

Row 1 (RS): P2, slip the next 2 sts onto cn and hold in front, k2, k2 from cn, p6, slip the next 2 sts onto cn and hold in back, k2, k2 from cn, p2.

Row 2 and all WS rows: Knit the knit sts and purl the purl sts.

Rows 3 and 15: P1, slip the next st onto cn and hold in back, k2, p1 from cn, slip the next 2 sts onto cn and hold in front, p1, k2 from cn, p4, slip the next st onto cn and hold in back, k2, p1 from cn, slip the next 2 sts onto cn and hold in front, p1, k2 from cn, p1.

Rows 5 and 17: Slip the next st onto cn and hold in back, k2, p1 from cn, p2, slip the next 2 sts onto cn and hold in front, p1, k2 from cn, p2, slip the next st onto cn and hold in back, k2, p1 from cn, p2, slip the next 2 sts onto cn and hold in front, p1, k2 from cn.

Rows 7 and 19: K2, p4, slip the next 2 sts onto cn #1 and hold in back, slip the next 2 sts onto cn #2 and hold in front, k2 from the left-hand needle, p2 from cn #2, k2 from cn #1, p4, k2.

Rows 9 and 21: Slip the next 2 sts onto cn and hold in front, p1, k2 from cn, p2, slip the next st onto cn and hold in back, k2, p1 from cn, p2, slip the next 2 sts onto cn and hold in front, p1, k2 from cn, p2, slip the next st onto cn and hold in back, k2, p1 from cn.

Rows 11 and 23: P1, slip the next 2 sts onto cn and hold in front, p1, k2 from cn, slip the next st onto cn and hold in back, k2, p1 from cn, p4, slip the next 2 sts onto cn and hold in front, p1, k2 from cn, slip the next st onto cn and hold in back, k2, p1 from cn, p1.

Row 13: P2, slip the next 2 sts onto cn and hold in back, k2, k2 from cn, p6, slip the next 2 sts onto cn and hold in front, k2, k2 from cn, p2.

Row 24: As Row 2.

Repeat Rows 1–24 for the pattern.

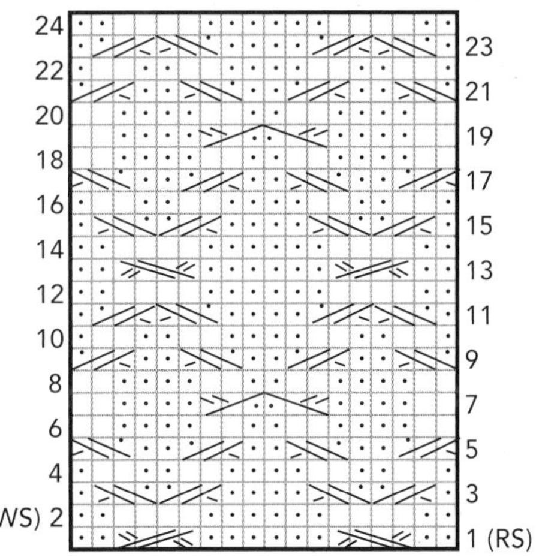

entwined diamonds panel 

(over 22 stitches on a reverse stockinette background)

Row 1 (RS): K2, p3, k4, p4, k4, p3, k2.

Row 2 and all WS rows: Knit the knit sts and purl the purl sts.

Row 3: Slip the next 2 sts onto cn and hold in front, p1, k2 from cn, p2, slip the next 2 sts onto cn and hold in back, k2, k2 from cn, p4, slip the next 2 sts onto cn and hold in back, k2, k2 from cn, p2, slip the next st onto cn and hold in back, k2, p1 from cn.

Row 5: P1, slip the next 2 sts onto cn and hold in front, p1, k2 from cn, slip the next st onto cn and hold in back, k2, p1 from cn, slip the next 2 sts onto cn and hold in front, p1, k2 from cn, p2, slip the next st onto cn and hold in back, k2, p1 from cn, slip the next 2 sts onto cn and hold in front, p1, k2 from cn, slip the next st onto cn and hold in back, k2, p1 from cn, p1.

Row 7: P2, slip the next 2 sts onto cn and hold in front, p2, k2 from cn, p2, slip the next 2 sts onto cn and hold in front, p1, k2 from cn, slip the next st onto cn and hold in back, k2, p1 from cn, p2, slip the next 2 sts onto cn and hold in back, k2, p2 from cn, p2.

Row 9: P4, slip the next 2 sts onto cn and hold in front, p1, k2 from cn, p2, slip the next 2 sts onto cn and hold in front, k2, k2 from cn, p2, slip the next st onto cn and hold in back, k2, p1 from cn, p4.

Row 11: P5, [slip the next 2 sts onto cn and hold in front, p1, k2 from cn, slip the next st onto cn and hold in back, k2, p1 from cn] twice, p5.

Row 13: P6, slip the next 2 sts onto cn and hold in back, k2, k2 from cn, p2, slip the next 2 sts onto cn and hold in back, k2, k2 from cn, p6.

Row 15: P5, [slip the next st onto cn and hold in back, k2, p1 from cn, slip the next 2 sts onto cn and hold in front, p1, k2 from cn] twice, p5.

Row 17: P4, slip the next st onto cn and hold in back, k2, p1 from cn, p2, slip the next 2 sts onto cn and hold in front, k2, k2 from cn, p2, slip the next 2 sts onto cn and hold in front, p1, k2 from cn, p4.

Row 19: P2, slip the next 2 sts onto cn and hold in back, k2, k2 from cn, p2, slip the next st onto cn and hold in back, k2, p1 from cn, slip the next 2 sts onto cn and hold in front, p1, k2 from cn, p2, slip the next 2 sts onto cn and hold in front, k2, k2 from cn, p2.

Row 21: P1, slip the next st onto cn and hold in back, k2, p1 from cn, slip the next 2 sts onto cn and hold in front, p1, k2 from cn, slip the next st onto cn and hold in back, k2, p1 from cn, p2, slip the next 2 sts onto cn and hold in front, p1, k2 from cn, slip the next st onto cn and hold in back, k2, p1 from cn, slip the next 2 sts onto cn and hold in front, p1, k2 from cn, p1.

Row 23: Slip the next st onto cn and hold in back, k2, p1 from cn, p2, slip the next 2 sts onto cn and hold in back, k2, k2 from cn, p4, slip the next 2 sts onto cn and hold in back, k2, k2 from cn, p2, slip the next 2 sts onto cn and hold in front, p1, k2 from cn.

Row 24: As Row 2.

Repeat Rows 1–24 for the pattern.

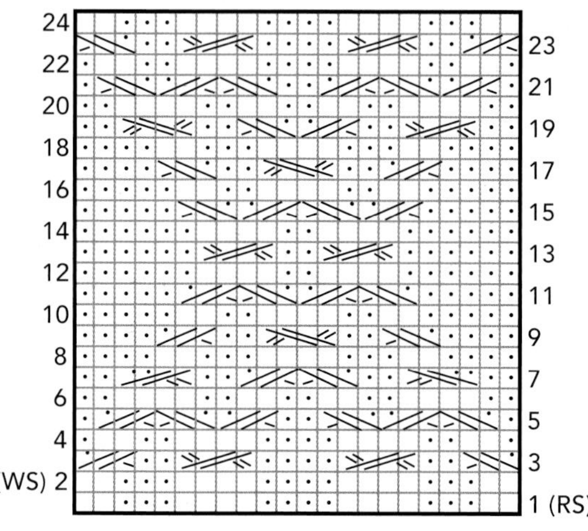

overlapping petals

easy

(multiple of 18 stitches plus 10 stitches)

Row 1 (RS): *P1, k8, p3, right twist (page 279), left twist (page 276), p2; repeat from the * across, ending with p1, k8, p1.

Row 2 and all WS rows: Knit the knit sts and purl the purl sts.

Row 3: *P1, k8, p2, right twist, k2, left twist, p1; repeat from the * across, ending with p1, k8, p1.

Row 5: *P1, k8, p1, right twist, k4, left twist; repeat from the * across, ending with p1, k8, p1.

Rows 7 and 15: *P1, k8; repeat from the * across, ending with p1, k8, p1.

Row 9: *P3, right twist, left twist, p3, k8; repeat from the * across, ending with p3, right twist, left twist, p3.

Row 11: *P2, right twist, k2, left twist, p2, k8; repeat from the * across, ending with p2, right twist, k2, left twist, p2.

Row 13: *P1, right twist, k4, left twist, p1, k8; repeat from the * across, ending with p1, right twist, k4, left twist, p1.

Row 16: As Row 2.

Repeat Rows 1–16 for the pattern.

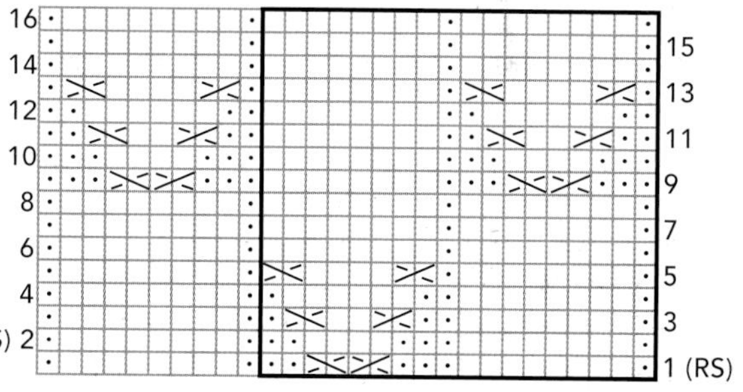

sailor's cables

(multiple of 26 stitches plus 14 stitches)

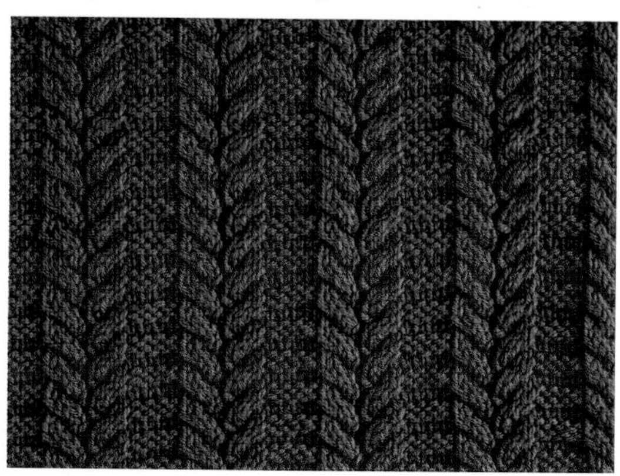

Row 1 (RS): *P1, slip the next 2 sts onto cn and hold in front, k2, k2 from cn, p4, slip the next 2 sts onto cn and hold in back, k2, k2 from cn, p1, k12; repeat from the * across, ending with p1, slip the next 2 sts onto cn and hold in front, k2, k2 from cn, p4, slip the next 2 sts onto cn and hold in back, k2, k2 from cn, p1.

Row 2: Knit the knit sts and purl the purl sts.

Row 3: *P1, k12, p1, slip the next 2 sts onto cn and hold in front, k2, k2 from cn, p4, slip the next 2 sts onto cn and hold in back, k2, k2 from cn; repeat from the * across, ending with p1, k12, p1.

Row 4: As Row 2.

Repeat Rows 1–4 for the pattern.

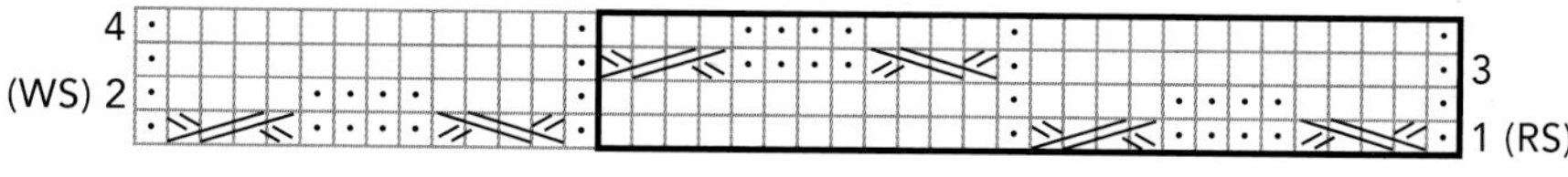

cinched cable

(over 12 stitches on a reverse stockinette background)

Rows 1, 3, 5, 7, 9, 21, 23, 25, 27, and 29 (RS): Knit across.

Row 2 and all WS rows: Purl across.

Rows 11, 15, and 19: K3, slip the next 3 sts onto cn and hold in front, k3, k3 from cn, k3.

Rows 13 and 17: [Slip the next 3 sts onto cn and hold in back, k3, k3 from cn] twice.

Row 30: As Row 2.

Repeat Rows 1–30 for the pattern.

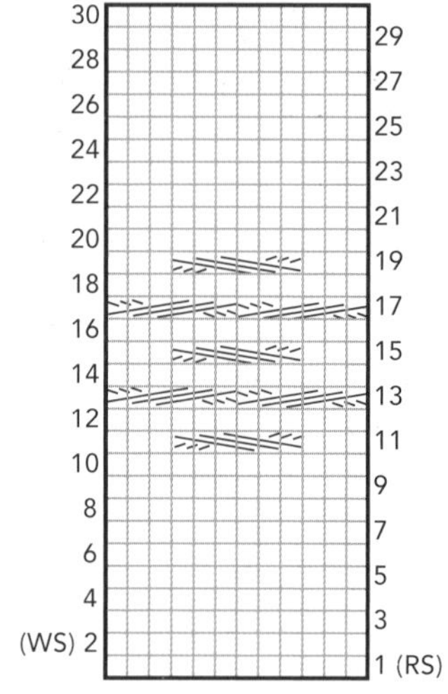

hanging fuchsia

(multiple of 8 stitches)

Rows 1, 3, and 5 (RS): *K2, p4, k2; repeat from the * across.

Row 2 and all WS rows: Knit the knit sts and purl the purl sts.

Row 7: Knit across.

Row 9: *Slip the next 2 sts onto cn and hold in back, k2, p2 from cn, slip the next 2 sts onto cn and hold in front, p2, k2 from cn; repeat from the * across.

Row 10: As Row 2.

Repeat Rows 1–10 for the pattern.

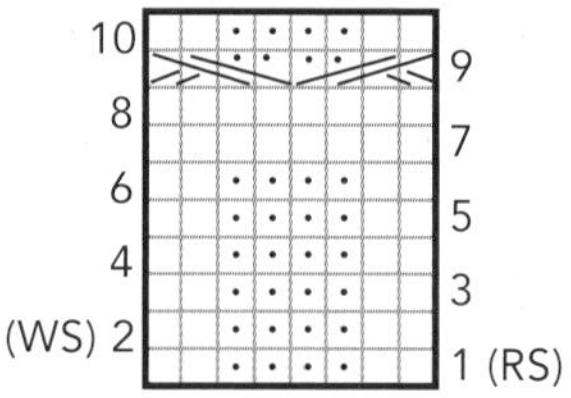

10, 9, 8, 7, 6, 5, 4, 3, (WS) 2, 1 (RS)

taffy cable

easy

(over 18 stitches on a reverse stockinette background)

Rows 1, 3, 5, 7, 9, 11, 23, 25, 27, 29, 31, and 33 (RS): Knit across.

Row 2 and all WS rows: Purl across.

Row 13: K6, [slip the next 3 sts onto cn and hold in back, k3, k3 from cn] twice.

Rows 15 and 19: K3, [slip the next 3 sts onto cn and hold in back, k3, k3 from cn] twice, k3.

Row 17: [Slip the next 3 sts onto cn and hold in back, k3, k3 from cn] 3 times.

Row 21: K6, slip the next 3 sts onto cn and hold in back, k3, k3 from cn, k6.

Row 34: As Row 2.

Repeat Rows 1–34 for the pattern.

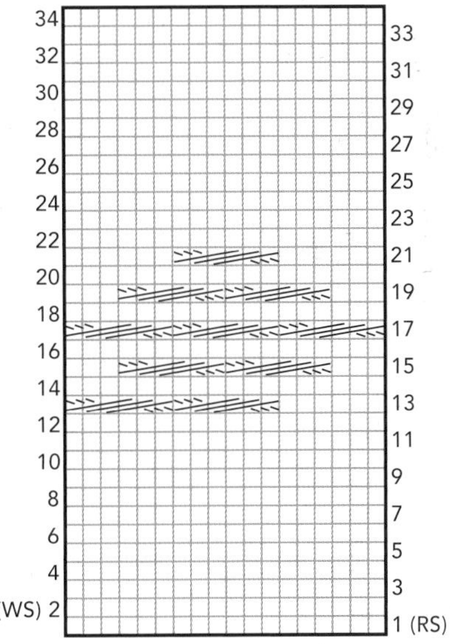

crests

easy

(multiple of 3 stitches plus 2 stitches)

Row 1 (RS): Knit across.

Row 2 and all WS rows: Purl across.

Row 3: K1, *slip the next 2 sts onto cn and hold in back, k1, k2 from cn; repeat from the * across, ending with k1.

Row 5: K1, *slip the next st onto cn and hold in front, k2, k1 from cn; repeat from the * across, ending with k1.

Row 6: As Row 2.

Repeat Rows 1–6 for the pattern.

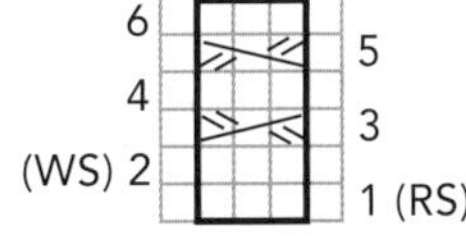

rippling cables

(multiple of 10 stitches plus 7 stitches)

Row 1 (RS): P2, slip the next 2 sts onto cn and hold in front, k1, k2 from cn, p1, *slip the next 2 sts onto cn and hold in front, p1, k2 from cn, slip the next st onto cn and hold in back, k1, p1 from cn, p1, slip the next 2 sts onto cn and hold in front, k1, k2 from cn, p1; repeat from the * across, ending with p1.

Row 2 and all WS rows: Knit the knit sts and purl the purl sts.

Row 3: P1, slip the next st onto cn and hold in back, k1, p1 from cn, slip the next 2 sts onto cn and hold in front, p1, k2 from cn, *p1, slip the next 2 sts onto cn and hold in front, p1, k2 from cn, p1, slip the next st onto cn and hold in back, k1, p1 from cn, slip the next 2 sts onto cn and hold in front, p1, k2 from cn; repeat from the * across, ending with p1.

Row 5: P1, k1, p2, k2, *p2, k2, p1, k1, p2, k2; repeat from the * across, ending with p1.

Row 7: P1, slip the next st onto cn and hold in front, p1, k1 from cn, slip the next st onto cn and hold in back, k2, p1 from cn, *p1, slip the next st onto cn and hold in back, k2, k1 from cn, p1, slip the next st onto cn and hold in front, p1, k1 from cn, slip the next st onto cn and hold in back, k2, p1 from cn; repeat from the * across, ending with p1.

Row 9: P2, slip the next st onto cn and hold in back, k2, p1 from cn, p1, *slip the next st onto cn and hold in back, k2, p1 from cn, slip the next st onto cn and hold in front, p1, k1 from cn, p1, slip the next st onto cn and hold in back, k2, p1 from cn, p1; repeat from the * across, ending with p1.

Row 11: P2, k2, p2, *k2, p2, k1, p1, k2, p2; repeat from the * across, ending with p1.

Row 12: As Row 2.

Repeat Rows 1–12 for the pattern.

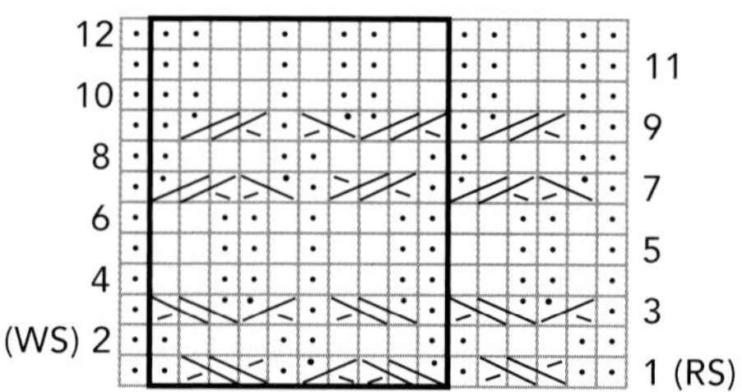

quilted cables 

(multiple of 18 stitches)

Rows 1, 3, 7, and 9 (RS): *K3, p3, k6, p3, k3; repeat from the * across.

Row 2 and all WS rows: Knit the knit sts and purl the purl sts.

Row 5: *Slip the next 3 sts onto cn and hold in back, k3, p3 from cn, k6, slip the next 3 sts onto cn and hold in front, p3, k3 from cn; repeat from the * across.

Row 11: *K3, slip the next 3 sts onto cn and hold in front, p3, k3 from cn, slip the next 3 sts onto cn and hold in back, k3, p3 from cn, k3; repeat from the * across.

Row 12: As Row 2.

Repeat Rows 1–12 for the pattern.

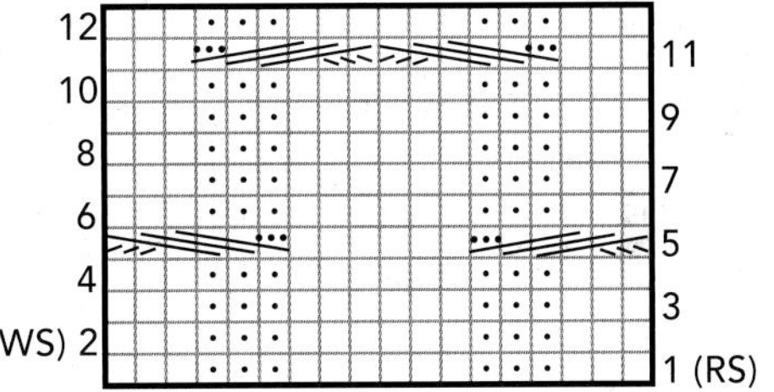

wexford braid 

(over 26 stitches on a reverse stockinette background)

Row 1 (RS): Right twist (page 279), p2, slip the next 3 sts onto cn and hold in front, k3, k3 from cn, k6, slip the next 3 sts onto cn and hold in back, k3, k3 from cn, p2, right twist.

Row 2 and all WS rows: Knit the knit sts and purl the purl sts.

Rows 3 and 7: Left twist (page 276), p2, k18, p2, left twist.

Row 5: Right Twist, p2, k3, slip the next 3 sts onto cn and hold in back, k3, k3 from cn, slip the next 3 sts onto cn and hold in front, k3, k3 from cn, k3, p2, right twist.

Row 8: As Row 2.

Repeat Rows 1–8 for the pattern.

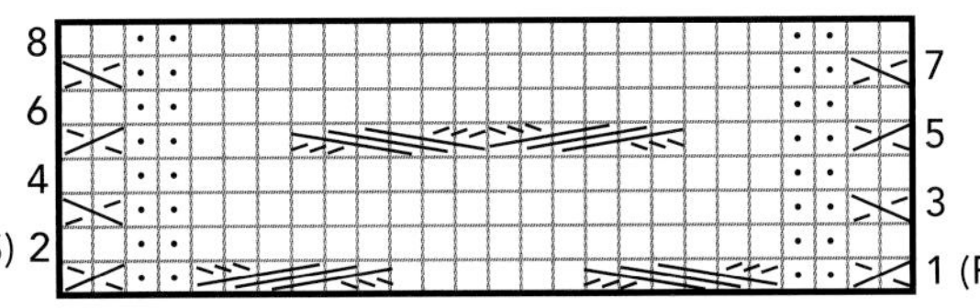

buckeye cables

(multiple of 24 stitches plus 12 stitches)

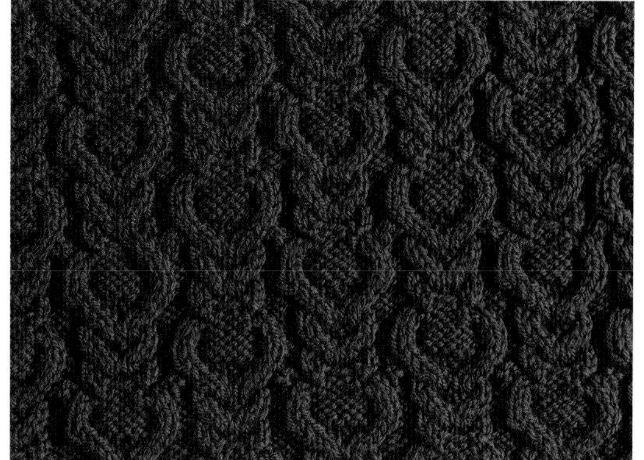

Row 1 (RS): P2, slip the next 2 sts onto cn and hold in back, k2, k2 from cn, *slip the next 2 sts onto cn and hold in front, k2, k2 from cn, slip the next 2 sts onto cn and hold in back, k2, p2 from cn, slip the next 2 sts onto cn and hold in back, k2, k2 from cn, slip the next 2 sts onto cn and hold in front, k2, k2 from cn, slip the next 2 sts onto cn and hold in front, p2, k2 from cn, slip the next 2 sts onto cn and hold in back, k2, k2 from cn; repeat from the * across, ending with slip the next 2 sts onto cn and hold in front, k2, k2 from cn, p2.

Row 2 and all WS rows: Knit the knit sts and purl the purl sts.

Row 3: Slip the next 2 sts onto cn and hold in back, k2, p2 from cn, p2, *p2, slip the next 2 sts onto cn and hold in front, p2, k2 from cn, p2, k8, p2, slip the next 2 sts onto cn and hold in back, k2, p2 from cn, p2; repeat from the * across, ending with p2, slip the next 2 sts onto cn and hold in front, p2, k2 from cn.

Row 5: K2, p4, *p4, k2, p2, slip the next 2 sts onto cn and hold in back, k2, k2 from cn, slip the next 2 sts onto cn and hold in front, k2, k2 from cn, p2, k2, p4; repeat from the * across, ending with p4, k2.

Row 7: *Slip the next 2 sts onto cn and hold in front, p2, k2 from cn, p2, *p2, slip the next 2 sts onto cn and hold in back, k2, p2 from cn, p2, k8, p2, slip the next 2 sts onto cn and hold in front, p2, k2 from cn, p2; repeat from the * across, ending with p2, slip the next 2 sts onto cn and hold in back, k2, p2 from cn.

Row 9: P2, slip the next 2 sts onto cn and hold in back, k2, k2 from cn, *slip the next 2 sts onto cn and hold in front, k2, k2 from cn, p4, slip the next 2 sts onto cn and hold in back, k2, k2 from cn; repeat from the * across, ending with slip the next 2 sts onto cn and hold in front, k2, k2 from cn, p2.

Row 11: P2, k4, *k4, p2, slip the next 2 sts onto cn and hold in back, k2, p2 from cn, p4, slip the next 2 sts onto cn and hold in front, p2, k2 from cn; p2, k4; repeat from the * across, ending with k4, p2.

Row 13: *P2, slip the next 2 sts onto cn and hold in back, k2, k2 from cn, slip the next 2 sts onto cn and hold in front, k2, k2 from cn, p2, k2, p8, k2, p2, slip the next 2 sts onto cn and hold in back, k2, k2 from cn; repeat from the * across, ending with slip the next 2 sts onto cn and hold in front, k2, k2 from cn, p2.

Row 15: *P2, k4, *k4, p2, slip the next 2 sts onto cn and hold in front, k2, k2 from cn, p4, slip the next 2 sts onto cn and hold in back, k2, k2 from cn, p2, k4; repeat from the * across, ending with k4, p2.

Row 16: As Row 2.

Repeat Rows 1–16 for the pattern.

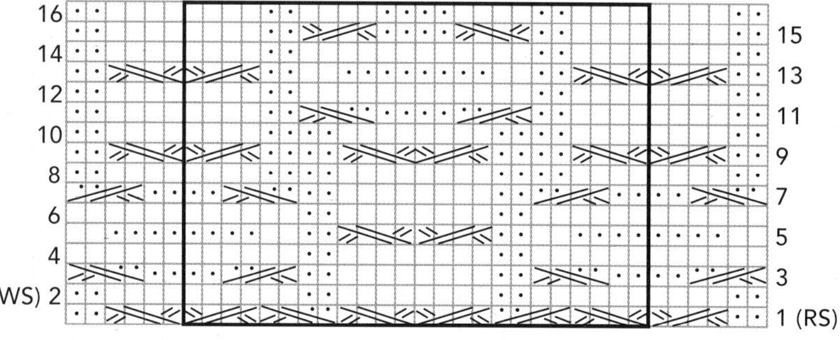

claddaghduff aran cable easy

(over 26 stitches on a reverse stockinette background)

Row 1 (RS): P9, slip the next 2 sts onto cn and hold in back, k2, k2 from cn, slip the next 2 sts onto cn and hold in front, k2, k2 from cn, p9.

Row 2 and all WS rows: Knit the knit sts and purl the purl sts.

Row 3: P7, slip the next 2 sts onto cn and hold in back, k2, p2 from cn, k4, slip the next 2 sts onto cn and hold in front, p2, k2 from cn, p7.

Row 5: P5, slip the next 2 sts onto cn and hold in back, k2, p2 from cn, p2, slip the next 2 sts onto cn and hold in front, k2, k2 from cn, p2, slip the next 2 sts onto cn and hold in front, p2, k2 from cn, p5.

Row 7: P3, slip the next 2 sts onto cn and hold in back, k2, p2 from cn, p2, slip the next 2 sts onto cn and hold in back, k2, p2 from cn, slip the next 2 sts onto cn and hold in front, p2, k2 from cn, p2, slip the next 2 sts onto cn and hold in front, p2, k2 from cn, p3.

Row 9: P1, slip the next 2 sts onto cn and hold in back, k2, p2 from cn, p2, slip the next 2 sts onto cn and hold in back, k2, k2 from cn, p4, slip the next 2 sts onto cn and hold in front, k2, k2 from cn, p2, slip the next 2 sts onto cn and hold in front, p2, k2 from cn, p1.

Row 11: Slip the next st onto cn and hold in back, k2, p1 from cn, p2, [slip the next 2 sts onto cn and hold in back, k2, p2 from cn, slip the next 2 sts onto cn and hold in front, p2, k2 from cn] twice, p2, slip the next 2 sts onto cn and hold in front, p1, k2 from cn.

Row 13: K2, p3, k2, p4, slip the next 2 sts onto cn and hold in back, k2, k2 from cn, p4, k2, p3, k2.

Row 15: Slip the next 2 sts onto cn and hold in front, p1, k2 from cn, p2, [slip the next 2 sts onto cn and hold in front, p2, k2 from cn, slip the next 2 sts onto cn and hold in back, k2, p2 from cn] twice, p2, slip the next st onto cn and hold in back, k2, p1 from cn.

Row 17: P1, slip the next 2 sts onto cn and hold in front, p2, k2 from cn, p2, slip the next 2 sts onto cn and hold in front, p2, k2 from cn, p4, slip the next 2 sts onto cn and hold in back, k2, p2 from cn, p2, slip the next 2 sts onto cn and hold in back, k2, p2 from cn, p1.

Row 19: P3, slip the next 2 sts onto cn and hold in front, p2, k2 from cn, p2, slip the next 2 sts onto cn and hold in front, p2, k2 from cn, slip the next 2 sts onto cn and hold in back, k2, p2 from cn, p2, slip the next 2 sts onto cn and hold in back, k2, p2 from cn, p3.

Row 21: P5, slip the next 2 sts onto cn and hold in front, p2, k2 from cn, p2, slip the next 2 sts onto cn and hold in front, k2, k2 from cn, p2, slip the next 2 sts onto cn and hold in back, k2, p2 from cn, p5.

Row 23: P7, slip the next 2 sts onto cn and hold in front, p2, k2 from cn, k4, slip the next 2 sts onto cn and hold in back, k2, p2 from cn, p7.

Row 25: P9, slip the next 2 sts onto cn and hold in front, p2, k2 from cn, slip the next 2 sts onto cn and hold in back, k2, p2 from cn, p9.

Row 27: P11, slip the next 2 sts onto cn and hold in back, k2, k2 from cn, p11.

Row 28: As Row 2.

Repeat Rows 1–28 for the pattern.

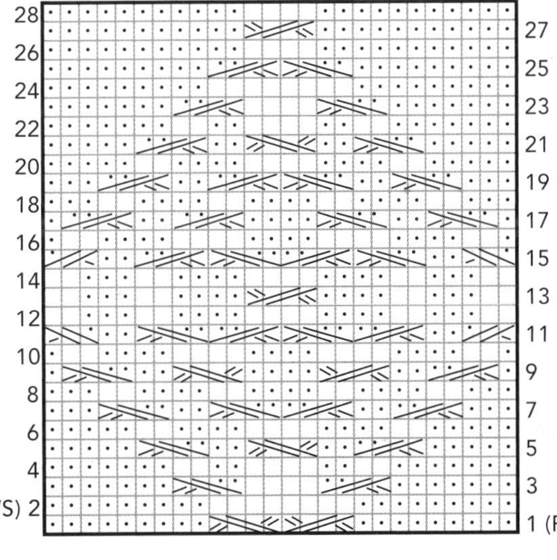

o'briensbridge cables 

(multiple of 28 stitches plus 28 stitches)

Rows 1 and 9 (RS): P1, [k3, p2] twice, *slip the next 3 sts onto cn and hold in back, k3, k3 from cn, [p2, k3] 4 times, p2; repeat from the * across, ending with slip the next 3 sts onto cn and hold in back, k3, k3 from cn, [p2, k3] twice, p1.

Row 2 and all WS rows: Knit the knit sts and purl the purl sts.

Rows 3 and 7: P1, k3, p2, slip the next 2 sts onto cn and hold in back, k1, k2 from cn, p2, k3, *k3 p2, slip the next st onto cn and hold in front, k2, k1 from cn, [p2, k3] twice, p2, slip the next 2 sts onto cn and hold in back, k1, k2 from cn, p2, k3; repeat from the * across, ending with k3, p2, slip the next st onto cn and hold in front, k2, k1 from cn, p2, k3, p1.

Row 5: P1, [k3, p2] twice, k3,*[k3, p2] twice, k3, p2, slip the next 3 sts onto cn #1 and hold in back, slip the next 2 sts onto cn #2 and hold in back, k3 from the left-hand needle, p2 from cn #2, k3 from cn #1, [p2, k3] twice; repeat from the * across, ending with k3, [p2, k3] twice, p1.

Row 11: P1, k3, p2, slip the next 2 sts onto cn and hold in back, k1, k2 from cn, p1, slip the next st onto cn and hold in back, k3, p1 from cn, *slip the next 3 sts onto cn and hold in front, p1, k3 from cn, p1, slip the next st onto cn and hold in front, k2, k1 from cn, [p2, k3] twice, p2, slip the next 2 sts onto cn and hold in back, k1, k2 from cn, p1, slip the next st onto cn and hold in back, k3, p1 from cn; repeat from the * across, ending with slip the next 3 sts onto cn and hold in front, p1, k3, from cn, p1, slip the next st onto cn and hold in front, k2, k1 from cn, p2, k3, p1.

Row 13: P1, k3, p2, k3, slip the next st onto cn and hold in back, k3, p1 from cn, p1, *p1, slip the next 3 sts onto cn and hold in front, p1, k3 from cn, [k3, p2] 3 times, k3, slip the next st onto cn and hold in back, k3, p1 from cn, p1; repeat from the * across, ending with p1, slip the next 3 sts onto cn and hold in front, p1, k3 from cn, k3, p2, k3, p1.

Row 15: P1, k3, p2, slip the next 3 sts onto cn and hold in back, k3, k3 from cn, p2, *p2, slip the next 3 sts onto cn and hold in front, k3, k3 from cn, [p2, k3] twice, p2, slip the next 3 sts onto cn and hold in back, k3, k3 from cn, p2; repeat from the * across, ending with p2, slip the next 3 sts onto cn and hold in front, k3, k3 from cn, p2, k3, p1.

Rows 17 and 21: Knit the knit sts and purl the purl sts.

Row 19: P1, slip the next 3 sts onto cn #1 and hold in back, slip the next 2 sts onto cn #2 and hold in back, k3 from the left-hand needle, p2 from cn #2, k3 from cn #1, k3, p2, *p2, k3, slip the next 3 sts onto cn #1 and hold in front, slip the next 2 sts onto cn #2 and hold in back, k3 from the left-hand needle, p2 from cn #2, k3 from cn #1, p2, slip the next 3 sts onto cn #1 and hold in back, slip the next 2 sts onto cn #2 and hold in back, k3 from the left-hand needle, p2 from cn #2, k3 from cn #1, k3, p2; repeat from the * across, ending with p2, k3, slip the next 3 sts onto cn #1 and hold in front, slip the next 2 sts onto cn #2 and hold in back, k3 from the left-hand needle, p2 from cn #2, k3 from cn #1, p1.

Row 23: P1, k3, p2, slip the next 2 sts onto cn and hold in back, k1, k2 from cn, k3, p2, *p2, k3, slip the next st onto cn and hold in front, k2, k1 from cn, [p2, k3] twice, p2, slip the next 2 sts onto cn and hold in back, k1, k2 from cn, k3, p2; repeat from the * across, ending with p2, k3, slip the next st onto cn and hold in front, k2, k1 from cn, p2, k3, p1.

Row 25: P1, k3, p2, k3, slip the next 3 sts onto cn and hold in front, p1, k3 from cn, p1, *p1, slip the next st onto cn and hold in back, k3, p1 from cn, [k3, p2] 3 times, k3, slip the next 3 sts onto cn and hold in front, p1, k3 from cn, p1; repeat from the * across, ending with p1, slip the next st onto cn and hold in back, k3, p1 from cn, k3, p2, k3, p1.

Row 27: P1, k3, p2, slip the next 2 sts onto cn and hold in back, k1, k2 from cn, p1, slip the next 3 sts onto cn and hold in front, p1, k3 from cn, *slip the next st onto cn and hold in back, k3, p1 from cn, p1, slip the next st onto cn and hold in front, k2, k1 from cn, [p2, k3] twice, p2, slip the next 2 sts onto cn and hold in back, k1, k2 from cn, p1, slip the next 3 sts onto cn and hold in front, p1, k3 from cn; repeat from the * across, ending with slip the next st onto cn and hold in back, k3, p1 from cn, p1, slip the next st onto cn and hold in front, k2, k1 from cn, p2, k3, p1.

Row 28: As Row 2.

Repeat Rows 1–28 for the pattern.

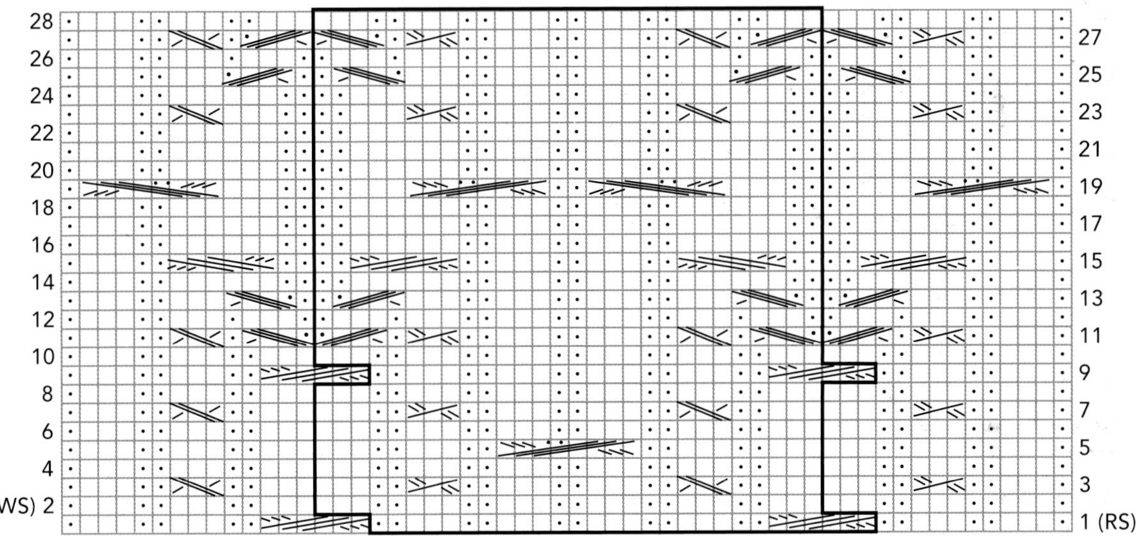

tipperary textile pattern easy

(multiple of 28 stitches)

Row 1 (RS): *K4, p4, slip the next st onto cn and hold in back, k1, p1 from cn, k8, slip the next st onto cn and hold in front, p1, k1 from cn, p4, k4; repeat from the * across.

Row 2 and all WS rows: Knit the knit sts and purl the purl sts.

Row 3: *Slip the next 2 sts onto cn and hold in back, k2, k2 from cn, p3, slip the next st onto cn and hold in back, k1, p1 from cn, p1, k8, p1, slip the next st onto cn and hold in front, p1, k1 from cn, p3, slip the next 2 sts onto cn and hold in front, k2, k2 from cn; repeat from the * across.

Row 5: *K4, p2, slip the next st onto cn and hold in back, k1, p1 from cn, p2, slip the next 2 sts onto cn and hold in front, k2, k2 from cn, slip the next 2 sts onto cn and hold in back, k2, k2 from cn, p2, slip the next st onto cn and hold in front, p1, k1 from cn, p2, k4; repeat from the * across.

Row 7: *Slip the next 2 sts onto cn and hold in back, k2, k2 from cn, p1, slip the next st onto cn and hold in back, k1, p1 from cn, p3, k8, p3, slip the next st onto cn and hold in front, p1, k1 from cn, p1, slip the next 2 sts onto cn and hold in front, k2, k2 from cn; repeat from the * across.

Row 9: *K4, slip the next st onto cn and hold in back, k1, p1 from cn, p4, slip the next 2 sts onto cn and hold in front, k2, k2 from cn, slip the next 2 sts onto cn and hold in back, k2, k2 from cn, p4, slip the next st onto cn and hold in front, p1, k1 from cn, k4; repeat from the * across.

Row 11: *K4, slip the next st onto cn and hold in front, p1, k1 from cn, p4, k8, p4, slip the next st onto cn and hold in back, k1, p1 from cn, k4; repeat from the * across.

Row 13: *K4, p1, slip the next st onto cn and hold in front, p1, k1 from cn, p3, slip the next 2 sts onto cn and hold in front, k2, k2 from cn, slip the next 2 sts onto cn and hold in back, k2, k2 from cn, p3, slip the next st onto cn and hold in back, k1, p1 from cn, p1, k4; repeat from the * across,

Row 15: *Slip the next 2 sts onto cn and hold in back, k2, k2 from cn, p2, slip the next st onto cn and hold in front, p1, k1 from cn, p2, k8, p2, slip the next st onto cn and hold in back, k1, p1 from cn, p2, slip the next 2 sts onto cn and hold in front, k2, k2 from cn; repeat from the * across.

Row 17: *K4, p3, slip the next st onto cn and hold in front, p1, k1 from cn, p1, slip the next 2 sts onto cn and hold in front, k2, k2 from cn, slip the next 2 sts onto cn and hold in back, k2, k2 from cn, p1, slip the next st onto cn and hold in back, k1, p1 from cn, p3, k4; repeat from the * across.

Row 19: *Slip the next 2 sts onto cn and hold in back, k2, k2 from cn, p4, slip the next st onto cn and hold in front, p1, k1 from cn, k8, slip the next st onto cn and hold in back, k1, p1 from cn, p4, slip the next 2 sts onto cn and hold in front, k2, k2 from cn; repeat from the * across.

Row 20: As Row 2.

Repeat Rows 1–20 for the pattern.

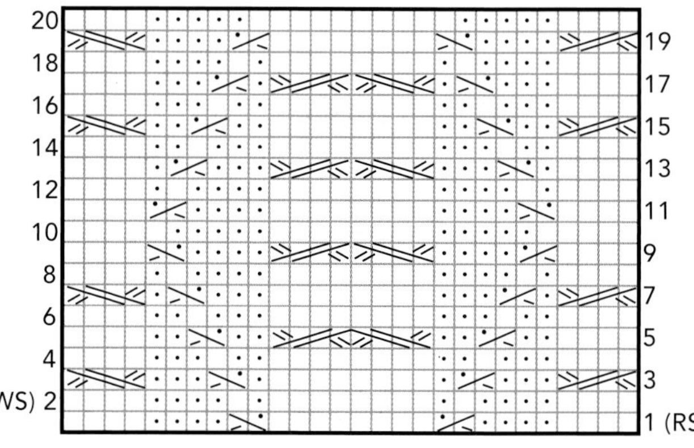

braided oval

easy

(over 20 stitches on a reverse stockinette background)

Row 1 (RS): P6, [slip the next 2 sts onto cn and hold in back, k2, k2 from cn] twice, p6.

Row 2 and all WS rows: Knit the knit sts and purl the purl sts.

Row 3: P4, slip the next 2 sts onto cn and hold in back, k2, p2 from cn, slip the next 2 sts onto cn and hold in front, k2, k2 from cn, slip the next 2 sts onto cn and hold in front, p2, k2 from cn, p4.

Row 5: P2, [slip the next 2 sts onto cn and hold in back, k2, p2 from cn] twice, [slip the next 2 sts onto cn and hold in front, p2, k2 from cn] twice, p2.

Row 7: P2, k2, slip the next 2 sts onto cn and hold in back, k2, p2 from cn, p4, slip the next 2 sts onto cn and hold in front, p2, k2 from cn, k2, p2.

Row 9: P2, slip the next 2 sts onto cn and hold in back, k2, k2 from cn, p8, slip the next 2 sts onto cn and hold in front, k2, k2 from cn, p2.

Row 11: Slip the next 2 sts onto cn and hold in back, k2, p2 from cn, slip the next 2 sts onto cn and hold in front, p2, k2 from cn, p4, slip the next 2 sts onto cn and hold in back, k2, p2 from cn, slip the next 2 sts onto cn and hold in front, p2, k2 from cn.

Row 13: [K2, p4] 3 times, k2.

Row 15: Slip the next 2 sts onto cn and hold in front, p2, k2 from cn, slip the next 2 sts onto cn and hold in back, k2, p2 from cn, p4, slip the next 2 sts onto cn and hold in front, p2, k2 from cn, slip the next 2 sts onto cn and hold in back, k2, p2 from cn.

Row 17: P2, slip the next 2 sts onto cn and hold in back, k2, k2 from cn, p8, slip the next 2 sts onto cn and hold in front, k2, k2 from cn, p2.

Row 19: P2, k2, slip the next 2 sts onto cn and hold in front, p2, k2 from cn, p4, slip the next 2 sts onto cn and hold in back, k2, p2 from cn, k2, p2.

Row 21: P2, [slip the next 2 sts onto cn and hold in front, p2, k2 from cn] twice, [slip the next 2 sts onto cn and hold in back, k2, p2 from cn] twice, p2.

Row 23: P4, slip the next 2 sts onto cn and hold in front, p2, k2 from cn, slip the next 2 sts onto cn and hold in front, k2, k2 from cn, slip the next 2 sts onto cn and hold in back, k2, p2 from cn, p4.

Row 24: As Row 2.

Repeat Rows 1–24 for the pattern.

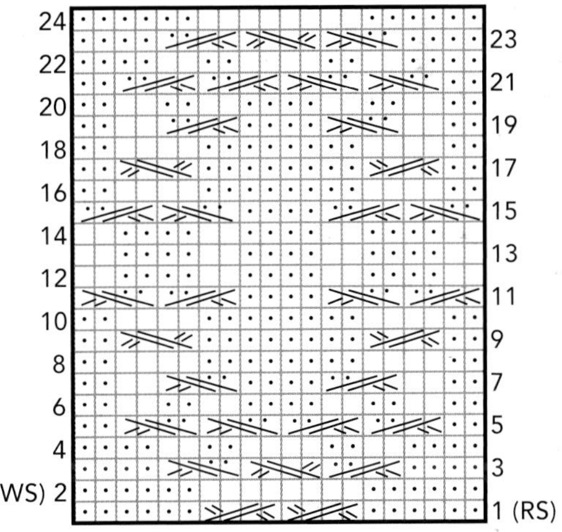

lamp posts

(over 20 stitches on a reverse stockinette background)

Row 1 (RS): [Slip the next 3 sts onto cn and hold in front, p1, k3 from cn, p2, slip the next st onto cn and hold in back, k3, p1 from cn] twice.

Row 2 and all WS rows: Knit the knit sts and purl the purl sts.

Row 3: [P1, slip the next 3 sts onto cn and hold in front, p1, k3 from cn, slip the next st onto cn and hold in back, k3, p1 from cn, p1] twice.

Rows 5 and 19: P2, slip the next 3 sts onto cn and hold in back, k3, k3 from cn , p4, slip the next 3 sts onto cn and hold in front, k3, k3 from cn, p2.

Rows 7, 9, 11, 13, 15, and 17: P2, k6, p4, k6, p2.

Row 21: [P1, slip the next st onto cn and hold in back, k3, p1 from cn, slip the next 3 sts onto cn and hold in front, p1, k3 from cn, p1] twice.

Row 23: [Slip the next st onto cn and hold in back, k3, p1 from cn, p2, slip the next 3 sts onto cn and hold in front, p1, k3 from cn] twice.

Row 24: As Row 2.

Repeat Rows 1–24 for the pattern.

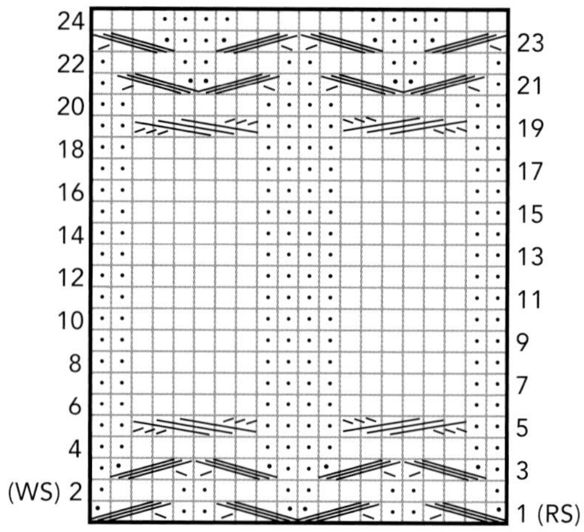

ribs on the move

easy

(multiple of 10 stitches plus 10 stitches)

Rows 1, 5, 7, and 11 (RS): P1, k3, p1, *p1, k3, p2, k3, p1; repeat from the * across, ending with p1, k3, p1.

Row 2 and all WS rows: Knit the knit sts and purl the purl sts.

Row 3: P1, k1, *slip the next 2 sts onto cn #1 and hold in front, slip the next 2 sts onto cn #2 and hold in back, k2 from the left-hand needle, p2 from cn #2, k2 from cn #1, k1, p2, k1, ending with slip the next 2 sts onto cn #1 and hold in front, slip the next 2 sts onto cn #2 and hold in back, k2 from the left-hand needle, p2 from cn #2, k2 from cn #1, k1, p1.

Row 9: P1, k3, p1, *p1, k1, slip the next 4 sts (2 knit sts and 2 purl sts) onto cn and hold in back, k2 from the left-hand needle, slip the 2 purl sts back to the left-hand needle, p2 from the left-hand needle, k2 from cn, k1, p1; repeat from the * across, ending with p1, k3, p1.

Row 12: As Row 2.

Repeat Rows 1–12 for the pattern.

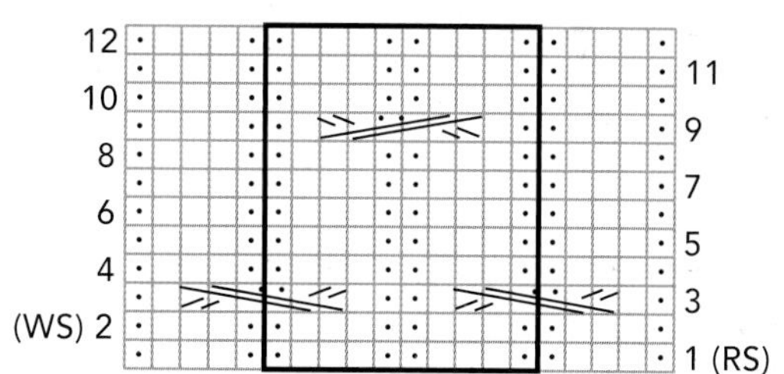

little crescents

(multiple of 4 stitches plus 4 stitches)

Row 1 (RS): P1, *p2, right twist (page 279); repeat from the * across, ending with p3.

Row 2 and all WS rows: Knit the knit sts and purl the purl sts.

Row 3: K1, *k2, left twist (page 276); repeat from the * across, ending with k3.

Row 5: P1, *right twist, p2; repeat from the * across, ending with right twist, p1.

Row 7: K1, *left twist, k2; repeat from the * across, ending with left twist, k1.

Row 8: Purl across.

Repeat Rows 1–8 for the pattern.

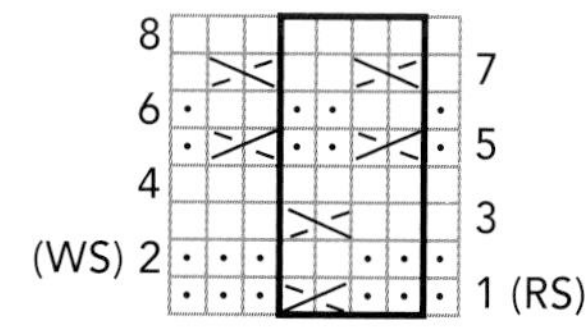

woven ribs

(multiple of 12 stitches plus 12 stitches)

Row 1 (RS): K2, p2, k2, *slip the next 6 sts onto cn and hold in front, [k2, p2, k2] from the left-hand needle, [k2, p2, k2] from the cn; repeat from the * across, ending with k2, p2, k2.

Row 2 and all WS rows: Knit the knit sts and purl the purl sts.

Rows 3 and 7: K2, p2, k2, *k2, p2, k4, p2, k2; repeat from the * across, ending with k2, p2, k2.

Row 5: *Slip the next 6 sts onto cn and hold in back, [k2, p2, k2] from the left-hand needle, [k2, p2, k2] from the cn; repeat from the * across.

Row 8: As Row 2.

Repeat Rows 1–8 for the pattern.

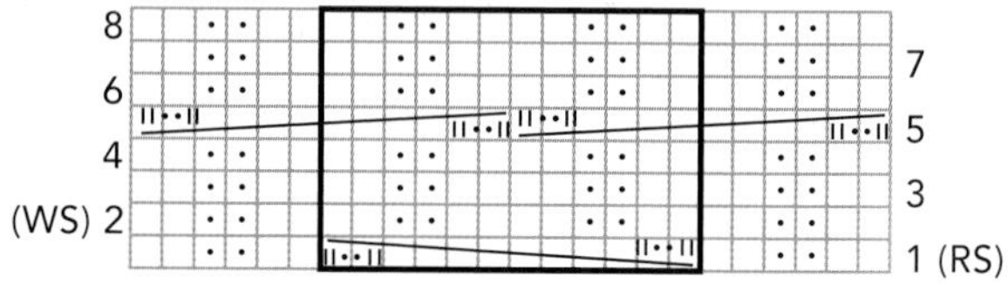

wrapped cable

(over 12 stitches on a reverse stockinette background)

Rows 1 and 5 (RS): P2, slip the next 2 sts onto cn and hold in front, k2, k2 from cn, slip the next 2 sts onto cn and hold in back, k2, k2 from cn, p2.

Row 2 and all WS rows: Knit the knit sts and purl the purl sts.

Rows 3 and 11: P2, k8, p2.

Row 7: P2, k2, slip the next 2 sts onto cn and hold in front, k2, k2 from cn, k2, p2.

Rows 9 and 13: P2, slip the next 2 sts onto cn and hold in back k2, k2 from cn, slip the next 2 sts onto cn and hold in front, k2, k2 from cn, p2.

Row 15: Slip the next 2 sts onto cn and hold in back, k2, p2 from cn, slip the next 2 sts onto cn and hold in front, k2, k2 from cn, slip the next 2 sts onto cn and hold in front, p2, k2 from cn.

Row 17: K2, p2, k4, p2, k2.

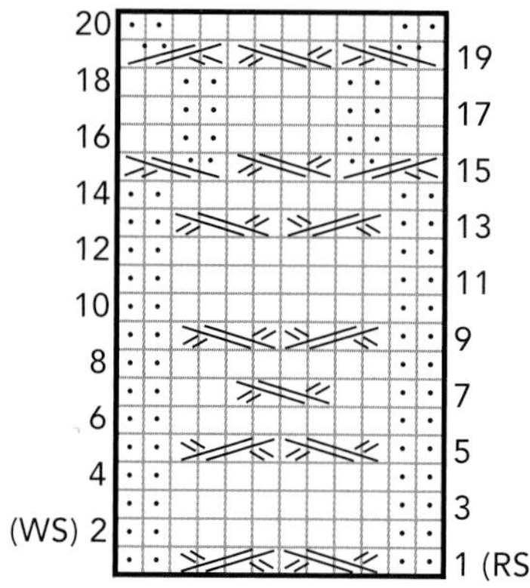

Row 19: Slip the next 2 sts onto cn and hold in front, p2, k2 from cn, slip the next 2 sts onto cn and hold in front, k2, k2 from cn, slip the next 2 sts onto cn and hold in back, k2, p2 from cn.

Row 20: As Row 2.

Repeat Rows 1–20 for the pattern.

intertwined ropes

(multiple of 22 stitches plus 1 stitch)

Rows 1, 5, 9, 13, 17, 21, 25, and 29 (RS): *P1, k10; repeat from the * across, ending with p1.

Row 2 and all WS rows: Knit the knit sts and purl the purl sts.

Rows 3, 7, and 11: *P1, slip the next 3 sts onto cn and hold in front, k3, k3 from cn, k4, p1, k4, slip the next 3 sts onto cn and hold in back, k3, k3 from cn; repeat from the * across, ending with p1.

Row 15: *P1, slip the next 6 sts onto cn and hold in back, k4, k6 from cn, p1, slip the next 4 sts onto cn and hold in front, k6, k4 from cn; repeat from the * across, ending with p1.

Rows 19, 23, and 27: *P1, k4, slip the next 3 sts onto cn and hold in front, k3, k3 from cn, p1, slip the next 3 sts onto cn and hold in back, k3, k3 from cn, k4; repeat from the * across, ending with p1.

Row 31: *P1, slip the next 4 sts onto cn #1 and hold in back, slip the next 3 sts onto cn #2 and hold in front, k3 from the left-hand needle, k3 from cn #2, k4 from cn #1, p1, slip the next 3 sts onto cn #1 and hold in back, slip the next 3 sts onto cn #2 and hold in front, k4 from the left-hand needle, k3 from cn #2, k3 from cn #1; repeat from the * across, ending with p1.

Row 32: As Row 2.

Repeat Rows 1–32 for the pattern.

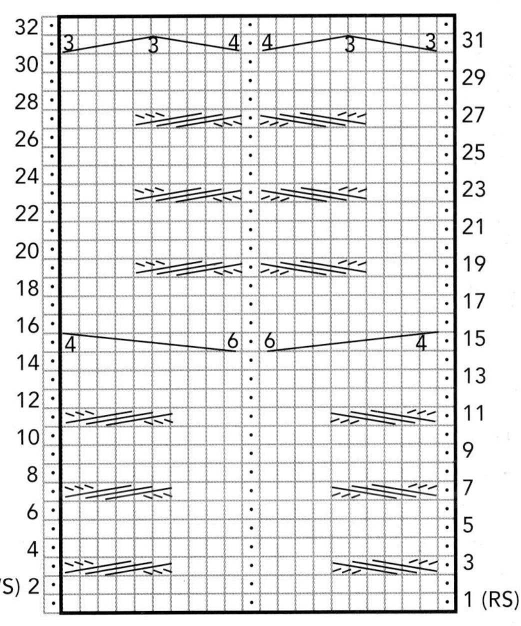

linked cables panel

(over 14 stitches on a reverse stockinette background)

Row 1 (RS): P1, slip the next 3 sts onto cn and hold in back, k3, p3 from cn, slip the next 3 sts onto cn and hold in front, p3, k3 from cn, p1.

Row 2 and all WS rows: Knit the knit sts and purl the purl sts.

Row 3: Slip the next st onto cn and hold in back, k3, p1 from cn, p6, slip the next 3 sts onto cn and hold in front, p1, k3 from cn.

Row 5: K3, p8, k3.

Row 7: Slip the next 3 sts onto cn and hold in front, p1, k3 from cn, p6, slip the next st onto cn and hold in back, k3, p1 from cn.

Row 9: P1, slip the next 3 sts onto cn and hold in front, p3, k3 from cn, slip the next 3 sts onto cn and hold in back, k3, p3 from cn, p1.

Row 11: P4, slip the next 6 sts onto cn and wrap the yarn counterclockwise around them 4 times just below the cn (page 282), k6 from cn, p4.

Rows 13–20: As Rows 1–8.

Row 21: P1, slip the next 3 sts onto cn and hold in front, k3, k3 from cn, slip the next 3 sts onto cn and hold in back, k3, k3 from cn, p1.

Rows 23 and 25: P1, k12, p1.

Row 27: As Row 21.

Rows 29 and 31: As Row 23.

Row 33: P1, slip the next 3 sts onto cn and hold in back, k3, k3 from cn, slip the next 3 sts onto cn and hold in front, k3, k3 from cn, p1.

Rows 35 and 37: As Row 23.

Row 38: As Row 2.

Repeat Rows 1–38 for the pattern.

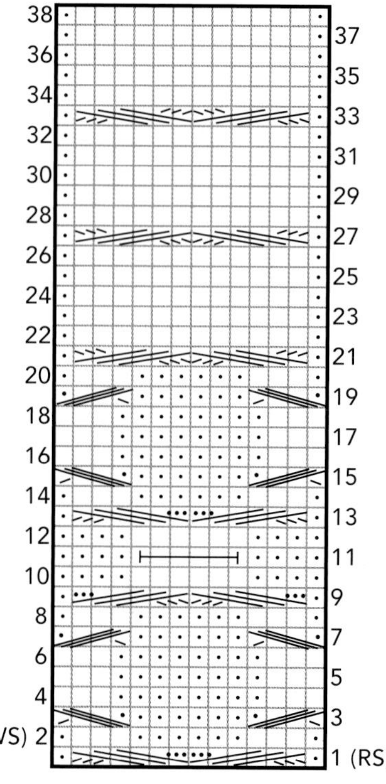

spinning tops

easy

(multiple of 16 stitches plus 14 stitches)

Row 1 (RS): P6, k1, *k1, p5, right twist (page 279), left twist (page 276), p5, k1; repeat from the * across, ending with k1, p6.

Row 2 and all WS rows: Knit the knit sts and purl the purl sts.

Row 3: P6, k1, *k1, p4, right twist, k2, left twist, p4, k1; repeat from the * across, ending with k1, p6.

Row 5: P6, k1, *k1, p3, right twist, k4, left twist, p3, k1; repeat from the * across, ending with k1, p6.

Row 7: P6, k1, *k1, p2, right twist, k6, left twist, p2, k1; repeat from the * across, ending with k1, p6.

Row 9: P6, k1, *k1, p2, slip the next 2 sts onto cn and hold in front, p2, k2 from cn, k2, slip the next 2 sts onto cn and hold in back, k2, p2 from cn, p2, k1; repeat from the * across, ending with k1, p6.

Row 11: P5, right twist, *left twist, p5, k2, p5, right twist; repeat from the * across, ending with left twist, p5.

Row 13: P4, right twist, k1, *k1, left twist, p4, k2, p4, right twist, k1; repeat from the * across, ending with k1, left twist, p4.

Row 15: P3, right twist, k2, *k2, left twist, p3, k2, p3, right twist, k2; repeat from the * across, ending with k2, left twist, p3.

Row 17: P2, right twist, k3, *k3, left twist, p2, k2, p2, right twist, k3; repeat from the * across, ending with k3, left twist, p2.

Row 19: P2, slip the next 2 sts onto cn and hold in front, p2, k2 from cn, k1, *k1, slip the next 2 sts onto cn and hold in back, k2, p2 from cn, p2, k2, p2, slip the next 2 sts onto cn and hold in front, p2, k2 from cn, k1; repeat from the * across, ending with k1, slip the next 2 sts onto cn and hold in back, k2, p2 from cn, p2.

Row 20: As Row 2.

Repeat Rows 1–20 for the pattern.

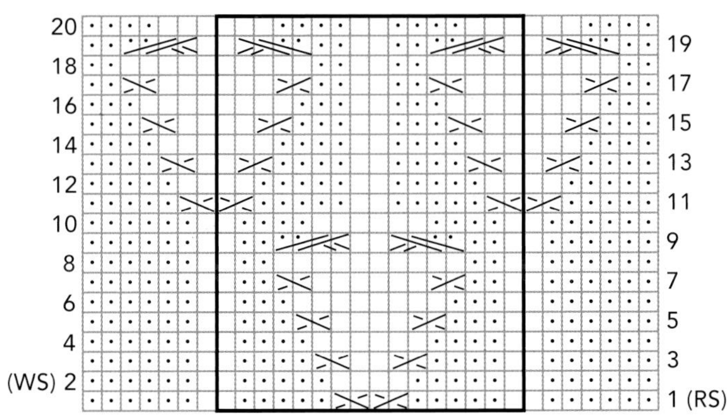

diverging cable

(over 19 stitches on a reverse stockinette background)

Rows 1, 5, and 9 (RS): K5, slip the next 2 sts onto cn and hold in back, k2, k2 from cn, p1, slip the next 2 sts onto cn and hold in front, k2, k2 from cn, k5.

Row 2 and all WS rows: Knit the knit sts and purl the purl sts.

Rows 3, 7, and 21: K9, p1, k9.

Row 11: K4, slip the next st onto cn and hold in back, k2, k1 from cn, k2, p1, k2, slip the next 2 sts onto cn and hold in front, k1, k2 from cn, k4.

Row 13: K3, slip the next st onto cn and hold in back, k2, k1 from cn, k3, p1, k3, slip the next 2 sts onto cn and hold in front, k1, k2 from cn, k3.

Row 15: K2, slip the next st onto cn and hold in back, k2, k1 from cn, k4, p1, k4, slip the next 2 sts onto cn and hold in front, k1, k2 from cn, k2.

Row 17: K1, slip the next st onto cn and hold in back, k2, k1 from cn, k5, p1, k5, slip the next 2 sts onto cn and hold in front, k1, k2 from cn, k1.

Row 19: Slip the next st onto cn and hold in back, k2, k1 from cn, k2, slip the next 2 sts onto cn and hold in back, k2, k2 from cn, p1, slip the next 2 sts onto cn and hold in front, k2, k2 from cn, k2, slip the next 2 sts onto cn and hold in front, k1, k2 from cn.

Row 22: As Row 2.

Repeat Rows 1–22 for the pattern.

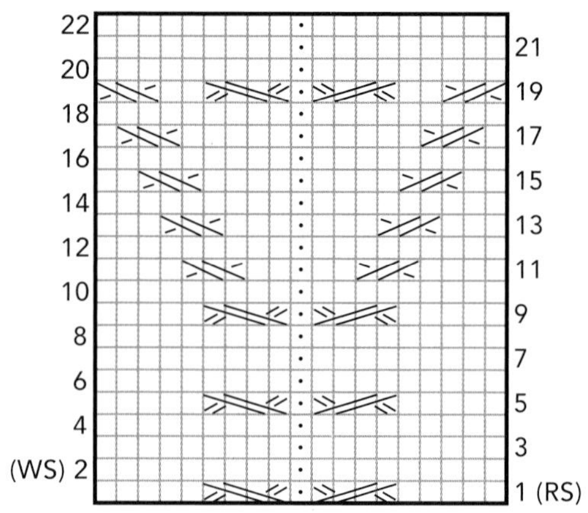

sheenagh panel

easy

(over 34 stitches on a reverse stockinette background)

Row 1 (RS): K2, p4, slip the next 2 sts onto cn and hold in back, k2, k2 from cn, p4, k2, p2, k2, p4, slip the next 2 sts onto cn and hold in front, k2, k2 from cn, p4, k2.

Row 2 and all WS rows: Knit the knit sts and purl the purl sts.

Row 3: Slip the next 2 sts onto cn and hold in front, p2, k2 from cn, slip the next 2 sts onto cn and hold in back, k2, p2 from cn, slip the next 2 sts onto cn and hold in front, p2, k2 from cn, [p2, k2] twice, p2, slip the next 2 sts onto cn and hold in back, k2, p2 from cn, slip the next 2 sts onto cn and hold in front, p2, k2 from cn, slip the next 2 sts onto cn and hold in back, k2, p2 from cn.

Row 5: P2, slip the next 2 sts onto cn and hold in front, k2, k2 from cn, p4, [k2, p2] 3 times, k2, p4, slip the next 2 sts onto cn and hold in back, k2, k2 from cn, p2.

Row 7: Slip the next 2 sts onto cn and hold in back, k2, p2 from cn, slip the next 2 sts onto cn and hold in front, p2, k2 from cn, slip the next 2 sts onto cn and hold in back, k2, p2 from cn, [p2, k2] twice, p2, slip the next 2 sts onto cn and hold in front, p2, k2 from cn, slip the next 2 sts onto cn and hold in back, k2, p2 from cn, slip the next 2 sts onto cn and hold in front, p2, k2 from cn.

Rows 9 and 13: K2, p4, slip the next 2 sts onto cn and hold in back, k2, k2 from cn, p4, k2, p2, k2, p4, slip the next 2 sts onto cn and hold in front, k2, k2 from cn, p4, k2.

Row 11: K2, p4, k4, p4, k2, p2, k2, p4, k4, p4, k2.

Row 15: K2, p2, slip the next 2 sts onto cn and hold in back, k2, p2 from cn, slip the next 2 sts onto cn and hold in front, p2, k2 from cn, slip the next 2 sts onto cn and hold in back, k2, p2 from cn, p2, slip the next 2 sts onto cn and hold in front, p2, k2 from cn, slip the next 2 sts onto cn and hold in back, k2, p2 from cn, slip the next 2 sts onto cn and hold in front, p2, k2 from cn, p2, k2.

Row 17: K2, p2, k2, p4, slip the next 2 sts onto cn and hold in front, k2, k2 from cn, p6, slip the next 2 sts onto cn and hold in back, k2, k2 from cn, p4, k2, p2, k2.

Row 19: K2, p2, slip the next 2 sts onto cn and hold in front, p2, k2 from cn, slip the next 2 sts onto cn and hold in back, k2, p2 from cn, slip the next 2 sts onto cn and hold in front, p2, k2 from cn, p2, slip the next 2 sts onto cn and hold in back, k2, p2 from cn, slip the next 2 sts onto cn and hold in front, p2, k2 from cn, slip the next 2 sts onto cn and hold in back, k2, p2 from cn, p2, k2.

Row 20: As Row 2.

Repeat Rows 1–20 for the pattern.

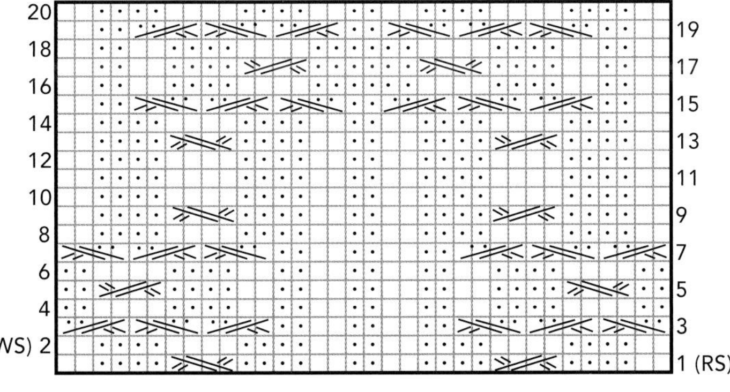

ballinlough cables 

(multiple of 32 stitches plus 16 stitches)

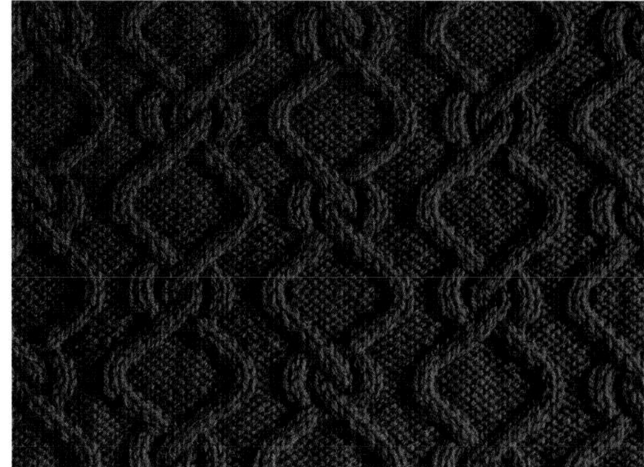

Row 1 (RS): P2, slip the next 2 sts onto cn and hold in back, k2, p2 from cn, p2, *p2, slip the next 2 sts onto cn and hold in front, p2, k2 from cn, p6, slip the next 2 sts onto cn and hold in front, k2, k2 from cn, slip the next 2 sts onto cn and hold in back, k2, k2 from cn, p6, slip the next 2 st onto cn and hold in back, k2, p2 from cn, p2; repeat from the * across, ending with p2, slip the next 2 sts onto cn and hold in front, p2, k2 from cn, p2.

Row 2 and all WS rows: Knit the knit sts and purl the purl sts.

Row 3: Slip the next 2 sts onto cn and hold in back, k2, p2 from cn, p4, *p4, slip the next 2 sts onto cn and hold in front, p2, k2 from cn, p2, slip the next 2 sts onto cn and hold in back, k2, p2 from cn, slip the next 2 sts onto cn and hold in back, k2, k2 from cn, slip the next 2 sts onto cn and hold in front, p2, k2 from cn, p2, slip the next 2 sts onto cn and hold in back, k2, p2 from cn, p4; repeat from the * across, ending with p4, slip the next 2 sts onto cn and hold in front, p2, k2 from cn.

Rows 5 and 15: As Row 2.

Row 7: Slip the next 2 sts onto cn and hold in front, p2, k2 from cn, p4, *p4, slip the next 2 sts onto cn and hold in back, k2, p2 from cn, p2, slip the next 2 sts onto cn and hold in front, p2, k2 from cn, slip the next 2 sts onto cn and hold in back, k2, k2 from cn, slip the next 2 sts onto cn and hold in back, k2, p2 from cn, p2, slip the next 2 sts onto cn and hold in front, p2, k2 from cn, p4; repeat from the * across, ending with p4, slip the next 2 sts onto cn and hold in back, k2, p2 from cn.

Row 9: P2, slip the next 2 sts onto cn and hold in front, p2, k2 from cn, p2, *p2, slip the next 2 sts onto cn and hold in back, k2, p2 from cn, p6, slip the next 2 sts onto cn and hold in back, k2, p2 from cn, slip the next 2 sts onto cn and hold in front, p2, k2 from cn, p6, slip the next 2 sts onto cn and hold in front, p2, k2 from cn, p2; repeat from the * across, ending with p2, slip the next 2 sts onto cn and hold in back, k2, p2 from cn, p2.

Row 11: P4, slip the next 2 sts onto cn and hold in front, k2, k2 from cn, *slip the next 2 sts onto cn and hold in back, k2, k2 from cn, p6, slip the next 2 sts onto cn and hold in back, k2, p2 from cn, p4, slip the next 2 sts onto cn and hold in front, p2, k2 from cn, p6, slip the next 2 sts onto cn and hold in front, k2, k2 from cn; repeat from the * across, ending with slip the next 2 sts onto cn and hold in back, k2, k2 from cn, p4.

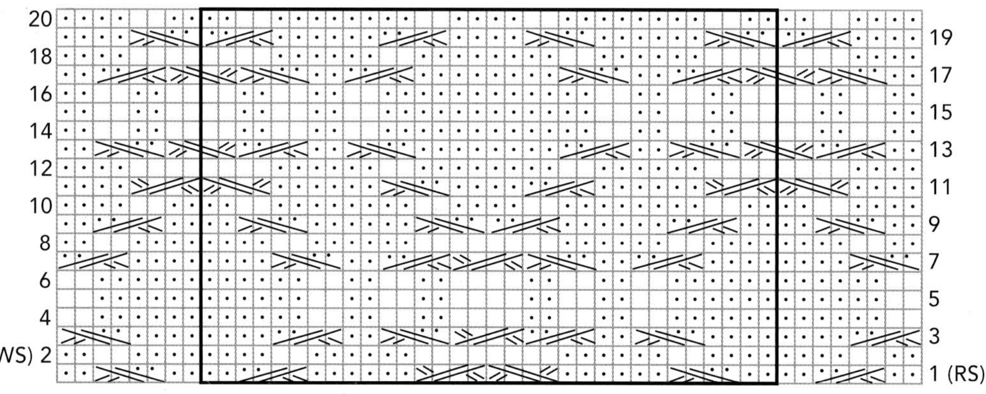

Row 13: P2, slip the next 2 sts onto cn and hold in back, k2, p2 from cn, *slip the next 2 sts onto cn and hold in front, k2, k2 from cn, slip the next 2 sts onto cn and hold in front, p2, k2 from cn, p2, slip the next 2 sts onto cn and hold in back, k2, p2 from cn, p8, slip the next 2 sts onto cn and hold in front, p2, k2 from cn, p2, slip the next 2 sts onto cn and hold in back, k2, p2 from cn; repeat from the * across, ending with slip the next 2 sts onto cn and hold in front, k2, k2 from cn, slip the next 2 sts onto cn and hold in front, p2, k2 from cn, p2.

Row 17: P2, slip the next 2 sts onto cn and hold in front, p2, k2 from cn, *slip the next 2 sts onto cn and hold in front, k2, k2 from cn, slip the next 2 sts onto cn and hold in back, k2, p2 from cn, p2, slip the next 2 sts onto cn and hold in front, p2, k2 from cn, p8, slip the next 2 sts onto cn and hold in back, k2, p2 from cn, p2, slip the next 2 sts onto cn and hold in front, p2, k2 from cn; repeat from the * across, ending with slip the next 2 sts onto cn and hold in front, k2, k2 from cn, slip the next 2 sts onto cn and hold in back, k2, p2 from cn, p2.

Row 19: P4, slip the next 2 sts onto cn and hold in back, k2, p2 from cn, *slip the next 2 sts onto cn and hold in front, p2, k2 from cn, p6, slip the next 2 sts onto cn and hold in front, p2, k2 from cn, p4, slip the next 2 sts onto cn and hold in back, k2, p2 from cn, p6, slip the next 2 sts onto cn and hold in back, k2, p2 from cn; repeat from the * across, ending with slip the next 2 sts onto cn and hold in front, p2, k2 from cn, p4.

Row 20: As Row 2.

Repeat Rows 1–20 for the pattern.

trellis and ribs

(multiple of 24 stitches plus 16 stitches)

Row 1 (RS): Slip the next 2 sts onto cn and hold in back, k2, k2 from cn, p4, *p4, slip the next 2 sts onto cn and hold in back, k2, k2 from cn, p8, slip the next 2 sts onto cn and hold in back, k2, k2 from cn, p4; repeat from * ending with p4, slip the next 2 sts onto cn and hold in back, k2, k2 from cn.

Rows 2, 4, 6, 8, 10, 12, 16, 18, 20, 22 and 24: Knit the knit sts and purl the purl sts.

Row 3: K2, slip the next 2 sts onto cn and hold in front, p2, k2 from cn, p2, *p2, slip the next 2 st onto cn and hold in back, k2, p2 from cn, k2, p8, k2, slip the next 2 sts onto cn and hold in front, p2, k2 from cn, p2; repeat from the * across, ending with p2, slip the next 2 st onto cn and hold in back, k2, p2 from cn, k2.

Row 5: K2, p2, slip the next 2 sts onto cn and hold in front, p2, k2 from cn, *slip the next 2 sts onto cn and hold in back, k2, p2 from cn, p2, k2, p8, k2, p2, slip the next 2 sts onto cn and hold in front, p2, k2 from cn; repeat from the * across, ending with slip the next 2 sts onto cn and hold in back, k2, p2 from cn, p2, k2.

Row 7: K2, p4, *slip the next 2 sts onto cn and hold in front, k2, k2 from cn, p4, k2, p8, k2, p4; repeat from the * across, ending with slip the next 2 sts onto cn and hold in front, k2, k2 from cn, p4, k2.

Row 9: K2, p2, slip the next 2 sts onto cn and hold in back, k2, p2 from cn, *slip the next 2 sts onto cn and hold in front, p2, k2 from cn, p2, k2, p8, k2, p2, slip the next 2 sts onto cn and hold in back, k2, p2 from

(continued on next page)

cn; repeat from the * across, ending with slip the next 2 sts onto cn and hold in front, p2, k2 from cn, p2, k2.

Row 11: K2, slip the next 2 sts onto cn and hold in back, k2, p2 from cn, p2, *p2, slip the next 2 sts onto cn and hold in front, p2, k2 from cn, k2, p8, k2, slip the next 2 sts onto cn and hold in back, k2, p2 from cn, p2; repeat from the * across, ending with p2, slip the next 2 sts onto cn and hold in front, p2, k2 from cn, k2.

Row 13: Slip the next 2 sts onto cn and hold in back, k2, k2 from cn, p4, *[p4, slip the next 2 sts onto cn and hold in back, k2, k2 from cn, p4] twice; repeat from the * across, ending with p4, slip the next 2 sts onto cn and hold in back, k2, k2 from cn.

Row 14: K2, p2, k4,*k4, p4, k8, p4, k4; repeat from * ending with k4, p2, k2.

Row 15: P2, k2, p4, *p4, k2, slip the next 2 sts onto cn and hold in front, p2, k2 from cn, p4, slip the next 2 sts onto cn and hold in back, k2, p2 from cn, k2, p4; repeat from the * across, ending with p4, k2, p2.

Row 17: P2, k2, p4, *p4, k2, p2, slip the next 2 sts onto cn and hold in front, p2, k2 from cn, slip the next 2 sts onto cn and hold in back, k2, p2 from cn, p2, k2, p4; repeat from the * across, ending with p4, k2, p2.

Row 19: P2, k2, p4,*p4, k2, p4, slip the next 2 sts onto cn and hold in front, k2, k2 from cn, p4, k2, p4; repeat from the * across, ending with p4, k2, p2.

Row 21: P2, k2, p4, *p4, k2, p2, slip the next 2 sts onto cn and hold in back, k2, p2 from cn, slip the next 2 sts onto cn and hold in front, p2, k2 from cn, p2, k2, p4; repeat from the * across, ending with p4, k2, p2.

Row 23: P2, k2, p4, *p4, k2, slip the next 2 sts onto cn and hold in back, k2, p2 from cn, p4, slip the next 2 sts onto cn and hold in front, p2, k2 from cn, k2, p4; repeat from the * across, ending with p4, k2, p2.

Row 24: As Row 2.

Repeat Rows 1–24 for the pattern.

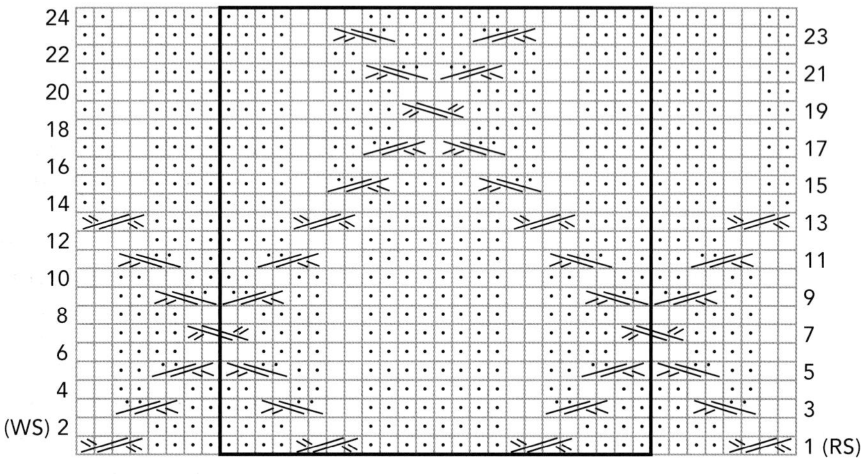

nautical braids

easy

(over 32 stitches on a reverse stockinette background)

Row 1 (RS): P2, [slip the next 2 sts onto cn and hold in back, k2, k2 from cn, p8] twice, slip the next 2 sts onto cn and hold in back, k2, k2 from cn, p2.

Row 2 and all WS rows: Knit the knit sts and purl the purl sts.

Row 3: [Slip the next 2 sts onto cn and hold in back, k2, p2 from cn, slip the next 2 sts onto cn and hold in front, p2, k2 from cn, p4] twice, slip the next 2 sts onto cn and hold in back, k2, p2 from cn, slip the next 2 sts onto cn and hold in front, p2, k2 from cn.

Row 5: K2, p4, [slip the next 2 sts onto cn and hold in front, p2, k2 from cn, slip the next 2 sts onto cn and hold in back, k2, p2 from cn, p4] twice, k2.

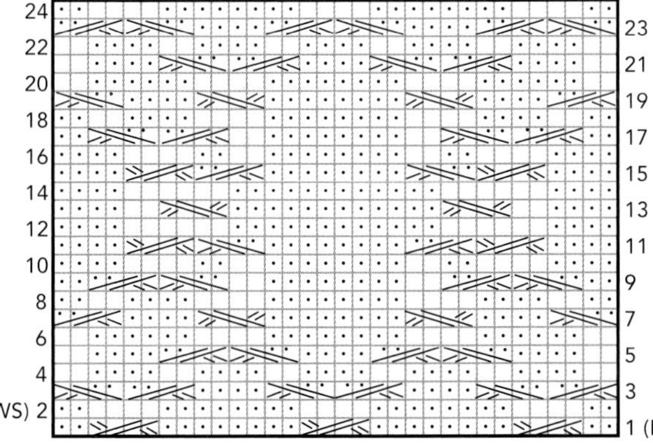

Row 7: Slip the next 2 sts onto cn and hold in front, p2, k2 from cn, p4, slip the next 2 sts onto cn and hold in front, k2, k2 from cn, p8, slip the next 2 sts onto cn and hold in front, k2, k2 from cn, p4, slip the next 2 sts onto cn and hold in back, k2, p2 from cn.

Row 9: P2, slip the next 2 sts onto cn and hold in front, p2, k2 from cn, slip the next 2 sts onto cn and hold in back, k2, p2 from cn, k2, p8, k2, slip the next 2 sts onto cn and hold in front, p2, k2 from cn, slip the next 2 sts onto cn and hold in back, k2, p2 from cn, p2.

Row 11: P4, slip the next 2 sts onto cn and hold in back, k2, k2 from cn, slip the next 2 sts onto cn and hold in back, k2, p2 from cn, p8, slip the next 2 sts onto cn and hold in front, p2, k2 from cn, slip the next 2 sts onto cn and hold in back, k2, k2 from cn, p4.

Row 13: P4, k2, slip the next 2 sts onto cn and hold in front, k2, k2 from cn, p12, slip the next 2 sts onto cn and hold in front, k2, k2 from cn, k2, p4.

Row 15: P4, slip the next 2 sts onto cn and hold in back, k2, k2 from cn, slip the next 2 sts onto cn and hold in front, p2, k2 from cn, p8, slip the next 2 sts onto cn and hold in back, k2, p2 from cn, slip the next 2 sts onto cn and hold in back, k2, k2 from cn, p4.

Row 17: P2, slip the next 2 sts onto cn and hold in back, k2, p2 from cn, slip the next 2 sts onto cn and hold in front, p2, k2 from cn, k2, p8, k2, slip the next 2 sts onto cn and hold in back, k2, p2 from cn, slip the next 2 sts onto cn and hold in front, p2, k2 from cn, p2.

Row 19: Slip the next 2 sts onto cn and hold in back, k2, p2 from cn, p4, slip the next 2 sts onto cn and hold in front, k2, k2 from cn, p8, slip the next 2 sts onto cn and hold in front, k2, k2 from cn, p4, slip the next 2 sts onto cn and hold in front, p2, k2 from cn.

Row 21: K2, p4, slip the next 2 sts onto cn and hold in back, k2, p2 from cn, slip the next 2 sts onto cn and hold in front, p2, k2 from cn, p4, slip the next 2 sts onto cn and hold in back, k2, p2 from cn, slip the next 2 sts onto cn and hold in front, p2, k2 from cn, p4, k2.

Row 23: [Slip the next 2 sts onto cn and hold in front, p2, k2 from cn, slip the next 2 sts onto cn and hold in back, k2, p2 from cn, p4] twice, slip the next 2 sts onto cn and hold in front, p2, k2 from cn, slip the next 2 sts onto cn and hold in back, k2, p2 from cn.

Row 24: As Row 2.

Repeat Rows 1–24 for the pattern.

braided lattice

(multiple of 12 stitches plus 14 stitches)

Row 1 (RS): P4, k1, slip the next st onto cn and hold in front, p1, k1 from cn, *slip the next st onto cn and hold in back, k1, p1 from cn, k1, p6, k1, slip the next st onto cn and hold in front, p1, k1 from cn; repeat from the * across, ending with slip the next st onto cn and hold in back, k1, p1 from cn, k1, p4.

Row 2 and all WS rows: Knit the knit sts and purl the purl sts.

Row 3: P4, slip the next st onto cn and hold in front, p1, k1 from cn, *right twist (page 279), slip the next st onto cn and hold in back, k1, p1 from cn, p6, slip the next st onto cn and hold in front, p1, k1 from cn; repeat from the * across, ending with right twist, slip the next st onto cn and hold in back, k1, p1 from cn, p4.

Row 5: P5, left twist (page 276), *right twist, p8, left twist; repeat from the * across, ending with right twist, p5.

Row 7: P4, slip the next st onto cn and hold in back, k1, p1 from cn, *right twist, slip the next st onto cn and hold in front, p1, k1 from cn, p6, slip the next st onto cn and hold in back, k1, p1 from cn; repeat from the * across, ending with right twist, slip the next st onto cn and hold in front, p1, k1 from cn, p4.

Row 9: P4, k1, slip the next st onto cn and hold in back, k1, p1 from cn, *slip the next st onto cn and hold in front, p1, k1 from cn, k1, p6, k1, slip the next st onto cn and hold in back, k1, p1 from cn; repeat from the * across, ending with slip the next st onto cn and hold in front, p1, k1 from cn, k1, p4.

Row 11: P3, slip the next st onto cn and hold in back, k2, p1 from cn, p1, *p1, slip the next 2 sts onto cn and hold in front, p1, k2 from cn, p4, slip the next st onto cn and hold in back, k2, p1 from cn, p1; repeat from the * across, ending with p1, slip the next 2 sts onto cn and hold in front, p1, k2 from cn, p3.

Row 13: P2, slip the next st onto cn and hold in back, k2, p1 from cn, p2, *p2, slip the next 2 sts onto cn and hold in front, p1, k2 from cn, p2, slip the next st onto cn and hold in back, k2, p1 from cn, p2; repeat from the * across, ending with p2, slip the next 2 sts onto cn and hold in front, p1, k2 from cn, p2.

Row 15: P1, slip the next st onto cn and hold in back, k1, p1 from cn, k1, p3, *p3, k1, slip the next st onto cn and hold in front, p1, k1 from cn, slip the next st onto cn and hold in back, k1, p1 from cn, k1, p3; repeat from the * across, ending with p3, k1, slip the next st onto cn and hold in front, p1, k1 from cn, p1.

Row 17: P1, k1, slip the next st onto cn and hold in back, k1, p1 from cn, p3, *p3, slip the next st onto cn and hold in front, p1, k1 from cn, left twist, slip the next st onto cn and hold in back, k1, p1 from cn, p3; repeat from the * across, ending with p3, slip the next st onto cn and hold in front, p1, k1 from cn, k1, p1.

Row 19: P1, right twist, p4, *p4, [right twist] twice, p4; repeat from the * across, ending with p4, right twist, p1.

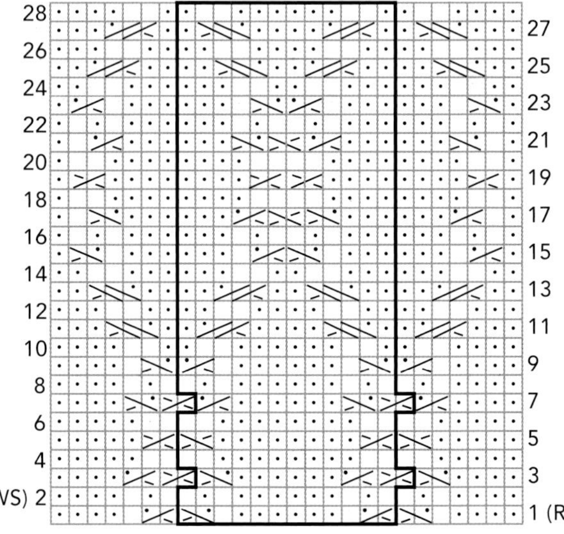

Row 21: P1, k1, slip the next st onto cn and hold in front, p1, k1 from cn, p3, *p3, slip the next st onto cn and hold in back, k1, p1 from cn, left twist, slip the next st onto cn and hold in front, p1, k1 from cn, p3; repeat from the * across, ending with p3, slip the next st onto cn and hold in back, k1, p1 from cn, k1, p1.

Row 23: P1, slip the next st onto cn and hold in front, p1, k1 from cn, k1, p3, *p3, k1, slip the next st onto cn and hold in back, k1, p1 from cn, slip the next st onto cn and hold in front, p1, k1 from cn, k1, p3; repeat from the * across, ending with p3, k1, slip the next st onto cn and hold in back, k1, p1 from cn, p1.

Row 25: P2, slip the next 2 sts onto cn and hold in front, p1, k2 from cn, p2, *p2, slip the next st onto cn and hold in back, k2, p1 from cn, p2, slip the next 2 sts onto cn and hold in front, p1, k2 from cn, p2; repeat from the * across, ending with p2, slip the next st onto cn and hold in back, k2, p1 from cn, p2.

Row 27: P3, slip the next 2 sts onto cn and hold in front, p1, k2 from cn, p1, *p1, slip the next st onto cn and hold in back, k2, p1 from cn, p4, slip the next 2 sts onto cn and hold in front, p1, k2 from cn, p1; repeat from the * across ending with p1, slip the next st onto cn and hold in back, k2, p1 from cn, p3.

Row 28: As Row 2.

Repeat Rows 1–28 for the pattern.

diamonds and kisses 

(multiple of 30 stitches plus 2 stitches)

Rows 1 and 5 (RS): *[P2, right twist (page 279)] 3 times, p2, slip the next 2 sts onto cn and hold in front, k2, k2 from cn, [p2, right twist] 3 times; repeat from the * across, ending with p2.

Row 2 and all WS rows: Knit the knit sts and purl the purl sts.

Row 3: *[P2, right twist] 3 times, p2, k4, [p2, right twist] 3 times; repeat from the * across, ending with p2.

Row 7: *[P2, right twist] 3 times, slip the next 2 sts onto cn and hold in back, k2, p2 from cn, slip the next 2 sts onto cn and hold in front, p2, k2 from cn, [right twist, p2] twice, right twist; repeat from the * across, ending with p2.

Row 9: *[P2, right twist] twice, p2, slip the next 2 sts onto cn and hold in back, k2, [p1, k1] from cn, p4, slip the next 2 sts onto cn and hold in front, [k1, p1] from the left-hand needle, k2 from cn, [p2, right twist] twice; repeat from the * across, ending with p2.

Row 11: *[P2, right twist] twice, slip the next 2 sts onto cn and hold in back, k2, [p1, k1] from cn, p1, slip the next st onto cn and hold in front, p1, k1 from cn, p2, slip the next st onto cn and hold in back, k1, p1 from cn, p1, slip the next 2 sts onto cn and hold in front, [k1, p1] from the left-hand needle, k2 from cn, right twist, p2, right twist; repeat from the * across, ending with p2.

Row 13: *P2, right twist, p2, slip the next 2 sts onto cn and hold in back, k2, p2 from cn, [p1, slip the next st onto cn and hold in front, p1, k1 from cn] twice, [slip the next st onto cn and hold in back, k1, p1 from cn, p1] twice, slip the next 2 sts onto cn and hold in front, p2, k2 from cn, p2, right twist; repeat from the * across, ending with p2.

Row 15: *P2, right twist, slip the next 2 sts onto cn and hold in back, k2, p2 from cn, p4, slip the next st onto cn and hold in front, p1, k1 from cn, p1, k2, p1, slip the next st onto cn and hold in back, k1, p1 from

(continued on next page)

cn, p4, slip the next 2 sts onto cn and hold in front, p2, k2 from cn, right twist; repeat from the * across, ending with p2.

Row 17: *P2, slip the next 2 sts onto cn and hold in back, k2, p2 from cn, p7, slip the next st onto cn and hold in front, p1, k1 from cn, k2, slip the next st onto cn and hold in back, k1, p1 from cn, p7, slip the next 2 sts onto cn and hold in front, p2, k2 from cn; repeat from the * across, ending with p2.

Row 19: *P2, k2, p10, slip the next 2 sts onto cn and hold in back, k2, k2 from cn, p10, k2; repeat from the * across, ending with p2.

Row 21: *P2, slip the next 2 sts onto cn and hold in front, k2, k2 from cn, p7, slip the next st onto cn and hold in back, k1, p1 from cn, k2, slip the next st onto cn and hold in front, p1, k1 from cn, p7, slip the next 2 sts onto cn and hold in back, k2, k2 from cn; repeat from the * across, ending with p2.

Row 23: *P2, right twist, slip the next 2 sts onto cn and hold in front, p2, k2 from cn, p4, slip the next st onto cn and hold in back, k1, p1 from cn, p1, k2, p1, slip the next st onto cn and hold in front, p1, k1 from cn, p4, slip the next 2 sts onto cn and hold in back, k2, p2 from cn, right twist; repeat from the * across, ending with p2.

Row 25: *P2, right twist, p2, slip the next 2 sts onto cn and hold in front, k2, k2 from cn, [p1, slip the next st onto cn and hold in back, k1, p1 from cn] twice, [slip the next st onto cn and hold in front, p1, k1 from cn, p1] twice, slip the next 2 sts onto cn and hold in back, k2, k2 from cn, p2, right twist; repeat from the * across, ending with p2.

Row 27: *[P2, right twist] twice, slip the next 2 sts onto cn and hold in front, p2, k2 from cn, p1, slip the next st onto cn and hold in back, k1, p1 from cn, p2, slip the next st onto cn and hold in front, p1, k1 from cn, p1, slip the next 2 sts onto cn and hold in back, k2, p2 from cn, right twist, p2, right twist; repeat from the * across, ending with p2.

Row 29: *[P2, right twist] twice, p2, slip the next 2 sts onto cn and hold in front, k2, k2 from cn, p4, slip the next 2 sts onto cn and hold in back, k2, k2 from cn, [p2, right twist] twice; repeat from the * across, ending with p2.

Row 31: *[P2, right twist] 3 times, slip the next 2 sts onto cn and hold in front, p2, k2 from cn, slip the next 2 sts onto cn and hold in back, k2, p2 from cn, [right twist, p2] twice, right twist; repeat from the * across, ending with p2.

Row 32: As Row 2.

Repeat Rows 1–32 for the pattern.

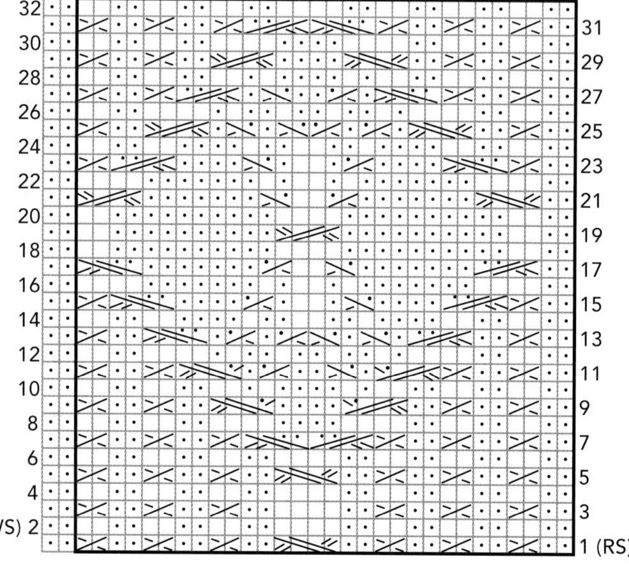

irish panel

easy

(over 24 stitches on a reverse stockinette background)

Row 1 (RS): Left twist (page 276), p8, slip the next 2 sts onto cn and hold in front, k2, k2 from cn, p8, left twist.

Row 2 and all WS rows: Knit the knit sts and purl the purl sts.

Row 3: Left twist, p6, slip the next 2 sts onto cn and hold in back,k2, k2 from cn, slip the next 2 sts onto cn and hold in front, k2, k2 from cn, p6, left twist.

Row 5: Left twist, p4, slip the next 2 sts onto cn and hold in back, k2, p2 from cn, slip the next 2 sts onto cn and hold in front, k2, k2 from cn, slip the next 2 sts onto cn and hold in front, p2, k2 from cn, p4, left twist.

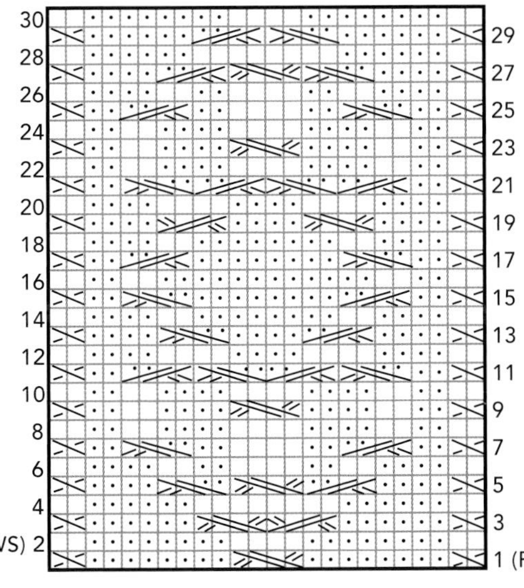

Row 7: Left twist, p2, slip the next 2 sts onto cn and hold in back, k2, p2 from cn, p2, k4, p2, slip the next 2 sts onto cn and hold in front, p2, k2 from cn, p2, left twist.

Rows 9 and 23: Left twist, p2, k2, p4, slip the next 2 sts onto cn and hold in front, k2, k2 from cn, p4, k2, p2, left twist.

Row 11: Left twist, p2, [slip the next 2 sts onto cn and hold in front, p2, k2 from cn, slip the next 2 sts onto cn and hold in back, k2, p2 from cn] twice, p2, left twist.

Row 13: Left twist, p4, slip the next 2 sts onto cn and hold in back, k2, p2 from cn, p4, slip the next 2 sts onto cn and hold in front, p2, k2 from cn, p4, left twist.

Row 15: Left twist, p2, slip the next 2 sts onto cn and hold in back,k2, p2 from cn, p8, slip the next 2 sts onto cn and hold in front, p2, k2 from cn, p2, left twist.

Row 17: Left twist, p2, slip the next 2 sts onto cn and hold in front, p2, k2 from cn, p8, slip the next 2 sts onto cn and hold in back, k2, p2 from cn, p2, left twist.

Row 19: Left twist, p4, slip the next 2 sts onto cn and hold in front, k2, k2 from cn, p4, slip the next 2 sts onto cn and hold in back, k2, k2 from cn, p4, left twist.

Row 21: Left twist, p2, [slip the next 2 sts onto cn and hold in back, k2, p2 from cn, slip the next 2 sts onto cn and hold in front, p2, k2 from cn] twice, p2, left twist.

Row 25: Left twist, p2, slip the next 2 sts onto cn and hold in front, p2, k2 from cn, p2, k4, p2, slip the next 2 sts onto cn and hold in back, k2, p2 from cn, p2, left twist.

Row 27: Left twist, p4, slip the next 2 sts onto cn and hold in front, p2, k2 from cn, slip the next 2 sts onto cn and hold in front, k2, k2 from cn, slip the next 2 sts onto cn and hold in back, k2, p2 from cn, p4, left twist.

Row 29: Left twist, p6, slip the next 2 sts onto cn and hold in front, p2, k2 from cn, slip the next 2 sts onto cn and hold in back, k2, p2 from cn, p6, left twist.

Row 30: As Row 2.

Repeat Rows 1–30 for the pattern.

wellingtonbridge cable easy

(over 32 stitches on a reverse stockinette background)

Row 1 (RS): P5, [slip the next 2 sts onto cn and hold in front, k2, k2 from cn, p2] 4 times, p3.

Row 2 and all WS rows: Knit the knit sts and purl the purl sts.

Row 3: P4, [slip the next st onto cn and hold in back, k2, p1 from cn, slip the next 2 sts onto cn and hold in front, p1, k2 from cn] 4 times, p4.

Row 5: P3, slip the next st onto cn and hold in back, k2, p1 from cn, [p2, slip the next 2 sts onto cn and hold in back, k2, k2 from cn] 3 times, p2, slip the next 2 sts onto cn and hold in front, p1, k2 from cn, p3.

Row 7: P2, slip the next st onto cn and hold in back, k2, p1 from cn, p2, [slip the next st onto cn and hold in back, k2, p1 from cn, slip the next 2 sts onto cn and hold in front, p1, k2 from cn] 3 times, p2, slip the next 2 sts onto cn and hold in front, p1, k2 from cn, p2.

Row 9: P1, [slip the next st onto cn and hold in back, k2, p1 from cn, p2] twice, [slip the next 2 sts onto cn and hold in front, k2, k2 from cn, p2] twice, slip the next 2 sts onto cn and hold in front, p1, k2 from cn, p2, slip the next 2 sts onto cn and hold in front, p1, k2 from cn, p1.

Row 11: [Slip the next st onto cn and hold in back, k2, p1 from cn, p2] twice, [slip the next st onto cn and hold in back, k2, p1 from cn, slip the next 2 sts onto cn and hold in front, p1, k2 from cn] twice, [p2, slip the next 2 sts onto cn and hold in front, p1, k2 from cn] twice.

Row 13: K2, p2, [slip the next st onto cn and hold in back, k2, p1 from cn, p2] twice, slip the next 2 sts onto cn and hold in back, k2, k2 from cn, [p2, slip the next 2 sts onto cn and hold in front, p1, k2 from cn] twice, p2, k2.

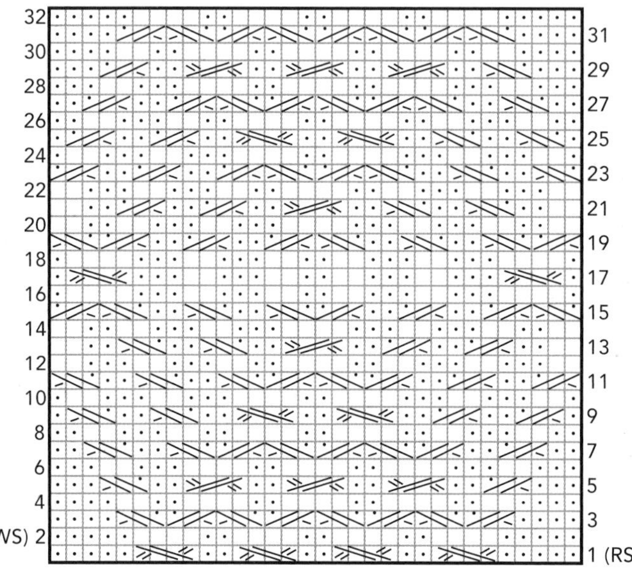

Row 15: Slip the next 2 sts onto cn and hold in front, p1, k2 from cn, slip the next st onto cn and hold in back, k2, p1 from cn, [p2, slip the next st onto cn and hold in back, k2, p1 from cn] twice, [slip the next 2 sts onto cn and hold in front, p1, k2 from cn, p2] twice, slip the next 2 sts onto cn and hold in front, p1, k2 from cn, slip the next st onto cn and hold in back, k2, p1 from cn.

Row 17: P1, slip the next 2 sts onto cn and hold in front, k2, k2 from cn, [p3, k2] twice, p2, [k2, p3] twice, slip the next 2 sts onto cn and hold in front, k2, k2 from cn, p1.

Row 19: Slip the next st onto cn and hold in back, k2, p1 from cn, slip the next 2 sts onto cn and hold in front, p1, k2 from cn, [p2, slip the next 2 sts onto cn and hold in front, p1, k2 from cn] twice, [slip the next st onto cn and hold in back, k2, p1 from cn, p2] twice, slip the next st onto cn and hold in back, k2, p1 from cn, slip the next 2 sts onto cn and hold in front, p1, k2 from cn.

Row 21: K2, p2, [slip the next 2 sts onto cn and hold in front, p1, k2 from cn, p2] twice, slip the next 2 sts onto cn and hold in back, k2, k2 from cn, [p2, slip the next st onto cn and hold in back, k2, p1 from cn] twice, p2, k2.

Row 23: [Slip the next 2 sts onto cn and hold in front, p1, k2 from cn, p2] twice, [slip the next 2 sts onto cn and hold in front, p1, k2 from cn, slip the next st onto cn and hold in back, k2, p1 from cn] twice, [p2, slip the next st onto cn and hold in back, k2, p1 from cn] twice.

Row 25: P1, [slip the next 2 sts onto cn and hold in front, p1, k2 from cn, p2] twice, slip the next 2 sts onto cn and hold in front, k2, k2 from cn, p2, slip the next 2 sts onto cn and hold in front, k2, k2 from cn, [p2, slip the next st onto cn and hold in back, k2, p1 from cn] twice, p1.

Row 27: [P2, slip the next 2 sts onto cn and hold in front, p1, k2 from cn] twice, [slip the next st onto cn and hold in back, k2, p1 from cn, slip the next 2 sts onto cn and hold in front, p1, k2 from cn] twice, [slip the next st onto cn and hold in back, k2, p1 from cn, p2] twice.

Row 29: P3, slip the next 2 sts onto cn and hold in front, p1, k2 from cn, [p2, slip the next 2 sts onto cn and hold in back, k2, k2 from cn] 3 times, p2, slip the next st onto cn and hold in back, k2, p1 from cn, p3.

Row 31: P4, [slip the next 2 sts onto cn and hold in front, p1, k2 from cn, slip the next st onto cn and hold in back, k2, p1 from cn] 4 times, p4.

Row 32: As Row 2.

Repeat Rows 1–32 for the pattern.

mariner's cables

(multiple of 12 stitches plus 12 stitches)

Rows 1 and 15 (RS): *K1, p4, k1; repeat from the * across.

Row 2 and all WS rows: Knit the knit sts and purl the purl sts.

Row 3: K1, p1, k4, *k4, p1, k2, p1, k4; repeat from the * across, ending with k4, p1, k1.

Row 5: K1, p1, slip the next st onto cn and hold in front, p1, k1 from cn, k2, *k2, slip the next st onto cn and hold in back, k1, p1 from cn, p1, k2, p1, slip the

(continued on next page)

next st onto cn and hold in front, p1, k1 from cn, k2; repeat from the * across, ending with k2, slip the next st onto cn and hold in back, k1, p1 from cn, p1, k1.

Row 7: *K1, p2, slip the next st onto cn and hold in front, p1, k1 from cn, k1, *k1, slip the next st onto cn and hold in back, k1, p1 from cn, p2, k2, p2, slip the next st onto cn and hold in front, p1, k1 from cn, k1; repeat from the * across, ending with k1, slip the next st onto cn and hold in back, k1, p1 from cn, p2, k1.

Row 9: K1, p3, *slip the next 2 sts onto cn and hold in front, k2, k2 from cn, p3, k2, p3; repeat from the * across, ending with slip the next 2 sts onto cn and hold in front, k2, k2 from cn, p3, k1.

Row 11: K1, p2, right twist (page 279), k1, *k1, left twist (page 276), p2, k2, p2, right twist, k1; repeat from the * across, ending with k1, left twist, p2, k1.

Row 13: K1, p1, right twist, k2, *k2, left twist, p1, k2, p1, right twist, k2; repeat from the * across, ending with k2, left twist, p1, k1.

Row 17: K4, p1, k1, *k1, p1, k8, p1, k1; repeat from the * across, ending with k1, p1, k4.

Row 19: K2, slip the next st onto cn and hold in back, k1, p1 from cn, p1, k1, *k1, p1, slip the next st onto cn and hold in front, p1, k1 from cn, k4, slip the next st onto cn and hold in back, k1, p1 from cn, p1, k1; repeat from the * across, ending with k1, p1, slip the next st onto cn and hold in front, p1, k1 from cn, k2.

Row 21: K1, slip the next st onto cn and hold in back, k1, p1 from cn, p2, k2, p2, slip the next st onto cn and hold in front, p1, k1 from cn, k2, slip the next st onto cn and hold in back, k1, p1 from cn, p2, k1; repeat from the * across, ending with k1, p2, slip the next st onto cn and hold in front, p1, k1 from cn, k1.

Row 23: K2, p3, k1, *k1, p3, slip the next 2 sts onto cn and hold in back, k2, k2 from cn, p3, k1; repeat from the * across, ending with k1, p3, k2.

Row 25: K1, left twist, p2, k1, *k1, p2, right twist, k2, left twist, p2, k1; repeat from the * across, ending with k1, p2, right twist, k1.

Row 27: K2, left twist, p1, k1, *k1, p1, right twist, k4, left twist, p1, k1; repeat from the * across, ending with k1, p1, right twist, k2.

Row 28: As Row 2.

Repeat Rows 1–28 for the pattern.

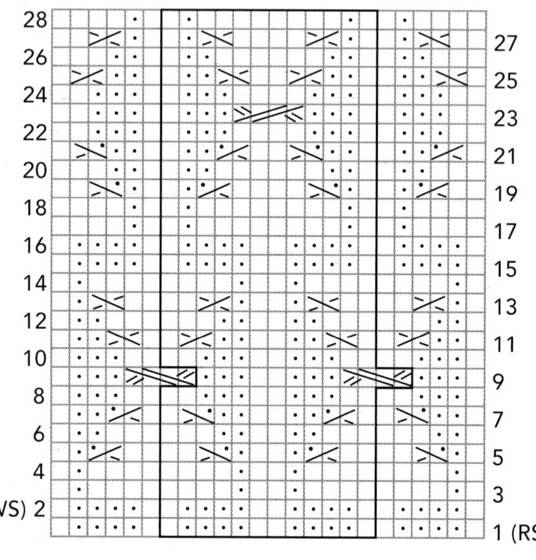

sweeping ribs

easy

(multiple of 40 stitches plus 22 stitches)

Row 1 (RS): *[P2, k2] 8 times, p2, slip the next 4 sts (2 knit sts and 2 purl sts) onto cn and hold in back, k2 from the left-hand needle, slip the 2 purl sts back to the left-hand needle, p2 from the left-hand needle, k2 from cn; repeat from the * across, ending with [p2, k2] 5 times, p2.

Row 2 and all WS rows: Knit the knit sts and purl the purl sts.

Row 3: *[P2, k2] 7 times, p2, slip the next 4 sts onto cn and hold in back, k2 from the left-hand needle, slip the 2 purl sts back to the left-hand needle, p2 from the left-hand needle, k2 from cn, p2, k2; repeat from the * across, ending with [p2, k2] 5 times, p2.

Rows 5, 9, and 13: *[P2, k2] 6 times, [p2, slip the next 4 sts onto cn and hold in back, k2 from the left-hand needle, slip the 2 purl sts back to the left-hand needle, p2 from the left-hand needle, k2 from cn] twice; repeat from the * across, ending with [p2, k2] 5 times, p2.

Rows 7, 11, and 15: *[P2, k2] 5 times, [p2, slip the next 4 sts onto cn and hold in back, k2 from the left-hand needle, slip the 2 purl sts back to the left-hand needle, p2 from the left-hand needle, k2 from cn] twice, p2, k2; repeat from the * across, ending with [p2, k2] 5 times, p2.

Row 17: *[P2, k2] 6 times, p2, slip the next 4 sts onto cn and hold in back, k2 from the left-hand needle, slip the 2 purl sts back to the left-hand needle, p2 from the left-hand needle, k2 from cn, [p2, k2] twice; repeat from the * across, ending with [p2, k2] 5 times, p2.

Row 19: *[P2, k2] 5 times, p2, slip the next 4 sts onto cn and hold in back, k2 from the left-hand needle, slip the 2 purl sts back to the left-hand needle, p2 from the left-hand needle, k2 from cn, [p2, k2] 3 times; repeat from the * across, ending with [p2, k2] 5 times, p2.

Row 21: *P2, slip the next 2 sts onto cn #1 and hold in front, slip the next 2 sts onto cn #2 and hold in back, k2, p2 from cn #2, k2 from cn #1, [p2, k2] 8 times; repeat from the * across, ending with p2, slip the next 2 sts onto cn #1 and hold in front, slip the next 2 sts onto cn #2 and hold in back, k2 from the left-hand needle, p2 from cn #2, k2 from cn #1, [p2, k2] 3 times, p2.

Row 23: *P2, k2, p2, slip the next 2 sts onto cn #1 and hold in front, slip the next 2 sts onto cn #2 and hold in back, k2 from the left-hand needle, p2 from cn #2, k2 from cn #1, [p2, k2] 7 times; repeat from the * across, ending with p2, k2, p2, slip the next 2 sts onto cn #1 and hold in front, slip the next 2 sts onto cn #2 and hold in back, k2 from the left-hand needle, p2 from cn #2, k2 from cn #1, [p2, k2] 2 times, p2.

Rows 25, 29, and 33: *[P2, slip the next 2 sts onto cn #1 and hold in front, slip the next 2 sts onto cn #2 and hold in back, k2 from the left-hand needle, p2 from cn #2, k2 from cn #1] twice, [p2, k2] 6 times; repeat from the * across, ending with [p2, slip the next 2 sts onto cn #1 and hold in front, slip the next 2 sts onto cn #2 and hold in back, k2 from the left-hand needle, p2 from cn #2, k2 from cn #1] twice, p2, k2, p2.

Rows 27, 31, and 35: *P2, k2, [p2, slip the next 2 sts onto cn #1 and hold in front, slip the next 2 sts onto cn #2 and hold in back, k2 from the left-hand needle, p2 from cn #2, k2 from cn #1] twice, [p2, k2] 5 times; repeat from the * across, ending with p2, k2, [p2, slip the next 2 sts onto cn #1 and hold in front, slip the next 2 sts onto cn #2 and hold in back, k2 from the left-hand needle, p2 from cn #2, k2 from cn #1] twice, p2.

Row 37: *[P2, k2] twice, p2, slip the next 2 sts onto cn #1 and hold in front, slip the next 2 sts onto cn #2 and hold in back, k2 from the left-hand needle, p2 from cn #2, k2 from cn #1, [p2, k2] 6 times; repeat

(continued on next page)

from the * across, ending with [p2, k2] twice, p2, slip the next 2 sts onto cn #1 and hold in front, slip the next 2 sts onto cn #2 and hold in back, k2 from the left-hand needle, p2 from cn #2, k2 from cn #1, p2, k2, p2.

Row 39: *[P2, k2] 3 times, p2, slip the next 2 sts onto cn #1 and hold in front, slip the next 2 sts onto cn #2 and hold in back, k2 from the left-hand needle, p2 from cn #2, k2 from cn #1, [p2, k2] 5 times; repeat from the * across, ending with [p2, k2] 3 times, p2, slip the next 2 sts onto cn #1 and hold in front, slip the next 2 sts onto cn #2 and hold in back, k2 from the left-hand needle, p2 from cn #2, k2 from cn #1, p2.

Row 40: As Row 2.

Repeat Rows 1–40 for the pattern.

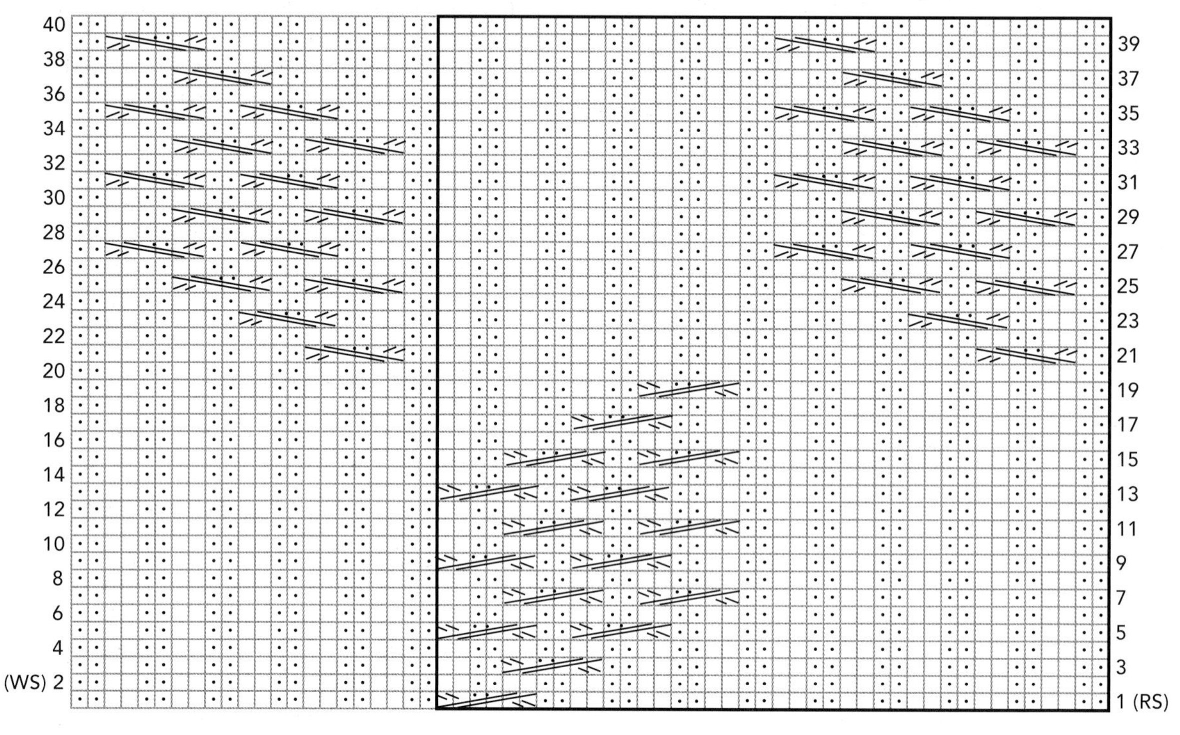

tuxedo cable

(over 29 stitches on a reverse stockinette background)

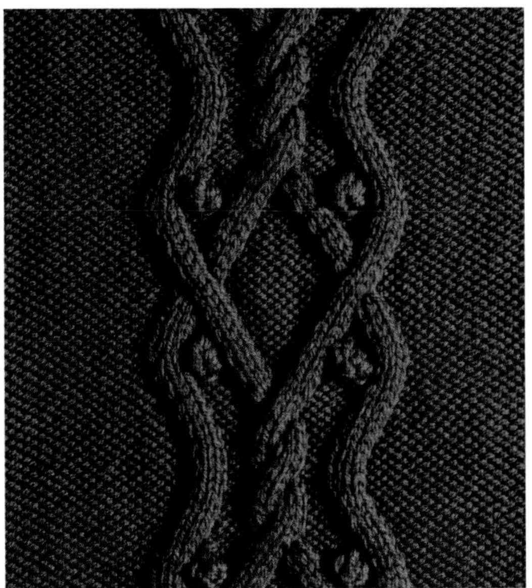

Row 1 (RS): P3, slip the next 3 sts onto cn and hold in back, k3, k3 from cn, p11, slip the next 3 sts onto cn and hold in front, k3, k3 from cn, p3.

Row 2 and all WS rows: Knit the knit sts and purl the purl sts, and purl the bobbles.

Row 3: P2, slip the next st onto cn and hold in back, k3, p1 from cn, slip the next 3 sts onto cn and hold in front, p1, k3 from cn, p9, slip the next st onto cn and hold in back, k3, p1 from cn, slip the next 3 sts onto cn and hold in front, p1, k3 from cn, p2.

Row 5: P1, slip the next st onto cn and hold in back, k3, p1 from cn, p2, slip the next 3 sts onto cn and hold in front, p1, k3 from cn, p7, slip the next st onto cn and hold in back, k3, p1 from cn, p2, slip the next 3 sts onto cn and hold in front, p1, k3 from cn, p1.

Row 7: Slip the next st onto cn and hold in back, k3, p1 from cn, p4, slip the next 3 sts onto cn and hold in front, p1, k3 from cn, p5, slip the next st onto cn and hold in back, k3, p1 from cn, p4, slip the next 3 sts onto cn and hold in front, p1, k3 from cn.

Row 9: Slip the next 3 sts onto cn and hold in front, p1, k3 from cn, p2, make a bobble (page 270), p2, slip the next 3 sts onto cn and hold in front, p1, k3 from cn, p3, slip the next st onto cn and hold in back, k3, p1 from cn, p2, make a bobble, p2, slip the next st onto cn and hold in back, k3, p1 from cn.

Row 11: P1, slip the next 3 sts onto cn and hold in front, p1, k3 from cn, p5, slip the next 3 sts onto cn and hold in front, p1, k3 from cn, p1, slip the next st onto cn and hold in back, k3, p1 from cn, p5, slip the next st onto cn and hold in back, k3, p1 from cn, p1.

Row 13: P2, slip the next 3 sts onto cn and hold in front, p1, k3 from cn, p5, slip the next 3 sts onto cn #1 and hold in back, slip the next st onto cn #2 and hold in back, k3 from the left-hand needle, p1 from cn #2, k3 from cn #1, p5, slip the next st onto cn and hold in back, k3, p1 from cn, p2.

Row 15: P3, slip the next 3 sts onto cn and hold in front, p1, k3 from cn, p4, k3, p1, k3, p4, slip the next st onto cn and hold in back, k3, p1 from cn, p3.

Row 17: P4, slip the next 3 sts onto cn and hold in front, p1, k3 from cn, p3, k3, p1, k3, p3, slip the next st onto cn and hold in back, k3, p1 from cn, p4.

Row 19: P5, k3, p3, slip the next 3 sts onto cn #1 and hold in back, slip the next st onto cn #2 and hold in back, k3 from the left-hand needle, p1 from cn #2, k3 from cn #1, p3, k3, p5.

Row 21: P4, slip the next st onto cn and hold in back, k3, p1 from cn, p3, k3, p1, k3, p3, slip the next 3 sts onto cn and hold in front, p1, k3 from cn, p4.

Row 23: P3, slip the next st onto cn and hold in back, k3, p1 from cn, p4, k3, p1, k3, p4, slip the next 3 sts onto cn and hold in front, p1, k3 from cn, p3.

Row 25: P2, slip the next st onto cn and hold in back, k3, p1 from cn, p5, slip the next 3 sts onto cn #1 and hold in back, slip the next st onto cn #2 and hold in back, k3 from the left-hand needle, p1 from cn #2, k3 from cn #1, p5, slip the next 3 sts onto cn and hold in front, p1, k3 from cn, p2.

Row 27: P1, slip the next st onto cn and hold in back, k3, p1 from cn, p5, slip the next st onto cn and hold in back, k3, p1 from cn, p1, slip the next 3 sts onto cn and hold in front, p1, k3 from cn, p5, slip the next 3 sts onto cn and hold in front, p1, k3 from cn, p1.

(continued on next page)

Row 29: Slip the next st onto cn and hold in back, k3, p1 from cn, p2, make a bobble, p2, slip the next st onto cn and hold in back, k3, p1 from cn, p3, slip the next 3 sts onto cn and hold in front, p1, k3 from cn, p2, make a bobble, p2, slip the next 3 sts onto cn and hold in front, p1, k3 from cn.

Row 31: Slip the next 3 sts onto cn and hold in front, p1, k3 from cn, p4, slip the next st onto cn and hold in back, k3, p1 from cn, p5, slip the next 3 sts onto cn and hold in front, p1, k3 from cn, p4, slip the next st onto cn and hold in back, k3, p1 from cn.

Row 33: P1, slip the next 3 sts onto cn and hold in front, p1, k3 from cn, p2, slip the next st onto cn and hold in back, k3, p1 from cn, p7, slip the next 3 sts onto cn and hold in front, p1, k3 from cn, p2, slip the next st onto cn and hold in back, k3, p1 from cn, p1.

Row 35: P2, slip the next 3 sts onto cn and hold in front, p1, k3 from cn, slip the next st onto cn and hold in back, k3, p1 from cn, p9, slip the next 3 sts onto cn and hold in front, p1, k3 from cn, slip the next st onto cn and hold in back, k3, p1 from cn, p2.

Row 36: As Row 2.

Repeat Rows 1–36 for the pattern.

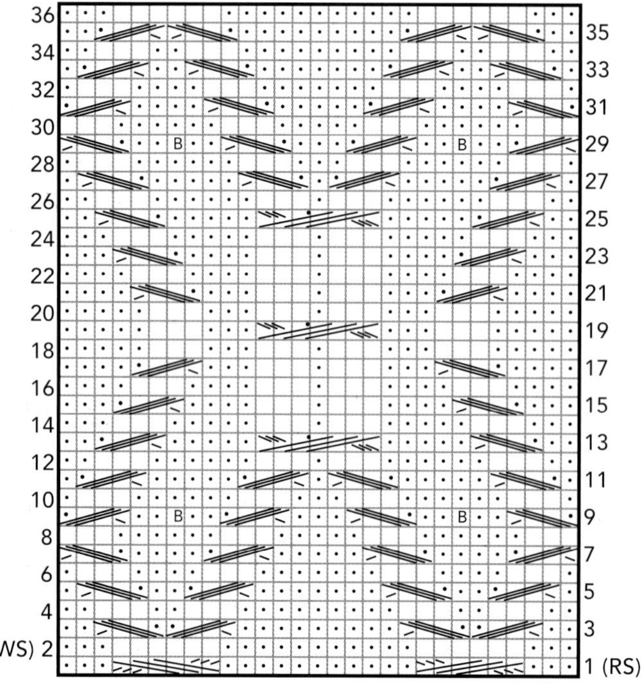

chain links

easy

(multiple of 16 stitches plus 10 stitches)

Rows 1, 3, 7, and 9 (RS): *P2, k2; repeat from the * across, ending with p2.

Row 2 and all WS rows: Knit the knit sts and purl the purl sts.

Row 5: *P2, slip the next 2 sts onto cn #1 and hold in back, slip the next 2 sts onto cn #2 and hold in front, k2 from the left-hand needle, p2 from cn #2, k2 from cn #1, [p2, k2] twice; repeat from the * across, ending with p2, slip the next 2 sts onto cn #1 and hold in back, slip the next 2 sts onto cn #2 and hold in front, k2 from the left-hand needle, p2 from cn #2, k2 from cn #1, p2.

Row 11: *[P2, k2] twice, p2, slip the next 2 sts onto cn #1 and hold in back, slip the next 2 sts onto cn #2 and hold in front, k2 from the left-hand needle, p2 from cn #2, k2 from cn #1; repeat from the * across, ending with [p2, k2] twice, p2.

Row 12: As Row 2.

Repeat Rows 1–12 for the pattern.

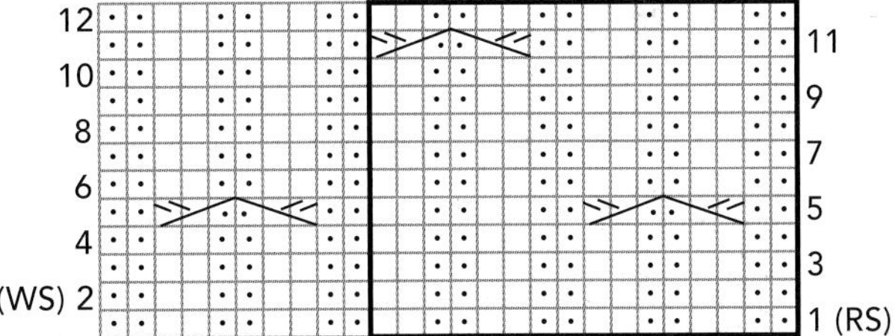

meandering cables

(multiple of 24 stitches plus 14 stitches)

Row 1 (RS): *P3, slip the next 4 sts onto cn and hold in front, k4, k4 from cn, p3, k4, p2, k4; repeat from the * across, ending with p3, slip the next 4 sts onto cn and hold in front, k4, k4 from cn, p3.

Row 2 and all WS rows: Knit the knit sts and purl the purl sts.

Rows 3 and 39: *P3, k8, p3, k4, p2, k4; repeat from the * across, ending with p3, k8, p3.

Row 5: *P2, slip the next st onto cn and hold in back, k4, p1 from cn, slip the next 4 sts onto cn and hold in front, p1, k4 from cn, p2, slip the next 2 sts onto cn and hold in front, k2, k2 from cn, p2, slip the next 2 sts onto cn and hold in back, k2, k2 from cn; repeat from the * across, ending with p2, slip the next st onto cn and hold in back, k4, p1 from cn, slip the next 4 sts onto cn and hold in front, p1, k4 from cn, p2.

Rows 7, 9, 11, 13, and 15: *P2, k4; repeat from the * across, ending with p2.

Row 17: *P2, slip the next 2 sts onto cn and hold in front, k2, k2 from cn, p2, slip the next 2 sts onto cn and hold in back, k2, k2 from cn, p2, slip the next 4 sts onto cn and hold in front, p1, k4 from cn, slip

(continued on next page)

the next st onto cn and hold in back, k4, p1 from cn; repeat from the * across, ending with p2, slip the next 2 sts onto cn and hold in front, k2, k2 from cn, p2, slip the next 2 sts onto cn and hold in back, k2, k2 from cn, p2.

Rows 19 and 23: *[P2, k4] twice, p3, k8, p1; repeat from the * across, ending with [p2, k4] twice, p2.

Row 21: *[P2, k4] twice, p3, slip the next 4 sts onto cn and hold in front, k4, k4 from cn, p1; repeat from the * across, ending with [p2, k4] twice, p2.

Row 25: *P2, slip the next 2 sts onto cn and hold in front, k2, k2 from cn, p2, slip the next 2 sts onto cn and hold in back, k2, k2 from cn, p2, slip the next st onto cn and hold in back, k4, p1 from cn, slip the next 4 sts onto cn and hold in front, p1, k4 from cn; repeat from the * across, ending with p2, slip the next 2 sts onto cn and hold in front, k2, k2 from cn, p2, slip the next 2 sts onto cn and hold in back, k2, k2 from cn, p2.

Rows 27, 29, 31, 33, and 35: *P2, k4; repeat from the * across, ending with p2.

Row 37: *P2, slip the next 4 sts onto cn and hold in front, p1, k4 from cn, slip the next st onto cn and hold in back, k4, p1 from cn, p2, slip the next 2 sts onto cn and hold in front, k2, k2 from cn, p2, slip the next 2 sts onto cn and hold in back, k2, k2 from cn; repeat from the * across, ending with p2, slip the next 4 sts onto cn and hold in front, p1, k4 from cn, slip the next st onto cn and hold in back, k4, p1 from cn, p2.

Row 40: As Row 2.

Repeat Rows 1–40 for the pattern.

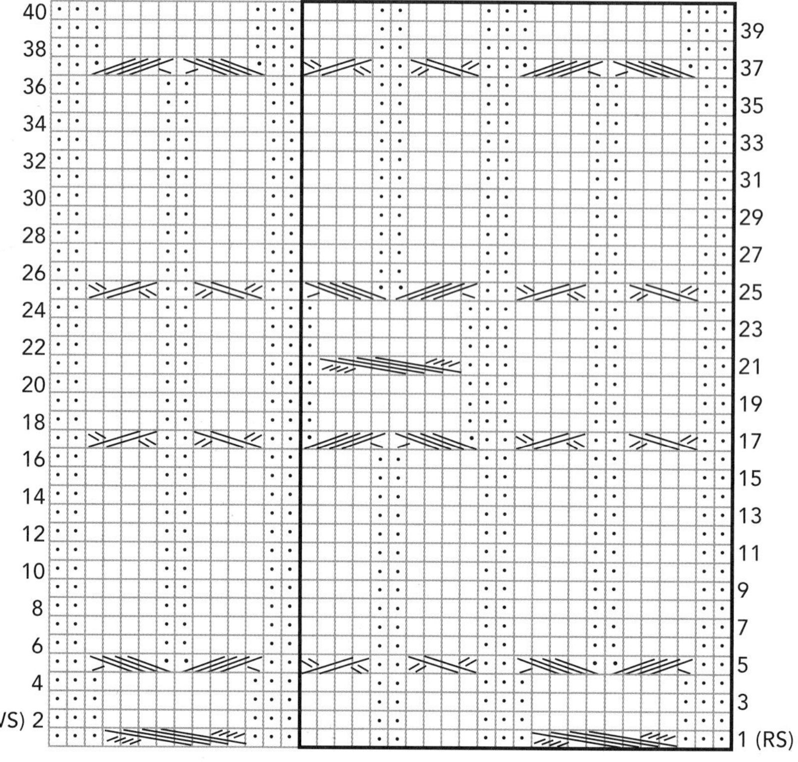

ribbed cable

(over 17 stitches on a reverse stockinette background)

Row 1 (RS): Slip the next st onto cn and hold in front, [k1, p1] from the left-hand needle, k1 from cn, [p1, k1] 7 times.

Row 2 and all WS rows: Knit the knit sts and purl the purl sts.

Row 3: K1, p1, slip the next st onto cn and hold in front, [k1, p1] from the left-hand needle, k1 from cn, [p1, k1] 6 times.

Row 5: [K1, p1] twice, slip the next st onto cn and hold in front, [k1, p1] from the left-hand needle, k1 from cn, [p1, k1] 5 times.

Row 7: Slip the next st onto cn and hold in front, [k1, p1] from the left-hand needle, k1 from cn, p1, k1, p1, slip the next st onto cn and hold in front, [k1, p1] from the left-hand needle, k1 from cn, [p1, k1] 4 times.

Row 9: K1, p1, slip the next st onto cn and hold in front, [k1, p1] from the left-hand needle, k1 from cn, p1, k1, p1, slip the next st onto cn and hold in front, [k1, p1] from the left-hand needle, k1 from cn, [p1, k1] 3 times.

Row 11: [K1, p1] twice, slip the next st onto cn and hold in front, [k1, p1] from the left-hand needle, k1 from cn, p1, k1, p1, slip the next st onto cn and hold in front, [k1, p1] from the left-hand needle, k1 from cn, [p1, k1] twice.

Row 13: [Slip the next st onto cn and hold in front, [k1, p1] from the left-hand needle, k1 from cn, p1, k1, p1] twice, slip the next st onto cn and hold in front, [k1, p1] from the left-hand needle, k1 from cn, p1, k1.

Row 15: K1, p1, [slip the next st onto cn and hold in front, [k1, p1] from the left-hand needle, k1 from cn, p1, k1, p1] twice, slip the next st onto cn and hold in front, [k1, p1] from the left-hand needle, k1 from cn.

Row 17: [K1, p1] twice, [slip the next st onto cn and hold in front, [k1, p1] from the left-hand needle, k1 from cn, p1, k1, p1] twice, k1.

Row 19: [K1, p1] 3 times, slip the next st onto cn and hold in front, [k1, p1] from the left-hand needle, k1 from cn, p1, k1, p1, slip the next st onto cn and hold in front, [k1, p1] from the left-hand needle, k1 from cn, p1, k1.

Row 21: [K1, p1] 4 times, slip the next st onto cn and hold in front, [k1, p1] from the left-hand needle, k1 from cn, p1, k1, p1, slip the next st onto cn and hold in front, [k1, p1] from the left-hand needle, k1 from cn.

Row 23: [K1, p1] 5 times, slip the next st onto cn and hold in front, [k1, p1] from the left-hand needle, k1 from cn, [p1, k1] twice.

Row 25: [K1, p1] 6 times, slip the next st onto cn and hold in front, [k1, p1] from the left-hand needle, k1 from cn, p1, k1.

Row 27: [K1, p1] 7 times, slip the next st onto cn and hold in front, [k1, p1] from the left-hand needle, k1 from cn.

Row 28: As Row 2.

Repeat Rows 1–28 for the pattern.

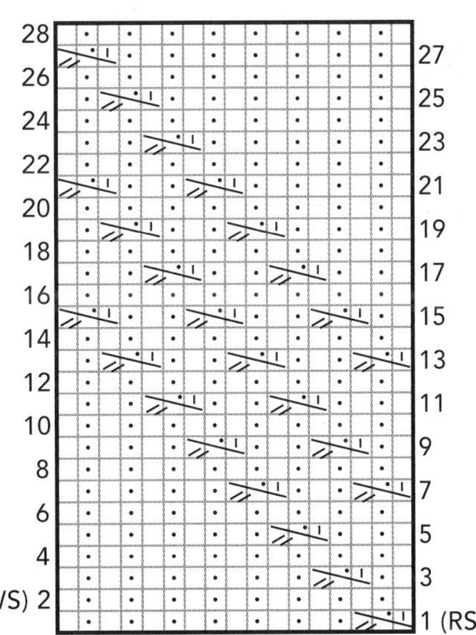

reversible rope cables  easy

(multiple of 8 stitches)

Row 1 (RS): *P4, slip the next 2 sts onto cn and hold in back, k2, k2 from cn; repeat from the * across.

Row 2 and all WS Rows: Knit the knit sts and purl the purl sts.

Row 3: *Slip the next 2 sts onto cn and hold in front, p2, p2 from cn, k4; repeat from the * across.

Row 4: As Row 2.

Repeat Rows 1–4 for the pattern.

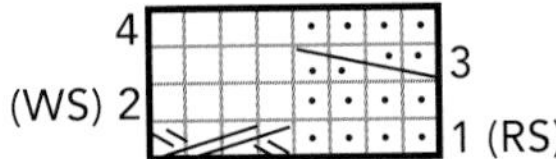

reversible zigzag cables  easy

(multiple of 8 stitches)

Row 1 (RS): *P4, slip the next 2 sts onto cn and hold in back, k2, k2 from cn; repeat from the * across.

Row 2 and all WS Rows: Knit the knit sts and purl the purl sts.

Row 3: *Slip the next 2 sts onto cn and hold in front, p2, p2 from cn, k4; repeat from the * across.

Row 5: *P4, slip the next 2 sts onto cn and hold in front, k2, k2 from cn; repeat from the * across.

Row 7: *Slip the next 2 sts onto cn and hold in back, p2, p2 from cn, k4; repeat from the * across.

Row 8: As Row 2.

Repeat Rows 1–8 for the pattern.

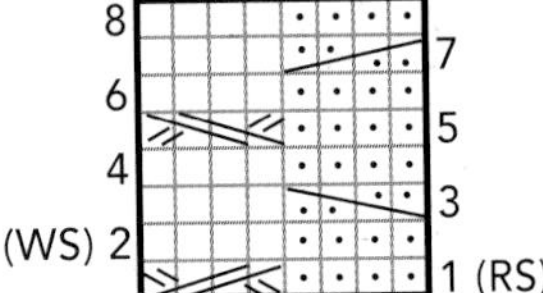

tiny braids

(multiple of 3 stitches)

Row 1 (RS): *Right twist (page 279), k1; repeat from the * across.

Row 2: *Skip the next st, p1-tbl (page 279), then purl the skipped st and slip both sts off at once, p1; repeat from the * across.

Repeat Rows 1 and 2 for the pattern.

(WS) 2 1 (RS)

cables and ridges

(multiple of 10 stitches plus 6 stitches)

Rows 1, 5, and 9 (RS): *P1, right twist (page 279), left twist (page 276), p1, k4; repeat from the * across, ending with p1, right twist, left twist, p1.

Row 2 and all WS rows: *K1, p4; repeat from the * across, ending with k1.

Rows 3, 7, and 11: *P1, left twist, right twist, p1, slip the next 2 sts onto cn and hold in front, k2, k2 from cn; repeat from the * across, ending with p1, left twist, right twist, p1.

Rows 13 and 15: Purl across.

Rows 17, 21, and 25: *P1, k4, p1, right twist, left twist; repeat from the * across, ending with p1, k4, p1.

Rows 19, 23, and 27: *P1, slip the next 2 sts onto cn and hold in back, k2, k2 from cn, p1, left twist, right twist; repeat from the * across, ending with p1, slip the next 2 sts onto cn and hold in back, k2, k2 from cn, p1.

Rows 29 and 31: As Rows 13 and 15.

Row 32: As Row 2.

Repeat Rows 1–32 for the pattern.

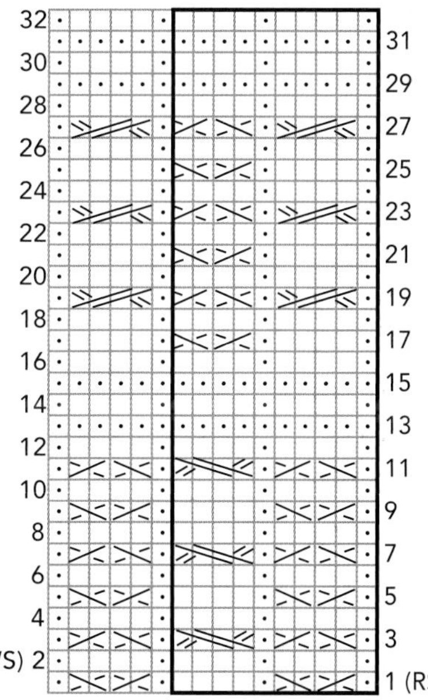

drapey cable

(over 20 stitches on a reverse stockinette background)

Row 1 (RS): K20.

Row 2: P6, [3X elongated purl st (page 274)] twice, p12.

Row 3: K12, slip the next 2 sts onto cn and hold in back *allowing the extra loops to drop*, k6, k2 from cn.

Row 4: P8, [3X elongated purl st] twice, p10.

Row 5: K10, slip the next 2 sts onto cn and hold in back *allowing the extra loops to drop*, k6, k2 from cn, k2.

Row 6: P10, [3X elongated purl st] twice, p8.

Row 7: K8, slip the next 2 sts onto cn and hold in back *allowing the extra loops to drop*, k6, k2 from cn, k4.

Row 8: P12, [3X elongated purl st] twice, p6.

Row 9: K6, slip the next 2 sts onto cn and hold in back *allowing the extra loops to drop*, k6, k2 from cn, k6.

Row 10: P14, [3X elongated purl st] twice, p4.

Row 11: K4, slip the next 2 sts onto cn and hold in back *allowing the extra loops to drop*, k6, k2 from cn, k8.

Row 12: P16, [3X elongated purl st] twice, p2.

Row 13: K2, slip the next 2 sts onto cn and hold in back *allowing the extra loops to drop*, k6, k2 from cn, k10.

Row 14: P18, [3X elongated purl st] twice.

Row 15: Slip the next 2 sts onto cn and hold in back *allowing the extra loops to drop*, k6, k2 from cn, k12.

Row 16: Purl across.

Repeat Rows 1–16 for the pattern.

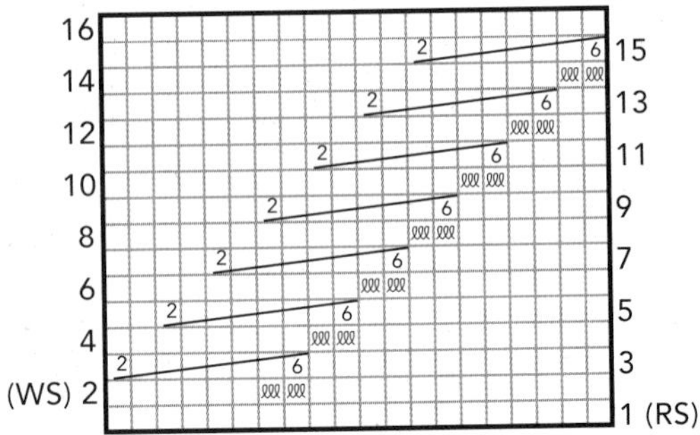

racked rib

(multiple of 2 stitches plus 2 stitches)

Row 1 (RS): K1, *slip the next st onto cn and hold in front, p1, k1 from cn; repeat from the * across, ending with k1.

Row 2: P1, *purl the next st in the row below (page 275), k1; repeat from the * across, ending with p1.

Row 3: K1, *slip the next st onto cn and hold in back, k1, p1 from cn; repeat from the * across, ending with k1.

Row 4: P1, *k1, purl the next st in the row below; repeat from the * across, ending with p1.

Repeat Rows 1–4 for the pattern.

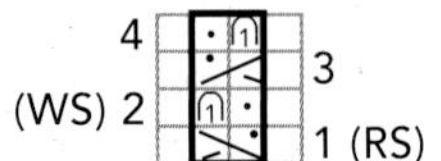

reverse ring cable panel

(over 20 stitches on a reverse stockinette background)

Rows 1, 3, 5, 7, 9, and 11 (RS): [K4, p4] twice, k4.

Row 2 and all WS rows except Rows 14 and 28: Knit the knit sts and purl the purl sts.

Row 13: Slip the next 4 sts onto cn and hold in front, k6, k4 from cn, slip the next 6 sts onto cn and hold in back, k4, k6 from cn.

Row 14: P6, k8, p6.

Rows 15, 17, 19, 21, 23, and 25: K6, p8, k6.

Row 27: Slip the next 6 sts onto cn and hold in back, k4, [p4, k2] from the cn, slip the next 4 sts onto cn and hold in front, [k2, p4] from the left-hand needle, k4 from the cn.

Row 28: [P4, k4] twice, p4.

Repeat Rows 1–28 for the pattern.

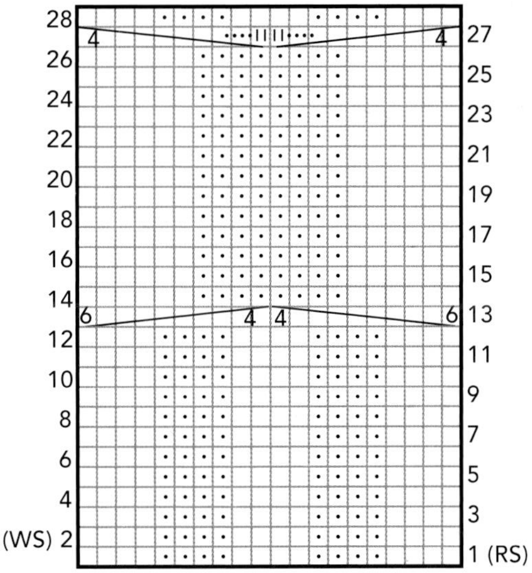

cabled argyle

(multiple of 14 stitches plus 10 stitches)

Row 1 (RS): P4, *slip the next st onto cn and hold in front, k1-tbl (page 275), k1-tbl from cn, p4, slip the next 2 sts onto cn and hold in front, k2, k2 from cn, p4; repeat from the * across, ending with slip the next st onto cn and hold in front, k1-tbl, k1-tbl from cn, p4.

Row 2 and all WS rows: Knit the knit sts and purl the purl sts, working sts that were worked in the back loop on the last row *through their back loops* again.

Row 3: P3, slip the next st onto cn and hold in back, k1-tbl, p1 from cn, *slip the next st onto cn and hold in front, p1, k1-tbl from cn, p2, slip the next st onto cn and hold in back, k2, p1 from cn, slip the next 2 sts onto cn and hold in front, p1, k2 from cn, p2, slip the next st onto cn and hold in back, k1-tbl, p1 from cn; repeat from the * across, ending with slip the next st onto cn and hold in front, p1, k1-tbl from cn, p3.

Row 5: P2, slip the next st onto cn and hold in back, k1-tbl, p1 from cn, p1, *p1, slip the next st onto cn and hold in front, p1, k1-tbl from cn, slip the next st onto cn and hold in back, k2, p1 from cn, p2, slip the next 2 sts onto cn and hold in front, p1, k2 from cn, slip the next st onto cn and hold in back, k1-tbl, p1 from cn, p1; repeat from the * across, ending with p1, slip the next st onto cn and hold in front, p1, k1-tbl from cn, p2.

Row 7: P1, right twist (page 279), p2,*p2, slip the next st onto cn and hold in back, k2, k1-tbl from cn, p4, slip the next 2 sts onto cn and hold in front, k1-tbl, k2 from cn, p2; repeat from the * across, ending with p2, left twist (page 276), p1.

Row 9: P1, slip the next 2 sts onto cn and hold in front, p1, k2 from cn, p1, *p1, slip the next st onto cn and hold in back, k2, p1 from cn, slip the next st onto cn and hold in front, p1, k1-tbl from cn, p2, slip the next st onto cn and hold in back, k1-tbl, p1 from cn, slip the next 2 sts onto cn and hold in front, p1, k2 from cn, p1; repeat from the * across, ending with p1, slip the next st onto cn and hold in back, k2, p1 from cn, p1.

Row 11: P2, slip the next 2 sts onto cn and hold in front, p1, k2 from cn, *slip the next st onto cn and hold in back, k2, p1 from the cn, p2, slip the next st onto cn and hold in front, p1, k1-tbl from cn, slip the next st onto cn and hold in back, k1-tbl, p1 from cn, p2, slip the next 2 sts onto cn and hold in front, p1, k2 from cn; repeat from the * across, ending with slip the next st onto cn and hold in back, k2, p1 from cn, p2.

Row 13: P3, *slip the next 2 sts onto cn and hold in back, k2, k2 from cn, p4, slip the next st onto cn and hold in back, k1-tbl, k1-tbl from cn, p4; repeat from the * across, ending with slip the next 2 sts onto cn and hold in back, k2, k2 from cn, p3.

Row 15: P2, slip the next st onto cn and hold in back, k2, p1 from cn, *slip the next 2 sts onto cn and hold in front, p1, k2 from cn, p2, slip the next st onto cn and hold in back, k1-tbl, p1 from cn, slip the next st onto cn and hold in front, p1, k1-tbl from cn, p2, slip the next st onto cn and hold in back, k2, p1 from cn; repeat from the * across, ending with slip the next 2 sts onto cn and hold in front, p1, k2 from cn, p2.

Row 17: P1, slip the next st onto cn and hold in back, k2, p1 from cn, p1, *p1, slip the next 2 sts onto cn and hold in front, p1, k2 from cn, slip the next st onto cn and hold in back, k1-tbl, p1 from cn, p2, slip the next st onto cn and hold in front, p1, k1-tbl from cn, slip the next st onto cn and hold in back, k2, p1 from cn, p1; repeat from the * across, ending with p1, slip the next 2 sts onto cn and hold in front, p1, k2 from cn, p1.

Row 19: P1, slip the next st onto cn and hold in front, p1, k1-tbl from cn, p2, *p2, slip the next 2 sts onto cn and hold in front, k1-tbl, k2 from cn, p4, slip the next st onto cn and hold in back, k2, k1-tbl from cn, p2; repeat from the * across, ending with p2, slip the next st onto cn and hold in back, k1-tbl, p1 from cn, p1.

Row 21: P2, slip the next st onto cn and hold in front, p1, k1-tbl from cn, p1, *p1, slip the next st onto cn and hold in back, k1-tbl, p1 from cn, slip the next 2 sts onto cn and hold in front, p1, k2 from cn, p2, slip the next st onto cn and hold in back, k2, p1 from cn, slip the next st onto cn and hold in front, p1, k1-tbl from cn, p1; repeat from the * across, ending with p1, slip the next st onto cn and hold in back, k1-tbl, p1 from cn, p2.

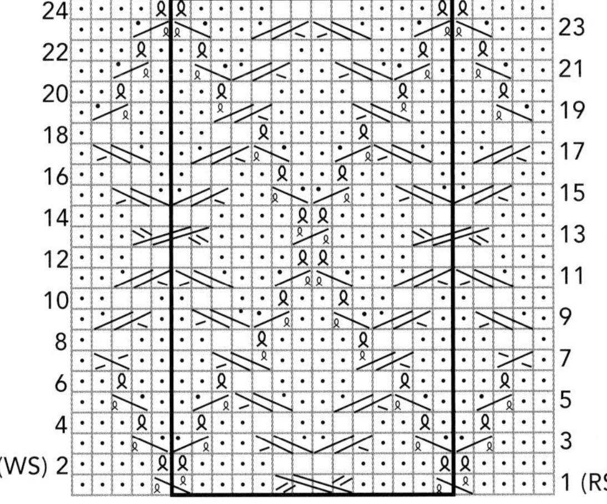

Row 23: P3, slip the next st onto cn and hold in front, p1, k1-tbl from cn, *slip the next st onto cn and hold in back, k1-tbl, p1 from cn, p2, slip the next 2 sts onto cn and hold in front, p1, k2 from cn, slip the next st onto cn and hold in back, k2, p1 from cn, p2, slip the next st onto cn and hold in front, p1, k1-tbl from cn; repeat from the * across, ending with slip the next st onto cn and hold in back, k1-tbl, p1 from cn, p3.

Row 24: As Row 2.

Repeat Rows 1–24 for the pattern.

cornflower panel

(over 24 stitches on a reverse stockinette background)

Row 1 (RS): P10, slip the next 2 sts onto cn and hold in front, k2, k2 from cn, p10.

Rows 2, 4, 6, 8, 10, 12, 14, and 16: Knit the knit sts and purl the purl sts.

Row 3: P8, slip the next 2 sts onto cn and hold in back, k2, k2 from cn, slip the next 2 sts onto cn and hold in front, k2, k2 from cn, p8.

Row 5: P6, slip the next 2 sts onto cn and hold in back, k2, p2 from cn, k4, slip the next 2 sts onto cn and hold in front, p2, k2 from cn, p6.

Row 7: P4, slip the next 2 sts onto cn and hold in back, k2, p2 from cn, p2, slip the next 2 sts onto cn and hold in front, k2, k2 from cn, p2, slip the next 2 sts onto cn and hold in front, p2, k2 from cn, p4.

Row 9: P2, slip the next 2 sts onto cn and hold in back, k2, p2 from cn, p3, slip the next st onto cn and hold in back, k2, p1 from cn, slip the next 2 sts onto cn and hold in front, p1, k2 from cn, p3, slip the next 2 sts onto cn and hold in front, p2, k2 from cn, p2.

(continued on next page)

Row 11: P1, slip the next st onto cn and hold in back, k1, p1 from cn, slip the next st onto cn and hold in front, p1, k1 from cn, p3, slip the next st onto cn and hold in back, k2, p1 from cn, p2, slip the next 2 sts onto cn and hold in front, p1, k2 from cn, p3, slip the next st onto cn and hold in back, k1, p1 from cn, slip the next st onto cn and hold in front, p1, k1 from cn, p1.

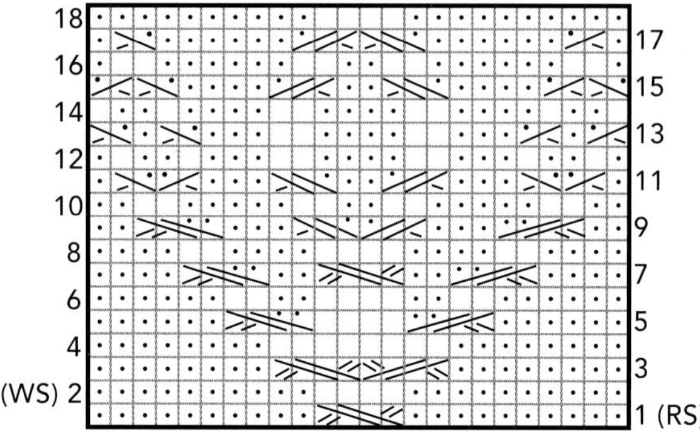

Row 13: Slip the next st onto cn and hold in back, k1, p1 from cn, p1, slip the next st onto cn and hold in back, k1, p1 from cn, p3, k2, p4, k2, p3, slip the next st onto cn and hold in front, p1, k1 from cn, p1, slip the next st onto cn and hold in front, p1, k1 from cn.

Row 15: Slip the next st onto cn and hold in front, p1, k1 from cn, slip the next st onto cn and hold in back, k1, p1 from cn, p4, slip the next 2 sts onto cn and hold in front, p1, k2 from cn, p2, slip the next st onto cn and hold in back, k2, p1 from cn, p4, slip the next st onto cn and hold in front, p1, k1 from cn, slip the next st onto cn and hold in back, k1, p1 from cn.

Row 17: P1, slip the next st onto cn and hold in back, k1, p1 from cn, p6, slip the next 2 sts onto cn and hold in front, p1, k2 from cn, slip the next st onto cn and hold in back, k2, p1 from cn, p6, slip the next st onto cn and hold in front, p1, k1 from cn, p1.

Row 18: K10, p4, k10.

Repeat Rows 1–18 for the pattern.

toggles and links

(multiple of 32 stitches plus 19 stitches)

Row 1 (RS): *P3, k13, p5, slip the next 3 sts onto cn #1 and hold in back, slip the next 3 sts onto cn #2 and hold in front, k3 from left-hand needle, k3 from cn #2, k3 from cn #1, p2; repeat from the * across, ending with p3, k13, p3.

Rows 2, 6, 12, and 16: Knit the knit sts and purl the purl sts.

Rows 3 and 19: *P3, k1, p11, k1, p5, k9, p2; repeat from the * across, ending with p3, k1, p11, k1, p3.

Rows 4 and 18: K3, p2, k9, p2, k3, *k2, p9, k5, p2, k9, p2, k3; repeat from the * across.

Row 5: *P3, k3, p7, k3, p3, slip the next 2 sts onto cn and hold in back, k3, p2 from cn, p3, slip the next 3 sts onto cn and hold in front, p2, k3 from cn; repeat from the * across, ending with p3, k3, p7, k3, p3.

Row 7: *P3, slip the next 3 sts onto cn and hold in front, p2, k3 from cn, p3, slip the next 2 sts onto cn and hold in back, k3, p2 from cn, p3, k3, p7, k3; repeat from the * across, ending with p3, slip the next 3 sts onto cn and hold in front, p2, k3 from cn, p3, slip the next 2 sts onto cn and hold in back, k3, p2 from cn, p3.

Row 8: K5, p9, k5, *p2, k9, p2, k5, p9, k5; repeat from the * across.

Rows 9 and 13: *P5, k9, p5, k1, p11, k1; repeat from the * across, ending with p5, k9, p5.

Row 10: K5, p9, k5, *p13, k5, p9, k5; repeat from the * across.

Row 11: *P5, slip the next 3 sts onto cn #1 and hold in back, slip the next 3 sts onto cn #2 and hold in front, k3 from the left-hand needle, k3 from cn #2, k3 from cn #1, p5, k13; repeat from the * across, ending with p5, slip the next 3 sts onto cn #1 and hold in back, slip the next 3 sts onto cn #2 and hold in front, k3 from the left-hand needle, k3 from cn #2, k3 from cn #1, p5.

Row 14: K5, p9, k5, *p2, k9, p2, k5, p9, k5; repeat from the * across.

Row 15: *P3, slip the next 2 sts onto cn and hold in back, k3, p2 from cn, p3, slip the next 3 sts onto cn and hold in front, p2, k3 from cn, p3, k3, p7, k3; repeat from the * across, ending with p3, slip the next 2 sts onto cn and hold in back, k3, p2 from cn, p3, slip the next 3 sts onto cn and hold in front, p2, k3 from cn, p3.

Row 17: *P3, k3, p7, k3, p3, slip the next 3 sts onto cn and hold in front, p2, k3 from cn, p3, slip the next 2 sts onto cn and hold in back, k3, p2 from cn; repeat from the * across, ending with p3, k3, p7, k3, p3.

Row 20: K3, p13, k3, *k2, p9, k5, p13, k3; repeat from the * across.

Repeat Rows 1–20 for the pattern.

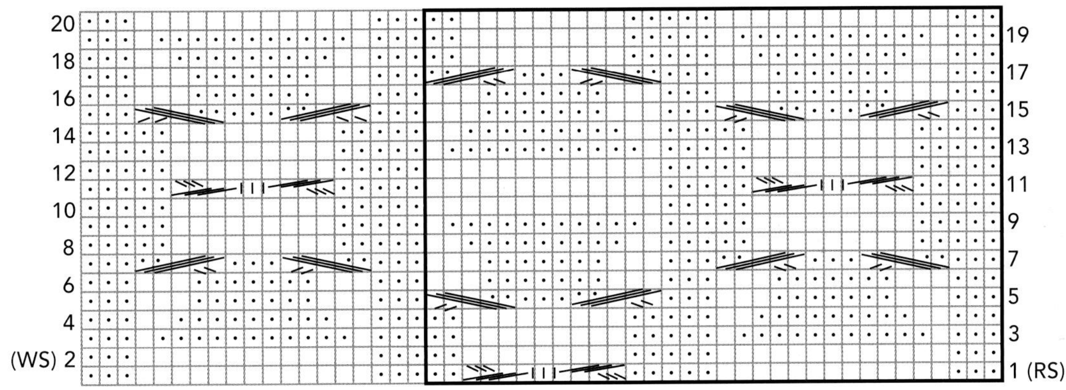

heart cable panel

(over 20 stitches on a reverse stockinette background)

Row 1 (RS): K1, p1, k2, p1, k1, p1, slip the next 3 sts onto cn and hold in front, [k1, p1, k1] from the left-hand needle, [k1, p1, k1] from cn, [k1, p1] 3 times, k1.

Row 2: P1, k1, p2, [k1, p1] twice, [k1, p2] twice, [k1, p1] 3 times.

Row 3: Slip the next 3 sts onto cn and hold in front, p1, [k1, p1, k1] from cn, p1, k1, slip the next st onto cn and hold in back, [k1, p1, k1] from the left-hand needle, k1 from cn, slip the next 3 sts onto cn and hold in front, p1, [k1, p1, k1] from cn, p1, k1, slip the next st onto cn and hold in back, [k1, p1, k1] from the left-hand needle, p1 from cn.

Row 4: [K1, p1] twice, [k1, p2] twice, [k1, p1] twice, k1, p2, k1, p1, k1.

Row 5: P1, slip the next 3 sts onto cn and hold in front, p1, [k1, p1, k1] from cn, slip the next st onto cn and hold in back, [k1, p1, k1] from the left-hand needle, p1 from cn, k1, p1, slip the next 3 sts onto cn and hold in front, k1, [k1, p1, k1] from cn, slip the next st onto cn and hold in back, [k1, p1, k1] from the left-hand needle, p1 from cn, p1.

Row 6: K2, p1, k1, p2, [k1, p1] twice, [k1, p2] twice, k1, p1, k2.

Row 7: P2, slip the next 3 sts onto cn and hold in back, [k1, p1, k1] from the left-hand needle, [k1, p1, k1] from cn, [p1, k1] twice, slip the next 3 sts onto cn and hold in front, [k1, p1, k1] from the left-hand needle, [k1, p1, k1] from cn, p2.

Row 8: K2, p1, k1, p2, [k1, p1] 6 times, k2.

Row 9: P1, slip the next st onto cn and hold in back, [k1, p1, k1] from the left-hand needle, p1 from cn, [k1, p1] 5 times, slip the next 3 sts onto cn and hold in front, k1, [k1, p1, k1] from cn, p1.

Row 10: [K1, p1] 7 times, k1, p2, k1, p1, k1.

Row 11: Slip the next st onto cn and hold in back, [k1, p1, k1] from the left-hand needle, k1 from cn, [p1, k1] 6 times, slip the next 3 sts onto cn and hold in front, p1, [k1, p1, k1] from cn.

Row 12: P1, k1, p2, [k1, p1] 8 times.

Repeat Rows 1–12 for the pattern.

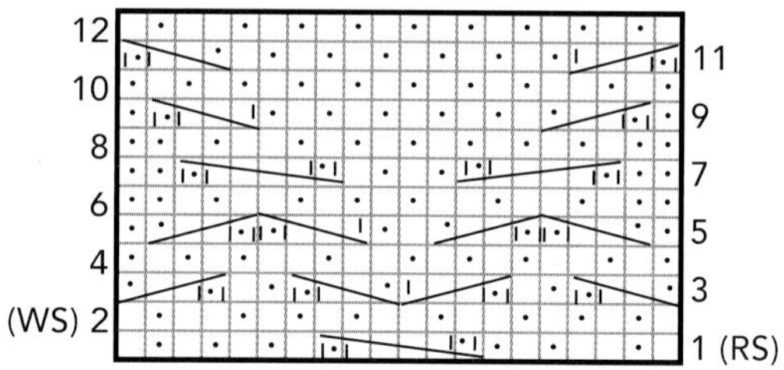

boxes 'n' braids

(multiple of 14 stitches plus 8 stitches)

Row 1 (RS): *P8, k6; repeat from the * across, ending with p8.

Rows 2 and 12: K8, *p6, k8; repeat from the * across.

Row 3: *P1, k6, p1, slip the next 2 sts onto cn and hold in back, k2, k2 from cn, k2; repeat from the * across, ending with p1, k6, p1.

Rows 4, 6 and 8: K1, p2, [k1, p1] twice, k1, *p6, k1, p2, [k1, p1] twice, k1; repeat from the * across.

Rows 5 and 9: *P1, k2, [p1, k1] twice, p1, k2, slip the next 2 sts onto cn and hold in front, k2, k2 from cn; repeat from the * across, ending with p1, k2, [p1, k1] twice, p1.

Row 7: *P1, k2, [p1, k1] twice, p1, slip the next 2 sts onto cn and hold in back, k2, k2 from cn, k2; repeat from the * across, ending with p1, k2, [p1, k1] twice, p1.

Rows 10 and 24: K1, p6, k1, *p6, k1, p6, k1; repeat from the * across.

Row 11: *P8, slip the next 2 sts onto cn and hold in back, k2, k2 from cn, k2; repeat from the * across, ending with p8.

Row 13: Knit across.

Row 14: Purl across.

Row 15: *P1, k6, p7; repeat from the * across, ending with p1, k6, p1.

Row 16: K1, p6, k1,*k7, p6, k1; repeat from the * across.

Row 17: *P1, slip the next 2 sts onto cn and hold in back, k2, k2 from cn, k2, p1, k6; repeat from the * across, ending with p1, slip the next 2 sts onto cn and hold in back, k2, k2 from cn, k2, p1.

Rows 18, 20, and 22: K1, p6, k1, *p2, [k1, p1] twice, k1, p6, k1; repeat from the * across.

Rows 19 and 23: *P1, k2, slip the next 2 sts onto cn and hold in front, k2, k2 from cn, p1, k2, [p1, k1] twice; repeat from the * across, ending with p1, k2, slip the next 2 sts onto cn and hold in front, k2, k2 from cn, p1.

Rows 21: *P1, slip the next 2 sts onto cn and hold in back, k2, k2 from cn, k2, p1, k2, [p1,k1] twice; repeat from the * across, ending with p1, slip the next 2 sts onto cn and hold in back, k2, k2 from cn, k2, p1.

Row 25: *P1, slip the next 2 sts onto cn and hold in back, k2, k2 from cn, k2, p7; repeat from the * across, ending with p1, slip the next 2 sts onto cn and hold in back, k2, k2 from cn, k2, p1.

Row 26: K1, p6, k1, *k7, p6, k1; repeat from the * across.

Rows 27 and 28: As Rows 13 and 14.

Repeat Rows 1–28 for the pattern.

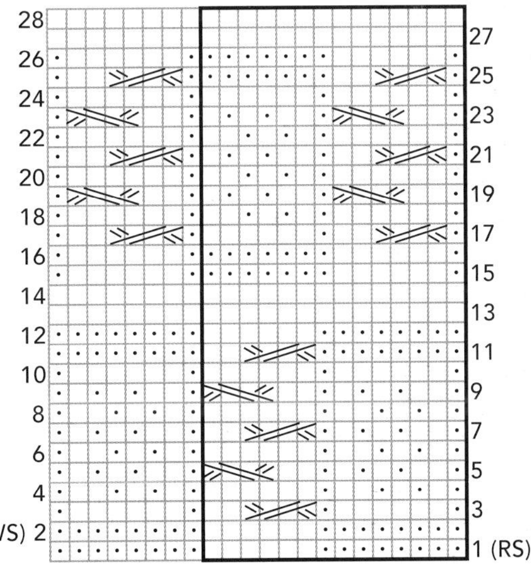

deconstructed cables

(multiple of 11 stitches plus 8 stitches, increases to multiple of 12 stitches plus 9 stitches)

NOTE

- Stitch count varies from row to row.

Row 1 (RS): *P3, left twist (page 276), p3, k3; repeat from the * across, ending with p3, left twist, p3.

Row 2: K3, p1, M1 (page 277), p1, k3, *p3, k3, p1, M1, p1, k3; repeat from the * across.

Rows 3, 5, 9, and 11: *P3, k3; repeat from the * across, ending with p3.

Rows 4 and 10: *K3, p3; repeat from the * across, ending with k3.

Row 6: K3, p3, k3, *p1, remove the next st from the left-hand needle and unravel it 10 rows (page 284), p1, k3, p3, k3; repeat from the * across.

Row 7: *P3, k3, p3, right twist (page 279); repeat from the * across, ending with p3, k3, p3.

Row 8: K3, p3, k3, *p1, M1, p1, k3, p3, k3; repeat from the * across.

Row 12: K3, p1, remove the next st from the left-hand needle and unravel it 10 rows, p1, k3, *p3, k3, p1, remove the next st from the left-hand needle and unravel it 10 rows, p1, k3; repeat from the * across.

Repeat Rows 1–12 for the pattern.

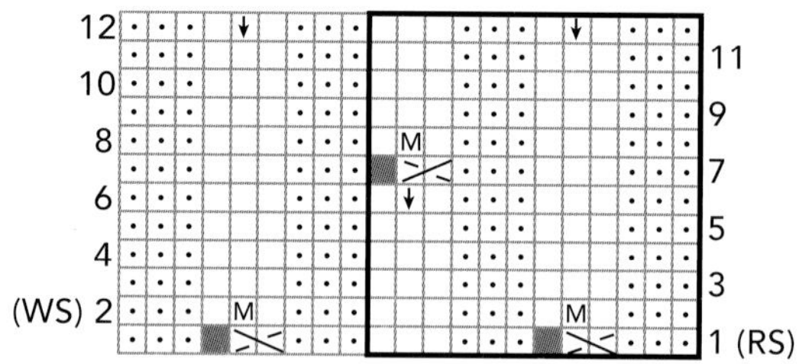

overlapping rings

(multiple of 10 stitches plus 11 stitches)

Row 1 (RS): P1, k1-tbl (page 275), *p7, slip the next st onto cn #1 and hold in back, slip the next st onto cn #2 and hold in back, k1-tbl, p1 from cn #2, k1-tbl from cn #1; repeat from the * across, ending with p7, k1-tbl, p1.

Row 2: K1, slip the next st onto cn and hold in back, k1, p1-tbl from cn (page 279), k5, *slip the next st onto cn and hold in front, p1-tbl, k1 from cn, k1, slip the next st onto cn and hold in back, k1, p1-tbl from cn, k5; repeat from the * across, ending with slip the next st onto cn and hold in front, p1-tbl, k1 from cn, k1.

Row 3: P2, *slip the next st onto cn and hold in front, p1, k1-tbl from cn, p3, slip the next st onto cn and hold in back, k1-tbl, p1 from cn, p3; repeat from the * across, ending with slip the next st onto cn and hold in front, p1, k1-tbl from cn, p3, slip the next st onto cn and hold in back, k1-tbl, p1 from cn, p2.

Row 4: K3, slip the next st onto cn and hold in back, k1, p1-tbl from cn, k1, slip the next st onto cn and hold in front, p1-tbl, k1 from cn, k1, *k4, slip the next st onto cn and hold in back, k1, p1-tbl from cn, k1, slip the next st onto cn and hold in front, p1-tbl, k1 from cn, k1; repeat from the * across, ending k2.

Row 5: P2, *p2, slip the next st onto cn #1 and hold in front, slip the next st onto cn #2 and hold in back, k1-tbl, p1 from cn #2, k1-tbl from cn #1, p5; repeat from the * across, ending with p2, slip the next st onto cn #1 and hold in front, slip the next st onto cn #2 and hold in back, k1-tbl, p1 from cn #2, k1-tbl from cn #1, p4.

Rows 6, 8, 10, 12, 14, and 16: K4, p1-tbl, k1, p1-tbl, k2, *k5, p1-tbl, k1, p1-tbl, k2; repeat from the * across, ending with k2.

Rows 7, 9, 11, 13, and 15: P2, *p2, k1-tbl, p1, k1-tbl, p5; repeat from the * across, ending with p2, k1-tbl, p1, k1-tbl, p4.

Row 17: P2, *p2, slip the next st onto cn #1 and hold in back, slip the next st onto cn #2 and hold in back, k1-tbl, p1 from cn #2, k1-tbl from cn #1, p5; repeat from the * across, ending with p2, slip the next st onto cn #1 and hold in back, slip the next st onto cn #2 and hold in back, k1-tbl, p1 from cn #2, k1-tbl from cn #1, p4.

Row 18: K3, slip the next st onto cn and hold in front, p1-tbl, k1 from cn, k1, slip the next st onto cn and hold in back, k1, p1-tbl from cn, k1, *k4, slip the next st onto cn and hold in front, p1-tbl, k1 from cn, k1, slip the next st onto cn and hold in back, k1, p1-tbl from cn, k1; repeat from the * across, ending with k2.

Row 19: P2, *slip the next st onto cn and hold in back, k1-tbl, p1 from cn, p3, slip the next st onto cn and hold in front, p1, k1-tbl from cn, p3; repeat from the * across, ending with slip the next st onto cn and hold in back, k1-tbl, p1 from cn, p3, slip the next st onto cn and hold in front, p1, k1-tbl from cn, p2.

Row 20: K1, slip the next st onto cn and hold in front, p1-tbl, k1 from cn, k5, *slip the next st onto cn and hold in back, k1, p1-tbl from cn, k1, slip the next st onto cn and hold in front, p1-tbl, k1 from cn, k5; repeat from the * across, ending with slip the next st onto cn and hold in back, k1, p1-tbl from cn, k1.

Row 21: P1, k1-tbl, *p7, slip the next st onto cn #1 and hold in front, slip the next st onto cn #2 and hold in back, k1-tbl, p1 from cn #2, k1-tbl from cn #1; repeat from the * across, ending with p7, k1-tbl, p1.

Rows 22, 24, 26, 28, 30, and 32: K1, p1-tbl, k7, *p1-tbl, k1, p1-tbl, k7; repeat from the * across, ending with p1-tbl, k1.

Rows 23, 25, 27, 29, and 31: P1, k1-tbl, *p7, k1-tbl, p1, k1-tbl; repeat from the * across, ending with p7, k1-tbl, p1.

Repeat Rows 1–32 for the pattern.

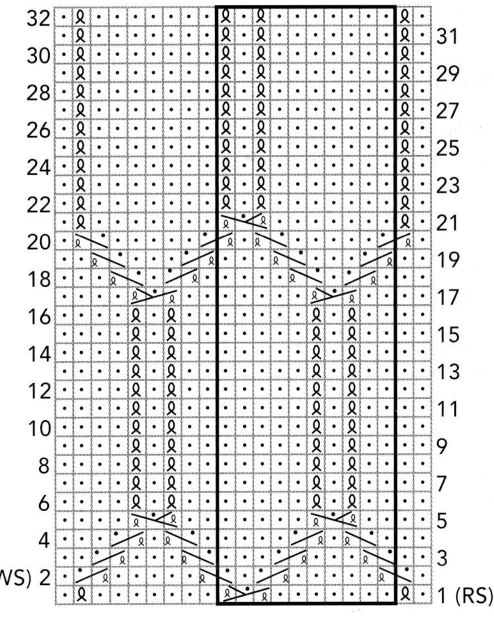

intertwined argyle

(multiple of 16 stitches plus 14 stitches)

Row 1 (RS): P4, slip the next st onto cn #1 and hold in back, slip the next st onto cn #2 and hold in back, k1-tbl (page 275), p1 from cn #2, k1-tbl from cn #1, *slip the next st onto cn #1 and hold in front, slip the next st onto cn #2 and hold in back, k1-tbl, p1 from cn #2, k1-tbl from cn #1, p3, k4, p3, slip the next st onto cn #1 and hold in back, slip the next st onto cn #2 and hold in back, k1-tbl, p1 from cn #2, k1-tbl from cn #1; repeat from the * across, ending with slip the next st onto cn #1 and hold in front, slip the next st onto cn #2 and hold in back, k1-tbl, p1 from cn #2, k1-tbl from cn #1, p4.

Row 2 and all WS rows: Knit the knit sts and purl the purl sts, working sts that were worked in the back loop on the last row *through their back loops* again.

Row 3: P4, k1-tbl, p1, *slip the next st onto cn and hold in front, k1-tbl, k1-tbl from cn, p1, k1-tbl, p2, slip the next st onto cn and hold in back, k2, p1 from cn, slip the next 2 sts onto cn and hold in front, p1, k2 from cn, p2, k1-tbl, p1; repeat from the * across, ending with slip the next st onto cn and hold in front, k1-tbl, k1-tbl from cn, p1, k1-tbl, p4.

Row 5: P3, [slip the next st onto cn and hold in back, k1-tbl, p1 from cn] twice, *[slip the next st onto cn and hold in front, p1, k1-tbl from cn] twice, slip the next st onto cn and hold in back, k2, p1 from cn, p2, slip the next 2 sts onto cn and hold in front, p1, k2 from cn, [slip the next st onto cn and hold in back, k1-tbl, p1 from cn] twice; repeat from the * across, ending with [slip the next st onto cn and hold in front, p1, k1-tbl from cn] twice, p3.

Row 7: P2, [slip the next st onto cn and hold in back, k1-tbl, p1 from cn] twice, p1, *p1, slip the next st onto cn and hold in front, p1, k1-tbl from cn, slip the next st onto cn and hold in back, k2, k1-tbl from cn, p4, slip the next 2 sts onto cn and hold in front, k1-tbl, k2 from cn, slip the next st onto cn and hold in back, k1-tbl, p1 from cn, p1; repeat from the * across, ending with p1, [slip the next st onto cn and hold in front, p1, k1-tbl from cn] twice, p2.

Row 9: P1, [slip the next st onto cn and hold in back, k1-tbl, p1] twice, p2, *p2, slip the next st onto cn and hold in back, k2, k1-tbl from cn, slip the next st onto cn and hold in front, p1, k1-tbl from cn, p2, slip the next st onto cn and hold in back, k1-tbl, p1 from cn, slip the next 2 sts onto cn and hold in front, k1-tbl, k2 from cn, p2; repeat from the * across, ending with p2, [slip the next st onto cn and hold in front, p1, k1-tbl from cn] twice, p1.

Row 11: [P1, k1-tbl] twice, p3, *p1, slip the next st onto cn and hold in back, k2, p1 from cn, [slip the next st onto cn and hold in front, p1, k1-tbl from cn] twice, [slip the next st onto cn and hold in back, k1-tbl, p1 from cn] twice, slip the next 2 sts onto cn and hold in front, p1, k2 from cn, p1; repeat from the * across, ending with p3, [k1-tbl, p1] twice.

Row 13: [P1, k1-tbl] twice, p3, *slip the next st onto cn and hold in back, k2, p1 from cn, p2, k1-tbl, p1, slip the next st onto cn and hold in back, k1-tbl, k1-tbl from cn, p1, k1-tbl, p2, slip the next 2 sts onto cn and hold in front, p1, k2 from cn; repeat from the * across, ending with p3, [k1-tbl, p1] twice.

Row 15: [P1, k1-tbl] twice, p3, *k2, p3, slip the next st onto cn #1 and hold in back, slip the next st onto cn #2 and hold in back, k1-tbl, p1 from cn #2, k1-tbl from cn #1, slip the next st onto cn #1 and hold in front, slip the next st onto cn #2 and hold in back, k1-tbl, p1 from cn #2, k1-tbl from cn #1, p3, k2; repeat from the * across, ending with p3, [k1-tbl, p1] twice.

Row 17: [P1, k1-tbl] twice, p3, *slip the next 2 sts onto cn and hold in front, p1, k2 from cn, p2, k1-tbl, p1, slip the next st onto cn and hold in back, k1-tbl, k1-tbl from cn, p1, k1-tbl, p2, slip the next st onto cn and hold in back, k2, p1 from cn; repeat from the * across, ending with p3, [k1-tbl, p1] twice.

Row 19: [P1, k1-tbl] twice, p3, *p1, slip the next 2 sts onto cn and hold in front, p1, k2 from cn, [slip the next st onto cn and hold in back, k1-tbl, p1 from cn] twice, [slip the next st onto cn and hold in front, p1, k1-tbl from cn] twice, slip the next st onto cn and hold in back, k2, p1 from cn, p1; repeat from the * across, ending with p3, [k1-tbl, p1] twice.

Row 21: P1, [slip the next st onto cn and hold in front, p1, k1-tbl from cn] twice, p2, *p2, slip the next 2 sts onto cn and hold in front, k1-tbl, k2 from cn, slip the next st onto cn and hold in back, k1-tbl, p1 from cn, p2, slip the next st onto cn and hold in front, p1, k1-tbl from cn, slip the next st onto cn and hold in back, k2, k1-tbl from cn, p2; repeat from the * across, ending with p2, [slip the next st onto cn and hold in back, k1-tbl, p1] twice, p1.

Row 23: P2, [slip the next st onto cn and hold in front, p1, k1-tbl from cn] twice, p1, *p1, slip the next st onto cn and hold in back, k1-tbl, p1 from cn, slip the next 2 sts onto cn and hold in front, k1-tbl, k2 from cn, p4, slip the next st onto cn and hold in back, k2, k1-tbl from cn, slip the next st onto cn and hold in front, p1, k1-tbl from cn, p1; repeat from the * across, ending with p1, [slip the next st onto cn and hold in back, k1-tbl, p1 from cn] twice, p2.

Row 25: P3, [slip the next st onto cn and hold in front, p1, k1-tbl from cn] twice, *[slip the next st onto cn and hold in back, k1-tbl, p1 from cn] twice, slip the next 2 sts onto cn and hold in front, p1, k2 from cn, p2, slip the next st onto cn and hold in back, k2, p1 from cn, [slip the next st onto cn and hold in front, p1, k1-tbl from cn] twice; repeat from the * across, ending with [slip the next st onto cn and hold in back, k1-tbl, p1 from cn] twice, p3.

Row 27: P4, k1-tbl, p1, *slip the next st onto cn and hold in front, k1-tbl, k1-tbl from cn, p1, k1-tbl, p2, slip the next 2 sts onto cn and hold in front, p1, k2 from cn, slip the next st onto cn and hold in back, k2, p1 from cn, p2, k1-tbl, p1; repeat from the * across, ending with slip the next st onto cn and hold in front, k1-tbl, k1-tbl from cn, p1, k1-tbl, p4.

Row 28: As Row 2.

Repeat Rows 1–28 for the pattern.

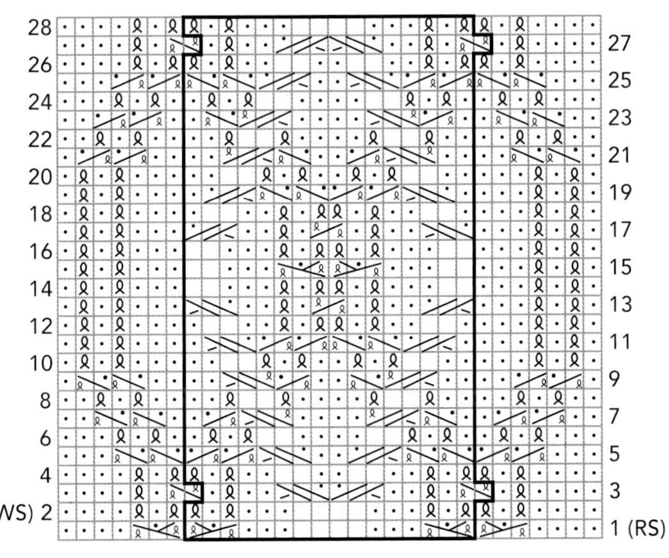

bavarian bells

(over 20 stitches on a reverse stockinette background)

Row 1 (RS): P5, slip the next st onto cn and hold in back, k1-tbl (page 275), k1-tbl from cn, p2, slip the next st onto cn and hold in front, k1-tbl, k1-tbl from cn, p2, slip the next st onto cn and hold in front, k1-tbl, k1-tbl from cn, p5.

Rows 2 and 6: K5, p1-tbl (page 279), [slip the next st onto cn and hold in back, k1, p1-tbl from cn, slip the next st onto cn and hold in front, p1-tbl, k1 from cn] twice, p1-tbl, k5.

Rows 3 and 7: P5, k1-tbl, p1, slip the next st onto cn and hold in front, k1-tbl, k1-tbl from cn, p2, slip the next st onto cn and hold in front, k1-tbl, k1-tbl from cn, p1, k1-tbl, p5.

Rows 4 and 8: K5, p1-tbl, [slip the next st onto cn and hold in front, p1-tbl, k1 from cn, slip the next st onto cn and hold in back, k1, p1-tbl from cn] twice, p1-tbl, k5.

Row 5: P5, slip the next st onto cn and hold in front, k1-tbl, k1-tbl from cn, p2, slip the next st onto cn and hold in back, k1-tbl, k1-tbl from cn, p2, slip the next st onto cn and hold in back, k1-tbl, k1-tbl from cn, p5.

Row 9: P5, slip the next st onto cn and hold in front, p1, k1-tbl from cn, p2, slip the next st onto cn and hold in back, k1-tbl, k1-tbl from cn, p2, slip the next st onto cn and hold in back, k1-tbl, p1 from cn, p5.

Row 10: K6, slip the next st onto cn and hold in back, k1, p1-tbl from cn, slip the next st onto cn and hold in front, p1-tbl, p1-tbl from cn, slip the next st onto cn and hold in back, p1-tbl, p1-tbl from cn, slip the next st onto cn and hold in front, p1-tbl, k1 from cn, k6.

Row 11: P7, slip the next st onto cn and hold in back, k1-tbl, k1-tbl from cn, [slip the next st onto cn and hold in front, k1-tbl, k1-tbl from the cn] twice, p7.

Row 12: K6, slip the next st onto cn and hold in front, [p1-tbl] twice, k1 from cn, [p1-tbl] twice, slip the next 2 sts onto cn and hold in back, k1, [p1-tbl] twice from cn, k6.

Row 13: P5, slip the next st onto cn and hold in back, [k1-tbl] twice, p1 from cn, p1, left twist (page 276), p1, slip the next 2 sts onto cn and hold in front, p1, [k1-tbl] twice from cn, p5.

Row 14: K4, slip the next st onto cn and hold in front, [p1-tbl] twice, k1 from cn, k2, p2, k2, slip the next 2 sts onto cn and hold in back, k1, [p1-tbl] twice from cn, k4.

Row 15: P3, slip the next st onto cn and hold in back, [k1-tbl] twice, p1 from cn, p3, left twist, p3, slip the next 2 sts onto cn and hold in front, p1, [k1-tbl] twice from cn, p3.

Row 16: K2, slip the next st onto cn and hold in front, [p1-tbl] twice, k1 from cn, k4, p2, k4, slip the next 2 sts onto cn and hold in back, k1, [p1-tbl] twice from cn, k2.

Row 17: P1, slip the next st onto cn and hold in back, [k1-tbl] twice, p1 from cn, p5, slip the next st onto cn and hold in front, k1-tbl, k1-tbl from cn, p5, slip the next 2 sts onto cn and hold in front, p1, [k1-tbl] twice from cn, p1.

Row 18: Slip the next st onto cn and hold in front, [p1-tbl] twice, k1 from cn, k5, slip the next st onto cn and hold in front, p1-tbl, k1 from cn, slip the next st onto cn and hold in back, k1, p1-tbl from cn, k5, slip the next 2 sts onto cn and hold in back, k1, [p1-tbl] twice from cn.

Row 19: [K1-tbl] twice, p3, [k1-tbl, p2] 3 times, k1-tbl, p3, [k1-tbl] twice.

Row 20: Slip the next st onto cn and hold in front, p1-tbl, p1-tbl from cn, k3, slip the next st onto cn and hold in back, k1, p1-tbl from cn, k1, p1-tbl, k2, p1-tbl, k1, slip the next st onto cn and hold in front, p1-tbl, k1 from cn, k3, slip the next st onto cn and hold in back, p1-tbl, p1-tbl from cn.

Row 21: [K1-tbl] twice, p4, k1-tbl, p1, slip the next st onto cn and hold in front, p1, k1-tbl from cn, slip the next st onto cn and hold in back, k1-tbl, p1 from cn, p1, k1-tbl, p4, [k1-tbl] twice.

Row 22: Slip the next st onto cn and hold in front, p1-tbl, p1-tbl from cn, k4, slip the next st onto cn and hold in back, k1, p1-tbl from cn, k1, slip the next st onto cn and hold in front, p1-tbl, p1-tbl from cn, k1, slip the next st onto cn and hold in front, p1-tbl, k1 from cn, k4, slip the next st onto cn and hold in back, p1-tbl, p1-tbl from cn.

Rows 23, 25, and 27: [K1-tbl] twice, p5, k1-tbl, p1, [k1-tbl] twice, p1, k1-tbl, p5, [k1-tbl] twice.

Rows 24, 26, and 28: Slip the next st onto cn and hold in front, p1-tbl, p1-tbl from cn, k5, p1-tbl, k1, [p1-tbl] twice, k1, p1-tbl, k5, slip the next st onto cn and hold in back, p1-tbl, p1-tbl from cn.

Row 29: [K1-tbl] twice, p5, slip the next st onto cn and hold in front, p1, k1-tbl from cn, slip the next st onto cn and hold in front, k1-tbl, k1-tbl from cn, slip the next st onto cn and hold in back, k1-tbl, p1 from cn, p5, [k1-tbl] twice.

Row 30: Slip the next st onto cn and hold in front, p1-tbl, p1-tbl from cn, k6, slip the next st onto cn and hold in back, k1, p1-tbl from cn, slip the next st onto cn and hold in front, p1-tbl, k1 from cn, k6, slip the next st onto cn and hold in back, p1-tbl, p1-tbl from cn.

Row 31: [K1-tbl] twice, p7, slip the next st onto cn and hold in front, k1-tbl, k1-tbl from cn, p7, [k1-tbl] twice.

Row 32: Slip the next 2 sts onto cn and hold in back, k1, [p1-tbl] twice from cn, k6, p2, k6, slip the next st onto cn and hold in front, [p1-tbl] twice, k1 from cn.

Row 33: P1, slip the next 2 sts onto cn and hold in front, p1, [k1-tbl] twice from cn, p5, left twist, p5, slip the next st onto cn and hold in back, [k1-tbl] twice, p1 from cn, p1.

Row 34: K2, slip the next 2 sts onto cn and hold in back, k1, [p1-tbl] twice from cn, k4, p2, k4, slip the next st onto cn and hold in front, [p1-tbl] twice, k1 from cn, k2.

Row 35: P3, slip the next 2 sts onto cn and hold in front, p1, [k1-tbl] twice from cn, p3, left twist, p3, slip the next st onto cn and hold in back, [k1-tbl] twice, p1 from cn, p3.

Row 36: K4, slip the next 2 sts onto cn and hold in back, k1, [p1-tbl] twice from cn, k2, p2, k2, slip the next st onto cn and hold in front, [p1-tbl] twice, k1 from cn, k4.

Repeat Rows 1–36 for the pattern.

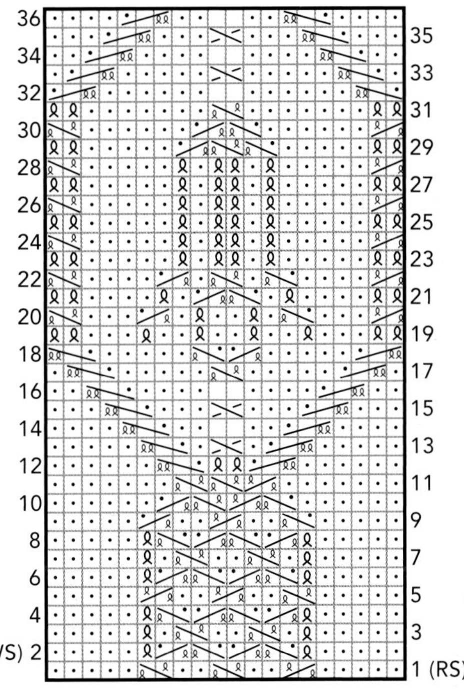

framed tulips

(over 22 stitches on a reverse stockinette background)

Row 1 (RS): P10, slip the next st onto cn and hold in back, k1-tbl (page 275), k1-tbl from cn, p10.

Row 2: K9, slip the next st onto cn and hold in front, p1-tbl (page 279), p1-tbl from cn, slip the next st onto cn and hold in back, p1-tbl, p1-tbl from cn, k9.

Row 3: P8, slip the next st onto cn and hold in back, k1-tbl, p1 from cn, slip the next st onto cn and hold in back, k1-tbl, k1-tbl from cn, slip the next st onto cn and hold in front, p1, k1-tbl from cn, p8.

Row 4: K7, slip the next st onto cn and hold in front, p1-tbl, k1 from cn, k1, [p1-tbl] twice, k1, slip the next st onto cn and hold in back, k1, p1-tbl from cn, k7.

Row 5: P6, slip the next st onto cn and hold in back, k1-tbl, p1 from cn, p2, slip the next st onto cn and hold in back, k1-tbl, k1-tbl from cn, p2, slip the next st onto cn and hold in front, p1, k1-tbl from cn, p6.

Row 6: K5, slip the next st onto cn and hold in front, p1-tbl, k1 from cn, k3, [p1-tbl] twice, k3, slip the next st onto cn and hold in back, k1, p1-tbl from cn, k5.

Row 7: P4, slip the next st onto cn and hold in back, k1-tbl, p1 from cn, p4, slip the next st onto cn and hold in back, k1-tbl, k1-tbl from cn, p4, slip the next st onto cn and hold in front, p1, k1-tbl from cn, p4.

Row 8: K3, slip the next st onto cn and hold in front, p1-tbl, k1 from cn, k4, slip the next st onto cn and hold in front, p1-tbl, p1-tbl from cn, slip the next st onto cn and hold in back, p1-tbl, p1-tbl from cn, k4, slip the next st onto cn and hold in back, k1, p1-tbl from cn, k3.

Row 9: P2, slip the next st onto cn and hold in back, k1-tbl, p1 from cn, p4, slip the next st onto cn and hold in back, k1-tbl, p1 from cn, [k1-tbl] twice, slip the next st onto cn and hold in front, p1, k1-tbl from cn, p4, slip the next st onto cn and hold in front, p1, k1-tbl from cn, p2.

Row 10: K1, slip the next st onto cn and hold in front, p1-tbl, k1 from cn, k5, p1-tbl, k1, [p1-tbl] twice, k1, p1-tbl, k5, slip the next st onto cn and hold in back, k1, p1-tbl from cn, k1.

Row 11: Slip the next st onto cn and hold in back, k1-tbl, p1 from cn, p6, k1-tbl, p1, [k1-tbl] twice, p1, k1-tbl, p6, slip the next st onto cn and hold in front, p1, k1-tbl from cn.

Row 12: P1-tbl, k7, p1-tbl, k1, [p1-tbl] twice, k1, p1-tbl, k7, p1-tbl.

Row 13: Slip the next st onto cn and hold in front, p1, k1-tbl from cn, p6, k1-tbl, p1, [k1-tbl] twice, p1, k1-tbl, p6, slip the next st onto cn and hold in back, k1-tbl, p1 from cn.

Row 14: K1, slip the next st onto cn and hold in back, k1, p1-tbl from cn, k5, p1-tbl, k1, [p1-tbl] twice, k1, p1-tbl, k5, slip the next st onto cn and hold in front, p1-tbl, k1 from cn, k1.

Row 15: P2, slip the next st onto cn and hold in front, p1, k1-tbl from cn, p4, k1-tbl, p1, slip the next st onto cn and hold in back, k1-tbl, k1-tbl from cn, p1, k1-tbl, p4, slip the next st onto cn and hold in back, k1-tbl, p1 from cn, p2.

Row 16: K3, slip the next st onto cn and hold in back, k1, p1-tbl from cn, k2, slip the next st onto cn and hold in front, p1-tbl, k1 from cn, k1, [p1-tbl] twice, k1, slip the next st onto cn and hold in back, k1, p1-tbl from cn, k2, slip the next st onto cn and hold in front, p1-tbl, k1 from cn, k3.

Row 17: P4, slip the next st onto cn and hold in front, p1, k1-tbl from cn, slip the next st onto cn and hold in back, k1-tbl, p1 from cn, p2, slip the next st onto cn and hold in back, k1-tbl, k1-tbl from cn, p2, slip the next st onto cn and hold in front, p1, k1-tbl from cn, slip the next st onto cn and hold in back, k1-tbl, p1 from cn, p4.

Row 18: K5, slip the next st onto cn and hold in back, k1, p1-tbl from cn, k3, [p1-tbl] twice, k3, slip the next st onto cn and hold in front, p1-tbl, k1 from cn, k5.

Row 19: P6, slip the next st onto cn and hold in front, p1, k1-tbl from cn, p2, slip the next st onto cn and hold in back, k1-tbl, k1-tbl from cn, p2, slip the next st onto cn and hold in back, k1-tbl, p1 from cn, p6.

Row 20: K7, slip the next st onto cn and hold in back, k1, p1-tbl from cn, k1, [p1-tbl] twice, k1, slip the next st onto cn and hold in front, p1-tbl, k1 from cn, k7.

Row 21: P8, slip the next st onto cn and hold in front, p1, k1-tbl from cn, slip the next st onto cn and hold in back, k1-tbl, k1-tbl from cn, slip the next st onto cn and hold in back, k1-tbl, p1 from cn, p8.

Row 22: K9, slip the next st onto cn and hold in back, k1, p1-tbl from cn, slip the next st onto cn and hold in front, p1-tbl, k1 from cn, k9.

Repeat Rows 1–22 for the pattern.

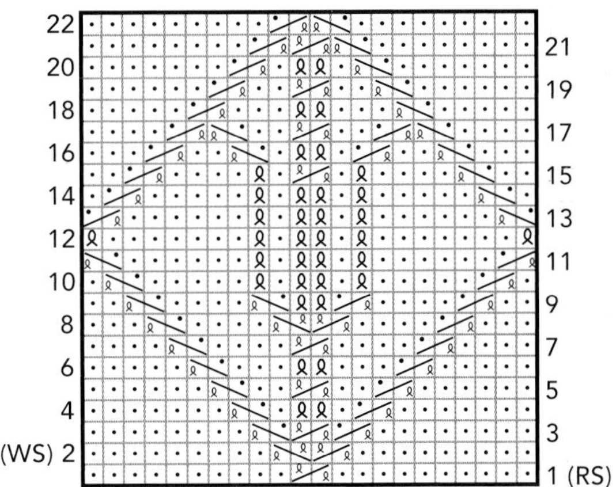

alpine tulips

(over 10 stitches on a reverse stockinette background)

NOTE

- Stitch count varies from row to row.

Rows 1 and 21 (RS): P4, slip the next st onto cn and hold in back, k1-tbl (page 275), k1-tbl from cn, p4.

Rows 2 and 22: K3, slip the next st onto cn and hold in front, p1-tbl (page 279), k1 from cn, slip the next st onto cn and hold in back, k1, p1-tbl from cn, k3.

Row 3: P2, slip the next st onto cn and hold in back, k1-tbl, k1-tbl from cn, p2, slip the next st onto cn and hold in front, k1-tbl, k1-tbl from cn, p2.

Row 4: K1, [slip the next st onto cn and hold in front, p1-tbl, k1 from cn, slip the next st onto cn and hold in back, k1, p1-tbl from cn] twice, k1.

(continued on next page)

Row 5: Slip the next st onto cn and hold in back, k1-tbl, p1 from cn, p2, slip the next st onto cn and hold in back, k1-tbl, k1-tbl from cn, p2, slip the next st onto cn and hold in front, p1, k1-tbl from cn.

Row 6: P1-tbl, k2, slip the next st onto cn and hold in front, p1-tbl, k1 from cn, slip the next st onto cn and hold in back, k1, p1-tbl from cn, k2, p1-tbl.

Row 7: [K1, yarn over, k1] all into one st (page 268), [p2, k1-tbl] twice, p2, [k1, yarn over, k1] all into one st.

Row 8: P3, [k2, p1-tbl] twice, k2, p3.

Row 9: K3, p2, slip the next st onto cn and hold in front, p1, k1-tbl from cn, slip the next st onto cn and hold in back, k1-tbl, p1 from cn, p2, k3.

Row 10: P3, k3, slip the next st onto cn and hold in back, p1-tbl, p1-tbl from cn, k3, p3.

Row 11: K3tog, p2, slip the next st onto cn and hold in back, k1-tbl, k1-tbl from cn, slip the next st onto cn and hold in front, k1-tbl, k1-tbl from cn, p2, sssk (page 281).

Row 12: K2, slip the next st onto cn and hold in front, p1-tbl, p1-tbl from cn, [p1-tbl] twice, slip the next st onto cn and hold in back, p1-tbl, p1-tbl from cn, k2.

Rows 13 and 15: P2, [k1-tbl] 6 times, p2.

Rows 14 and 16: K2, [p1-tbl] 6 times, k2.

Row 17: P1, slip the next st onto cn and hold in back, [k1-tbl] twice, p1 from cn, slip the next st onto cn and hold in back, k1-tbl, k1-tbl from cn, slip the next 2 sts onto cn and hold in front, p1, [k1-tbl] twice from cn, p1.

Row 18: K1, slip the next st onto cn and hold in front, p1-tbl, k1 from cn, k1, [p1-tbl] twice, k1, slip the next st onto cn and hold in back, k1, p1-tbl from cn, k1.

Row 19: P1, k1-tbl, p2, slip the next st onto cn and hold in back, k1-tbl, k1-tbl from cn, p2, k1-tbl, p1.

Row 20: K4, [p1-tbl] twice, k4.

Rows 23 and 25: P3, k1-tbl, p2, k1-tbl, p3.

Row 24: K3, p1-tbl, k2, p1-tbl, k3.

Row 26: K3, slip the next st onto cn and hold in back, k1, p1-tbl, slip the next st onto cn and hold in front, p1-tbl, k1 from cn, k3.

Repeat Rows 1–26 for the pattern.

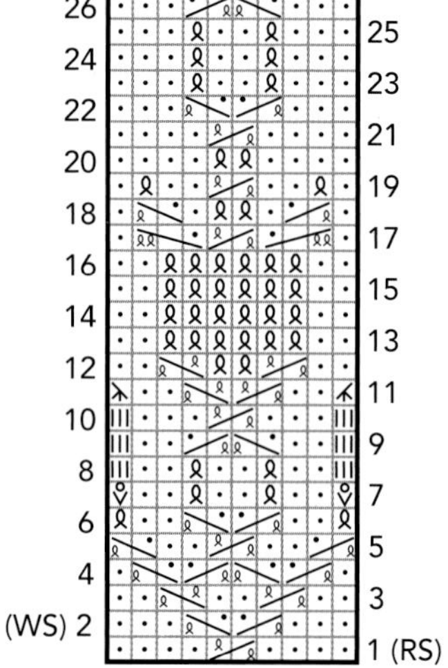

laced cables

(multiple of 40 stitches plus 2 stitches)

NOTES

- Use stranded technique (page 282) for the colorwork.
- Work the stitches in the colors on your needles even when knitting the cables.

Foundation Row (WS): *P2 with A, p2 with B; repeat from the * across, ending with p2 with A.

Row 1 (RS): *K2 with A, slip the next 4 sts onto cn and hold in front, [k2 with B, k2 with A] from the left-hand needle, [k2 with B, k2 with A] from the cn, k2 with B, slip the next 4 sts onto cn and hold in back, [k2 with A, k2 with B] from the left-hand needle, [k2 with A, k2 with B] from the cn, k2 with A, slip the next 4 sts onto cn and hold in back, [k2 with B, k2 with A] from the left-hand needle, [k2 with B, k2 with A] from the cn, k2 with B, slip the next 4 sts onto cn and hold in front, [k2 with A, k2 with B] from the left-hand needle, [k2 with A, k2 with B] from the cn; repeat from the * across, ending with k2 with A.

Row 2 and all WS rows: P2 with A, *p2 with B, p2 with A; repeat from the * across.

Row 3: *[K2 with A, k2 with B] twice, slip the next 2 sts onto cn #1 and hold in front, slip the next 2 sts onto cn #2 and hold in back, k2 with A from the left-hand needle, k2 with B from cn #2, k2 with A from cn #1, [k2 with B, k2 with A] 6 times, k2 with B; repeat from the * across, ending with k2 with A.

Row 5: *K2 with A, slip the next 4 sts onto cn and hold in back, [k2 with B, k2 with A] from the left-hand needle, [k2 with B, k2 with A] from the cn, k2 with B, slip the next 4 sts onto cn and hold in front, [k2 with A, k2 with B] from the left-hand needle, [k2 with A, k2 with B] from the cn, k2 with A, slip the next 4 sts onto cn and hold in front, [k2 with B, k2 with A] from the left-hand needle, [k2 with B, k2 with A] from the cn, k2 with B, slip the next 4 sts onto cn and hold in back, [k2 with A, k2 with B] from the left-hand needle, [k2 with A, k2 with B] from the cn; repeat from the * across, ending with k2 with A.

Row 7: *[K2 with A, k2 with B] 7 times, slip the next 2 sts onto cn #1 and hold in front, slip the next 2 sts onto cn #2 and hold in back, k2 with A from the left-hand needle, k2 with B from cn #2, k2 with A from cn #1, k2 with B, k2 with A, k2 with B; repeat from the * across, ending with k2 with A.

Row 8: As Row 2.

Repeat Rows 1–8 for the pattern.

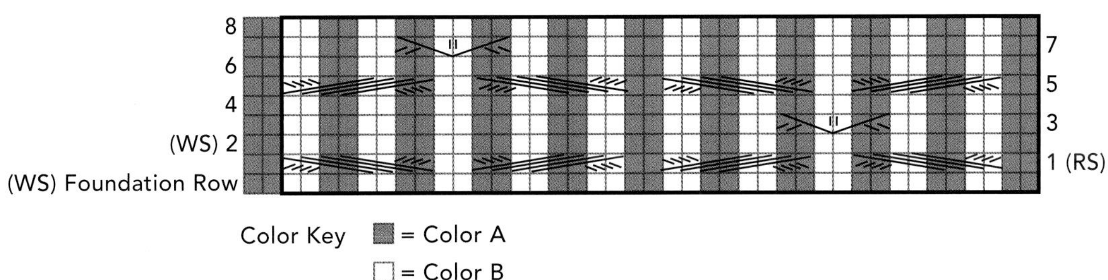

zigzag cables

(multiple of 12 stitches plus 2 stitches)

NOTES

- Use stranded technique (page 282) for the colorwork.
- Work the stitches in the colors on your needles even when knitting the cables.

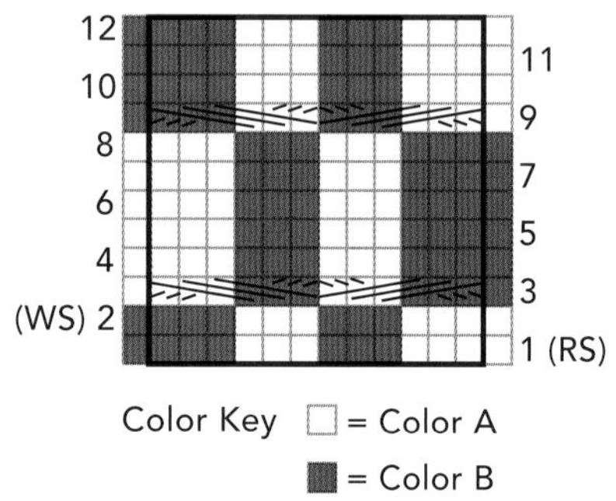

Rows 1 and 11 (RS): K1 with A, *k3 with A, k3 with B; repeat from the * across, ending with k1 with B.

Rows 2 and 10: P1 with B, *p3 with B, p3 with A; repeat from the * across, ending with p1 with A.

Row 3: K1 with B, *slip the next 3 sts onto cn and hold in back, k3 with B, k3 with A from the cn, slip the next 3 sts onto cn and hold in front, k3 with B, k3 with A from cn; repeat from the * across, ending with k1 with A.

Rows 4, 6, and 8: P1 with A, *p3 with A, p3 with B; repeat from the * across, ending with p1 with B.

Rows 5 and 7: K1 with B, *k3 with B, k3 with A; repeat from the * across, ending with k1 with A.

Row 9: K1 with A, *slip the next 3 sts onto cn and hold in back, k3 with A, k3 with B from cn, slip the next 3 sts onto cn and hold in front, k3 with A, k3 from cn with B; repeat from the * across, ending with k1 with B.

Row 12: As Row 2.

Repeat Rows 1–12 for the pattern.

two-color rope cables

(multiple of 20 stitches plus 2 stitches)

Rows 1, 3, and 7 (RS): *K2 with A, k2 with B; repeat from the * across, ending with k2 with A.

Row 2 and all WS rows: P2 with A, *p2 with B, p2 with A; repeat from the * across.

Row 5: *K2 with A, slip the next 4 sts onto cn and hold in back, [k2 with B, k2 with A] from the left-hand needle, [k2 with B, k2 with A] from the cn, k2 with B, slip the next 4 sts onto cn and hold in front, [k2 with A, k2 with B] from the left-hand needle, [k2 with A, k2 with B] from the cn; repeat from the * across, ending with k2 with A.

Row 8: As Row 2.

Repeat Rows 1–8 for the pattern.

NOTES

- Use stranded technique (page 282) for the colorwork.
- Work the stitches in the colors on your needles even when knitting the cables.

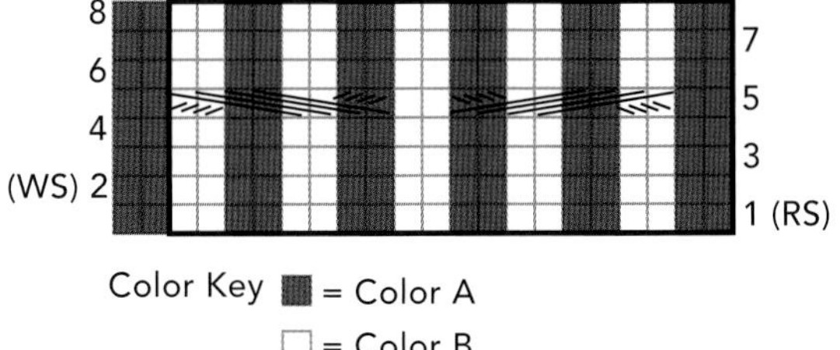

two-color wishbone cables

(multiple of 8 stitches)

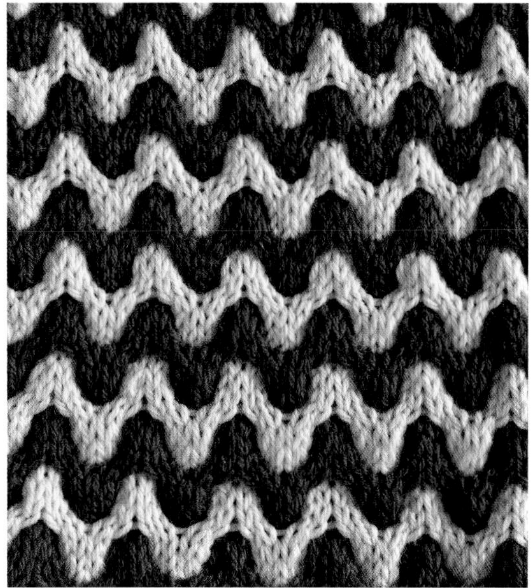

NOTE

- Use stranded technique (page 282) for the colorwork.
- Work the stitches in the colors on your needles even when knitting the cables.

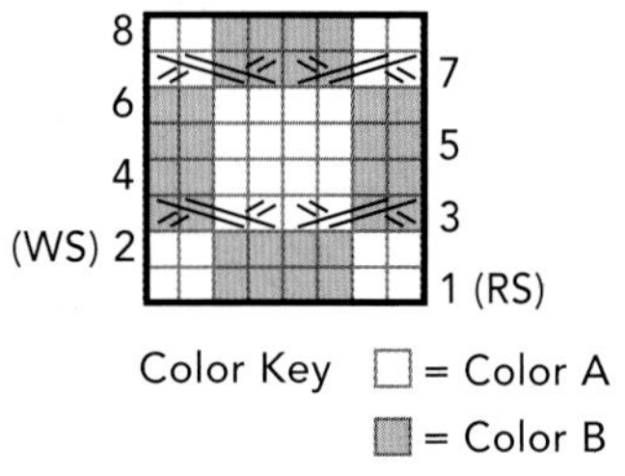

Row 1 (RS): *K2 with A, k4 with B, k2 with A; repeat from the * across.

Row 2: *P2 with A, p4 with B, p2 with A; repeat from the * across.

Row 3: *Slip the next 2 sts onto cn and hold in back, k2 with B from the left-hand needle, k2 with A from the cn, slip the next 2 sts onto cn and hold in front, k2 with A from the left-hand needle, k2 with B from the cn; repeat from the * across.

Rows 4 and 6: *P2 with B, p4 with A, p2 with B; repeat from the * across.

Row 5: *K2 with B, k4 with A, k2 with B; repeat from the * across.

Row 7: *Slip the next 2 sts onto cn and hold in back, k2 with A from the left-hand needle, k2 with B from the cn, slip the next 2 sts onto cn and hold in front, k2 with B from the left-hand needle, k2 with A from the cn; repeat from the * across.

Row 8: As Row 2.

Repeat Rows 1–8 for the pattern.

two-color hanover cables

(multiple of 40 stitches plus 2 stitches)

NOTE

- Use stranded technique (page 282) for the colorwork.
- Work the stitches in the colors on your needles even when knitting the cables.

Foundation Row (WS): *P2 with B, p2 with A; repeat from the * across, ending with p2 with B.

Row 1 (RS): *K2 with B, slip the next 4 sts onto cn and hold in back, [k2 with A, k2 with B] from the left-hand needle, [k2 with A, k2 with B] from the cn, k2 with A, slip the next 4 sts onto cn and hold in front, [k2 with B, k2 with A] from the left-hand needle, [k2 with B, k2 with A] from the cn, k2 with B, slip the next 4 sts onto cn and hold in front, [k2 with A, k2 with B] from the left-hand needle, [k2 with A, k2 with B] from the cn, k2 with A, slip the next 4 sts onto cn and hold in back, [k2 with B, k2 with A] from the left-hand needle, [k2 with B, k2 with A] from the cn; repeat from the * across, ending with k2 with B.

Row 2 and all WS rows: P2 with B, *p2 with A, p2 with B; repeat from the * across.

Row 3: *[K2 with B, k2 with A] twice, slip the next 2 sts onto cn #1 and hold in front, slip the next 2 sts onto cn #2 and hold in back, k2 with B from the left-hand needle, k2 with A from cn #2, k2 with B from cn #1, [k2 with A, k2 with B] 6 times, k2 with A; repeat from the * across, ending with k2 with B.

Row 5: *K2 with B, slip the next 4 sts onto cn and hold in front, [k2 with A, k2 with B] from the left-hand needle, [k2 with A, k2 with B] from the cn, k2 with A, slip the next 4 sts onto cn and hold in back, [k2 with B, k2 with A] from the left-hand needle, [k2 with B, k2 with A] from the cn, k2 with B, slip the next 4 sts onto cn and hold in back, [k2 with A, k2 with B] from the left-hand needle, [k2 with A, k2 with B] from the cn, k2 with A, slip the next 4 sts onto cn and hold in front, [k2 with B, k2 with A] from the left-hand needle, [k2 with B, k2 with A] from the cn; repeat from the * across, ending with k2 with B.

Row 7: *[K2 with B, k2 with A] 7 times, slip the next 2 sts onto cn #1 and hold in front, slip the next 2 sts onto cn #2 and hold in back, k2 with B from the left-hand needle, k2 with A from cn #2, k2 with B from cn #1, k2 with A, k2 with B, k2 with A; repeat from the * across, ending with k2 with B.

Row 8: As Row 2.

Repeat Rows 1–8 for the pattern.

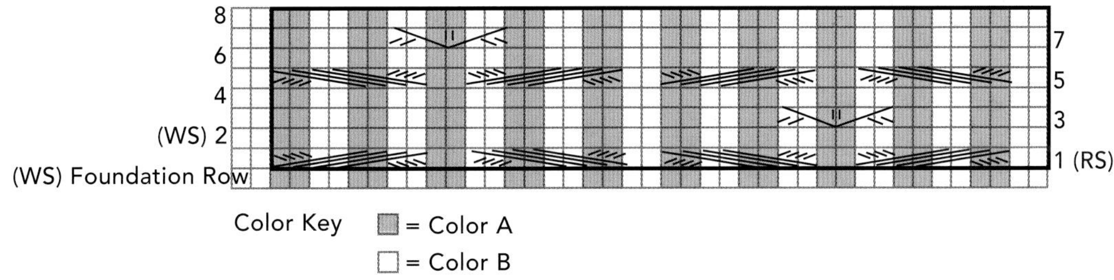

"awareness ribbon" cable

(over 11 stitches, increases to 17 stitches, on a reverse stockinette background)

NOTE

- Stitch count varies from row to row.

Row 1 (RS): M1 (page 277), p11, M1.

Rows 2, 4, 6, 8, 10, 12, 14, 16, 18, 20, 22, 24, and 26: Knit the knit sts and purl the purl sts.

Row 3: M1, k1, p11, k1, M1.

Row 5: M1, k2, p11, k2, M1.

Row 7: Slip the next 3 sts onto cn and hold in front, p1, k3 from cn, p9, slip the next st onto cn and hold in back, k3, p1 from cn.

Row 9: P1, slip the next 3 sts onto cn and hold in front, p1, k3 from cn, p7, slip the next st onto cn and hold in back, k3, p1 from cn, p1.

Row 11: P2, slip the next 3 sts onto cn and hold in front, p1, k3 from cn, p5, slip the next st onto cn and hold in back, k3, p1 from cn, p2.

Row 13: P3, slip the next 3 sts onto cn and hold in front, p1, k3 from cn, p3, slip the next st onto cn and hold in back, k3, p1 from cn, p3.

Row 15: P4, slip the next 3 sts onto cn and hold in front, p1, k3 from cn, p1, slip the next st onto cn and hold in back, k3, p1 from cn, p4.

Row 17: P5, slip the next 3 sts onto cn #1 and hold in back, slip the next st onto cn #2 and hold in back, k3 from the left-hand needle, p1 from cn #2, k3 from cn #1, p5.

Row 19: P4, slip the next st onto cn and hold in back, k3, p1 from cn, p1, slip the next 3 sts onto cn and hold in front, p1, k3 from cn, p4.

Row 21: P3, slip the next st onto cn and hold in back, k3, p1 from cn, p3, slip the next 3 sts onto cn and hold in front, p1, k3 from cn, p3.

Row 23: P3, k3, p5, k3, p3.

Row 25: P3, slip the next 3 sts onto cn and hold in front, p1, k3 from cn, p3, slip the next st onto cn and hold in back, k3, p1 from cn, p3.

Row 27: P4, slip the next 3 sts onto cn and hold in front, p1, k3 from cn, p1, slip the next st onto cn and hold in back, k3, p1 from cn, p4.

Row 28: K5, 7-to-1 st decrease (page 269), k5.

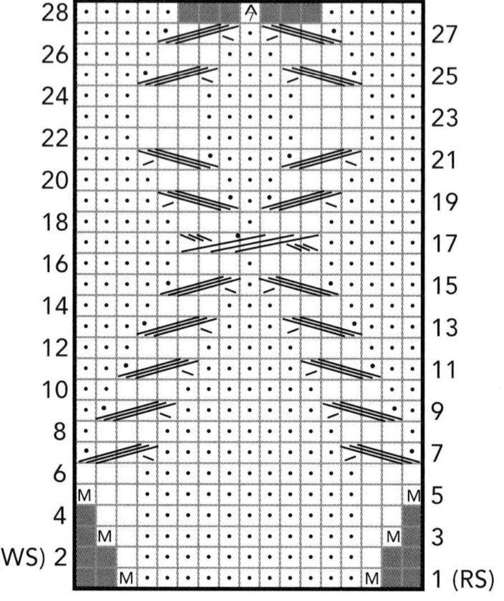

enniskerry cable

(over 22 stitches, increases to 30 stitches, on a reverse stockinette background)

NOTE

- Stitch count varies from row to row.

Rows 1, 3, and 5 (RS): P5, k2, p2, k4, p2, k2, p5.

Rows 2, 4, 6, 8, 12, 14, and 18: Knit the knit sts and purl the purl sts.

Row 7: P5, slip the next 2 sts onto cn and hold in front, p2, k2 from cn, slip the next 2 sts onto cn and hold in front, k2, k2 from cn, slip the next 2 sts onto cn and hold in back, k2, p2 from cn, p5.

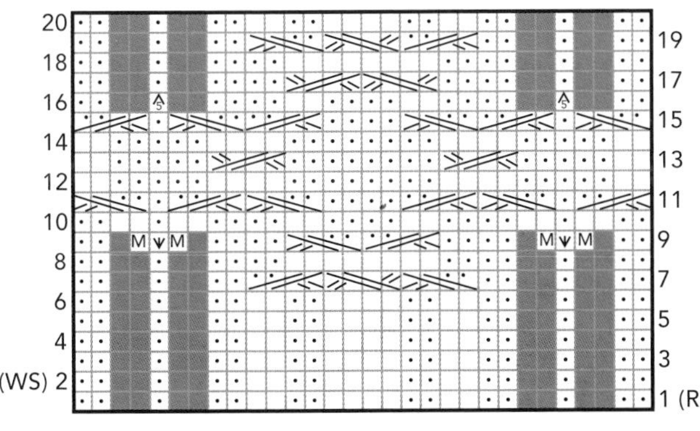

Row 9: P2, M1 (page 277), make a central double increase (page 273), M1, p4, slip the next 2 sts onto cn and hold in back, k2, p2 from cn, slip the next 2 sts onto cn and hold in front, p2, k2 from cn, p4, M1, make a central double increase, M1, p2.

Row 10: K2, p2, k1, [p2, k4] 3 times, p2, k1, p2, k2.

Row 11: Slip the next 2 sts onto cn and hold in back, k2, p2 from cn, p1, slip the next 2 sts onto cn and hold in front, p2, k2 from cn, slip the next 2 sts onto cn and hold in back, k2, p2 from cn, p4, slip the next 2 sts onto cn and hold in front, p2, k2 from cn, slip the next 2 sts onto cn and hold in back, k2, p2 from cn, p1, slip the next 2 sts onto cn and hold in front, p2, k2 from cn.

Row 13: K2, p5, slip the next 2 sts onto cn and hold in back, k2, k2 from cn, p8, slip the next 2 sts onto cn and hold in back, k2, k2 from cn, p5, k2.

Row 15: Slip the next 2 sts onto cn and hold in front, p2, k2 from cn, p1, slip the next 2 sts onto cn and hold in back, k2, p2 from cn, slip the next 2 sts onto cn and hold in front, p2, k2 from cn, p4, slip the next 2 sts onto cn and hold in back, k2, p2 from cn, slip the next 2 sts onto cn and hold in front, p2, k2 from cn, p1, slip the next 2 sts onto cn and hold in back, k2, p2 from cn.

Row 16: K2, 5-to-1 decrease (page 269), [k4, p2] twice, k4, 5-to-1 decrease, k2.

Row 17: P7, slip the next 2 sts onto cn and hold in front, k2, k2 from cn, slip the next 2 sts onto cn and hold in back, k2, k2 from cn, p7.

Row 19: P5, slip the next 2 sts onto cn and hold in back, k2, p2 from cn, slip the next 2 sts onto cn and hold in front, k2, k2 from cn, slip the next 2 sts onto cn and hold in front, p2, k2 from cn, p5.

Row 20: Knit the knit sts and purl the purl sts.

Repeat Rows 1–20 for the pattern.

caedmon celtic knot

(over 27 stitches, increases to 45 stitches, on a reverse stockinette background)

NOTE

- Stitch count varies from row to row.

Row 1 (RS): [P4, M1 (page 277), make a central double increase (page 273), M1, p4] 3 times.

Row 2: [K4, p2, [p1, yarn over, p1] into the next st (page 268), p2, k4] 3 times.

Row 3: [P2, slip the next 2 sts onto cn and hold in back, k3, p2 from cn, p1-tbl (page 279), slip the next 3 sts onto cn and hold in front, p2, k3 from cn, p2] 3 times.

Row 4 and all remaining WS rows *except for Rows 12, 22, 52, 62, and 72:* Knit the knit sts and purl the purl sts.

Row 5: [Slip the next 2 sts onto cn and hold in back, k3, p2 from cn, p5, slip the next 3 sts onto cn and hold in front, p2, k3 from cn] 3 times.

Row 7: K3, [p9, slip the next 3 sts onto cn and hold in front, k3, k3 from cn] twice, p9, k3.

Row 9: [Slip the next 3 sts onto cn and hold in front, p2, k3 from cn, p5, slip the next 2 sts onto cn and hold in back, k3, p2 from cn] 3 times.

Row 11: [P2, slip the next 3 sts onto cn and hold in front, p2, k3 from cn, p1, slip the next 2 sts onto cn and hold in back, k3, p2 from cn, p2] 3 times.

Row 12: K4, 7-to-1 st decrease (page 269), k8, p3, k1, p3, k8, 7-to-1 st decrease, k4.

Row 13: P13, slip the next 3 sts onto cn #1 and hold in back, slip the next st onto cn #2 and hold in back, k3 from the left-hand needle, p1 from cn #2, k3 from cn #1, p13.

Row 15: P11, slip the next 2 sts onto cn and hold in back, k3, p2 from cn, p1, slip the next 3 sts onto cn and hold in front, p2, k3 from cn, p11.

Row 17: P9, slip the next 2 sts onto cn and hold in back, k3, p2 from cn, p5, slip the next 3 sts onto cn and hold in front, p2, k3 from cn, p9.

Row 19: [P9, k3] twice, p9.

Row 21: M1, make a central double increase, M1, p8, slip the next 3 sts onto cn and hold in front, p2, k3 from cn, p5, slip the next 2 sts onto cn and hold in back, k3, p2 from cn, p8, M1, central double increase, M1.

Row 22: P2, [p1, yarn over, p1] into the next st, p2, k10, p3, k5, p3, k10, p2, [p1, yarn over, p1] into the next st, p2.

Row 23: K3, p1-tbl, slip the next 3 sts onto cn and hold in front, p2, k3 from cn, p8, slip the next 3 sts onto cn and hold in front, p2, k3 from cn, p1, slip the next 2 sts onto cn and hold in back, k3, p2 from cn, p8, slip the next 2 sts onto cn and hold in back, k3, p2 from cn, p1-tbl, k3.

Row 25: K3, p3, slip the next 3 sts onto cn and hold in front, p2, k3 from cn, p8, slip the next 3 sts onto cn #1 and hold in back, slip the next st onto cn #2 and hold in back, k3 from the left-hand needle; p1 from cn #2, k3 from cn #1, p8, slip the next 2 sts onto cn and hold in back, k3, p2 from cn, p3, k3.

Row 27: K3, p5, [slip the next 3 sts onto cn and hold in front, p2, k3 from cn, p4, slip the next 2 sts onto cn and hold in back, k3, p2 from cn, p1] twice, p4, k3.

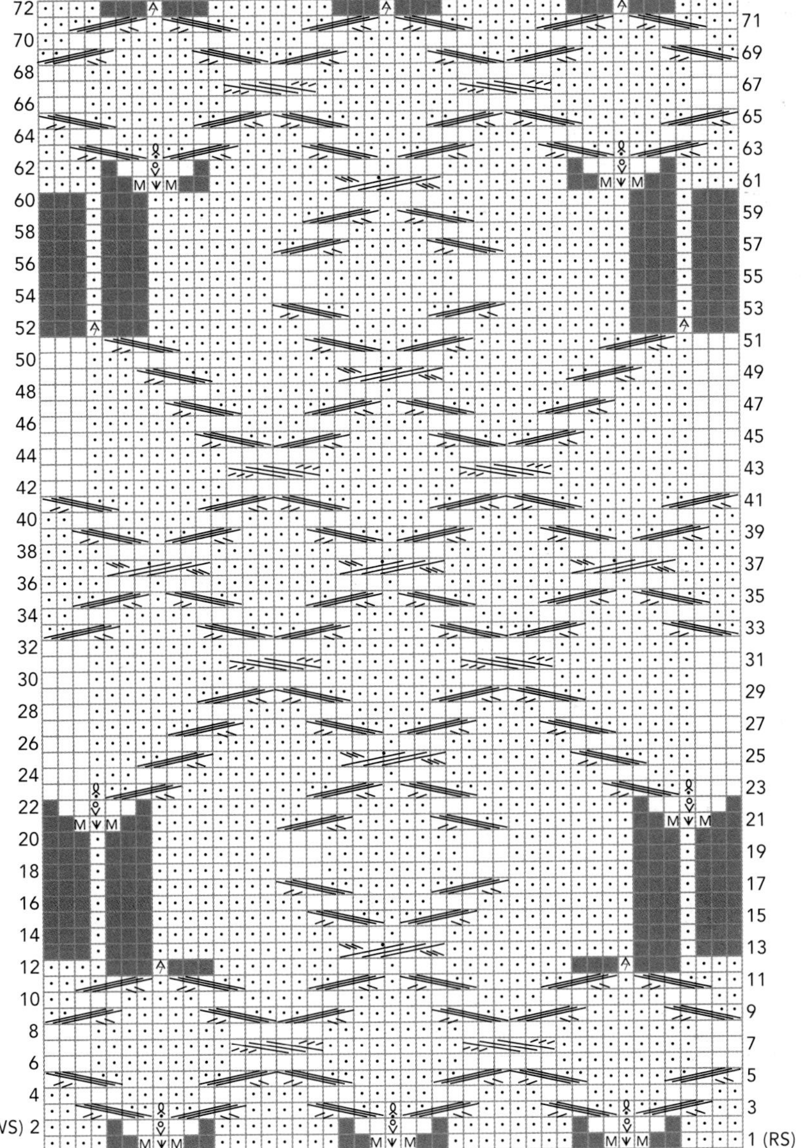

Row 29: K3, p7, [slip the next 3 sts onto cn and hold in front, p2, k3 from cn, slip the next 2 sts onto cn and hold in back, k3, p2 from cn, p5] twice, p2, k3.

Rows 31–35: As Rows 7–11.

Row 36: As Row 4.

Row 37: [P4, slip the next 3 sts onto cn #1 and hold in back, slip the next st onto cn #2 and hold in back, k3 from the left-hand needle, p1 from cn #2, k3 from cn #1, p4] 3 times.

Row 39: [P2, slip the next 2 sts onto cn and hold in back, k3, p2 from cn, p1, slip the next 3 sts onto cn and hold in front, p2, k3 from cn, p2] 3 times.

Rows 41–44: As Rows 5–8.

Row 45: K3, p7, [slip the next 2 sts onto cn and hold in back, k3, p2 from cn, slip the next 3 sts onto cn and hold in front, p2, k3 from cn, p5] twice, p2, k3.

(continued on next page)

Row 47: K3, p5, [slip the next 2 sts onto cn and hold in back, k3, p2 from cn, p4, slip the next 3 sts onto cn and hold in front, p2, k3 from cn, p1] twice, p4, k3.

Row 49: K3, p3, slip the next 2 sts onto cn and hold in back, k3, p2 from cn, p8, slip the next 3 sts onto cn #1 and hold in back, slip the next st onto cn #2 and hold in back, k3 from the left-hand needle, p1 from cn #2, k3 from cn #1, p8, slip the next 3 sts onto cn and hold in front, p2, k3 from cn, p3, k3.

Row 51: K3, p1, slip the next 2 sts onto cn and hold in back, k3, p2 from cn, p8, slip the next 2 sts onto cn and hold in back, k3, p2 from cn, p1, slip the next 3 sts onto cn and hold in front, p2, k3 from cn, p8, slip the next 3 sts onto cn and hold in front, p2, k3 from cn, p1, k3.

Row 52: 7-to-1 st decrease, k10, p3, k5, p3, k10, 7-to-1 st decrease.

Rows 53–56: As Rows 17–20.

Row 57: P9, slip the next 3 sts onto cn and hold in front, p2, k3 from cn, p5, slip the next 2 sts onto cn and hold in back, k3, p2 from cn, p9.

Row 59: P11, slip the next 3 sts onto cn and hold in front, p2, k3 from cn, p1, slip the next 2 sts onto cn and hold in back, k3, p2 from cn, p11.

Row 61: P4, M1, make a central double increase, M1, p8, slip the next 3 sts onto cn #1 and hold in back, slip the next st onto cn #2 and hold in back, k3 from the left-hand needle, p1 from cn #2, k3 from cn #1, p8, M1, central double increase, M1, p4.

Row 62: K4, p2, [p1, yarn over, p1] into the next st, p2, k8, p3, k1, p3, k8, p2, [p1, yarn over, p1] into the next st, p2, k4.

Row 63: P2, slip the next 2 sts onto cn and hold in back, k3, p2 from cn, p1-tbl, slip the next 3 sts onto cn and hold in front, p2, k3 from cn, p4, slip the next 2 sts onto cn and hold in back, k3, p2 from cn, p1, slip the next 3 sts onto cn and hold in front, p2, k3 from cn, p4, slip the next 2 sts onto cn and hold in back, k3, p2 from cn, p1-tbl, slip the next 3 sts onto cn and hold in front, p2, k3 from cn, p2.

Rows 65–71: As Rows 5–11.

Row 72: [K4, 7-to-1 st decrease, k4] 3 times.

celtic swirl

(over 39 stitches, increases to 45 stitches, on a reverse stockinette background)

NOTE

- Stitch count varies from row to row.

Row 1 (RS): P4, slip the next 3 sts onto cn and hold in front, p1, k3 from cn, p8, slip the next 3 sts onto cn #1 and hold in front, slip the next st onto cn #2 and hold in back, k3 from the left-hand needle, p1 from cn #2, k3 from cn #1, p8, slip the next 3 sts onto cn and hold in front, p1, k3 from cn, p4.

Rows 2, 4, 6, 8, 12, 14, 16, 18, 20, 22, 24, 26, 28, 30, 34, 36, and 38: Knit the knit sts and purl the purl sts.

Row 3: P5, slip the next 3 sts onto cn and hold in front, p1, k3 from cn, p5, slip the next 2 sts onto cn and hold in back, k3, p2 from cn, p1, slip the next 3 sts onto cn and hold in front, p2, k3 from cn, p7, slip the next 3 sts onto cn and hold in front, p1, k3 from cn, p3.

Row 5: P6, slip the next 3 sts onto cn and hold in front, p1, k3 from cn, p3, slip the next st onto cn and hold in back, k3, p1 from cn, p5, slip the next 3 sts onto cn and hold in front, p2, k3 from cn, p6, slip the next 3 sts onto cn and hold in front, p1, k3 from cn, p2.

Row 7: P7, slip the next 3 sts onto cn and hold in front, p1, k3 from cn, p1, slip the next st onto cn and hold in back, k3, p1 from cn, p8, slip the next 3 sts onto cn and hold in front, p2, k3 from cn, p5, slip the next 3 sts onto cn and hold in front, p1, k3 from cn, p1.

Row 9: P8, slip the next 3 sts onto cn #1 and hold in back, slip the next st onto cn #2 and hold in back, k3 from the left-hand needle, p1 from cn #2, k3 from cn #1, p6, M1 (page 277), central double increase (page 273), M1, p4, slip the next 3 sts onto cn and hold in front, p1, k3 from cn, p5, k3, p1.

Row 10: K1, [p3, k5] twice, p2, [p1, yarn over, p1] into the next st (page 268), p2, k6, p3, k1, p3, k8.

Row 11: P6, slip the next 2 sts onto cn and hold in back, k3, p2 from cn, p1, slip the next 3 sts onto cn and hold in front, p1, k3 from cn, p3, slip the next 2 sts onto cn and hold in back, k3, p2 from cn, p1-tbl (page 279), slip the next 3 sts onto cn and hold in front, p2, k3 from cn, p3, k3, p5, k3, p1.

Row 13: P5, slip the next st onto cn and hold in back, k3, p1 from cn, p4, slip the next 3 sts onto cn and hold in front, p1, k3 from cn, slip the next 2 sts onto cn and hold in back, k3, p2 from cn, p4, slip the next st onto cn and hold in back, k3, p1 from cn, p3, k3, p5, k3, p1.

Row 15: P4, slip the next st onto cn and hold in back, k3, p1 from cn, p6, slip the next 3 sts onto cn and hold in front, k3, k3 from cn, p5, slip the next st onto cn and hold in back, k3, p1 from cn, p4, k3, p5, k3, p1.

Row 17: P3, slip the next st onto cn and hold in back, k3, p1 from cn, p6, slip the next st onto cn and hold in back, k3, p1 from cn, slip the next 3 sts onto cn and hold in front, p1, k3 from cn, p3, slip the next st onto cn and hold in back, k3, p1 from cn, p4, slip the next st onto cn and hold in back, k3, p1 from cn, p5, k3, p1.

Row 19: P2, slip the next st onto cn and hold in back, k3, p1 from cn, p6, slip the next st onto cn and hold in back, k3, p1 from cn, p2, slip the next 3 sts onto cn and hold in front, p1, k3 from cn, p1, slip the next st onto cn and hold in back, k3, p1 from cn, p4, slip the next st onto cn and hold in back, k3, p1 from cn, p6, k3, p1.

Row 21: P1, slip the next st onto cn and hold in back, k3, p1 from cn, p6, slip the next st onto cn and hold in back, k3, p1 from cn, p4, slip the next 3 sts onto cn #1 and hold in back, slip the next st onto cn #2 and hold in back, k3 from the left-hand needle, p1 from cn #2, k3 from cn #1, p4, slip the next st onto cn and hold in back, k3, p1 from cn, p6, slip the next st onto cn and hold in back, k3, p1 from cn, p1.

Row 23: P1, k3, p6, slip the next st onto cn and hold in back, k3, p1 from cn, p4, slip the next st onto cn and hold in back, k3, p1 from cn, p1, slip the next 3 sts onto cn and hold in front, p1, k3 from cn, p2, slip the next st onto cn and hold in back, k3, p1 from cn, p6, slip the next st onto cn and hold in back, k3, p1 from cn, p2.

Row 25: P1, k3, p5, slip the next st onto cn and hold in back, k3, p1 from cn, p4, slip the next st onto cn and hold in back, k3, p1 from cn, p3, slip the next 3 sts onto cn and hold in front, p1, k3 from cn, slip the next st onto cn and hold in back, k3, p1 from cn, p6, slip the next st onto cn and hold in back, k3, p1 from cn, p3.

Row 27: P1, k3, p5, k3, p4, slip the next st onto cn and hold in back, k3, p1 from cn, p5, slip the next 3 sts onto cn and hold in front, k3, k3 from cn, p6, slip the next st onto cn and hold in back, k3, p1 from cn, p4.

Row 29: P1, k3, p5, k3, p3, slip the next st onto cn and hold in back, k3, p1 from cn, p4, slip the next 2 sts onto cn and hold in back, k3, p2 from cn, slip the next 3 sts onto cn and hold in front, p1, k3 from cn, p4, slip the next st onto cn and hold in back, k3, p1 from cn, p5.

Row 31: P1, k3, p5, k3, p3, slip the next 3 sts onto cn and hold in front, p2, k3 from cn, p1, slip the next 2 sts onto cn and hold in back, k3, p2 from cn, p3,

(continued on next page)

slip the next 3 sts onto cn and hold in front, p1, k3 from cn, p1, slip the next 2 sts onto cn and hold in back, k3, p2 from cn, p6.

Row 32: K8, p3, k1, p3, k6, 7-to-1 st decrease (page 269), [k5, p3] twice, p1.

Row 33: P1, k3, p5, slip the next 3 sts onto cn and hold in front, p1, k3 from cn, p11, slip the next 3 sts onto cn #1 and hold in back, slip the next st onto cn #2 and hold in back, k3 from the left-hand needle, p1 from cn #2, k3 from cn #1, p8.

Row 35: P1, slip the next 3 sts onto cn and hold in front, p1, k3 from cn, p5, slip the next 3 sts onto cn and hold in front, p2, k3 from cn, p8, slip the next st onto cn and hold in back, k3, p1 from cn, p1, slip the next 3 sts onto cn and hold in front, p1, k3 from cn, p7.

Row 37: P2, slip the next 3 sts onto cn and hold in front, p1, k3 from cn, p6, slip the next 3 sts onto cn and hold in front, p2, k3 from cn, p5, slip the next st onto cn and hold in back, k3, p1 from cn, p3, slip the next 3 sts onto cn and hold in front, p1, k3 from cn, p6.

Row 39: P3, slip the next 3 sts onto cn and hold in front, p1, k3 from cn, p7, slip the next 3 sts onto cn and hold in front, p2, k3 from cn, p1, slip the next 2 sts onto cn and hold in back, k3, p2 from cn, p5, slip the next 3 sts onto cn and hold in front, p1, k3 from cn, p5.

Row 40: As Row 2.

Repeat Rows 1–40 for the pattern.

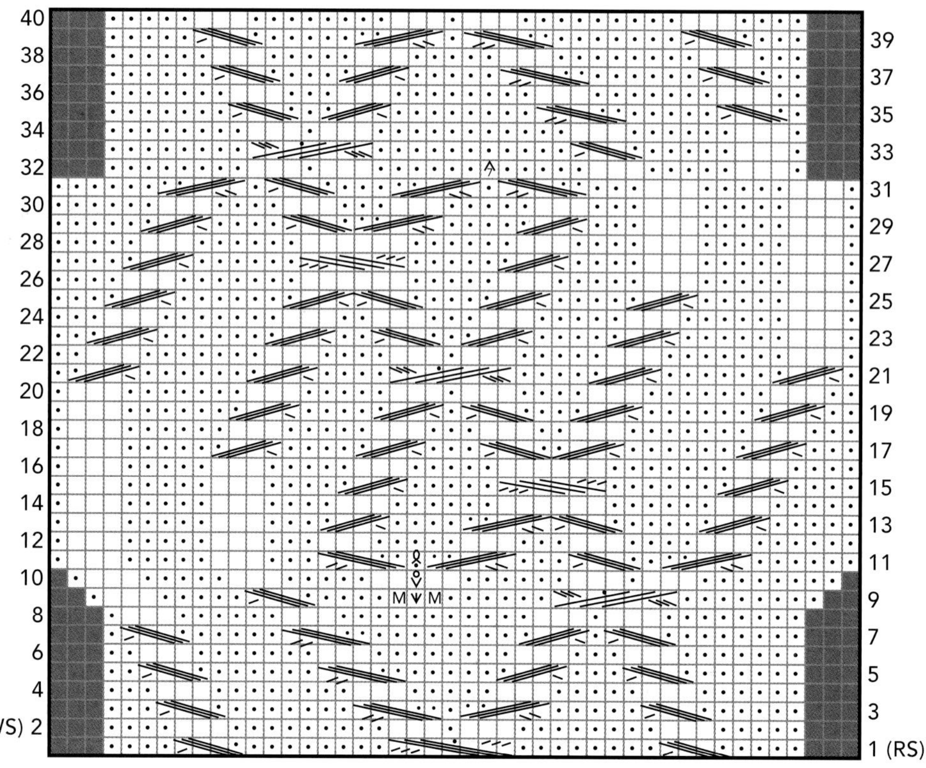

reversible kerry braids 

(multiple of 24 stitches plus 6 stitches)

NOTES

- Always slip stitches purlwise (page 279) unless told otherwise.
- Odd-numbered rows are worked on Side A; even-numbered rows are worked on Side B of this fabric.
- Work Chart A on all odd-numbered rows; work Chart B on all even-numbered rows. Because this pattern results in a reversible fabric, both charts and all symbols are read as right-side rows, from right to left.

Rows 1 and 2: Slip the next 2 sts with the yarn in back, p1, *slip the next 2 sts onto cn #1 and hold in front, slip the next 2 sts onto cn #2 and hold in back, k2 from the left-hand needle, p2 from cn #2, k2 from cn #1, [p2, k2] twice, p2, slip the next 4 sts (2 knit sts and 2 purl sts) onto cn and hold in back, k2 from the left-hand needle, slip the 2 purl sts back onto the left-hand needle and hold the 2 knit sts on the cn in front, p2 from the left-hand needle, k2 from cn, p2; repeat from the * across, ending with k1, p2.

Rows 3 and 4: Slip the next 2 sts with the yarn in back, p1, *k2, p2, slip the next 2 sts onto cn #1 and hold in front, slip the next 2 sts onto cn #2 and hold in back, k2 from the left-hand needle, p2 from cn #2, k2 from cn #1, p2, slip the next 4 sts onto cn and hold in back, k2 from the left-hand needle, slip the 2 purl sts back onto the left-hand needle and hold the 2 knit sts on the cn in front, p2 from the left-hand needle, k2 from cn, p2, k2, p2; repeat from the * across ending with k1, p2.

Rows 5 and 6: Slip the next 2 sts with the yarn in back, p1, *[k2, p2] twice, slip the next 2 sts onto cn #1 and hold in front, slip the next 2 sts onto cn #2 and hold in back, k2 from the left-hand needle, p2 from cn #2, k2 from cn #1, [p2, k2] twice, p2; repeat from the * across, ending with k1, p2.

Repeat Rows 1–6 for the pattern.

Chart A

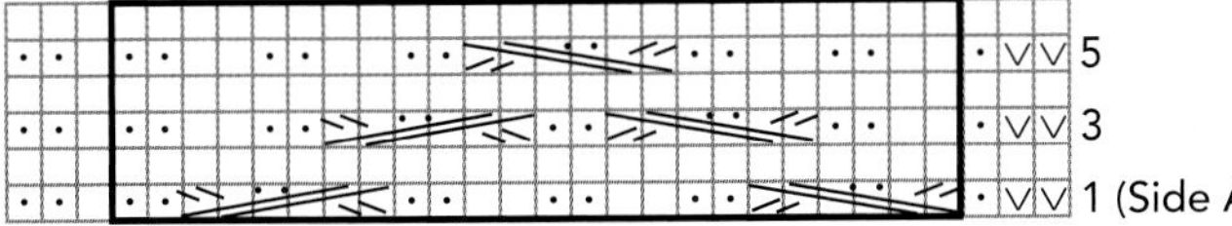

Chart B

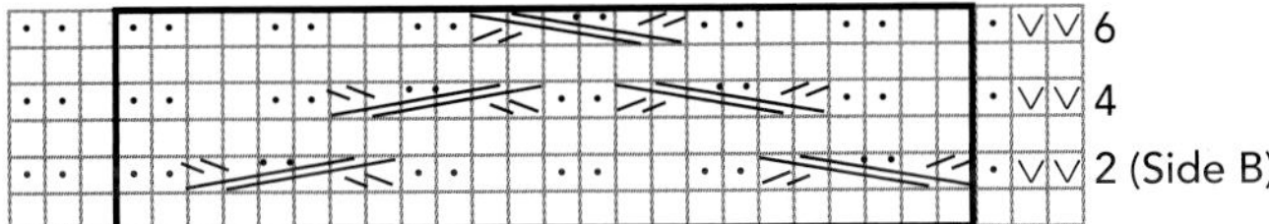

reversible dungourney cables 

(multiple of 24 stitches plus 6 stitches)

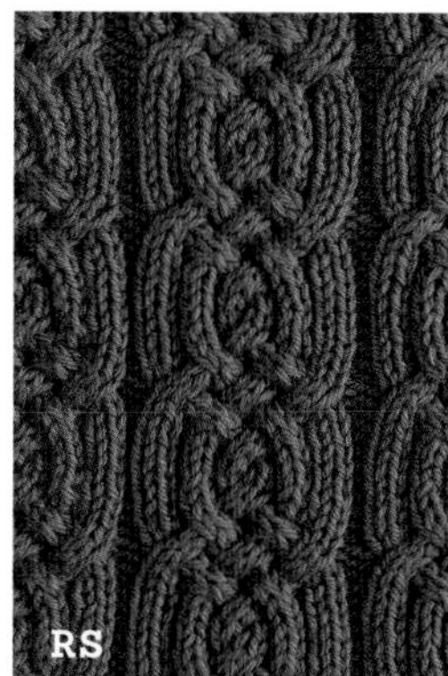

NOTE

- Always slip stitches purlwise (page 279) unless told otherwise.
- Work Chart A on all odd-numbered rows; work Chart B on all even-numbered rows. Because this pattern results in a reversible fabric, both charts and all symbols are read as right-side rows, from right to left.

Rows 1 and 9 (Side A): Slip the next 2 sts with the yarn in back, p1, *[k2, p2] twice, slip the next 4 sts (2 knit sts and 2 purl sts) onto cn and hold in back, k2 from the left-hand needle, slip the 2 purl sts back to the left-hand needle and hold the 2 knit sts on the cn in front, p2 from the left-hand needle, k2 from cn, [p2, k2] twice, p2; repeat from the * across, ending with k1, p2.

Rows 2, 6, and 10: Slip the next 2 sts with the yarn in back, p1, *k2, p2, slip the next 2 sts onto cn #1 and hold in front, slip the next 2 sts onto cn #2 and hold in back, k2 from the left-hand needle, p2 from cn #2, k2 from cn #1, p2; repeat from the * across, ending with k1, p2.

Rows 3 and 7: Slip the next 2 sts with the yarn in back, p1, *k2, p2, [slip the next 2 sts onto cn #1 and hold in front, slip the next 2 sts onto cn #2 and hold in back, k2 from the left-hand needle, p2 from cn #2, k2 from cn #1, p2] twice, k2, p2; repeat from the * across, ending with k1, p2.

Rows 4 and 8: Slip the next 2 sts with the yarn in back, p1, *k2, p2; repeat from the * across, ending with k1, p2.

Row 5: Slip the next 2 sts with the yarn in back, p1, * slip the next 4 sts on cn and hold in back; k2 from the left-hand needle; slip the 2 purl sts back to the left-hand needle, and hold the 2 knit sts on the cn in front; p2 from the left-hand needle; k2 from cn, p2; repeat from the * across, ending with k1, p2.

Rows 11 and 12: Slip the next 2 sts with the yarn in back, p1, *k2, p2; repeat from the * across, ending with k1, p2.

Repeat Rows 1–12 for the pattern.

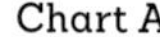

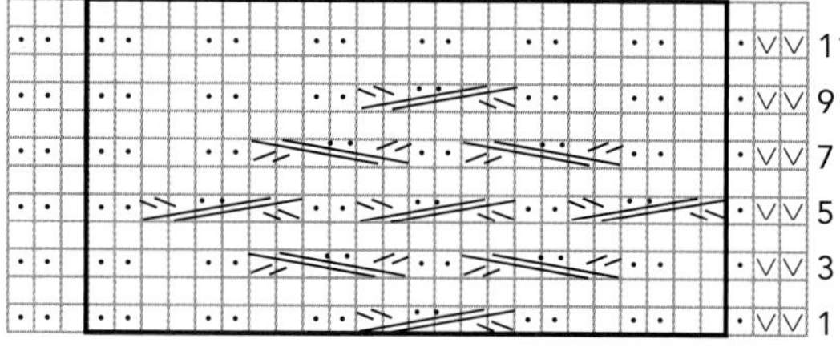

Chart B

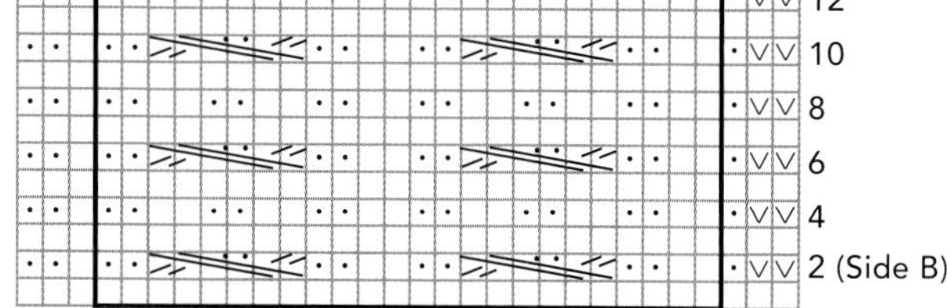

chapter **four**

slip **stitch patterns**

It is amazing how a few simple slipped stitches can affect a knitted fabric. Worked in a solid color, unusual textures result; worked with more than one color, fantastic mosaic effects are possible, even though just one color is used per row. Add cables to the mix, and the design possibilities increase!

slip stitch rib

(multiple of 3 stitches plus 2 stitches)

(WS) 2 1 (RS)

NOTES

- Always slip stitches purlwise (page 279) unless told otherwise.
- When slipping stitches in this pattern, the working yarn will be on the wrong side of the fabric.

Row 1 (RS): *P2, slip the next st with the yarn in back; repeat from the * across, ending with p2.

Row 2: K2, *p1, k2; repeat from the * across.

Repeat Rows 1 and 2 for the pattern.

textured ribbons

(multiple of 6 stitches plus 1 stitch)

NOTES

- Always slip stitches purlwise (page 279) unless told otherwise.
- When slipping stitches in this pattern, the working yarn will be on the wrong side of the fabric.

Rows 1 and 7 (RS): Knit across.

Rows 2 and 8: Purl across.

Rows 3 and 5: *Slip the next st with the yarn in back, p5; repeat from the * across, ending with slip the next st with the yarn in back.

Rows 4 and 6: Slip the next st with the yarn in front, *k5, slip the next st with the yarn in front; repeat from the * across.

Rows 9 and 11: *P3, slip the next st with the yarn in back, p2; repeat from the * across, ending with p1.

Rows 10 and 12: K1, *k2, slip the next st with the yarn in front, k3; repeat from the * across.

Repeat Rows 1–12 for the pattern.

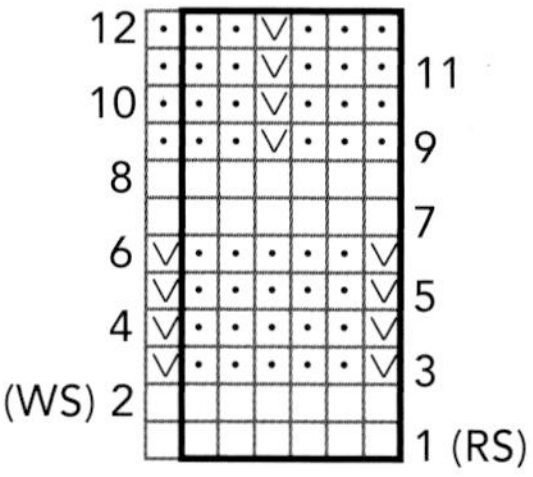

gulls

(multiple of 7 stitches plus 1 stitch)

Row 1 (RS): *K1, slip the next st with the yarn in back, k4, slip the next st with the yarn in back; repeat from the * across, ending with k1.

Row 2: P1, *slip the next st with the yarn in front, p4, slip the next st with the yarn in front, p1; repeat from the * across.

Row 3: *K1, slip the next st onto cn and hold in front, k2, k1 from cn, slip the next 2 sts onto cn and hold in back, k1, k2 from cn; repeat from the * across, ending with k1.

Row 4: Purl across.

Repeat Rows 1–4 for the pattern.

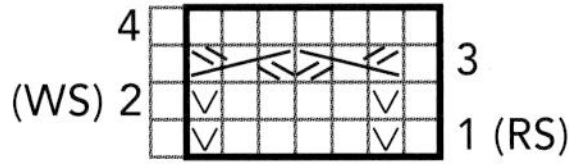

NOTES

- Always slip stitches purlwise (page 279) unless told otherwise.
- When slipping stitches in this pattern, the working yarn will be on the wrong side of the fabric.

tweed rib

(multiple of 2 stitches plus 1 stitch)

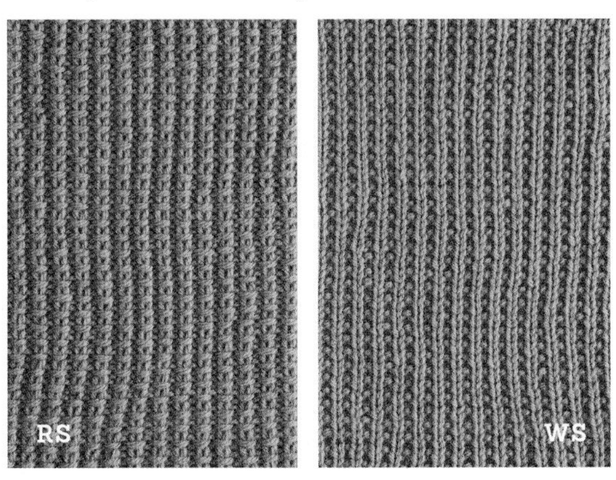

(WS) 2

(WS) Foundation Row

1 (RS)

NOTES

- Always slip stitches purlwise (page 279) unless told otherwise.
- When slipping stitches in this pattern, the working yarn will be on the right side of the fabric.

Foundation Row (WS): K1, *p1, k1; repeat from the * across.

Row 1 (RS): *P1, slip the next st with the yarn in front; repeat from the * across, ending with p1.

Row 2: K1, *p1, k1; repeat from the * across.

Repeat Rows 1 and 2 for the pattern.

drifting sand

(multiple of 4 stitches plus 5 stitches)

NOTES

- Always slip stitches purlwise (page 279) unless told otherwise.
- When slipping stitches in this pattern, the working yarn will be on the wrong side of the fabric.

Row 1 (RS): K1, slip the next st with the yarn in back, *k3, slip the next st with the yarn in back; repeat from the * across, ending with k3.

Row 2: P3, *slip the next st with the yarn in front, p3; repeat from the * across, ending with slip the next st with the yarn in front, p1.

Row 3: K1, *slip the next st onto cn and hold in front, k2, k1 from cn, k1; repeat from the * across.

Row 4: Purl across.

Row 5: K2, *k3, slip the next st with the yarn in back; repeat from the * across, ending with k3.

Row 6: P3, *slip the next st with the yarn in front, p3; repeat from the * across, ending with p2.

Row 7: K2, *k1, slip the next 2 sts onto cn and hold in back, k1, k2 from cn; repeat from the * across, ending with k3.

Row 8: As Row 4.

Repeat Rows 1–8 for the pattern.

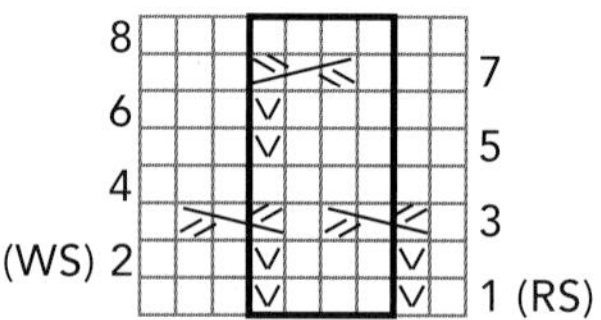

waffle pattern

(multiple of 3 stitches plus 2 stitches)

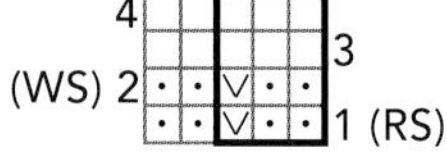

NOTES

- Always slip stitches purlwise (page 279) unless told otherwise.
- When slipping stitches in this pattern, the working yarn will be on the wrong side of the fabric.

Row 1 (RS): *P2, slip the next st with the yarn in back; repeat from the * across, ending with p2.

Row 2: K2, *slip the next st with the yarn in front, k2; repeat from the * across.

Row 3: Knit across.

Row 4: Purl across.

Repeat Rows 1–4 for the pattern.

slip stitch cables

(multiple of 12 stitches plus 8 stitches)

NOTES

- Always slip stitches purlwise (page 279) unless told otherwise.
- When slipping stitches in this pattern, the working yarn will be on the wrong side of the fabric.

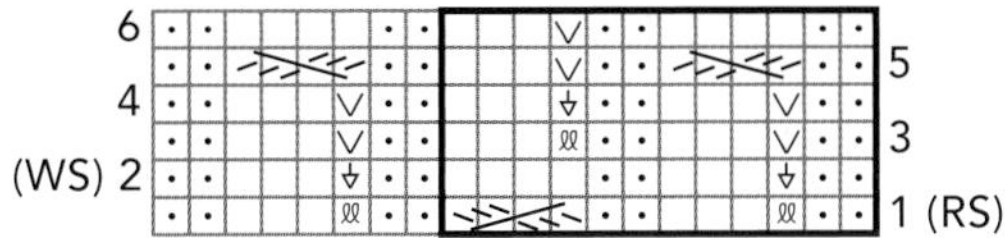

Row 1 (RS): *P2, 2X elongated knit st (page 274), k3, p2, slip the next 3 sts onto cn and hold in back, k1, k3 from cn; repeat from the * across, ending with p2, 2X elongated st, k3, p2.

Row 2: K2, p3, purl the next st, allowing the extra loop to drop, k2, *p4, k2, p3, purl the next st, allowing the extra loop to drop, k2; repeat from the * across.

Row 3: *P2, slip the next st with the yarn in back, k3, p2, 2X elongated knit st, k3; repeat from the * across, ending with p2, slip the next st with the yarn in back, k3, p2.

Row 4: K2, p3, slip the next st with the yarn in front, k2, *p3, purl the next st, allowing the extra loop to drop, k2, p3, slip the next st with the yarn in front, k2; repeat from the * across.

Row 5: *P2, slip the next st onto cn and hold in front, k3, k1 from cn, p2, slip the next st with the yarn in back, k3; repeat from the * across, ending with p2, slip the next st onto cn and hold in front, k3, k1 from cn, p2.

Row 6: K2, p4, k2, *p3, slip the next st with the yarn in front, k2, p4, k2; repeat from the * across.

Repeat Rows 1–6 for the pattern.

woolen stitch

(multiple of 4 stitches)

4
3
(WS) 2
1 (RS)

NOTES

- Always slip stitches purlwise (page 279) unless told otherwise.
- When slipping stitches in this pattern, the working yarn will be on the wrong side of the fabric.

Row 1 (RS): *K2, slip the next 2 sts with the yarn in back; repeat from the * across.

Row 2: *P2, k2; repeat from the * across.

Row 3: *K1, slip the next 2 sts with the yarn in back, k1; repeat from the * across.

Row 4: *K2, p2; repeat from the * across.

Repeat Rows 1–4 for the pattern.

dotted stripes

(multiple of 4 stitches plus 3 stitches)

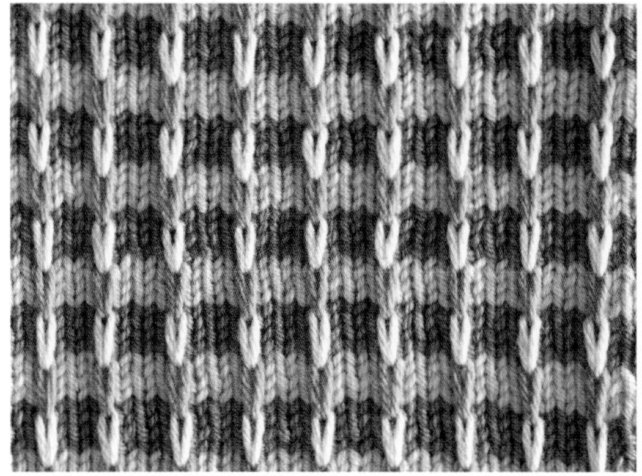

NOTES

- Always slip stitches purlwise (page 279) unless told otherwise.
- When slipping stitches in this pattern, the working yarn will be on the wrong side of the fabric.

Foundation Row (WS): With A, purl across.

Rows 1 and 3 (RS): With B, *k3, slip the next st with the yarn in back; repeat from the * across, ending with k3.

Row 2: With B, p3, *slip the next st with the yarn in front, p3; repeat from the * across.

Row 4: With B, purl across.

Rows 5 and 7: With A, *k3, slip the next st with the yarn in back; repeat from the * across, ending with k3.

Row 6: With A, p3,*slip the next st with the yarn in front, p3; repeat from the * across.

Row 8: With A, purl across.

Repeat Rows 1–8 for the pattern.

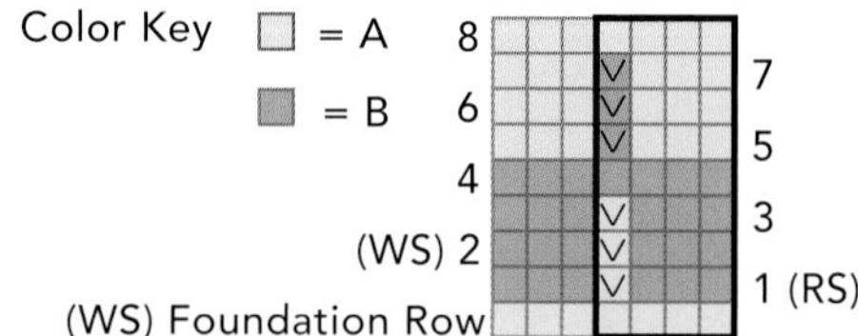

serrated ribs

(multiple of 3 stitches)

NOTES

- Always slip stitches purlwise (page 279) unless told otherwise.
- When slipping stitches in this pattern, the working yarn will be on the wrong side of the fabric.

Row 1 (RS): Knit across.

Row 2: *Slip the next st with the yarn in front, p1, k1; repeat from the * across.

Row3: *Slip the next st onto cn and hold in back, k2, k1 from cn; repeat from the * across.

Row 4: *P1, slip the next st with the yarn in front, k1; repeat from the * across.

Row 5: *P1, left twist (page 276); repeat from the * across.

Row 6: Purl across.

Repeat Rows 1–6 for the pattern.

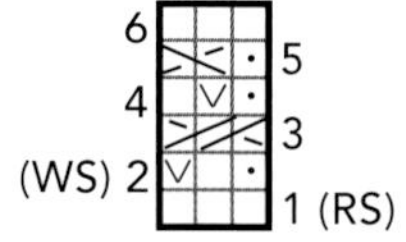

elm tweed

(multiple of 4 stitches plus 2 stitches)

NOTES

- Always slip stitches purlwise (page 279) unless told otherwise.
- When slipping stitches in this pattern, the working yarn will be on the wrong side of the fabric.

Foundation Row (WS): With C, purl across.

Row 1 (RS): With A, k1, *slip the next 2 sts with the yarn in back, k2; repeat from the * across, ending with k1.

Row 2: With A, p1, *p2, left twist (page 276); repeat from the * across, ending with p1.

Row 3: With B, k1, *k2, slip the next 2 sts with the yarn in back; repeat from the * across, ending with k1.

Row 4: With B, p1, left twist, p2; repeat from the * across, ending with p1.

Rows 5 and 6: With C, as Rows 1 and 2.

Rows 7 and 8: With A, as Rows 3 and 4.

Rows 9 and 10: With B, as Rows 1 and 2.

Rows 11 and 12: With C, as Rows 3 and 4.

Repeat Rows 1–12 for the pattern.

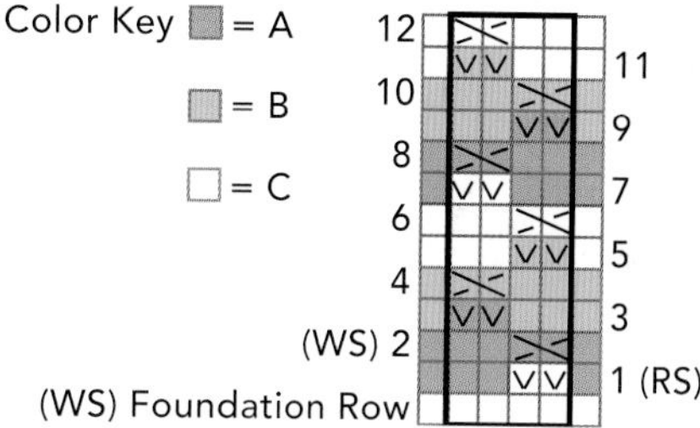

garden paths

(multiple of 6 stitches plus 5 stitches)

Row 1 (RS): With A, knit across.

Row 2: With A, knit across.

Row 3: With B, k1, *k3, slip the next st with the yarn in back, k1, slip the next st with the yarn in back; repeat from the * across, ending with k4.

Row 4: With B, p4, *slip the next st with the yarn in front, k1, slip the next st with the yarn in front, p3; repeat from the * across, ending with p1.

Rows 5 and 6: With A, knit across.

Row 7: With B, k1, *slip the next st with the yarn in back, k1, slip the next st with the yarn in back, k3; repeat from the * across, ending with [slip the next st with the yarn in back, k1] twice.

Row 8: With B, p1, slip the next st with the yarn in front, k1, slip the next st with the yarn in front, *p3, slip the next st with the yarn in front, k1, slip the next st with the yarn in front; repeat from the * across, ending with p1.

Repeat Rows 1–8 for the pattern.

NOTES

- Always slip stitches purlwise (page 279) unless told otherwise.
- When slipping stitches in this pattern, the working yarn will be on the wrong side of the fabric.

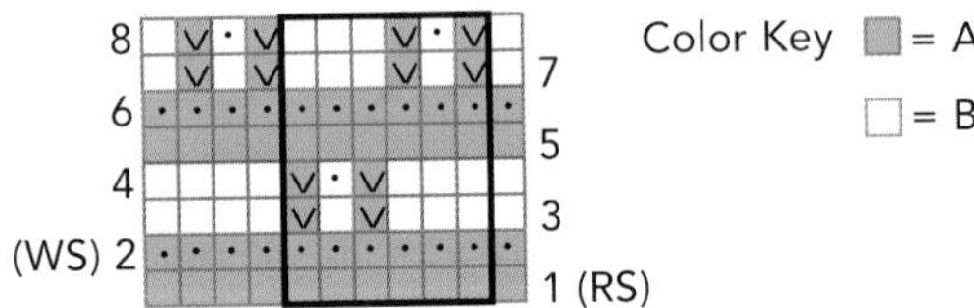

blazing stripes

(multiple of 6 stitches plus 2 stitches)

NOTES

- Always slip stitches purlwise (page 279) unless told otherwise.
- When slipping stitches in this pattern, the working yarn will be on the wrong side of the fabric.

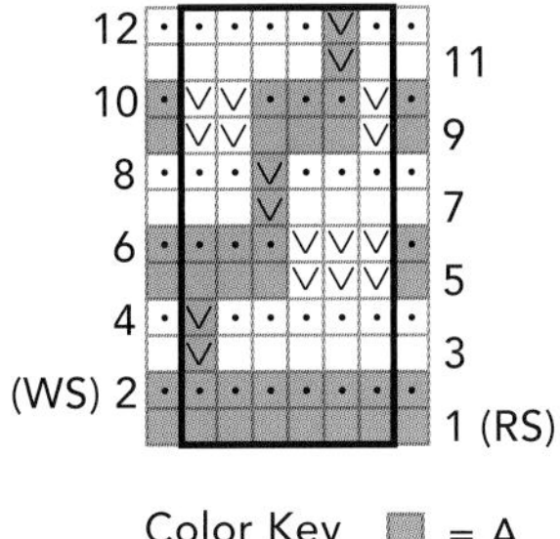

Color Key ■ = A

□ = B

Row 1 (RS): With A, knit across.

Row 2: With A, knit across.

Row 3: With B, k1, *k5, slip the next st with the yarn in back; repeat from the * across, ending with k1.

Row 4: With B, k1, *slip the next st with the yarn in front, k5; repeat from the * across, ending with k1.

Row 5: With A, k1, *slip the next 3 sts with the yarn in back, k3; repeat from the * across, ending with k1.

Row 6: With A, k1, *k3, slip the next 3 sts with the yarn in front; repeat from the * across, ending with k1.

Row 7: With B, k1, *k3, slip the next st with the yarn in back, k2; repeat from the * across, ending with k1.

Row 8: With B, k1, *k2, slip the next st with the yarn in front, k3; repeat from the * across, ending with k1.

Row 9: With A, k1, *slip the next st with the yarn in back, k3, slip the next 2 sts with the yarn in back; repeat from the * across, ending with k1.

Row 10: With A, k1, *slip the next 2 sts with the yarn in front, k3, slip the next st with the yarn in front; repeat from the * across, ending with k1.

Row 11: With B, k1, *k1, slip the next st with the yarn in back, k4; repeat from the * across, ending with k1.

Row 12: With B, k1, *k4, slip the next st with the yarn in front, k1; repeat from the * across, ending with k1.

Repeat Rows 1–12 for the pattern.

bargello pattern

(multiple of 4 stitches plus 1 stitch)

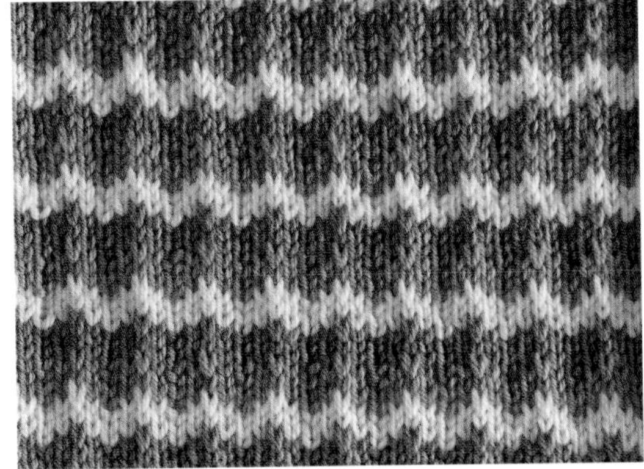

Row 1 (RS): With A, knit across.

Row 2: With A, purl across.

Row 3: With B, *k1, slip the next 3 sts with the yarn in back; repeat from the * across, ending with k1.

Row 4: With B, p1, *p1, slip the next st with the yarn in front, p2; repeat from the * across.

Rows 5 and 6: With B, as Rows 1 and 2.

Rows 7–10: With C, as Rows 3–6.

Rows 11 and 12: With A, as Rows 3 and 4.

Repeat Rows 1–12 for the pattern.

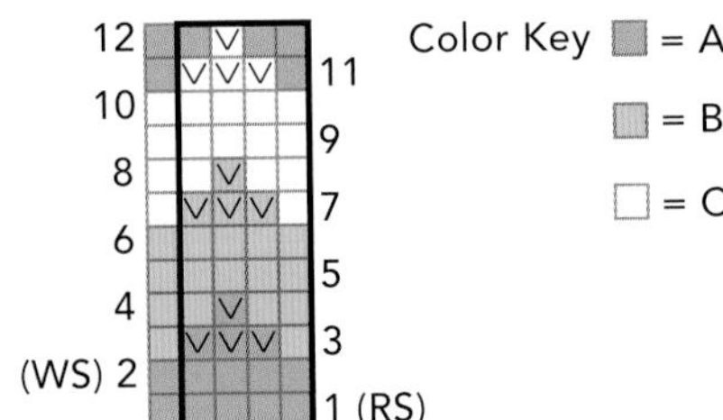

NOTES

- Always slip stitches purlwise (page 279) unless told otherwise.
- When slipping stitches in this pattern, the working yarn will be on the wrong side of the fabric.

roof tiles

(multiple of 7 stitches plus 1 stitch)

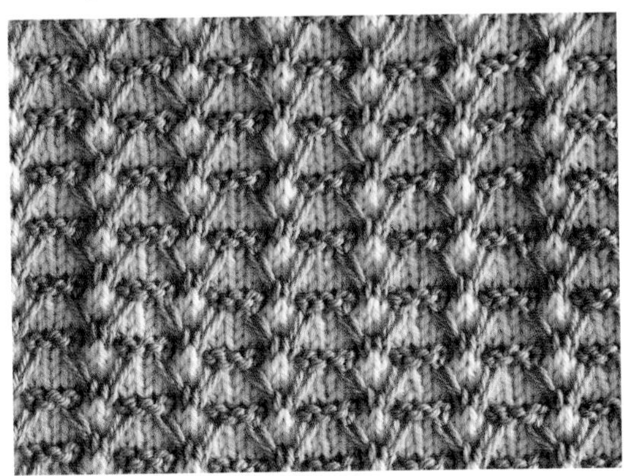

Foundation Row (WS): With A, knit across.

Rows 1 and 3 (RS): With B, *k3, slip the next 2 sts with the yarn in back, k2; repeat from the * across, ending with k1.

Rows 2 and 4: With B, p1,*p2, slip the next 2 sts with the yarn in front, p3; repeat from the * across.

Row 5: With A, *k1, slip the next 2 sts onto cn and hold in back, k1, k2 from cn, slip the next st onto cn and hold in front, k2, k1 from cn; repeat from the * across, ending with k1.

Row 6: With A, k1,*k2, p2, k3; repeat from the * across.

Repeat Rows 1–6 for the pattern.

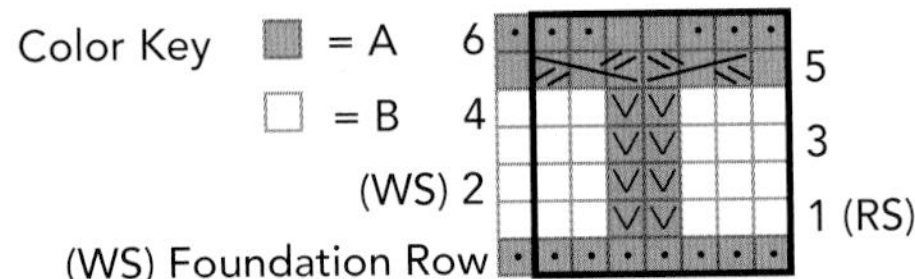

NOTES

- Always slip stitches purlwise (page 279) unless told otherwise.
- When slipping stitches in this pattern, the working yarn will be on the wrong side of the fabric.

perpendicular tiles

(multiple of 8 stitches plus 7 stitches)

NOTES

- Always slip stitches purlwise (page 279) unless told otherwise.
- When slipping stitches in this pattern, the working yarn will be on the wrong side of the fabric.

Foundation Row: With B, purl across.

Rows 1 and 5 (RS): With A, k1, *[slip the next st with the yarn in back, k1] twice, slip the next st with the yarn in back, k3; repeat from the * across, ending with [slip the next st with the yarn in back, k1] 3 times.

Rows 2 and 6: With A, [p1, slip the next st with the yarn in front] 3 times, *k3 [slip the next st with the yarn in front, p1] twice, slip the next st with the yarn in front; repeat from the * across, ending with p1.

Row 3: With B, k1, *[k1, slip the next st with the yarn in back] twice, k4; repeat from the * across, ending with [k1, slip the next st with the yarn in back] twice, k2.

Row 4: With B, p2, [slip the next st with the yarn in front, p1] twice, *p4, [slip the next st with the yarn in front, p1] twice; repeat from the * across, ending with p1.

Rows 7 and 15: With B, knit across.

Row 8: With B, purl across.

Rows 9 and 13: With A, k1, *slip the next st with the yarn in back, k3, [slip the next st with the yarn in back, k1] twice; repeat from the * across, ending with slip the next st with the yarn in back, k3, slip the next st with the yarn in back, k1.

Rows 10 and 14: With A, p1, slip the next st with the yarn in front, k3, slip the next st with the yarn in front, *[p1, slip the next st with the yarn in front] twice, k3, slip the next st with the yarn in front; repeat from the * across, ending with p1.

Row 11: With B, k1, *k5, slip the next st with the yarn in back, k1, slip the next st with the yarn in back; repeat from the * across, ending with k6.

Row 12: With B, p6, *slip the next st with the yarn in front, p1, slip the next st with the yarn in front, p5; repeat from the * across, ending with p1.

Row 16: With B, as Row 8.

Repeat Rows 1–16 for the pattern.

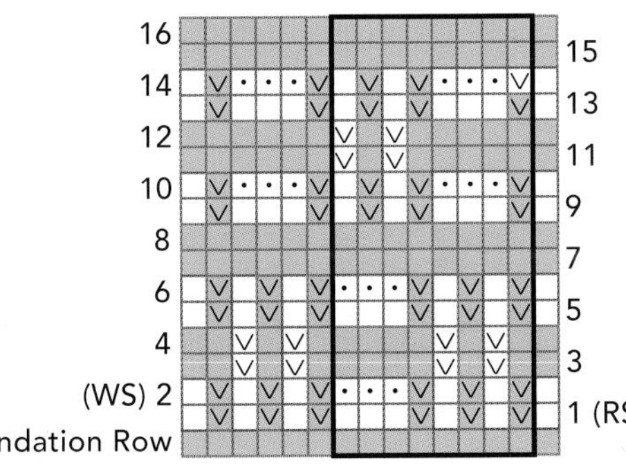

Color Key
□ = A
■ = B

moroccan tiles

(multiple of 16 stitches plus 1 stitch)

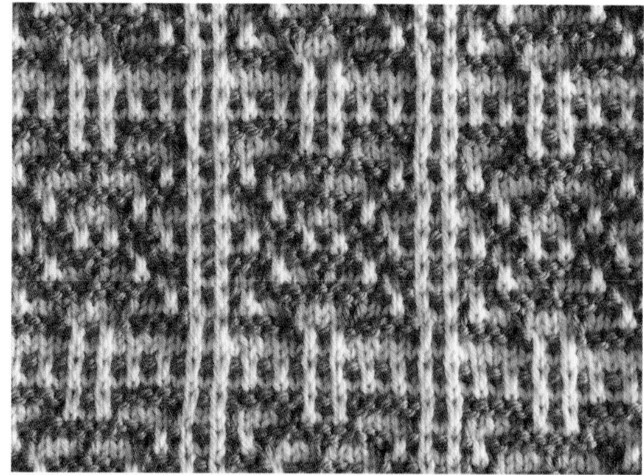

NOTES

- Always slip stitches purlwise (page 279) unless told otherwise.
- When slipping stitches in this pattern, the working yarn will be on the wrong side of the fabric.

Foundation Row (WS): With A, purl across.

Row 1 (RS): With B, *k1, slip the next st with the yarn in back; repeat from the * across, ending with k1.

Row 2: With B, k1, *slip the next st with the yarn in front, k1; repeat from the * across.

Rows 3 and 31: With A, knit across.

Row 4: With A, purl across.

Rows 5 and 29: With B, *[k1, slip the next st with the yarn in back, k5, slip the next st with the yarn in back] twice; repeat from the * across, ending with k1.

Rows 6 and 30: With B, k1, *[slip the next st with the yarn in front, k5, slip the next st with the yarn in front, k1] twice; repeat from the * across.

Rows 7 and 27: With A, *k2, slip the next st with the yarn in back, [k3, slip the next st with the yarn in back] 3 times, k1; repeat from the * across, ending with k1.

Rows 8 and 28: With A, p1,*p1, slip the next st with the yarn in front, [p3, slip the next st with the yarn in front] 3 times, p2; repeat from the * across.

Rows 9 and 25: With B, *[k1, slip the next st with the yarn in back] twice, k9, slip the next st with the yarn in back, k1, slip the next st with the yarn in back; repeat from the * across, ending with k1.

Rows 10 and 26: With B, k1, *slip the next st with the yarn in front, k1, slip the next st with the yarn in front, k9, [slip the next st with the yarn in front, k1] twice; repeat from the * across.

Rows 11 and 23: With A, *k2, slip the next st with the yarn in back, k1, [slip the next st with the yarn in back, k3] twice, [slip the next st with the yarn in back, k1] twice; repeat from the * across, ending with k1.

Rows 12 and 24: With A, p1,*[p1, slip the next st with the yarn in front] twice, [p3, slip the next st with the yarn in front] twice, p1, slip the next st with the yarn in front, p2; repeat from the * across.

Rows 13 and 21: With B, *k1, slip the next st with the yarn in back, k3, slip the next st with the yarn in back, k5, slip the next st with the yarn in back, k3, slip the next st with the yarn in back; repeat from the * across, ending with k1.

Rows 14 and 22: With B, k1, *slip the next st with the yarn in front, k3, slip the next st with the yarn in front, k5, slip the next st with the yarn in front, k3, slip the next st with the yarn in front, k1; repeat from the * across.

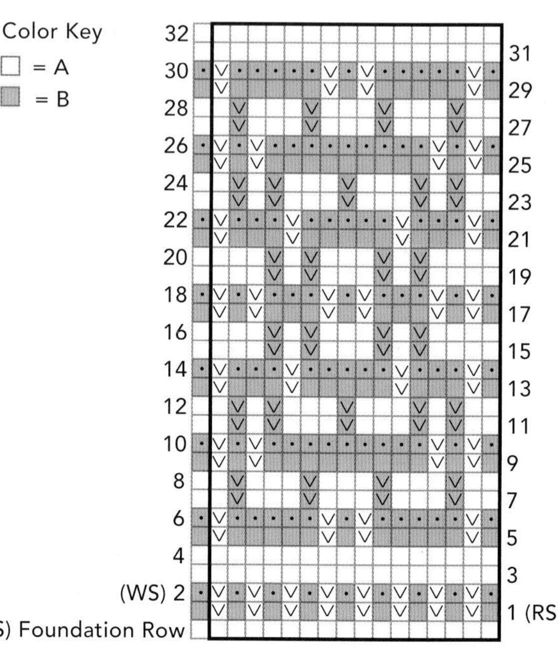

Rows 15 and 19: With A,*k4, [slip the next st with the yarn in back, k1, slip the next st with the yarn in back, k3] twice; repeat from the * across, ending with k1.

Rows 16 and 20: With A, p1, *[p3, slip the next st with the yarn in front, p1, slip the next st with the yarn in front] twice, p4; repeat from the * across.

Row 17: With B, *[k1, slip the next st with the yarn in back] twice, [k3, slip the next st with the yarn in back, k1, slip the next st with the yarn in back] twice; repeat from the * across, ending with k1.

Row 18: With B, k1, *[slip the next st with the yarn in front, k1, slip the next st with the yarn in front, k3] twice, [slip the next st with the yarn in front, k1] twice; repeat from the * across.

Row 32: With A, as Row 4.

Repeat Rows 1–32 for the pattern.

faux fair isle

(multiple of 8 stitches plus 3 stitches)

NOTES

- Always slip stitches purlwise (page 279) unless told otherwise.
- When slipping stitches in this pattern, the working yarn will be on the wrong side of the fabric.

Row 1 (RS): With B, knit across.

Row 2: With B, purl across.

Row 3: With A, k1, *slip the next st with the yarn in back, k2, slip the next 3 sts with the yarn in back, k2; repeat from the * across, ending with slip the next st with the yarn in back, k1.

Row 4: With A, p1, slip the next st with the yarn in front, *p2, slip the next 3 sts with the yarn in front, p2, slip the next st with the yarn in front; repeat from the * across, ending with, p1.

Row 5: With B, k1, *k1, slip the next 2 sts with the yarn in back, k3, slip the next 2 sts with the yarn in back; repeat from the * across, ending with k2.

Row 6: With B, p2, *slip the next 2 sts with the yarn in front, p3, slip the next 2 sts with the yarn in front, p1; repeat from the * across, ending with p1.

Row 7: With A, k1, *k3, slip the next st with the yarn in back, k1, slip the next st with the yarn in back, k2; repeat from the * across, ending with k2.

Row 8: With A, p2, *p2, slip the next st with the yarn in front, p1, slip the next st with the yarn in front, p3; repeat from the * across, ending with p1.

Row 9: With B, k1, *slip the next st with the yarn in back, k3; repeat from the * across, ending with slip the next st with the yarn in back, k1.

Row 10: With B, p1, slip the next st with the yarn in front, *p3, slip the next st with the yarn in front; repeat from the * across, ending with p1.

Row 11: With A, k1, *k1, slip the next 2 sts with the yarn in back, k3, slip the next 2 sts with the yarn in back; repeat from the * across, ending with k2.

Row 12: With A, p2, *slip the next 2 sts with the yarn in front, p3, slip the next 2 sts with the yarn in front, p1; repeat from the * across, ending with p1.

Row 13: With B, k1, *slip the next st with the yarn in back, k3; repeat from the * across, ending with slip the next st with the yarn in back, k1.

(continued on next page)

Row 14: With B, p1, slip the next st with the yarn in front, *p3, slip the next st with the yarn in front; repeat from the * across, ending with p1.

Row 15: With A, k1, *k3, slip the next st with the yarn in back, k1, slip the next st with the yarn in back, k2; repeat from the * across, ending with k2.

Row 16: With A, p2, *p2, slip the next st with the yarn in front, p1, slip the next st with the yarn in front, p3; repeat from the * across, ending with p1.

Row 17: With B, k1, *k1, slip the next 2 sts with the yarn in back, k3, slip the next 2 sts with the yarn in back; repeat from the * across, ending with k2.

Row 18: With B, p2, *slip the next 2 sts with the yarn in front, p3, slip the next 2 sts with the yarn in front, p1; repeat from the * across, ending with p1.

Row 19: With A, k1, *slip the next st with the yarn in back, k2, slip the next 3 sts with the yarn in back, k2; repeat from the * across, ending with slip the next st with the yarn in back, k1.

Row 20: With A, p1, slip the next st with the yarn in front, *p2, slip the next 3 sts with the yarn in front, p2, slip the next st with the yarn in front; repeat from the * across, ending with p1.

Row 21 and 22: With B, as Rows 1 and 2.

Row 23: With A, k1, *slip the next 2 sts with the yarn in back, [k2, slip the next st with the yarn in back] twice; repeat from the * across, ending with slip the next st with the yarn in back, k1.

Row 24: With A, p1, slip the next st with the yarn in front, *[slip the next st with yarn in front, p2] twice, slip the next 2 sts with the yarn in front; repeat from the * across, ending with p1.

Row 25: With B, k1, *k2, slip the next 2 sts with the yarn in back, k1, slip the next 2 sts with the yarn in back, k1; repeat from the * across, ending with k2.

Row 26: With B, p2, *[p1, slip the next 2 sts with the yarn in front] twice, p2; repeat from the * across, ending with p1.

Row 27: With A, k1, *k1, slip the next st with the yarn in back, k5, slip the next st with the yarn in back; repeat from the * across, ending with k2.

Row 28: With A, p2, *slip the next st with the yarn in front, p5, slip the next st with the yarn in front, p1; repeat from the * across, ending with p1.

Row 29: With B, k1, *slip the next st with the yarn in back, k3; repeat from the * across, ending with slip the next st with the yarn in back, k1.

Row 30: With B, p1, slip the next st with the yarn in front, *p3, slip the next st with the yarn in front; repeat from the * across, ending with p1.

Row 31: With A, k1, *k2, slip the next 2 sts with the yarn in back, k1, slip the next 2 sts with the yarn in back, k1; repeat from the * across, ending with k2.

Row 32: With A, p2, *[p1, slip the next 2 sts with the yarn in front] twice, p2; repeat from the * across, ending with p1.

Rows 33 and 34: With B, as Rows 13 and 14.

Rows 35 and 36: With A, as Rows 27 and 28.

Rows 37 and 38: With B, as Rows 25 and 26.

Rows 39 and 40: With A, as Rows 23 and 24.

Repeat Rows 1–40 for the pattern.

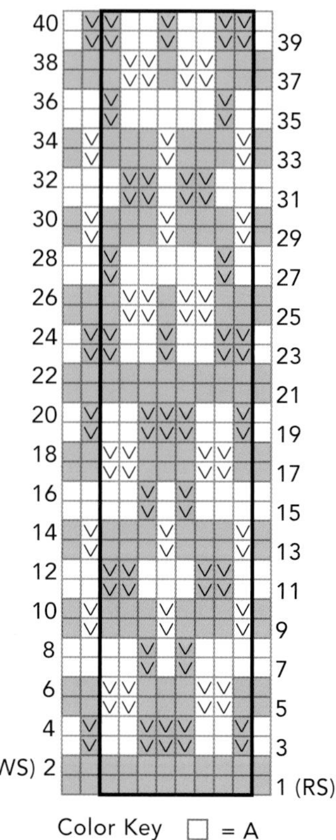

Color Key □ = A
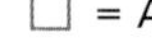 = B

byzantine mosaic

(multiple of 10 stitches plus 3 stitches)

NOTES

- Always slip stitches purlwise (page 279) unless told otherwise.
- When slipping stitches in this pattern, the working yarn will be on the wrong side of the fabric.

Foundation Row (WS): With A, knit across.

Rows 1 and 17 (RS): With B, k1, *slip the next st with the yarn in back, k9; repeat from the * across, ending with slip the next st with the yarn in back, k1.

Rows 2 and 18: With B, k1, slip the next st with the yarn in front, *k9, slip the next st with the yarn in front; repeat from the * across, ending with k1.

Rows 3 and 15: With A, k1, *[k1, slip the next st with the yarn in back] twice, k3, slip the next st with the yarn in back, k1, slip the next st with the yarn in back; repeat from the * across, ending with k2.

Rows 4 and 16: With A, k2, *slip the next st with the yarn in front, k1, slip the next st with the yarn in front, k3, [slip the next st with the yarn in front, k1] twice; repeat from the * across, ending with k1.

Rows 5 and 13: With B, k1, *slip the next st with the yarn in back, k3, slip the next st with the yarn in back, k1, slip the next st with the yarn in back, k3; repeat from the * across, ending with slip the next st with the yarn in back, k1.

Rows 6 and 14: With B, k1, slip the next st with the yarn in front, *k3, slip the next st with the yarn in front, k1, slip the next st with the yarn in front, k3, slip the next st with the yarn in front; repeat from the * across, ending with k1.

Rows 7 and 11: With A, k1, *k1, [slip the next st with the yarn in back, k3] twice, slip the next st with the yarn in back; repeat from the * across, ending with k2.

Rows 8 and 12: With A, k2, *[slip the next st with the yarn in front, k3] twice, slip the next st with the yarn in front, k1; repeat from the * across, ending with k1.

Row 9: With B, k1, *slip the next st with the yarn in back, k1, slip the next st with the yarn in back, k5, slip the next st with the yarn in back, k1; repeat from the * across, ending with slip the next st with the yarn in back, k1.

Row 10: With B, k1, slip the next st with the yarn in front, *k1, slip the next st with the yarn in front, k5, slip the next st with the yarn in front, k1, slip the next st with the yarn in front; repeat from the * across, ending with k1.

Row 19: With A, knit across.

Row 20: With A, as Row 19.

Repeat Rows 1–20 for the pattern.

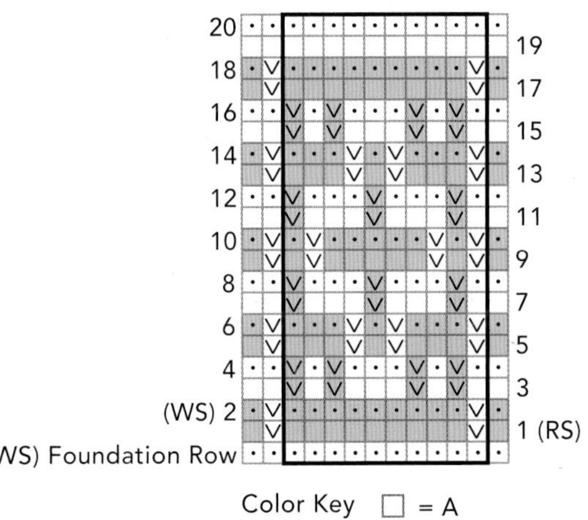

woven stripes

(multiple of 10 stitches plus 2 stitches)

NOTES

- Always slip stitches purlwise (page 279) unless told otherwise.
- When slipping stitches in this pattern, the working yarn will be on the right side of the fabric.

Rows 1, 11, and 19 (RS): K1, *k2, slip the next 3 sts with the yarn in front; repeat from the * across, ending with k1.

Rows 2, 10, 18, and 20: P1, *p1, slip the next 3 sts with the yarn in back, p1; repeat from the * across, ending with p1.

Rows 3, 9, 17, and 21: K1, *slip the next 3 sts with the yarn in front, k2; repeat from the * across, ending with k1.

Rows 4, 8, 16, and 22: P1, *slip the next st with the yarn in back, p2, slip the next 3 sts with the yarn in back, p2, slip the next 2 sts with the yarn in back; repeat from the * across, ending p1.

Rows 5, 7, 15, and 23: K1, *slip the next st with the yarn in front, k2, slip the next 3 sts with the yarn in front, k2, slip the next 2 sts with the yarn in front; repeat from the * across, ending with k1.

Rows 6, 14, and 24: P1, *slip the next 3 sts with the yarn in back, p2; repeat from the * across, ending with p1.

Row 12: Purl across.

Rows 13 and 25: Knit across.

Row 26: As Row 12.

Repeat Rows 1–26 for the pattern.

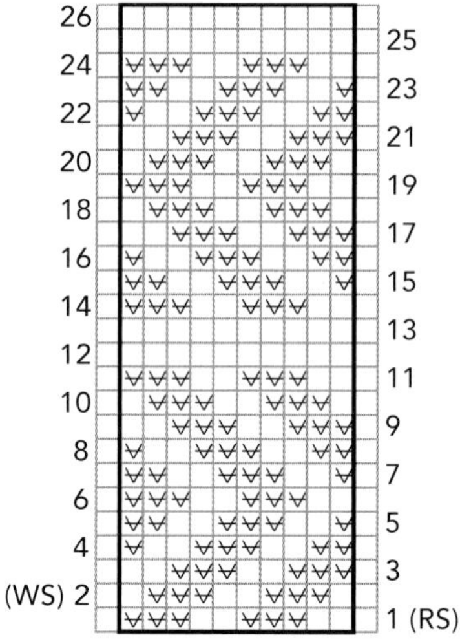

half linen stitch

(multiple of 2 stitches plus 3 stitches)

Foundation Row (WS): With A, purl across.

Row 1 (RS): With B, k1, *k1, slip the next st with the yarn in front; repeat from the * across, ending with k2.

Row 2: With B, purl across.

Row 3: With A, k1, *slip the next st with the yarn in front, k1; repeat from the * across.

Row 4: With A, purl across.

Repeat Rows 1–4 for the pattern.

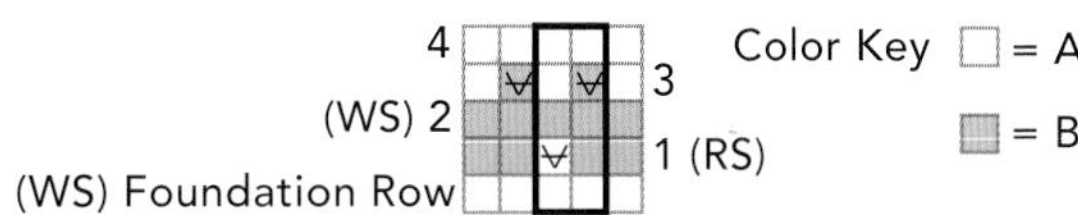

NOTES

- Always slip stitches purlwise (page 279) unless told otherwise.
- When slipping stitches in this pattern, the working yarn will be on the right side of the fabric.

linen stitch 

(multiple of 2 stitches plus 3 stitches)

Foundation Row (WS): With A, purl across.

Row 1 (RS): With B, k1, *k1, slip the next st with the yarn in front; repeat from the * across, ending with k2.

Row 2: With C, *p1, slip the next st with the yarn in back; repeat from the * across, ending with p1.

Row 3: With A, as Row 1.

Row 4: With B, same as Row 2.

Row 5: With C, as Row 1.

Row 6: With A, as Row 2.

Repeat Rows 1–6 for the pattern.

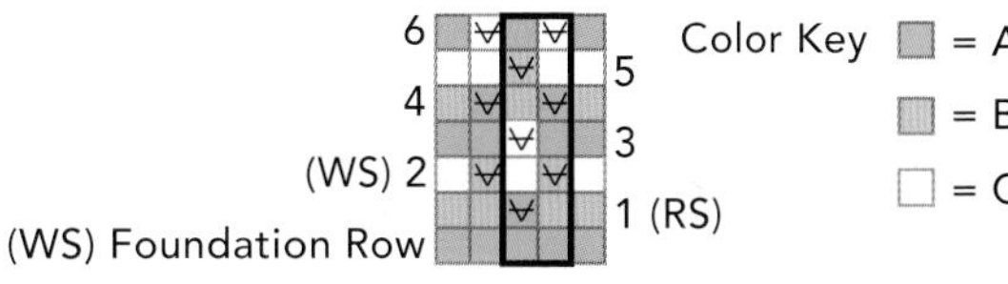

NOTES

- Always slip stitches purlwise (page 279) unless told otherwise.
- When slipping stitches in this pattern, the working yarn will be on the right side of the fabric.

diagonal tweed

(multiple of 6 stitches plus 2 stitches)

Row 1 (RS): K1, *k1, slip the next 3 sts with the yarn in front, k2; repeat from the * across, ending with k1.

Row 2: P1, *p3, slip the next 3 sts with the yarn in back; repeat from the * across, ending with p1.

Row 3: K1, *slip the next 2 sts with the yarn in front, k3, slip the next st with the yarn in front; repeat from the * across, ending with k1.

Row 4: P1, *slip the next 2 sts with the yarn in back, p3, slip the next st with the yarn in back; repeat from the * across, ending with p1.

Row 5: K1, *k3, slip the next 3 sts with the yarn in front; repeat from the * across, ending with k1.

Row 6: P1, *p1, slip the next 3 sts with the yarn in back, p2; repeat from the * across, ending with p1.

Repeat Rows 1–6 for the pattern.

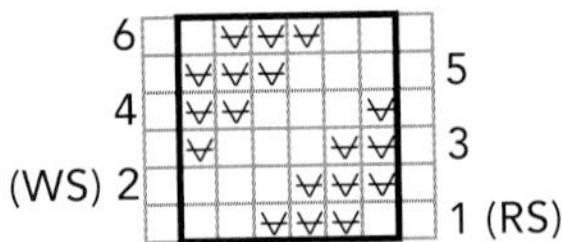

NOTES

- Always slip stitches purlwise (page 279) unless told otherwise.
- When slipping stitches in this pattern, the working yarn will be on the right side of the fabric.

zigzag

(multiple of 6 stitches plus 2 stitches)

Row 1 (RS): K1, *slip the next 2 sts with the yarn in front, k4; repeat from the * across, ending with k1.

Row 2: P1, *p3, slip the next 2 sts with the yarn in back, p1; repeat from the * across, ending with p1.

Rows 3 and 7: K1, *k2, slip the next 2 sts with the yarn in front, k2; repeat from the * across, ending with k1.

Rows 4 and 6: P1, *p1, slip the next 2 sts with the yarn in back, p3; repeat from the * across, ending with p1.

Row 5: K1, *k4, slip the next 2 sts with the yarn in front; repeat from the * across, ending with k1.

Row 8: As Row 2.

Repeat Rows 1–8 for the pattern.

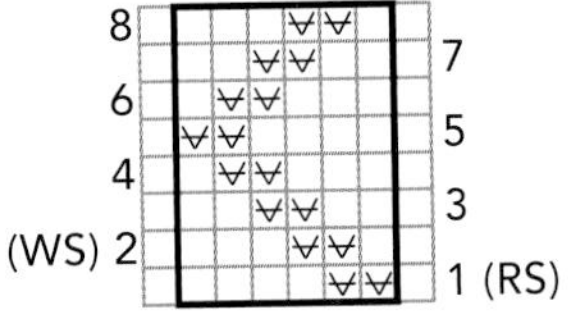

NOTES

- Always slip stitches purlwise (page 279) unless told otherwise.
- When slipping stitches in this pattern, the working yarn will be on the right side of the fabric.

woven relief

(multiple of 8 stitches plus 2 stitches)

NOTES

- Always slip stitches purlwise (page 279) unless told otherwise.
- When slipping stitches in this pattern, the working yarn will be on the right side of the fabric.

Row 1 (RS): K1, *k4, slip the next 4 sts with the yarn in front; repeat from the * across, ending with k1.

Row 2: P1, *p1, slip the next 4 sts with the yarn in back, p3; repeat from the * across, ending with p1.

Row 3: K1, *k2, slip the next 4 sts with the yarn in front, k2; repeat from the * across, ending with k1.

Row 4: P1, *p3, slip the next 4 sts with the yarn in back, p1; repeat from the * across, ending with p1.

Row 5: K1, *slip the next 4 sts with the yarn in front, k4; repeat from the * across, ending with k1.

Row 6: Purl across.

Row 7: K1, *k4, slip the next 4 sts with the yarn in front; repeat from the * across, ending with k1.

Row 8: P1, *slip the next 3 sts with the yarn in back, p4, slip the next st with the yarn in back; repeat from the * across, ending with p1.

Row 9: K1, *slip the next 2 sts with the yarn in front, k4, slip the next 2 sts with the yarn in front; repeat from the * across, ending with k1.

Row 10: P1, *slip the next st with the yarn in back, p4, slip the next 3 sts with the yarn in back; repeat from the * across, ending with p1.

Row 11: K1, *slip the next 4 sts with the yarn in front, k4; repeat from the * across, ending with k1.

Row 12: Purl across.

Repeat Rows 1–12 for the pattern.

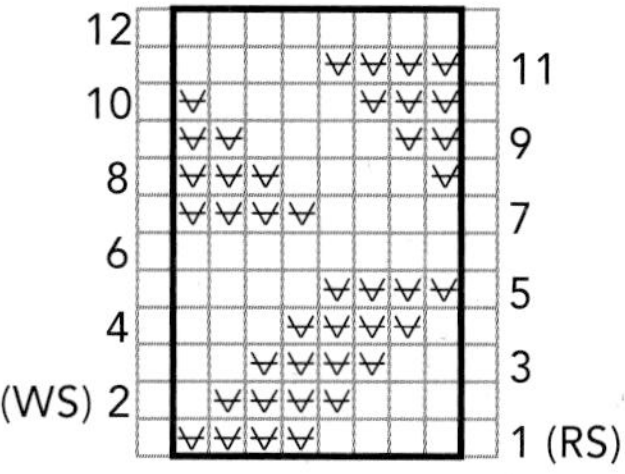

herringbone twill

(multiple of 4 stitches plus 2 stitches)

NOTES

- Always slip stitches purlwise (page 279) unless told otherwise.
- When slipping stitches in this pattern, the working yarn will be on the right side of the fabric.

Rows 1, 5, 9, 15, 19, and 23 (RS): K1, *k2, slip the next 2 sts with the yarn in front; repeat from the * across, ending with k1.

Rows 2, 6, 10, 14, 18, and 22: P1, *p1, slip the next 2 sts with the yarn in back, p1; repeat from the * across, ending with p1.

Rows 3, 7, 11, 13, 17, and 21: K1, *slip the next 2 sts with the yarn in front, k2; repeat from the * across, ending with k1.

Rows 4, 8, 12, 16, 20, and 24: P1, *slip the next st with the yarn in back, p2, slip the next st with the yarn in back; repeat from the * across, ending with p1.

Repeat Rows 1–24 for the pattern.

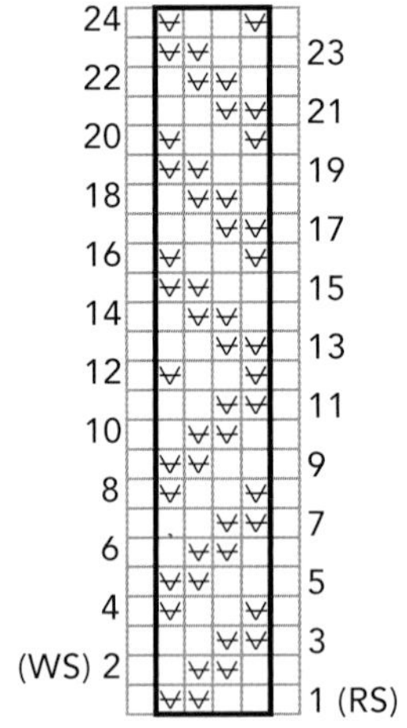

slip stitch bands

(multiple of 2 stitches plus 1 stitch)

NOTES

- Always slip stitches purlwise (page 279) unless told otherwise.
- When slipping stitches in this pattern, the working yarn will be on the right side of the fabric.

Row 1 (RS): Knit across.

Rows 2, 3, 5, and 9: As Row 1.

Row 4: Purl across.

Rows 6 and 8: K1, *slip the next st with the yarn in back, k1; repeat from the * across.

Row 7: *Slip the next st with the yarn in front, p1; repeat from the * across, ending with slip the next st with the yarn in front.

Row 10: As Row 4.

Repeat Rows 1–10 for the pattern.

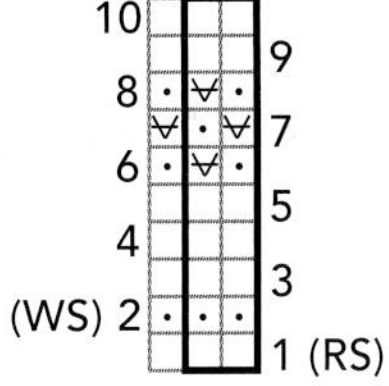

diagonal steps

(multiple of 4 stitches plus 2 stitches)

NOTES

- Always slip stitches purlwise (page 279) unless told otherwise.
- When slipping stitches in this pattern, the working yarn will be on the wrong side of the fabric.

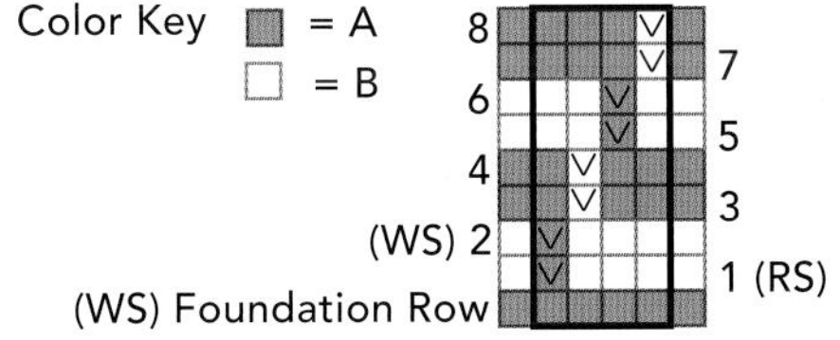

Foundation Row (WS): With A, purl across.

Row 1 (RS): With B, k1, *k3, slip the next st with the yarn in back; repeat from the * across, ending with k1.

Row 2: With B, p1, *slip the next st with the yarn in front, p3; repeat from the * across, ending with p1.

Row 3: With A, k1, *k2, slip the next st with the yarn in back, k1; repeat from the * across, ending with k1.

Row 4: With A, p1, *p1, slip the next st with the yarn in front, p2; repeat from the * across, ending with p1.

Row 5: With B, k1, *k1, slip the next st with the yarn in back, k2; repeat from the * across, ending with k1.

Row 6: With B, p1, *p2, slip the next st with the yarn in front, p1; repeat from the * across, ending with p1.

Row 7: With A, k1, *slip the next st with the yarn in back, k3; repeat from the * across, ending with k1.

Row 8: With A, p1, *p3, slip the next st with the yarn in front; repeat from the * across, ending with p1.

Repeat Rows 1–8 for the pattern.

multicolored tweed

(multiple of 4 stitches plus 1 stitch)

Foundation Row (WS): With C, knit across.

Row 1 (RS): With A, *k1, slip the next st with the yarn in back, k2; repeat from the * across, ending with k1.

Row 2: With A, k1, *k2, slip the next st with the yarn in front, k1; repeat from the * across.

Row 3: With B, *k2, slip the next st with the yarn in back, k1; repeat from the * across, ending with k1.

Row 4: With B, k1, *k1, slip the next st with the yarn in front, k2; repeat from the * across.

Row 5: With C, *k3, slip the next st with the yarn in back; repeat from the * across, ending with k1.

Row 6: With C, k1, *slip the next st with the yarn in front, k3; repeat from the * across.

Repeat Rows 1–6 for the pattern.

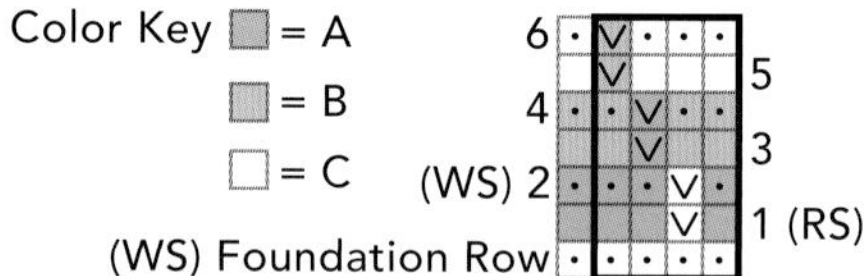

NOTES

- Always slip stitches purlwise (page 279) unless told otherwise.
- When slipping stitches in this pattern, the working yarn will be on the wrong side of the fabric.

simple slipped stripes

(multiple of 2 stitches plus 1 stitch)

Rows 1, 3, and 5 (RS): Knit across.

Rows 2, 4, and 6: Purl across.

Row 7: *P1, slip the next st with the yarn in front; repeat from the * across, ending with p1.

Row 8: Slip the next st with the yarn in back, *k1, slip the next st with the yarn in back; repeat from the * across.

Repeat Rows 1–8 for the pattern.

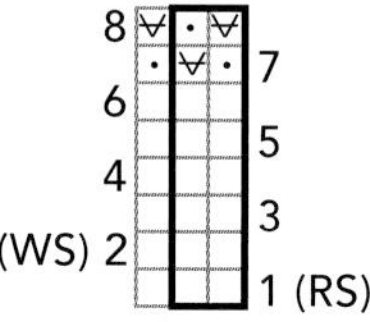

NOTES

- Always slip stitches purlwise (page 279) unless told otherwise.
- When slipping stitches in this pattern, the working yarn will be on the right side of the fabric.

quilted diamonds

easy

(multiple of 6 stitches plus 7 stitches)

NOTES

- Always slip stitches purlwise (page 279) unless told otherwise.
- When slipping stitches in this pattern, the working yarn will be on the right side of the fabric.

Row 1 (RS): K1, *slip the next 5 sts with the yarn in front, k1; repeat from the * across.

Row 2 and all WS rows: Purl across.

Row 3: K3, *insert the right-hand needle under the loose strand 2 rows below and knit the next stitch, catching the strand (page 280), k5; repeat from the * across, ending with insert the right-hand needle under the loose strand 2 rows below and knit the next stitch, catching the strand, k3.

Row 5: K3, *k1, slip the next 5 sts with the yarn in front; repeat from the * across, ending with k4.

Row 7: K3, *k3, insert the right-hand needle under the loose strand 2 rows below and knit the next stitch, catching the strand, k2; repeat from the * across, ending with k4.

Row 8: As Row 2.

Repeat Rows 1–8 for the pattern.

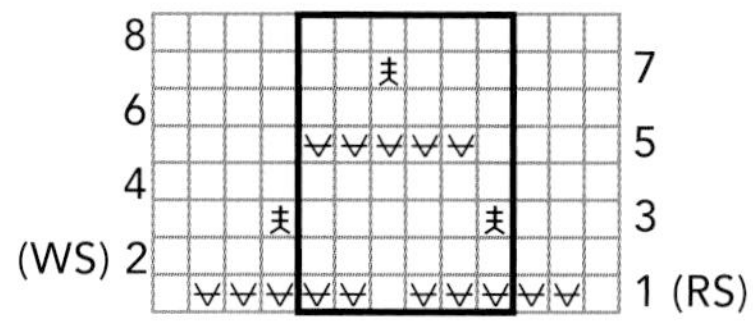

chutes and ladders

(multiple of 6 stitches plus 4 stitches)

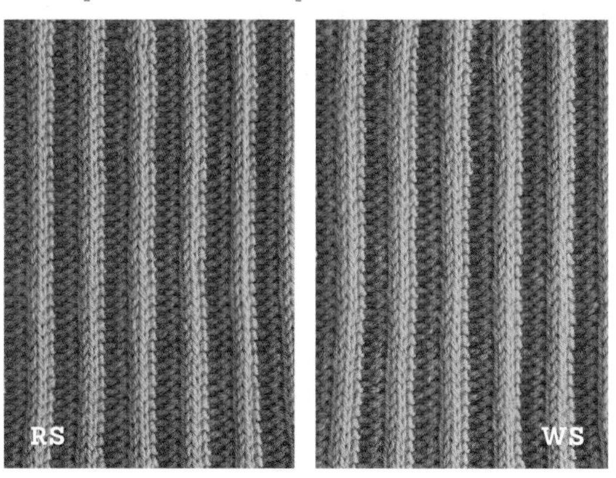

(WS) 2
1 (RS)

NOTES

- Always slip stitches purlwise (page 279) unless told otherwise.
- When slipping stitches in this pattern, the working yarn will be on the right side of the fabric on right-side rows and on the wrong side on wrong-side rows.

Row 1 (RS): *K4, slip the next 2 sts with the yarn in front; repeat from the * across, ending with k4.

Row 2: K1, *slip the next 2 sts with the yarn in front, k1, *k3, slip the next 2 sts with the yarn in front, k1; repeat from the * across.

Repeat Rows 1 and 2 for the pattern.

coverlet pattern

(multiple of 4 stitches plus 5 stitches)

Foundation Row 1 (RS): Knit across.

Foundation Row 2: P1, slip the next 2 sts with the yarn in back, *slip the next st with the yarn in back, k1, slip the next 2 sts with the yarn in back; repeat from the * across, ending with slip the next st with the yarn in back, p1.

Row 1 (RS): K1, slip the next st with the yarn in front, *slip the next 2 sts with the yarn in front, p1, slip the next st with the yarn in front; repeat from the * across, ending with slip the next 2 sts with the yarn in front, k1.

Rows 2, 4, 8, and 10: Purl across.

Rows 3 and 9: Knit across.

Row 5: K2, *insert the right-hand needle under the 2 loose strands several rows below and knit the next stitch, catching the strands (page 280), k3; repeat from the * across, ending with insert the right-hand needle under the 2 loose strands several rows below and knit the next stitch, catching the strands, k2.

Row 6: P2, k1, *slip the next 3 sts with the yarn in back, k1; repeat from the * across, ending with p2.

Row 7: K2, *p1, slip the next 3 sts with the yarn in front; repeat from the * across, ending with p1, k2.

Row 11: K2, *k2, insert the right-hand needle under the 2 loose strands several rows below, and knit the next stitch, catching the strands, k1; repeat from the * across, ending with k3.

Row 12: As Foundation Row 2.

Repeat Rows 1–12 for the pattern.

NOTES

- Always slip stitches purlwise (page 279) unless told otherwise.
- When slipping stitches in this pattern, the working yarn will be on the right side of the fabric.

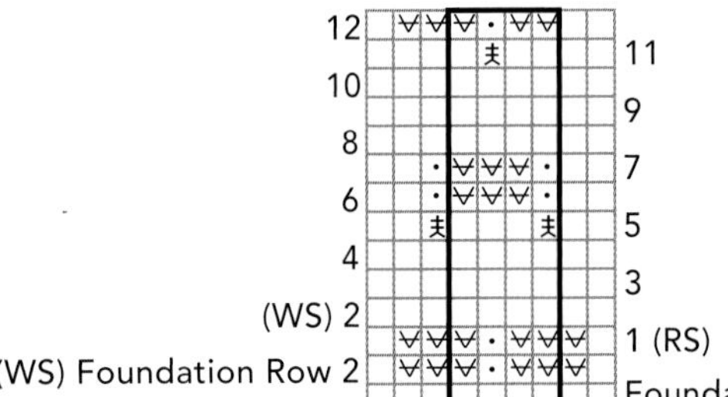

swags

(multiple of 12 stitches plus 7 stitches)

NOTES

- Always slip stitches purlwise (page 279) unless told otherwise.

Rows 1, 3, 5, 9, 11, 13, 15, and 19 (RS): Knit across.

Rows 2, 4, and 6: K7, *slip the next 5 sts with the yarn in back, k7; repeat from the * across.

Row 7: *K9, insert the right-hand needle under the 3 loose strands several rows below and knit the next stitch, catching the strands (page 280), k2; repeat from the * across, ending with k7.

Rows 8, 10, and 18: Purl across.

Rows 12, 14, and 16: K1, slip the next 5 sts with the yarn in back, k1, *k6, slip the next 5 sts with the yarn in back, k1; repeat from the * across.

Row 17: *K3, insert the right-hand needle under the 3 loose strands several rows below and knit the next stitch, catching the strands, k8; repeat from the * across, ending with k3, insert the right-hand needle under the 3 loose strands several rows below and knit the next stitch, catching the strands, k3.

Row 20: Purl across.

Repeat Rows 1–20 for the pattern.

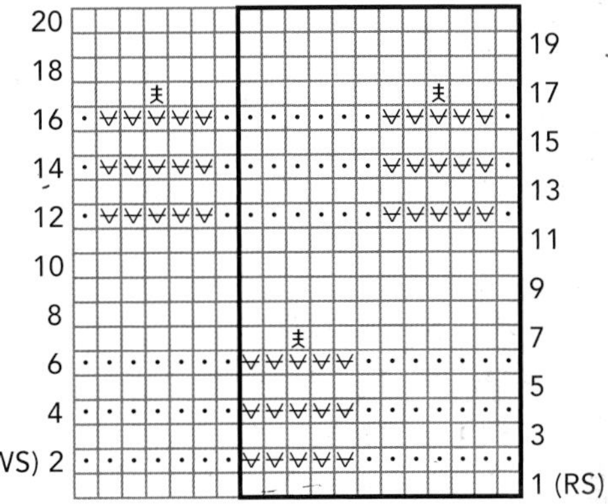

archways

(multiple of 10 stitches plus 7 stitches)

NOTES

- Always slip stitches purlwise (page 279) unless told otherwise.
- When slipping stitches in this pattern, the working yarn will be on the right side of the fabric.

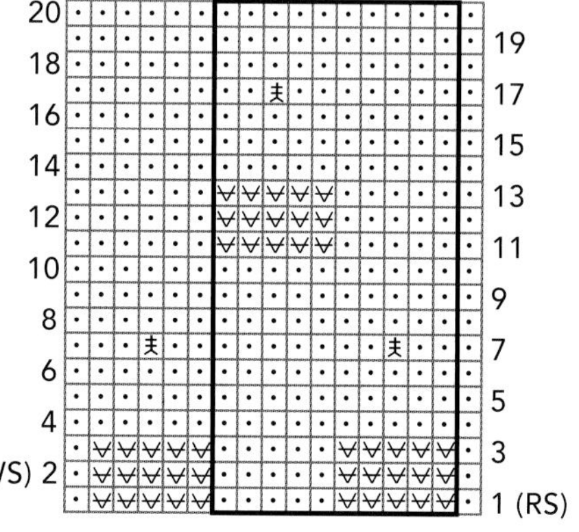

Rows 1 and 3 (RS): P1, *slip the next 5 sts with the yarn in front, p5; repeat from the * across, ending with slip the next 5 sts with the yarn in front, p1.

Row 2: K1, slip the next 5 sts with the yarn in back, *k5, slip the next 5 sts with the yarn in back; repeat from the * across, ending with k1.

Rows 4, 6, 8, 10, 14, 16, and 18: Knit across.

Rows 5, 9, 15, and 19: Purl across.

Row 7: P1, *p2, insert the right-hand needle under the 3 loose strands several rows below and knit the next st, catching the strands (page 280), p7; repeat from the * across, ending with p2, insert the right-hand needle under the 3 loose strands several rows below and knit the next st, catching the strands, p3.

Rows 11 and 13: P1, *p5, slip the next 5 sts with the yarn in front; repeat from the * across, ending with p6.

Row 12: K6, *slip the next 5 sts with the yarn in back, k5; repeat from the * across, ending with k1.

Row 17: P1, *p7, insert the right-hand needle under the 3 loose strands several rows below and knit the next st, catching the strands, p2; repeat from the * across, ending with p6.

Row 20: Knit across.

Repeat Rows 1–20 for the pattern.

cat's whiskers 

(multiple of 6 stitches plus 5 stitches, increases to a multiple of 7 stitches plus 6 stitches)

NOTES

- Always slip stitches purlwise (page 279) unless told otherwise.
- When slipping stitches in this pattern, the working yarn will be on the right side of the fabric.
- Stitch count varies from row to row.

Foundation Row (WS): Purl across.

Row 1 (RS): K1, *k3, slip the next 3 sts with the yarn in front, yarn over; repeat from the * across, ending with k4.

Rows 2 and 4: P4, *drop the yarn over, slip the next 3 sts with the yarn in back, yarn over, p3; repeat from the * across, ending with p1.

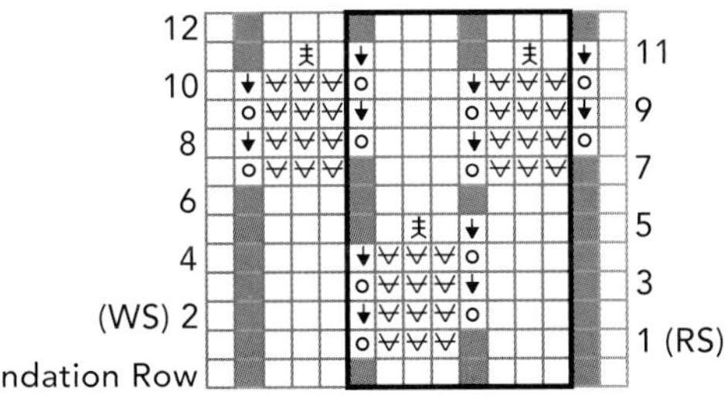

Row 3: K1, *k3, drop the yarn over, slip the next 3 sts with the yarn in front, yarn over; repeat from the * across, ending with k4.

Row 5: K1, *k3, drop the yarn over, k1, insert the right-hand needle under the 4 loose strands several rows below and knit the next stitch, catching the strands (page 280), k1; repeat from the * across, ending k4.

Row 6: Purl across.

Row 7: K1, *slip the next 3 sts with the yarn in front, yarn over, k3; repeat from the * across, ending with slip the next 3 sts with the yarn in front, yarn over, k1.

Rows 8 and 10: P1, drop the yarn over, slip the next 3 sts with the yarn in back, *yarn over, p3, drop the yarn over, slip the next 3 sts with the yarn in back, ending with yarn over, p1.

Row 9: K1, drop the yarn over, *slip the next 3 sts with the yarn in front, yarn over, k3, drop the yarn over; repeat from the * across, ending with slip the next 3 sts with the yarn in front, yarn over, k1.

Row 11: K1, drop the yarn over, *k1, insert the right-hand needle under the 4 loose strands several rows below and knit the next stitch, catching the strands, k4, drop the yarn over; repeat from the * across, ending with k1, insert the right-hand needle under the 4 loose strands several rows below and knit the next stitch, catching the strands, k2.

Row 12: Purl across.

Repeat Rows 1–12 for the pattern.

boxes 'n' bows

(multiple of 13 stitches plus 2 stitches)

NOTES

- Always slip stitches purlwise (page 279) unless told otherwise.
- When slipping stitches in this pattern, the working yarn will be on the right side of the fabric.

Row 1 (RS): Knit across.

Rows 2, 3, 4, 5, 7, 9, 11, 13, and 17: Knit across.

Rows 6, 8, 14, and 16: K2, *p11, k2; repeat from the * across.

Rows 10 and 12: K2, *p3, slip the next 5 sts with the yarn in back, p3, k2; repeat from the * across.

Row 15: *K7, insert the right-hand needle under the 2 loose strands several rows below and knit the next st, catching the strands (page 280), k5; repeat from the * across, ending with k2.

Row 18: As Row 6.

Repeat Rows 1–18 for the pattern.

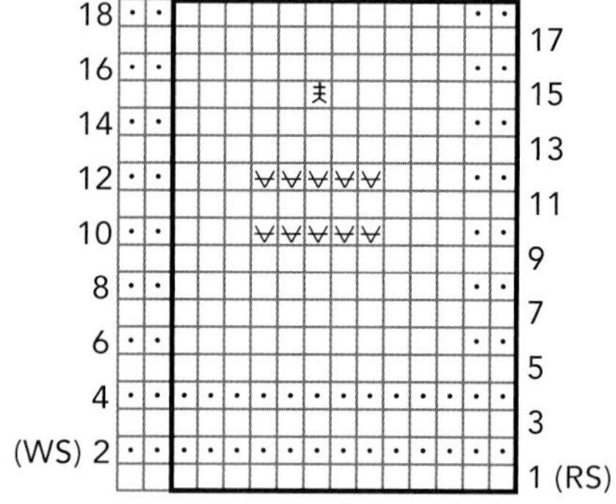

simple double knitting

(multiple of 2 stitches)

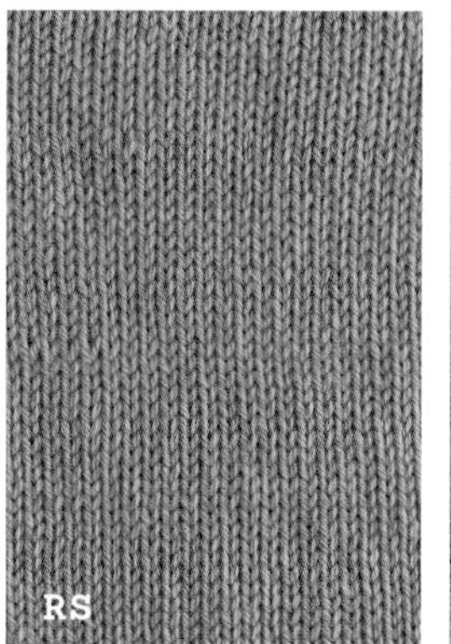

Row 1 (RS): *K1, slip the next st with the yarn in front; repeat from the * across.

Row 2: As Row 1.

Repeat Rows 1 and 2 for the pattern.

NOTES

- Always slip stitches purlwise (page 279) unless told otherwise.
- When slipping stitches in this pattern, the working yarn will always be in front of the slipped stitch. It will end up hidden between the stitches on each side of the fabric.
- This pattern is most effective when worked at a tight gauge; use knitting needles two sizes smaller than you would normally use for the yarn you choose.

(WS) 2 1 (RS)

overlay pattern

(multiple of 10 stitches plus 7 stitches)

NOTES

- Always slip stitches purlwise (page 279) unless told otherwise.
- When slipping stitches in this pattern, the working yarn will be on the right side of the fabric.

Foundation Row 1 (WS): With A, purl across.

Foundation Row 2: With B, k1, *k5, slip the next 5 sts with the yarn in front; repeat from the * across, ending with k6.

Foundation Row 3: With B, k6, *slip the next 5 sts with the yarn in back, k5; repeat from the * across, ending with k1.

Rows 1 and 3 (RS): With B, knit across.

Rows 2 and 4: With B, purl across.

Row 5: With A, k1, *slip the next 5 sts with the yarn in front, k2, insert the right-hand needle under the 2 loose strands several rows below, and knit the next stitch, catching the strands (page 280), k2; repeat from the * across, ending with slip the next 5 sts with the yarn in front, k1.

Row 6: With A, k1, slip the next 5 sts with the yarn in back, *k5, slip the next 5 sts with the yarn in back; repeat from the * across, ending with k1.

Rows 7 and 9: With A, knit across.

Rows 8 and 10: With A, purl across.

Row 11: With B, k1, *k2, insert the right-hand needle under the 2 loose strands several rows below, and knit the next stitch, catching the strands, k2, slip the next 5 sts with the yarn in front; repeat from the * across, ending with k2, insert the right-hand needle under the 2 loose strands several rows below, and knit the next stitch, catching the strands, k3.

Row 12: With B, k6, *slip the next 5 sts with the yarn in back, k5; repeat from the * across, ending with k1.

Repeat Rows 1–12 for the pattern.

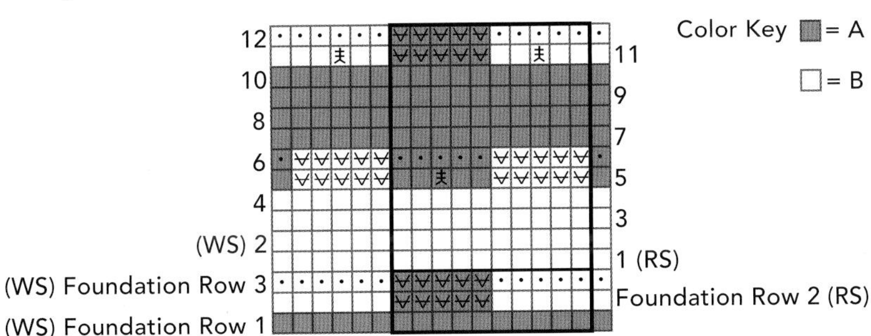

dragon skin

(multiple of 6 stitches plus 5 stitches)

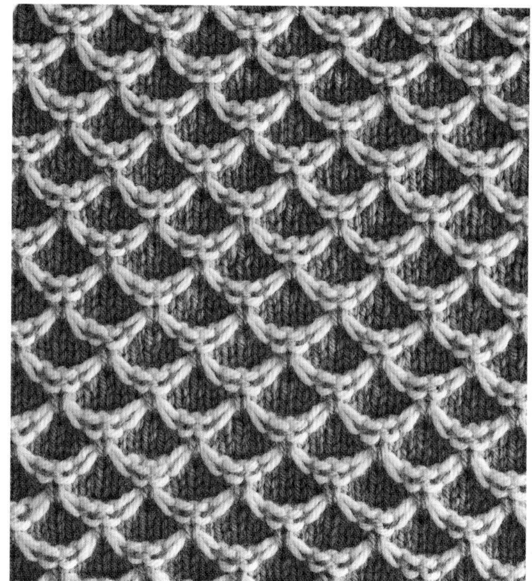

Foundation Row 1 (RS): With A, knit across.

Foundation Row 2: With A, purl across.

Row 1 (RS): With B, p1, *p3, slip the next 3 sts with the yarn in front; repeat from the * across, ending with p4.

Row 2: With B, k4, *slip the next 3 sts with the yarn in back, k3; repeat from the * across, ending with k1.

Rows 3 and 9: With A, knit across.

Rows 4, 6, and 10: With A, purl across.

Row 5: With A, k1,*k4, insert the right-hand needle under the 2 loose strands several rows below and knit the next stitch, catching the strands (page 280), k1; repeat from the * across, ending with k4.

Row 7: With B, p1, *slip the next 3 sts with the yarn in front, p3; repeat from the * across, ending with slip the next 3 sts with the yarn in front, p1.

Row 8: With B, k1, slip the next 3 sts with the yarn in back, *k3, slip the next 3 sts with the yarn in back; repeat from the * across, ending with k1.

Row 11: With A, k1, *k1, insert the right-hand needle under the 2 loose strands several rows below and knit the next stitch, catching the strands, k4; repeat from the * across, ending with k1, insert the right-hand needle under the 2 loose strands several rows below and knit the next stitch, catching the strands, k2.

Row 12: With B, purl across.

Repeat Rows 1–12 for the pattern.

NOTES

- Always slip stitches purlwise (page 279) unless told otherwise.
- When slipping stitches in this pattern, the working yarn will be on the right side of the fabric.

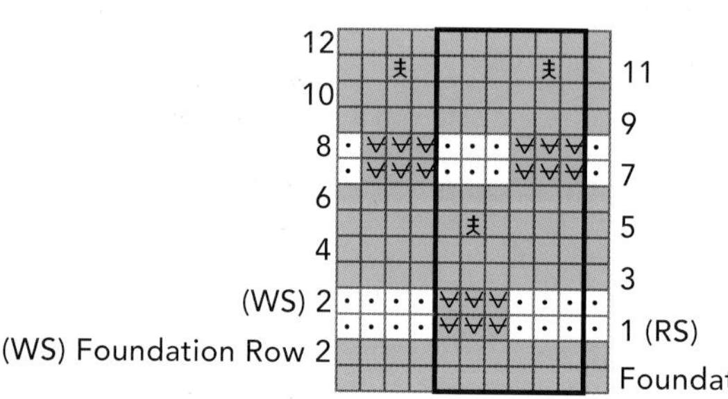

Color Key ▨ = A

□ = B

vertical welts

(multiple of 6 stitches plus 4 stitches)

(WS) 2

1 (RS)

NOTES

- Always slip stitches purlwise (page 279) unless told otherwise.
- When slipping stitches in this pattern, the working yarn will be on the right side of the fabric on Row 1 and on the wrong side on Row 2.

Row 1 (RS): *P1, k2, p1, slip the next 2 sts with the yarn in front; repeat from the * across, ending with p1, k2, p1.

Row 2: K1, slip the next 2 sts with the yarn in front, k1, *p2, k1, slip the next 2 sts with the yarn in front, k1; repeat from the * across.

Repeat Rows 1 and 2 for the pattern.

kendall tweed

(multiple of 4 stitches plus 3 stitches)

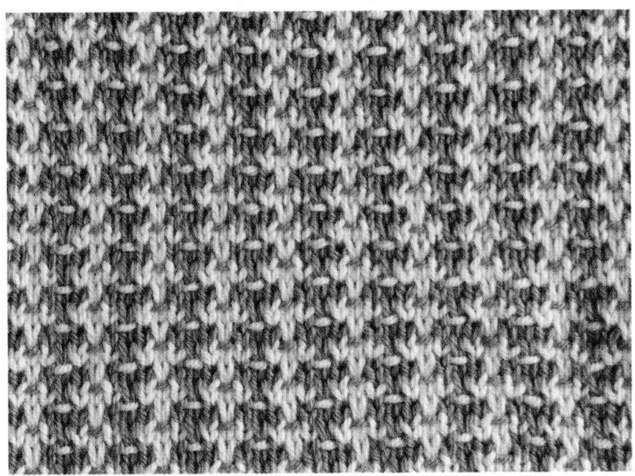

NOTES

- Always slip stitches purlwise (page 279) unless told otherwise.
- When slipping stitches in this pattern, the working yarn will be on the right side of the fabric on Rows 1 and 3; it will be on the wrong side on Rows 2 and 4.

Foundation Row (WS): With A, purl across.

Row 1 (RS): With B, *k1, slip the next st with the yarn in front, k2; repeat from the * across, ending with k1, slip the next st with the yarn in front, k1.

Row 2: With B, p1, slip the next st with the yarn in front, p1, *p2, slip the next st with the yarn in front, p1; repeat from the * across.

Row 3: With A, *k3, slip the next st with the yarn in front; repeat from the * across, ending with k3.

Row 4: With A, p3, *slip the next st with the yarn in front, p3; repeat from the * across.

Repeat Rows 1–4 for the pattern.

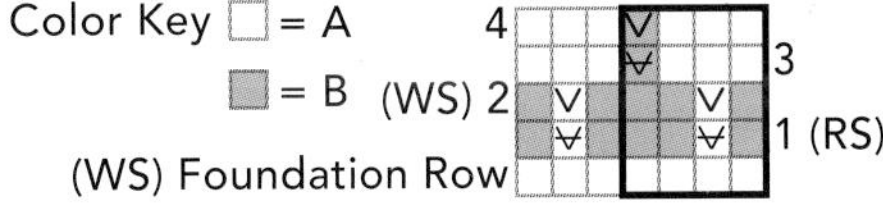

slip stitch lattice

(multiple of 8 stitches plus 10 stitches)

NOTES

- Always slip stitches purlwise (page 279) unless told otherwise.
- When slipping stitches in this pattern, the working yarn will be on the wrong side of the fabric.

Foundation Row (WS): With A, purl across.

Row 1 (RS): With B, k3, *slip the next 2 sts onto cn and hold in front, k2, k2 from cn, k4; repeat from the * across, ending with slip the next 2 sts onto cn and hold in front, k2, k2 from cn, k3.

Rows 2, 6, 10, 14, 18, and 22: With B, purl across.

Rows 3 and 23: With A, k3, slip the next 2 sts with the yarn in back, *slip the next 2 sts with the yarn in back, k4, slip the next 2 sts with the yarn in back; repeat from the * across, ending with slip the next 2 sts with the yarn in back, k3.

Row 4: With A, p3, slip the next 2 sts with the yarn in front, *slip the next 2 sts with the yarn in front, p4, slip the next 2 sts with the yarn in front; repeat from the * across, ending with slip the next 2 sts with the yarn in front, p3.

Row 5: With B, k2, slip the next st onto cn and hold in back, k2, k1 from cn, *slip the next 2 sts onto cn and hold in front, k1, k2 from cn, k2, slip the next st onto cn and hold in back, k2, k1 from cn; repeat from the * across, ending with slip the next 2 sts onto cn and hold in front, k1, k2 from cn, k2.

Rows 7 and 19: With A, *k2, slip the next 2 sts with the yarn in back; repeat from the * across.

Rows 8 and 20: With A, *p2, slip the next 2 sts with the yarn in front; repeat from the * across.

Row 9: With B, k1, slip the next st onto cn and hold in back, k2, k1 from cn, k1, *k1, slip the next 2 sts onto cn and hold in front, k1, k2 from cn, slip the next st onto cn and hold in back, k2, k1 from cn, k1; repeat from the * across, ending with k1, slip the next 2 sts onto cn and hold in front, k1, k2 from cn, k1.

Rows 11 and 15: With A, k1, slip the next 2 sts with the yarn in back, k2, *k2, slip the next 4 sts with the yarn in back, k2; repeat from the * across, ending with k2, slip the next 2 sts with the yarn in back, k1.

Rows 12 and 16: With A, p1, slip the next 2 sts with the yarn in front, p2, *p2, slip the next 4 sts with the yarn in front, p2; repeat from the * across, ending with p2, slip the next 2 sts with the yarn in front, p1.

Row 13: With B, k5, *k2, slip the next 2 sts onto cn and hold in back, k2, k2 from cn, k2; repeat from the * across, ending with k5.

Row 17: With B, k1, slip the next 2 sts onto cn and hold in front, k1, k2 from cn, k1, *k1, slip the next st onto cn and hold in back, k2, k1 from cn, slip the next

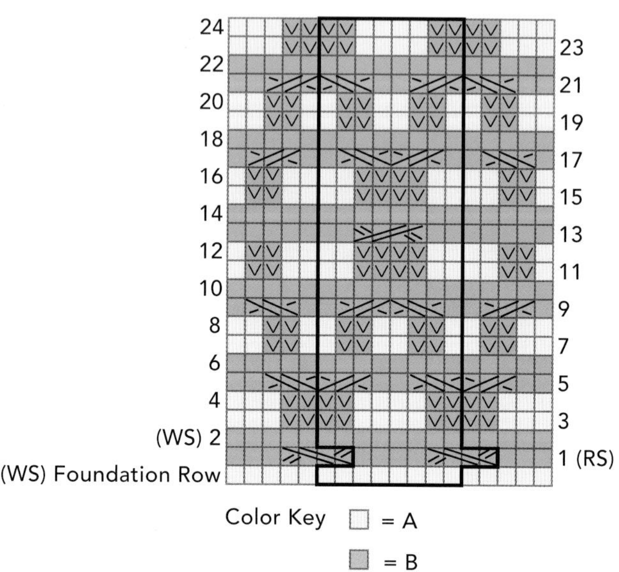

2 sts onto cn and hold in front, k1, k2 from cn, k1; repeat from the * across, ending with k1, slip the next st onto cn and hold in back, k2, k1 from cn, k1.

Row 21: With B, k2, slip the next 2 sts onto cn and hold in front, k1, k2 from cn, *slip the next st onto cn and hold in back, k2, k1 from cn, k2, slip the next 2 sts onto cn and hold in front, k1, k2 from cn; repeat from the * across, ending with slip the next st onto cn and hold in back, k2, k1 from cn, k2.

Row 24: As Row 4.

Repeat Rows 1–24 for the pattern.

acorns

(multiple of 4 stitches plus 3 stitches)

NOTES

- Always slip stitches purlwise (page 279) unless told otherwise.
- When slipping stitches in this pattern, the working yarn will be on the wrong side of the fabric.

Foundation Row (WS): With B, knit across.

Rows 1 and 3 (RS): With A, *k3, slip the next st with the yarn in back; repeat from the * across, ending with k3.

Row 2: With A, p3, *slip the next st with the yarn in front, p3; repeat from the * across.

Row 4: With A, k3, *p1, k3; repeat from the * across.

Rows 5 and 7: With B, *k1, slip the next st with the yarn in back, k2; repeat from the * across, ending with k1, slip the next st with the yarn in back, k1.

Row 6: With B, p1, slip the next st with the yarn in front, p1, *p2, slip the next st with the yarn in front, p1; repeat from the * across.

Row 8: With B, k1, p1, k1, *k2, p1, k1; repeat from the * across.

Repeat Rows 1–8 for the pattern.

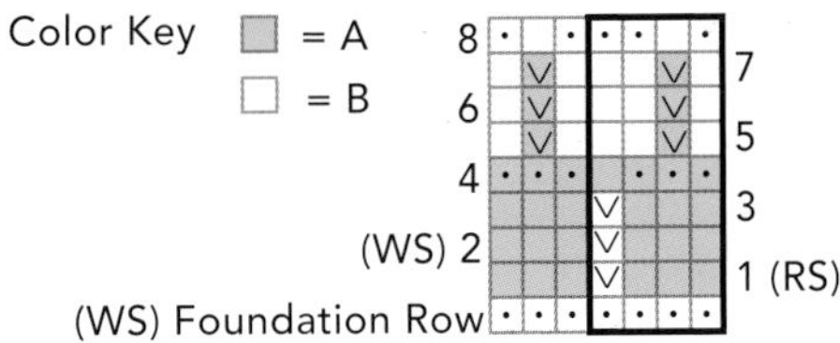

string of pearls

(multiple of 2 stitches plus 2 stitches)

Rows 1 and 3 (RS): With A, knit across.

Rows 2 and 4: With A, purl across.

Row 5: With B, k1, *[k1, yarn over, k1] all into the next st, slip the next st with the yarn in back; repeat from the * across, ending with k1.

Row 6: With B, p1, *slip the next st with the yarn in back, k3tog-tbl; repeat from the * across, ending with p1.

Repeat Rows 1–6 for the pattern.

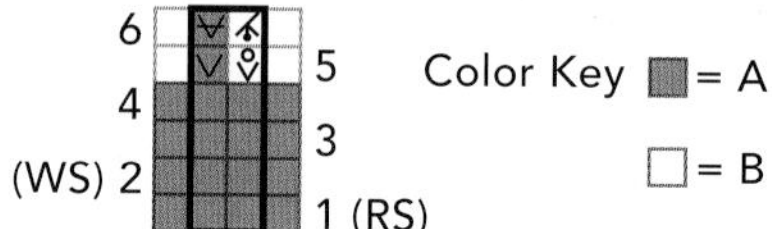

NOTES

- Always slip stitches purlwise (page 279) unless told otherwise.
- When slipping stitches in this pattern, the working yarn will be on the wrong side of the fabric on Row 5 and on the right side of the fabric on Row 6.

cables and tweed

(multiple of 7 stitches plus 3 stitches)

Row 1 (RS): With A, knit across.

Rows 2 and 6: With A, purl across.

Rows 3 and 7: With B, *p3, slip the next 4 sts with the yarn in back; repeat from the * across, ending with p3.

Row 4: With B, k3, *slip the next 4 sts with the yarn in front; repeat from the * across, ending with k3.

Row 5: With A, *k3, slip the next 2 sts onto cn and hold in front, k2, k2 from cn; repeat from the * across, ending with k3.

Row 8: As Row 4.

Repeat Rows 1–8 for the pattern.

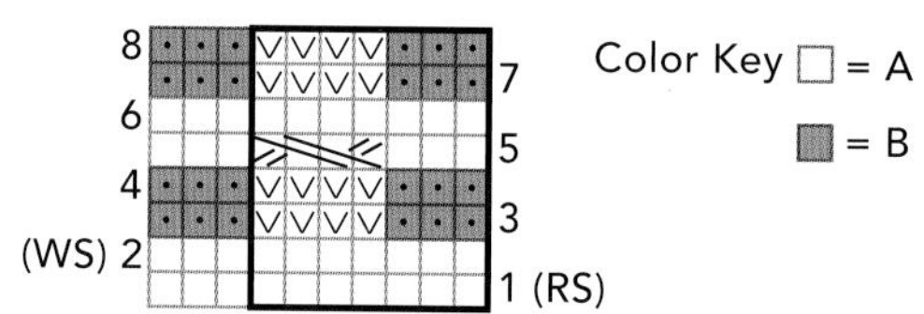

NOTES

- Always slip stitches purlwise (page 279) unless told otherwise.
- When slipping stitches in this pattern, the working yarn will be on the wrong side of the fabric.

chapter **five**

novelty **stitch patterns**

Knitting can utilize unusual techniques to create show-stopping fabrics. Intentionally unraveling a stitch makes tuck stitch patterns. Wrapping the yarn around your thumb creates a faux-fur fabric. Cleverly appliquéd pieces help to create a unique Butterfly Motif (page 244) or a textural Vineyard Lattice (page 254). I bet you'll agree that the stitch designs in this section are great fun to knit.

horizontal ruching

(any number of stitches)

NOTES

- Stitch count varies from row to row.
- This pattern requires the use of 2 sizes of knitting needles, one for the stockinette bands and one for the ruching. Actual size will depend on your yarn choice and gauge, but the larger needle should be approximately twice the size of the smaller needle.

Foundation Row 1 (RS): Knit across.

Foundation Row 2: As Foundation Row 1.

Row 1 (RS): With the smaller needles, knit across.

Rows 2, 3, and 4: As Row 1.

Row 5: With the larger needles, *k1f&b (page 274); repeat from the * across.

Rows 6, 8, and 10: With the larger needles, purl across.

Rows 7 and 9: With the larger needles, knit across.

Row 11: With the smaller needles, *k2tog; repeat from the * across.

Row 12: As Row 1.

Repeat Rows 1–12 for the pattern.

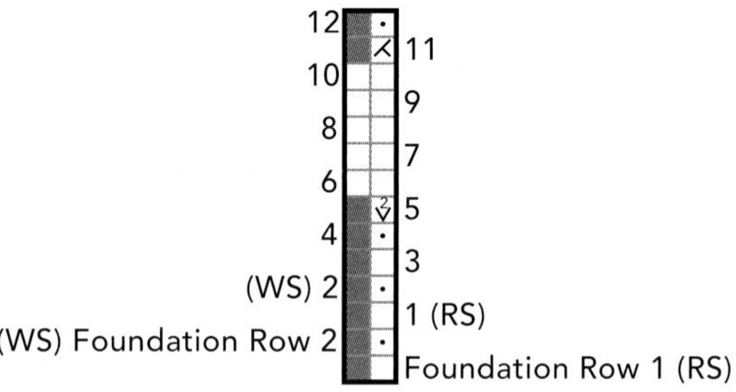

hexagon cells

(multiple of 6 stitches plus 9 stitches)

Row 1: K3, *yarn over, k3, pass the yarn over loop over the 3 sts just knit, k3; repeat from the * across.

Row 2: Purl across.

Row 3: K3, *k3, yarn over, k3, pass the yarn over loop over the 3 sts just knit; repeat from the * across, ending with k6.

Row 4: As Row 2.

Repeat Rows 1–4 for the pattern.

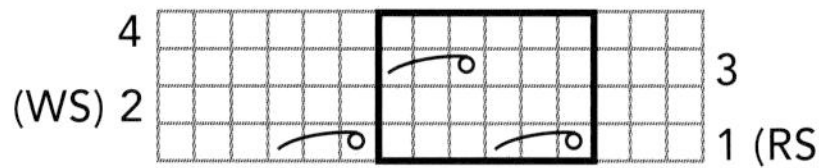

waves

(multiple of 14 stitches plus 1 stitch)

Row 1 (RS): With A, knit across.

Rows 2, 3, 4, 13, 14, 15, and 16: With A, as Row 1.

Rows 5, 7, 9, 11, 17, 19, 21, and 23: With B, as Row 1.

Rows 6, 8, 10, 18, 20, and 22: With B, purl across.

Row 12: With B, p1, *p3, [purl the next st together with the st 7 rows directly below it] 7 times, p4; repeat from the * across.

Row 24: With B, purl the next st together with the st 7 rows directly below it, *[purl the next st together with the st 7 rows directly below it] 3 times, p7, [purl the next st together with the st 7 rows directly below it] 4 times; repeat from the * across.

Repeat Rows 1–24 for the pattern.

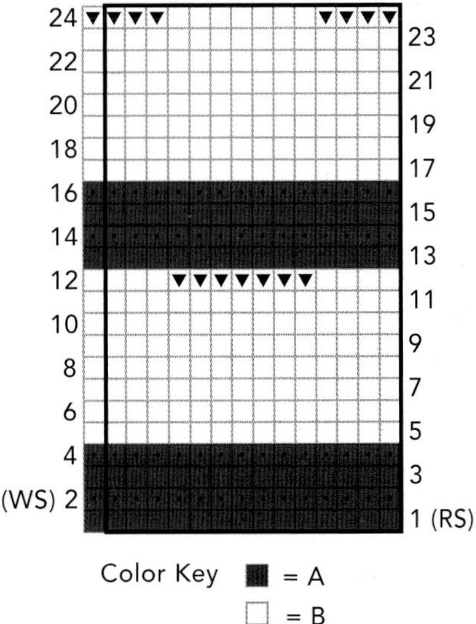

alternating pearls

easy

(multiple of 8 stitches plus 5 stitches)

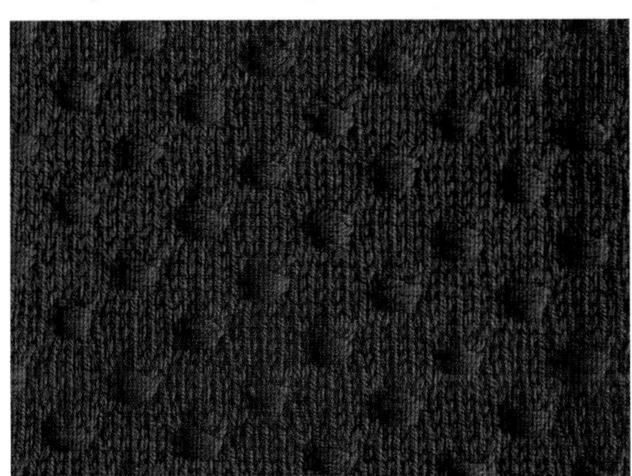

Rows 1 and 5 (RS): Knit across.

Row 2 and all WS rows: Purl across.

Row 3: K1, *k4, slip the next 3 sts onto cn and wrap the yarn counterclockwise 6 times around them just below the cn (page 282), knit these 3 sts, k1; repeat from the * across, ending with k4.

Row 7: K1, *slip the next 3 sts onto cn and wrap the yarn counterclockwise 6 times around them just below the cn, k3 from cn, k5; repeat from the * across, ending with slip the next 3 sts onto cn and wrap the yarn counterclockwise 6 times around them just below the cn, knit these 3 sts, k1.

Row 8: As Row 2.

Repeat Rows 1–8 for the pattern.

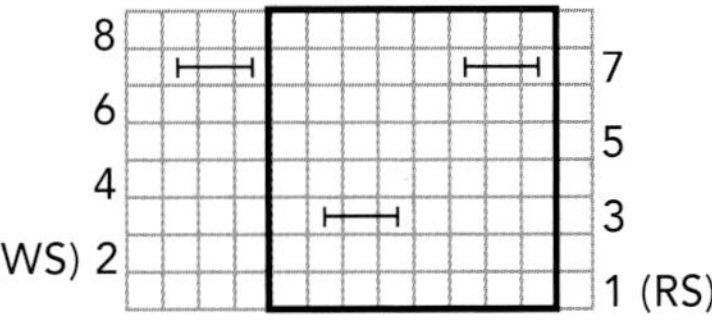

fountains

easy

(multiple of 24 stitches plus 25 stitches)

Row 1 (RS): K2tog, k5, M1 (page 277), k4, M1, *s2kp2 (page 272), M1, k4, M1, k5, s2kp2, k5, M1, k4, M1; repeat from the * across, ending with s2kp2, M1, k4, M1, k5, ssk.

Row 2 and all WS rows: Purl across.

Row 3: K2tog, k4, M1, k1, M1, k4, *s2kp2, k4, M1, k1, M1, k4; repeat from the * across, ending with ssk.

Row 5: K2tog, k3, [M1, k3] twice, *s2kp2, k3, [M1, k3] twice; repeat from the * across, ending with ssk.

Row 7: K2tog, k2, M1, k5, M1, k2, *s2kp2, k2, M1, k5, M1, k2; repeat from the * across, ending with ssk.

Row 9: K2tog, k1, M1, k7, M1, k1, *s2kp2, k1, M1, k7, M1, k1; repeat from the * across, ending with ssk.

Row 10: As Row 2.

Repeat Rows 1–10 for the pattern.

little blossoms

(multiple of 6 stitches plus 5 stitches)

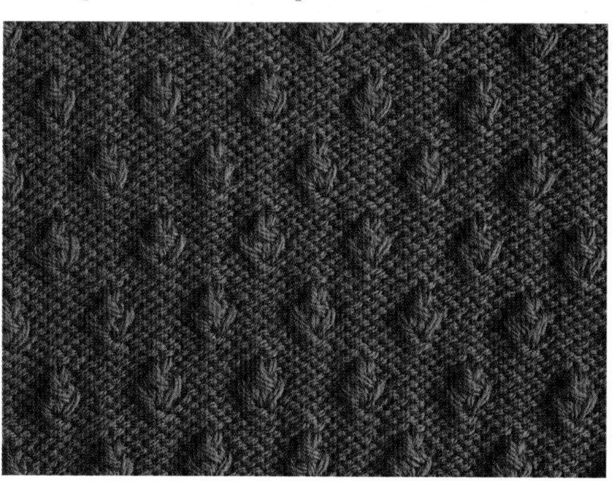

NOTE

- Stitch count varies from row to row.

Row 1: *P2, [k1, yarn over, k1] all into one st (page 268), p3; repeat from the * across, ending with p2, [k1, yarn over, k1] all into one st, p2.

Row 2 and all WS rows: Knit the knit sts, purl the purl sts, and purl the yarn overs.

Row 3: *P2, k3tog, p3; repeat from the * across, ending with p2, k3tog, p2.

Rows 5 and 11: Purl across.

Row 7: *P5, [k1, yarn over, k1] all into one st; repeat from the * across, ending with p5.

Row 9: *P5, k3tog; repeat from the * across, ending with p5.

Row 12: As Row 2.

Repeat Rows 1–12 for the pattern.

petite flowers

easy

(multiple of 22 stitches plus 13 stitches)

Row 1 (RS): K1, *slip the next 4 sts onto cn and hold in back, k1, k4 from cn, make a bobble (page 270), slip the next st onto cn and hold in front, k4, k1 from cn, k5, p1, k5; repeat from the * across, ending with slip the next 4 sts onto cn and hold in back, k1, k4 from cn, make a bobble, slip the next st onto cn and hold in front, k4, k1 from cn, k1.

Row 2 and all WS rows: Knit the knit sts and bobble sts, and purl the purl sts.

Row 3: K1, *k1, slip the next 3 sts onto cn and hold in back, k1, k3 from cn, p1, slip the next st onto cn and hold in front, k3, k1 from cn, k6, p1, k5; repeat from the * across, ending with k1, slip the next 3 sts onto cn and hold in back, k1, k3 from cn, p1, slip the next st onto cn and hold in front, k3, k1 from cn, k2.

Row 5: K1, *k2, slip the next 2 sts onto cn and hold in back, k1, k2 from cn, p1, slip the next st onto cn and hold in front, k2, k1 from cn, k7, p1, k5; repeat from the * across, ending with k2, slip the next 2 sts onto cn and hold in back, k1, k2 from cn, p1, slip the next st onto cn and hold in front, k2, k1 from cn, k3.

Row 7: K1, *k3, right twist (page 279), p1, left twist (page 276), k8, p1, k5; repeat from the * across, ending with k3, right twist, p1, left twist, k4.

Row 9: K1, *k5, p1, k5, slip the next 4 sts onto cn and hold in back, k1, k4 from cn, make a bobble, slip the next st onto cn and hold in front, k4, k1 from cn; repeat from the * across, ending with k5, p1, k6.

Row 11: K1, *k5, p1, k6, slip the next 3 sts onto cn and hold in back, k1, k3 from cn, p1, slip the next st onto cn and hold in front, k3, k1 from cn, k1; repeat from the * across, ending with k5, p1, k6.

Row 13: K1, *k5, p1, k7, slip the next 2 sts onto cn and hold in back, k1, k2 from cn, p1, slip the next st onto cn and hold in front, k2, k1 from cn, k2; repeat from the * across, ending with k5, p1, k6.

Row 15: K1, *k5, p1, k8, right twist, p1, left twist, k3; repeat from the * across, ending with k5, p1, k6.

Row 16: Same as Row 2.

Repeat Rows 1–16 for the pattern.

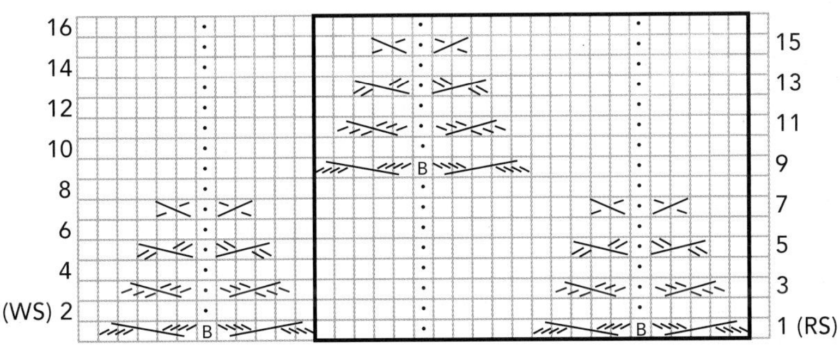

petals

(multiple of 6 stitches plus 5 stitches, increases to multiple of 10 stitches plus 9 stitches)

NOTE

- Stitch count varies from row to row.

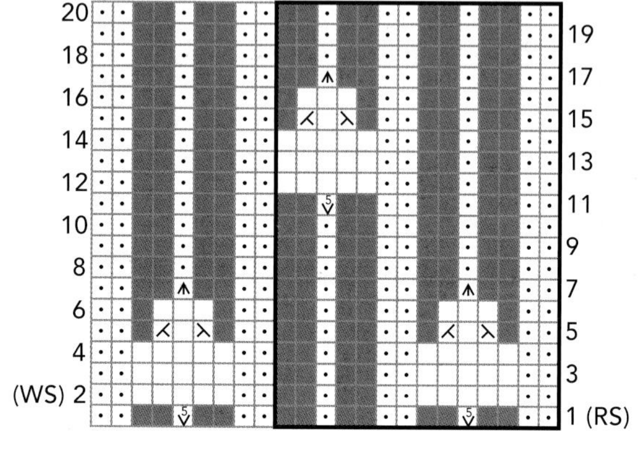

Row 1: *P2, [[k1, yarn over] twice, k1] all into one st (page 268), p3; repeat from the * across, ending with p2, [[k1, yarn over] twice, k1] all into one st, p2.

Rows 2, 4, 6, 12, 14, and 16: Knit the knit sts and purl the purl sts.

Row 3: *P2, k5, p3; repeat from the * across, ending with p2, k5, p2.

Row 5: *P2, ssk, k1, k2tog, p3; repeat from the * across, ending with p2, ssk, k1, k2tog, p2.

Row 7: *P2, s2kp2 (page 272), p3; repeat from the * across, ending with p2, s2kp2, p2.

Rows 8, 10, and 18: Knit across.

Rows 9 and 19: Purl across.

Row 11: *P5, [[k1, yarn over] twice, k1] all into one st; repeat from the * across, ending with p5.

Row 13: *P5, k5; repeat from the * across, ending with p5.

Row 15: *P5, ssk, k1, k2tog; repeat from the * across, ending with p5.

Row 17: *P5, s2kp2; repeat from the * across, ending with p5.

Row 20: As Row 2.

Repeat Rows 1–20 for the pattern.

raised leaves

(multiple of 6 stitches plus 5 stitches, increases to multiple of 10 stitches plus 9 stitches)

NOTE

- Stitch count varies from row to row.

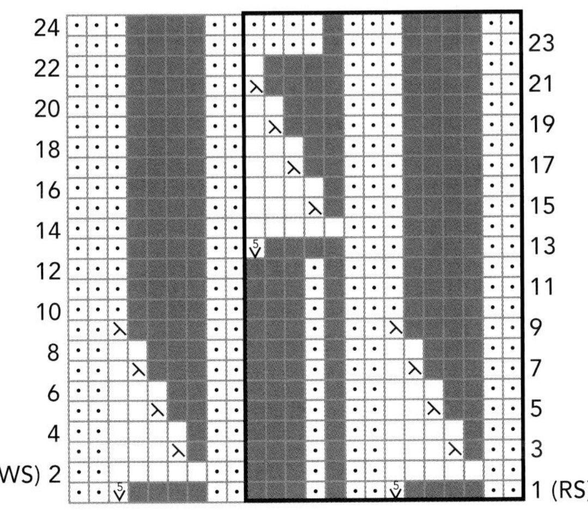

Row 1: *P2, [[k1, yarn over] twice, k1] all into one st, p3; repeat from the * across, ending with p2, [[k1, yarn over] twice, k1] all into one st, p2.

Row 2 and all WS rows *except Row 10*: Knit the knit sts and purl the purl sts.

Row 3: *P2, ssk, k3, p3; repeat from the * across, ending with p2, ssk, k3, p2.

Row 5: *P2, ssk, k2, p3; repeat from the * across, ending with p2, ssk, k2, p2.

Row 7: *P2, ssk, k1, p3; repeat from the * across, ending with p2, ssk, k1, p2.

Row 9: *P2, ssk, p3; repeat from the * across, ending with p2, ssk, p2.

Row 10: Knit across.

Rows 11 and 23: Purl across.

Row 13: *P5, [[k1, yarn over] twice, k1] all into one st; repeat from the * across, ending with p5.

Row 15: *P5, ssk, k3; repeat from the * across, ending with p5.

Row 17: *P5, ssk, k2; repeat from the * across, ending with p5.

Row 19: *P5, ssk, k1; repeat from the * across, ending with p5.

Row 21: *P5, ssk; repeat from the * across, ending with p5.

Row 24: As Row 2.

Repeat Rows 1–24 for the pattern.

quatrefoil

(multiple of 8 stitches plus 7 stitches, increases to multiple of 16 sts plus 15 stitches)

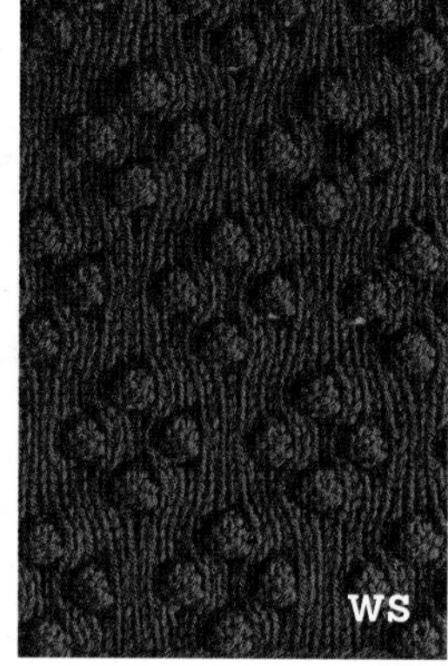

NOTE

- Stitch count varies from row to row.

Foundation Row 1 (RS): *P7, [[k1, yarn over] twice, k1] all into one st (page 268); repeat from the * across, ending with p7.

Foundation Row 2: *K7, p5; repeat from the * across, ending with k7.

Row 1: P5, *p2, k5, p5; repeat from the * across, ending with p2.

Row 2 and all WS rows: Knit the knit sts and purl the purl sts.

Row 3: *P5, [[k1, yarn over] twice, k1] all into one st, p1, 5-to-1 st decrease (page 269), p1, [[k1, yarn over] twice, k1] all into one st, p3; repeat from the * across, ending with p2.

Rows 5, 9, 13, 17, and 21: As Row 2.

Row 7: P5, *5-to-1 st decrease, p1, [[k1, yarn over] twice, k1] all into one st, p1, 5-to-1 st decrease, p3; repeat from the * across, ending with p2.

Row 11: P3, [[k1, yarn over] twice, k1] all into one st, p1, *p2, 5-to-1 st decrease, p3, [[k1, yarn over] twice, k1] all into one st, p1; repeat from the * across, ending with p2.

Row 15: P1, [[k1, yarn over] twice, k1] all into one st, p1, 5-to-1 st decrease, p1, *[[k1, yarn over] twice, k1] all into one st, p3, [[k1, yarn over] twice, k1] all into one st, p1, 5-to-1 st decrease, p1; repeat from the * across, ending with [[k1, yarn over] twice, k1] all into one st, p1.

Row 19: P1, 5-to-1 st decrease, p1, [[k1, yarn over] twice, k1] all into one st, p1, *5-to-1 st decrease, p3, 5-to-1 st decrease, p1, [[k1, yarn over] twice, k1] all into one st, p1; repeat from the * across, ending with 5-to-1 st decrease, p1.

Row 23: P3, 5-to-1 st decrease, p1, *p2, [[k1, yarn over] twice, k1] all into one st, p3, 5-to-1 st decrease, p1; repeat from the * across, ending with p2.

Row 24: As Row 2.

Repeat Rows 1–24 for the pattern.

24, 23, 22, 21, 20, 19, 18, 17, 16, 15, 14, 13, 12, 11, 10, 9, 8, 7, 6, 5, 4, 3
(WS) 2
1 (RS)
(WS) Foundation Row 2
Foundation Row 1 (RS)

textured bow ties 

(multiple of 14 stitches plus 7 stitches)

NOTE

- Long Stitch = Insert the right-hand needle into the indicated stitch 8 rows below and knit it, drawing up a long loop; transfer the loop onto the left-hand needle and knit it together with the next stitch on the needle.

Rows 1 and 7 (RS): *K7, p7; repeat from the * across, ending with k7.

Row 2 and all WS rows: Knit the knit sts and purl the purl sts.

Rows 3, 5, 13, and 15: Knit across.

Row 9: *K10, make a long stitch, k3; repeat from the * across, ending with k7.

Rows 11 and 17: *P7, k7; repeat from the * across, ending with p7.

Row 19: *K3, make a long stitch, k10; repeat from the * across, ending with k3, make a long stitch, k3.

Row 20: As Row 2.

Repeat Rows 1–20 for the pattern.

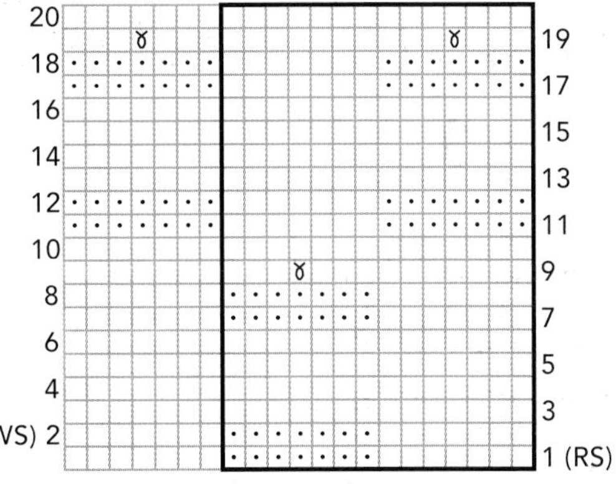

trinity stitch 

(multiple of 4 stitches plus 2 stitches)

Foundation Row (WS): Purl across.

Row 1 (RS): K1, *p3tog, [k1, p1, k1] into the next st; repeat from the * across, ending with k1.

Row 2: Purl across.

Row 3: K1, *[k1, p1, k1] into the next st, p3tog; repeat from the * across, ending with k1.

Row 4: Purl across.

Repeat Rows 1–4 for the pattern.

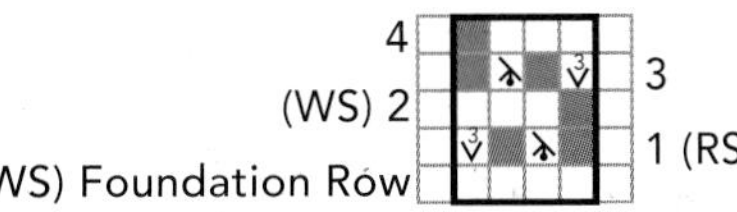

daisy stitch

easy

(multiple of 4 stitches plus 5 stitches)

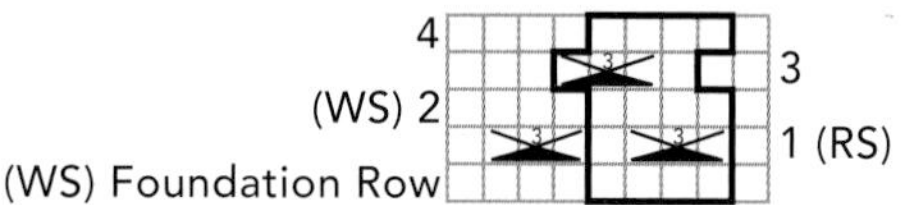

Foundation Row (WS): Purl across.

Row 1 (RS): K1, *k3tog but do not remove them from the left-hand needle, yarn over, then knit the 3 sts together again before removing them from the left-hand needle, k1; repeat from the * across.

Row 2: Purl across.

Row 3: K2, *k1, k3tog but do not remove them from the left-hand needle, yarn over, then knit the 3 sts together again before removing them from the left-hand needle; repeat from the * across, ending with k3.

Row 4: As Row 2.

Repeat Rows 1–4 for the pattern.

diamond jubilee

easy

(multiple of 4 stitches plus 5 stitches)

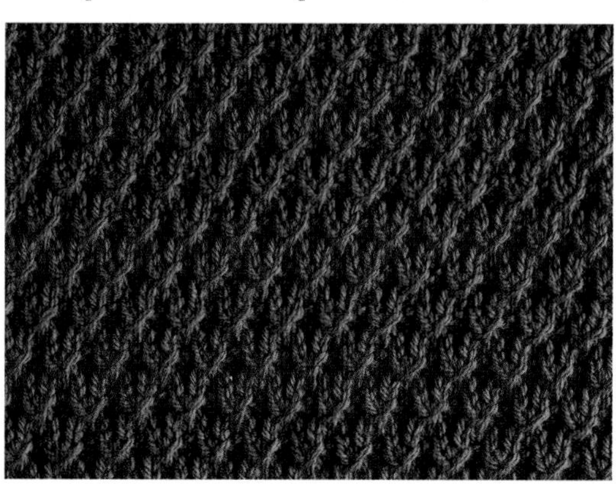

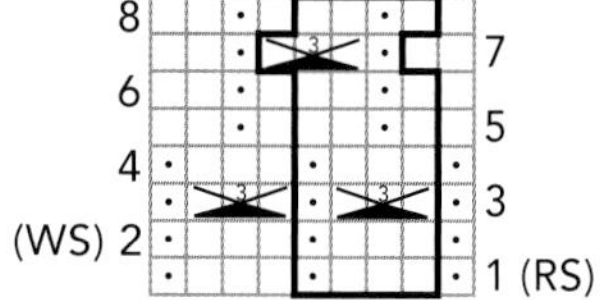

Row 1 (RS): P1, *k3, p1; repeat from the * across.

Row 2 and all WS rows: Knit the knit sts and purl the purl sts.

Row 3: P1, *k3tog but do not remove them from the left-hand needle, yarn over, then knit the 3 sts together again before removing them from the left-hand needle, p1; repeat from the * across.

Row 5: K2, *p1, k3, k2; repeat from the * across.

Row 7: K2, *p1, k3, k3tog but do not remove them from the left-hand needle, yarn over, then knit the 3 sts together again before removing them from the left-hand needle; repeat from the * across, ending with p1, k2.

Row 8: As Row 2.

Repeat Rows 1–8 for the pattern.

oyster rib

(multiple of 7 stitches)

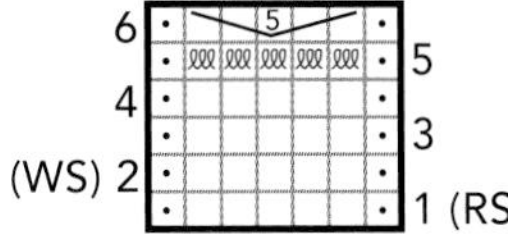

Rows 1 and 3 (RS): *P1, k5, p1; repeat from the * across.

Rows 2 and 4: *K1, p5, k1; repeat from the * across.

Row 5: *P1, k5, *wrapping yarn 3 times as you make each elongated st* (page 274), p1; repeat from the * across.

Row 6: *K1, slip 5 sts purlwise, *allowing the extra loops to drop*, then return the 5 sts to the left-hand needle, insert the right-hand needle knitwise into all 5 sts at once and [k1, p1, k1, p1, k1] into them, k1; repeat from the * across.

Repeat Rows 1–6 for the pattern.

mock broomstick pattern

(multiple of 5 stitches plus 2 stitches)

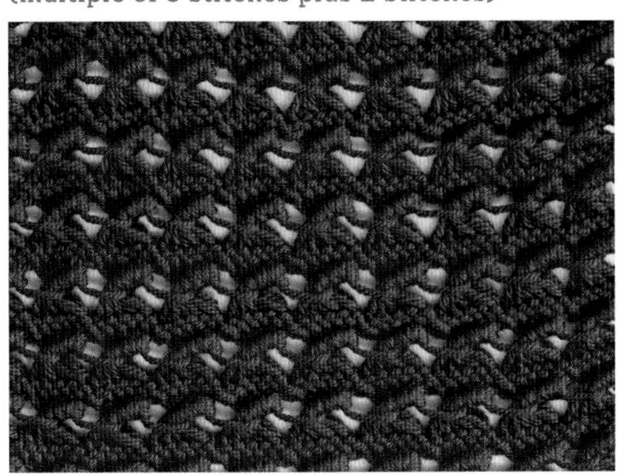

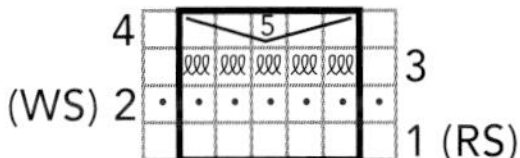

Row 1 (RS): Knit across.

Row 2: As Row 1.

Row 3: K1, *k5, *wrapping yarn 3 times as you make each elongated st* (page 274); repeat from the * across, ending with k1.

Row 4: P1, *slip 5 sts purlwise, *allowing the extra loops to drop*, then return the 5 sts to the left-hand needle, insert the right-hand needle knitwise into all 5 sts at once and [k1, p1, k1, p1, k1] into them; repeat from the * across, ending with p1.

Repeat Rows 1–4 for the pattern.

half brioche

(multiple of 2 stitches)

Row 1 (RS): Knit across.

Row 2: *K1, knit the next st in the row below (page 275); repeat from the * across.

Row 3: As Row 1.

Row 4: *Knit the next st in the row below, k1; repeat from the * across.

Repeat Rows 1–4 for the pattern.

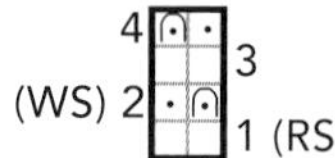

brioche ribbing

(multiple of 2 stitches plus 2 stitches)

Foundation Row (WS): Knit across.

Row 1 (RS): K1, *knit the next st in the row below (page 275), k1; repeat from the * across, ending with knit the next st in the row below.

Row 2: As Row 1.

Repeat Rows 1 and 2 for the pattern.

(WS) 2
1 (RS)
(WS) Foundation Row

bee stitch

(multiple of 2 stitches)

Foundation Row (WS): With B, knit across.

Row 1 (RS): With A, *knit the next st in the row below (page 275), k1; repeat from the * across.

Row 2: With A, knit across.

Row 3: With B, *k1, knit the next st in the row below; repeat from the * across.

Row 4: With B, knit across.

Repeat Rows 1–4 for the pattern.

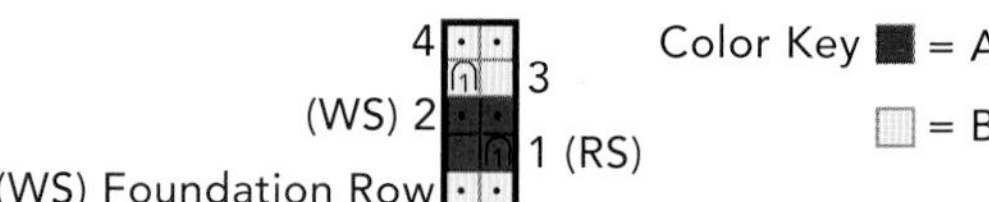

broken brioche rib

(multiple of 2 stitches)

Foundation Row (WS): Purl across.

Rows 1 and 3 (RS): *Purl the next st in the row below (page 275), p1; repeat from the * across.

Rows 2 and 4: As Row 1.

Rows 5 and 7: *P1, purl the next st in the row below; repeat from the * across.

Rows 6 and 8: As Rows 5 and 7.

Repeat Rows 1–8 for the pattern.

8 7
6 5
4 3
(WS) 2 1 (RS)
(WS) Foundation Row

checkerboard tuck pattern

(multiple of 10 stitches plus 5 stitches)

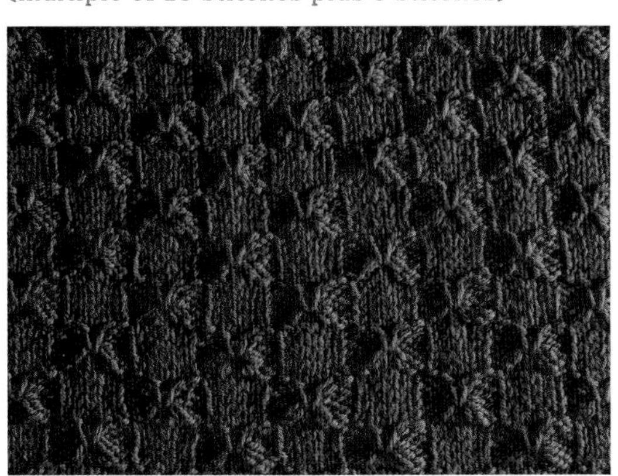

Foundation Row (WS): Purl across.

Rows 1, 3, and 5 (RS): *K5, p5; repeat from the * across, ending with k5.

Rows 2 and 4: P5, *k5, p5; repeat from the * across.

Row 6: P5, *k2, make a 6-row tuck stitch (page 284), k2, p5; repeat from the * across.

Rows 7, 9, and 11: *P5, k5; repeat from the * across, ending with p5.

Rows 8 and 10: K5, *p5, k5; repeat from the * across.

Row 12: K2, make a 6-row tuck stitch, k2, *p5, k2, make a 6-row tuck stitch, k2; repeat from the * across.

Repeat Rows 1–12 for the pattern.

12 11
10 9
8 7
6 5
4 3
(WS) 2 1 (RS)
(WS) Foundation Row

alternating tuck stitch 

(multiple of 4 stitches plus 3 stitches)

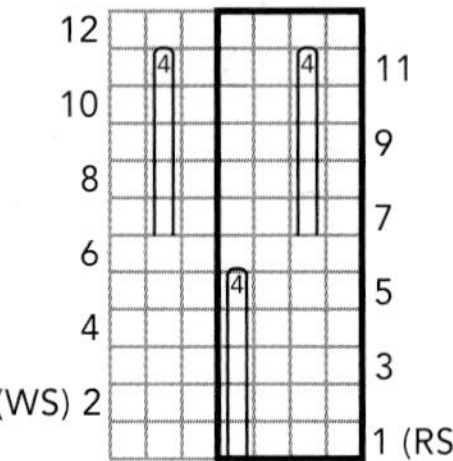

Rows 1, 3, 7, and 9 (RS): Knit across.

Row 2 and all WS rows: Purl across.

Row 5: *K3, drop the next st off the left-hand needle and, using the tip of the right-hand needle, unravel the st 4 rows down, then insert the right-hand needle into the live st and knit it, catching the 4 loose strands into the st as you knit (page 283); repeat from the * across, ending with k3.

Row 11: *K1, drop the next st off the left-hand needle and, using the tip of the right-hand needle, unravel the st 4 rows down, then insert the right-hand needle into the live st and knit it, catching the 4 loose strands into the st as you knit, k2; repeat from the * across, ending with k1, drop the next st off the left-hand needle and, using the tip of the right-hand needle, unravel the st 4 rows down, then insert the right-hand needle into the live st and knit it, catching the 4 loose strands into the st as you knit, k1.

Row 12: As Row 2.

Repeat Rows 1–12 for the pattern.

aligned tuck stitch 

(multiple of 4 stitches plus 3 stitches)

Rows 1 and 3 (RS): *P3, k1; repeat from the * across, ending with p3.

Row 2 and all WS rows: Knit the knit sts and purl the purl sts.

Row 5: *P3, make a 4-row tuck stitch (page 284); repeat from the * across, ending with p3.

Row 6: As Row 2.

Repeat Rows 1–6 for the pattern.

6
4
(WS) 2
5
3
1 (RS)

tucked lattice

(multiple of 6 stitches plus 5 stitches)

Foundation Row (WS): Knit across.

Rows 1, 3, 7, and 9 (RS): P2, *k1, p2; repeat from the * across.

Row 2 and all WS rows: *K2, p1; repeat from the * across, ending k2.

Row 5: P2, *make a 5-row tuck stitch (page 284), p2, k1, p2; repeat from the * across, ending with a 5-row tuck stitch, p2.

Row 11: P2, *k1, p2, make a 5-row tuck stitch, p2; repeat from the * across, ending with k1, p2.

Row 12: As Row 2.

Repeat Rows 1–12 for the pattern.

two-color garter tuck stitch

(multiple of 4 stitches plus 3 stitches)

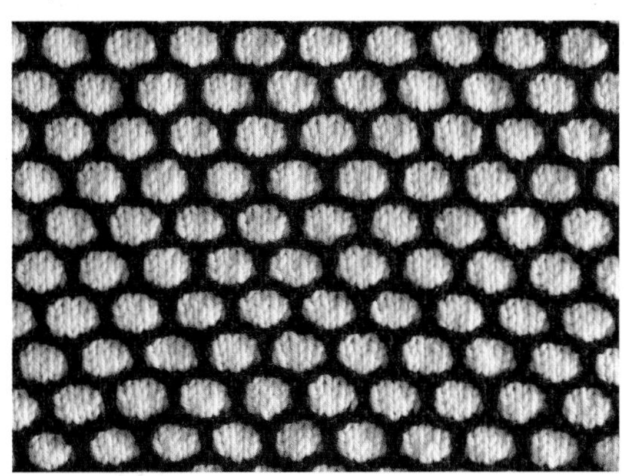

Rows 1, 3, 7, and 9 (RS): With A, knit across.

Rows 2, 4, 8, and 10: With A, purl across.

Row 5: With B, *k3, make a 4-row tuck stitch (page 284); repeat from the * across, ending with k3.

Row 6: With B, knit across.

Row 11: With B, *k1, make a 4-row tuck stitch, k2; repeat from the * across, ending with k1, make a 4-row tuck stitch, k1.

Row 12: With B, knit across.

Repeat Rows 1–12 for the pattern.

Color Key □ = A ■ = B

sunflower motif

(over 17 stitches on a reverse stockinette background)

Row 1 (RS): P7, k1, p1, k1, p7.

Row 2 and all WS rows: Knit the knit sts, knit the bobble stitches, and purl the purl sts.

Row 3: P6, right twist (page 279), p1, left twist (page 276), p6.

Row 5: P5, right twist, k1, p1, k1, left twist, p5.

Row 7: P4, right twist, k2, p1, k2, left twist, p4.

Row 9: P3, right twist, k3, p1, k3, left twist, p3.

Row 11: P2, right twist, k4, p1, k4, left twist, p2.

Row 13: P1, right twist, k5, p1, k5, left twist, p1.

Row 15: Right twist, k4, slip the next st onto cn and hold in back, k1, p1 from cn, p1, slip the next st onto cn and hold in front, p1, k1 from cn, k4, left twist.

Row 17: K5, slip the next st onto cn and hold in back, k1, p1 from cn, p1, k1, p1, slip the next st onto cn and hold in front, p1, k1 from cn, k5.

Row 19: K4, slip the next st onto cn and hold in back, k1, p1 from cn, p2, k1, p2, slip the next st onto cn and hold in front, p1, k1 from cn, k4.

Row 21: K3, slip the next st onto cn and hold in back, k1, p1 from cn, p3, k1, p3, slip the next st onto cn and hold in front, p1, k1 from cn, k3.

Row 23: K2, slip the next st onto cn and hold in back, k1, p1 from cn, p4, k1, p4, slip the next st onto cn and hold in front, p1, k1 from cn, k2.

Row 25: K1, slip the next st onto cn and hold in back, k1, p1 from cn, p4, Bobble (page 270), k1, Bobble, p4, slip the next st onto cn and hold in front, p1, k1 from cn, k1.

Row 27: Slip the next st onto cn and hold in back, k1, p1 from cn, p3, Bobble, [p1, k1] twice, p1, Bobble, p3, slip the next st onto cn and hold in front, p1, k1 from cn.

Row 29: P3, Bobble, [k1, p1] 4 times, k1, Bobble, p3.

Row 31: P1, Bobble, [p1, k1] 6 times, p1, Bobble, p1.

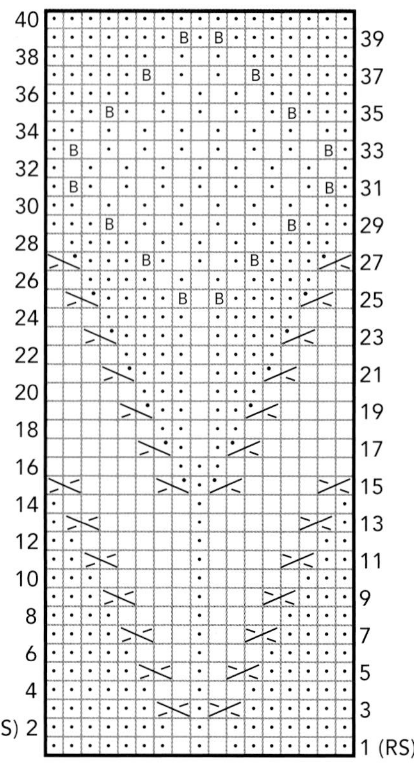

Row 33: P1, Bobble, [k1, p1] 6 times, k1, Bobble, p1.

Row 35: P3, Bobble, [p1, k1] 4 times, p1, Bobble, p3.

Row 37: P5, Bobble, [k1, p1] twice, k1, Bobble, p5.

Row 39: P7, Bobble, p1, Bobble, p7.

Row 40: Knit across.

posy

(over 9 stitches, increases to 15 stitches, on a reverse stockinette background)

NOTE

- Stitch count varies from row to row.

Row 1 (RS): P4, M1 (page 277), make a central double increase (page 273), M1, p4.

Row 2: K4, p2, [p1, yarn over, p1] into the next st (page 268), p2, k4.

Row 3: P3, k2tog, k2, M1 purlwise (page 278), k1-tbl (page 275), M1 purlwise, k2, ssk, p3.

Row 4: K3, p3, k1, p1-tbl (page 279), k1, p3, k3.

Row 5: P2, k2tog, k2, M1 purlwise, p1, k1-tbl, p1, M1 purlwise, k2, ssk, p2.

Row 6: K2, p3, k2, p1-tbl, k2, p3, k2.

Row 7: P1, k2tog, k2, M1 purlwise, p2, k1-tbl, p2, M1 purlwise, k2, ssk, p1.

Row 8: K1, p3, k3, p1-tbl, k3, p3, k1.

Row 9: [K2tog] twice, p3, k1-tbl, p3, [ssk] twice.

Row 10: P2, k3, p1-tbl, k3, p2.

Row 11: K2tog, p3, k1-tbl, p3, ssk.

Row 12: K4, p1-tbl, k4.

Row 13: P3, Bobble (page 270), k1-tbl, Bobble, p3.

Rows 14 and 16: Knit across.

Row 15: P2, Bobble, p3, Bobble, p2.

Row 17: P4, Bobble, p4.

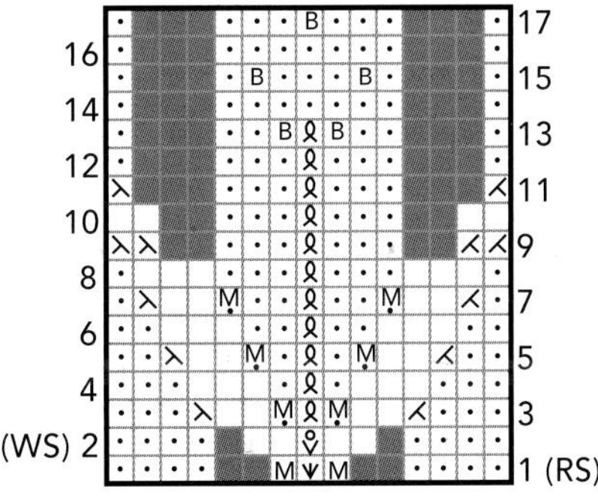

heart motif

(over 11 stitches, increases to 19 stitches, on a reverse stockinette background)

NOTE

- Stitch count varies from row to row.

Row 1 (RS): P5, M1 (page 277), make a central double increase (page 273), M1, p5.

Rows 2, 4, 6, 8, 10, 12, 14, 16, 18, 20, and 22: Knit the knit sts and purl the purl sts.

Row 3: P5, k1, right lifted increase (page 276), k1, left lifted increase (page 276), k1, p5.

Row 5: P5, k1, right lifted increase, k3, left lifted increase, k1, p5.

Row 7: P4, slip the next st onto cn and hold in back, k2, k1 from cn, k5, slip the next 2 sts onto cn and hold in front, k1, k2 from cn, p4.

Row 9: P3, slip the next st onto cn and hold in back, k2, k1 from cn, k7, slip the next 2 sts onto cn and hold in front, k1, k2 from cn, p3.

Row 11: P2, slip the next st onto cn and hold in back, k2, k1 from cn, k9, slip the next 2 sts onto cn and hold in front, k1, k2 from cn, p2.

Row 13: P1, slip the next st onto cn and hold in back, k2, k1 from cn, k11, slip the next 2 sts onto cn and hold in front, k1, k2 from cn, p1.

Row 15: Slip the next st onto cn and hold in back, k2, k1 from cn, k13, slip the next 2 sts onto cn and hold in front, k1, k2 from cn.

Rows 17 and 19: Knit across.

Row 21: K6, slip the next 2 sts onto cn and hold in back, k1, p2 from cn, p1, slip the next st onto cn and hold in front, p2, k1 from cn, k6.

Row 23: Slip the next 2 sts onto cn and hold in front, p1, k2 from cn, k2, slip the next st onto cn and hold in back, k1, p1 from cn, p5, slip the next st onto cn and hold in front, p1, k1 from cn, k2, slip the next st onto cn and hold in back, k2, p1 from cn.

Row 24: K1, 5-to-1 st decrease (page 269), k7, 5-to-1 st decrease, k1.

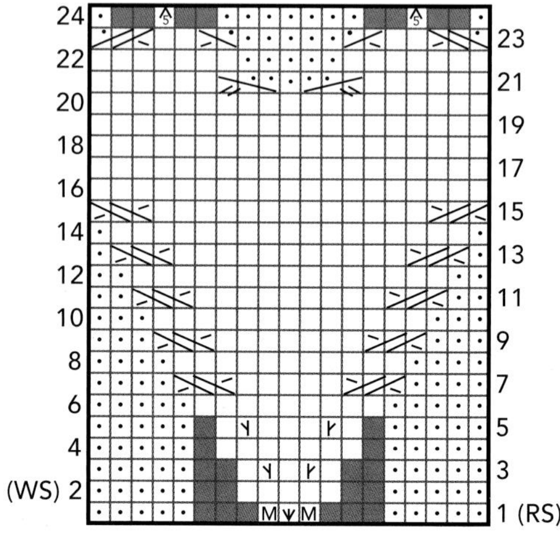

foxglove

(multiple of 4 stitches, increases to multiple of 14 stitches)

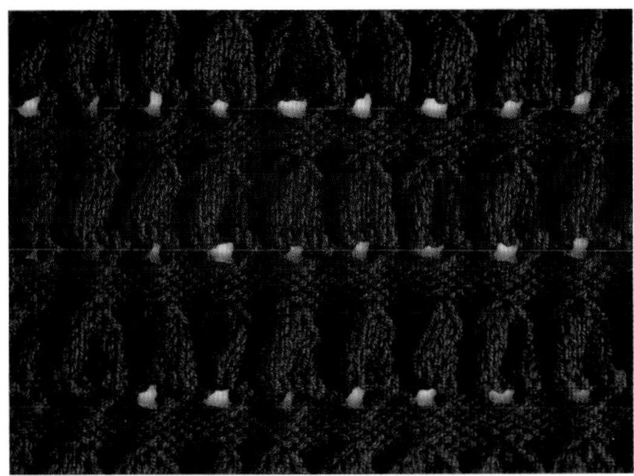

NOTE

- Stitch count varies from row to row.

Row 1 (RS): Purl across.

Row 2: Knit across.

Row 3: *P2, then use the cable cast-on technique (page 272) to cast on 10 new sts, p2; repeat from the * across.

Rows 4 and 6: *K2, p10, k2; repeat from the * across.

Row 5: *P2, k10, p2; repeat from the * across.

Row 7: *P2, ssk, k6, k2tog, p2; repeat from the * across.

Row 8: *K2, p2tog, p4, ssp (page 281), k2; repeat from the * across.

Row 9: *P2, ssk, k2, k2tog, p2; repeat from the * across.

Row 10: *K2, p2tog, ssp, k2; repeat from the * across.

Row 11: *P1, [p2tog] twice, p1; repeat from the * across.

Row 12: Knit across.

Repeat Rows 1–12 for the pattern.

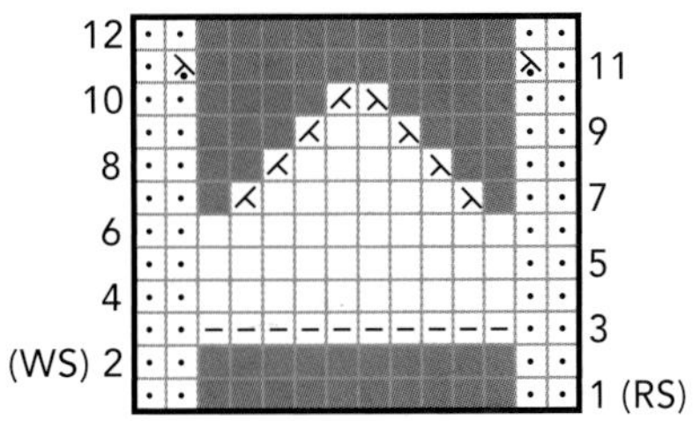

fur stitch

(multiple of 2 stitches plus 2 stitches)

Row 1 (RS): K1, *loop stitch (page 277), k1; repeat from the * across, ending with k1.

Row 2: Knit across.

Row 3: K1, *k1, loop stitch; repeat from the * across, ending with k1.

Row 4: Knit across.

Repeat Rows 1–4 for the pattern.

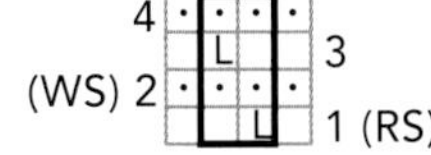

butterfly motif

(over 7 stitches, increases to 9 stitches, on a reverse stockinette background)

NOTE

- Stitch count varies from row to row.

Body

Row 1 (RS): P3, make a central double increase (page 273), p3.

Rows 2, 4, 6, 8, 10, 12, and 14: Knit the knit sts and purl the purl sts.

Rows 3, 5, 7, 9, 11, and 13: P3, k3, p3.

Row 15: P1, slip the next st onto cn and hold in back, k1-tbl (page 275), p1 from cn, s2kp2 (page 272), slip the next st onto cn and hold in front, p1, k1-tbl from cn, p1.

Rows 16 and 18: K1, p1-tbl (page 279), k3, p1-tbl, k1.

Row 17: P1, k1-tbl, p3, k1-tbl, p1.

Row 19: P1, make a knot (page 276), p3, make a knot, p1.

Upper Wing

Row 1 (RS): On the right-hand side of the body, with the right-side facing, pick up and knit 7 stitches where indicated in red on the chart.

Row 2: P7.

Row 3: K3, yarn over, k1, yarn over, k3.

Row 4: P4, k1, p4.

Row 5: K3, yarn over, p1, k1, p1, yarn over, k3.

Row 6: P3, [k1, p1] 3 times, p2.

Row 7: K3, yarn over, [k1, p1] twice, k1, yarn over, k3.

Row 8: P4, [k1, p1] twice, k1, p4.

Row 9: K3, yarn over, [p1, k1] 3 times, p1, yarn over, k3.

Row 10: P3, [k1, p1] 4 times, k1, p3.

Row 11: Using the cable cast-on technique (page 272), *cast on 1 st, then bind off the next 3 sts as you purl them; repeat from the * across, ending with cast on 1 st, bind off the last 2 sts. Fasten off.

Repeat for the left-hand side of the body.

Body

Upper Wing

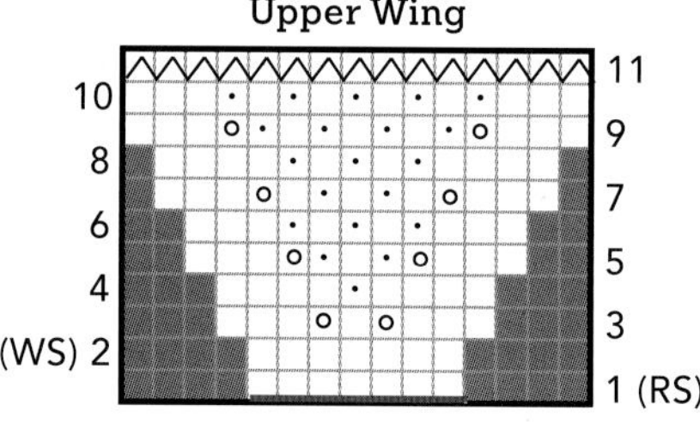

Lower Wing

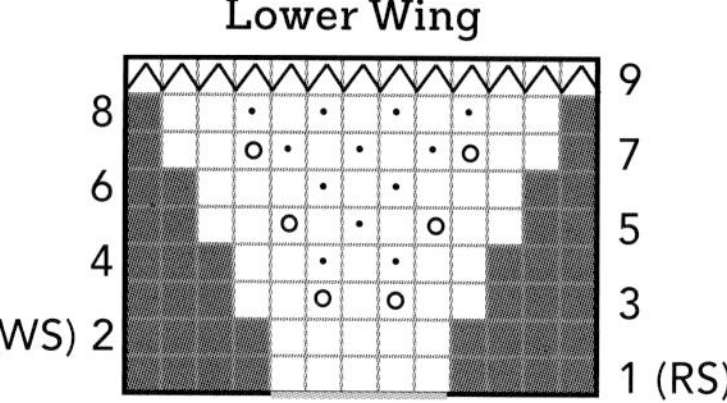

Lower Wing

Row 1 (RS): On the right-hand side of the body, with the right side facing, pick up and knit 5 stitches where indicated in blue on the chart, working behind the upper wing.

Row 2: P5.

Row 3: K2, yarn over, k1, yarn over, k2.

Row 4: P2, k1, p1, k1, p2.

Row 5: K2, yarn over, k1, p1, k1, yarn over, k2.

Row 6: P3, k1, p1, k1, p3.

Row 7: K2, yarn over, [p1, k1] twice, p1, yarn over, k2.

Row 8: P2, [k1, p1] 3 times, k1, p2.

Row 9: Using the cable cast-on technique, *cast on 1 st, bind off the next 3 sts as you purl them; repeat from the * across, ending with cast on 1 st, bind off the last 2 sts. Fasten off.

Repeat for the left-hand side of the body.

smocked ribbing

(multiple of 8 stitches plus 6 stitches)

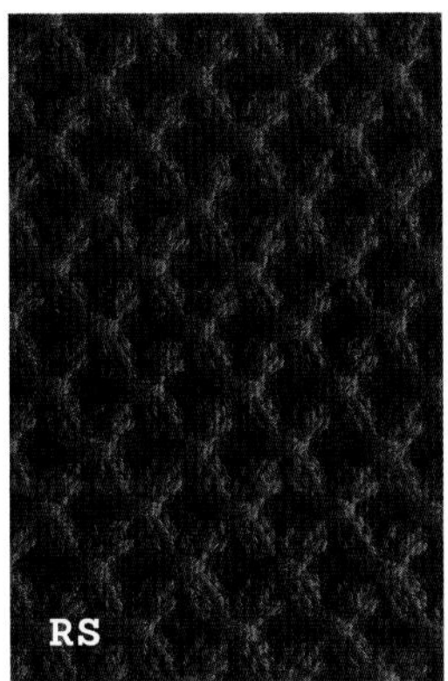

Rows 1 and 5 (RS): *K2, p2; repeat from the * across, ending with k2.

Row 2 and all WS rows: Knit the knit sts and purl the purl sts.

Row 3: *Slip the next 6 sts onto cn and wrap the yarn counterclockwise 4 times around them just below the cn (page 282), [k2, p2, k2] from cn, p2; repeat from the * across, ending with slip the next 6 sts onto cn and wrap the yarn counterclockwise 4 times around them just below the cn, [k2, p2, k2] the 6 sts on cn.

Row 7: K2, p1, *p1, slip the next 6 sts onto cn and wrap the yarn counterclockwise 4 times around them just below the cn, [k2, p2, k2] from cn, p1; repeat from the * across, ending with p1, k2.

Row 8: As Row 2.

Repeat Rows 1–8 for the pattern.

flora

(over 33 stitches, on a reverse stockinette background)

NOTE

- On the first repeat of the pattern, work the highlighted stitches as purl on the right side and knit on the wrong side.

Row 1 (RS): P6, right twist (page 279), slip the next 3 sts onto cn and hold in front, p2, k3 from cn, p9, make a knot (page 276), p4, make a knot, k1, p4.

Rows 2, 4, 6, 8, 10, 12, 14, 18, 20, 24, 26, 28, 30, 32, 34, 36, 40, and 42: Knit the knit sts, knit the knots, purl the purl sts, and purl the yarn over sts.

Row 3: P4, k3tog, yarn over, k1, yarn over, p2, slip the next 3 sts onto cn and hold in front, k2, k3 from cn, p13, make a knot, p4.

Row 5: P2, k3tog, [k1, yarn over] twice, k1, p1, slip the next st onto cn and hold in back, k1, p1 from cn, k1, slip the next 3 sts onto cn and hold in front, p2, k3 from cn, p16.

Row 7: K3tog, k2, yarn over, k1, yarn over, k2, p1, k1, p1, left twist (page 276), p1, slip the next 3 sts onto cn and hold in front, p2, k3 from cn, p14.

Row 9: K6, k2tog, M1 purlwise (page 278), p1, k1, p1, yarn over, k1, yarn over, sssk (page 281), p1, slip the next 3 sts onto cn and hold in front, p2, k3 from cn, p12.

Row 11: M1 purlwise, ssk, k3, k2tog, M1 purlwise, p1, slip the next st onto cn and hold in back, k1, p1 from cn, p1, [k1, yarn over] twice, k1, sssk, p1, slip the next 3 sts onto cn and hold in front, p2, k3 from cn, p10.

Row 13: P1, M1 purlwise, ssk, k1, k2tog, M1 purlwise, p2, k1, p2, k2, yarn over, k1, yarn over, k2, sssk, p1, slip the next 3 sts onto cn and hold in front, p2, k3 from cn, p8.

Row 15: P2, M1 purlwise, k3tog, M1 purlwise, p2, right twist, p2, M1 purlwise, ssk, k6, p3, slip the next 3 sts onto cn and hold in front, p1, k3 from cn, p7.

Row 16: K7, p3, k4, p7, k3, p2, k7.

Row 17: P6, slip the next st onto cn and hold in back, k1, p1 from cn, slip the next st onto cn and hold in front, p1, k1 from cn, p2, M1 purlwise, ssk, k3, k2tog, M1 purlwise, p4, k3, p7.

Row 19: P5, slip the next st onto cn and hold in back, k1, p1 from cn, p2, slip the next st onto cn and hold in front, p1, k1 from cn, make a knot, p1, M1 purlwise, ssk, k1, k2tog, M1 purlwise, p5, k3, p7.

Row 21: P3, make a knot, slip the next st onto cn and hold in back, k1, p1 from cn, p3, make a knot, k1, p3, M1 purlwise, k3tog, M1 purlwise, p5, slip the next st onto cn and hold in back, k3, k1 from cn, p7.

Row 22: K7, p4, k11, p1, k5, p1, k4.

Row 23: P4, k1, make a knot, p4, make a knot, p9, slip the next 2 sts onto cn and hold in back, k3, p2 from cn, left twist, p6.

Row 25: P4, make a knot, p13, slip the next 2 sts onto cn and hold in back, k3, k2 from cn, p2, yarn over, k1, yarn over, sssk, p4.

Row 27: P16, slip the next 2 sts onto cn and hold in back, k3, p2 from cn, k1, slip the next st onto cn and hold in front, p1, k1 from cn, p1, [k1, yarn over] twice, k1, sssk, p2.

Row 29: P14, slip the next 2 sts onto cn and hold in back, k3, p2 from cn, p1, right twist, p1, k1, p1, k2, yarn over, k1, yarn over, k2, sssk.

Row 31: P12, slip the next 2 sts onto cn and hold in back, k3, p2 from cn, p1, k3tog, yarn over, k1, yarn over, p1, k1, p1, M1 purlwise, ssk, k6.

Row 33: P10, slip the next 2 sts onto cn and hold in back, k3, p2 from cn, p1, k3tog, [k1, yarn over] twice, k1, p1, slip the next st onto cn and hold in front, p1, k1 from cn, p1, M1 purlwise, ssk, k3, k2tog, M1 purlwise.

Row 35: P8, slip the next 2 sts onto cn and hold in back, k3, p2 from cn, p1, k3tog, k2, yarn over, k1, yarn over, k2, p2, k1, p2, M1 purlwise, ssk, k1, k2tog, M1 purlwise, p1.

Row 37: P7, slip the next st onto cn and hold in back, k3, p1 from cn, p3, k6, k2tog, M1 purlwise, p2, left twist, p2, M1 purlwise, sssk, M1 purlwise, p2.

Row 38: K7, p2, k3, p7, k4, p3, k7.

Row 39: P7, k3, p4, M1 purlwise, ssk, k3, k2tog, M1 purlwise, p2, slip the next st onto cn and hold in back, k1, p1 from cn, slip the next st onto cn and hold in front, p1, k1 from cn, p6.

Row 41: P7, k3, p5, M1 purlwise, ssk, k1, k2tog, M1 purlwise, p1, make a knot, slip the next st onto cn and hold in back, k1, p1 from cn, p2, slip the next st onto cn and hold in front, p1, k1 from cn, p5.

Row 43: P7, slip the next 3 sts onto cn and hold in front, k1, k3 from cn, p5, M1 purlwise, sssk, M1 purlwise, p3, k1, make a knot, p3, slip the next st onto cn and hold in front, p1, k1 from cn, make a knot, p3.

Row 44: K4, p1, k5, p1, k11, p4, k7.

Repeat Rows 1–44 for the pattern.

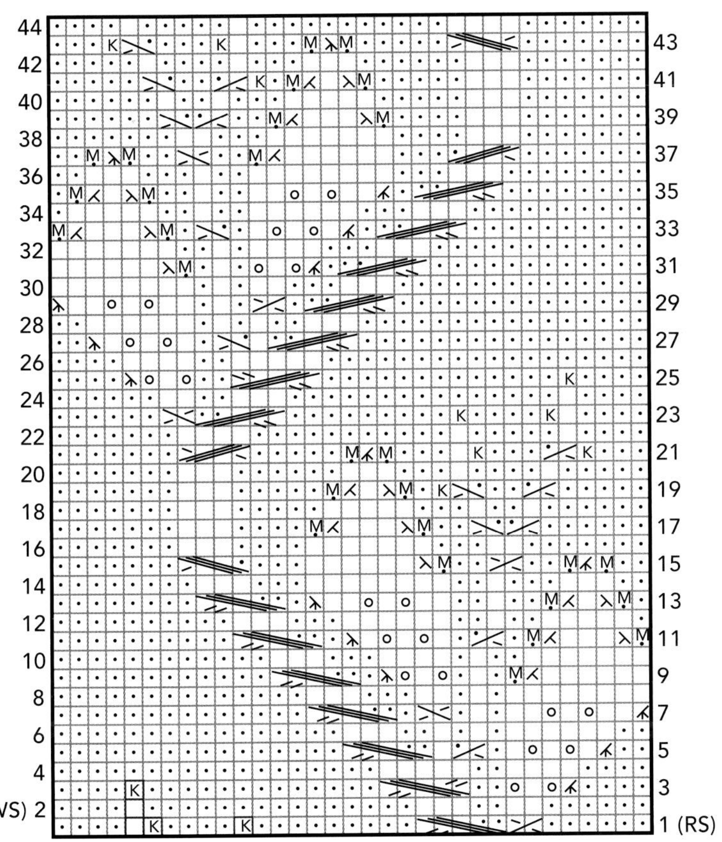

□ = On the first repeat of the pattern, work these 5 sts as follows: purl on the right-side; knit on the wrong-side

lamb's tails

(multiple of 4 stitches plus 3 stitches)

NOTES

- A crochet hook is required; use one that is the same millimeter size as your knitting needles for the project.
- Crocheted Chain Loop = Insert a crochet hook into the next st on the left-hand needle, yarn over the hook and pull it through the st, leaving the original st on the left-hand needle; make 11 more chain sts in this way, then insert the hook into the same original st on the left-hand needle, yarn over hook, and draw it through the original st and the last chain on the hook; slip this chain st to the right-hand needle.

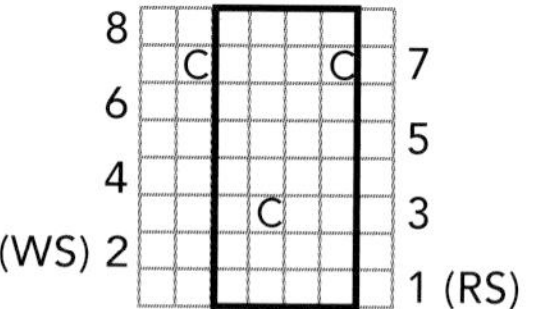

Rows 1 and 5 (RS): Knit across.

Row 2 and all WS rows: Purl across.

Row 3: K1, *k2, make a crocheted chain loop (see Notes), k1; repeat from the * across, ending with k2.

Row 7: K1, *make a crocheted chain loop, k3; repeat from the * across, ending with make a crocheted chain loop, k1.

Row 8: As Row 2.

Repeat Rows 1–8 for the pattern.

chain faux fur

(multiple of 2 stitches plus 2 stitches)

NOTES

- A crochet hook is required; use one that is the same millimeter size as your knitting needles for the project.
- Crocheted Chain Loop = Insert a crochet hook into the next st on the left-hand needle, yarn over the hook and pull it through the st, leaving the original st on the left-hand needle; make 11 more chain sts in this way, then insert the hook into the same original st on the left-hand needle, yarn over hook, and draw it through the original st and the last chain on the hook; slip this chain st to the right-hand needle.

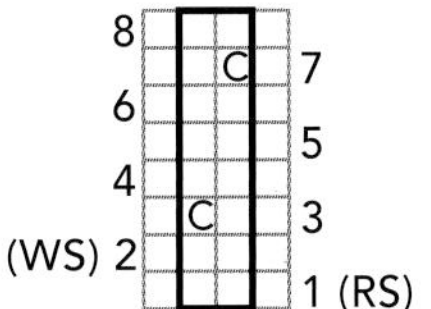

Rows 1 and 5 (RS): Knit across.

Row 2 and all WS rows: Purl across.

Row 3: K1, *k1, make a crocheted chain loop (see Notes); repeat from the * across, ending with k1.

Row 7: K1, *make a crocheted chain loop, k1; repeat from the * across, ending with k1.

Row 8: As Row 2.

Repeat Rows 1–8 for the pattern.

oak leaf

(over 11 stitches, increases to 23 stitches, on a reverse stockinette background)

NOTE

- Stitch count varies from row to row.

Row 1 (RS): P10, k1.

Rows 2, 4, 6, 8, 10, 12, 14, 16, 20, 22, 26, 28, 32, 34, 36, and 38: Knit the knit sts and purl the purl sts.

Row 3: P9, slip the next st onto cn and hold in back, k1, p1 from cn.

Row 5: P7, slip the next 2 sts onto cn and hold in back, k1 p2 from cn, p1.

Row 7: P6, slip the next st onto cn and hold in back k1, p1 from cn, p3.

Row 9: P5, slip the next st onto cn and hold in back k1, p1 from cn, p4.

Row 11: P5, M1 (page 277), make a central double increase (page 273), M1, p5.

Row 13: P5, [k1, M1] 4 times, k1, p5.

Row 15: P5, k1, [M1, k3, M1, k1] twice, p5.

Row 17: P2, slip the next 3 sts onto cn and hold in back, [ssk, k2tog] from the left-hand needle, turn, p2, turn, k2tog from the left-hand needle, p3 from cn, k5, slip the next 4 sts onto cn and hold in front, p3, [ssk, k2tog] from cn, turn, p2, turn, ssk, p2.

Row 18: K2, k2tog, k2, p5, k2, ssk, k2.

Rows 19–30: As Rows 13–18.

Rows 31 and 32: As Rows 13 and 14.

Row 33: P5, ssk, k5, k2tog, p5.

Row 35: P5, ssk, k3, k2tog, p5.

Row 37: P5, ssk, k1, k2tog, p5.

Row 39: P5, s2kp2 (page 272), p5.

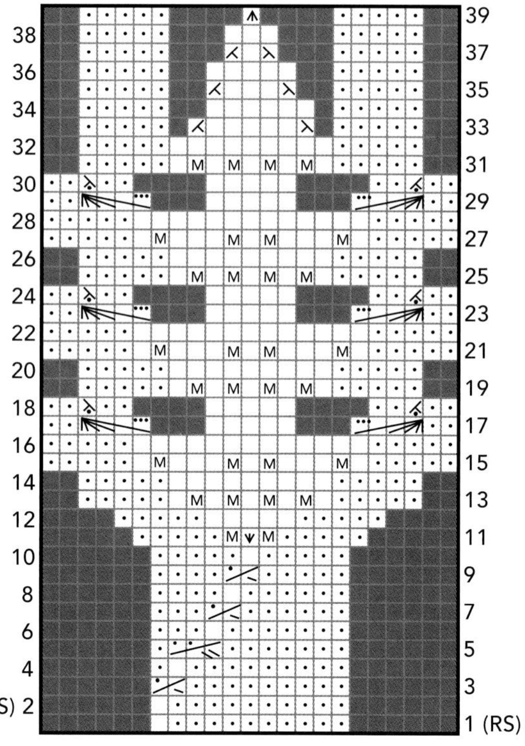

knotted cable

(over 16 stitches on a reverse stockinette background)

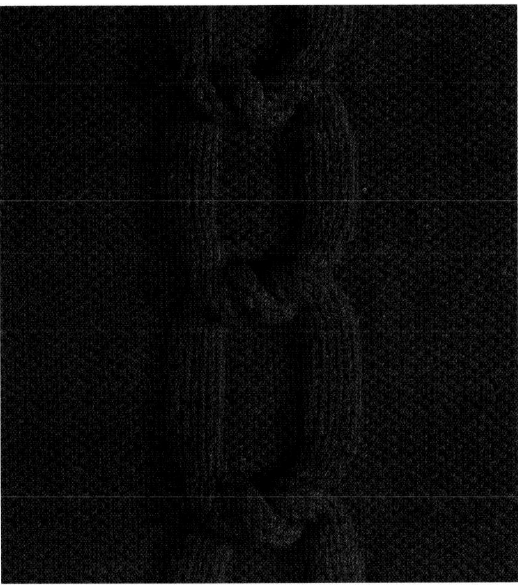

NOTE

- This pattern requires 3 safety pins or stitch holders and an extra knitting needle.

Rows 1, 3, 5, 17, and 19 (RS): K4, p8, k4.

Row 2 and all WS rows: Knit the knit sts and purl the purl sts.

Row 7: Slip the next 4 sts onto cn and hold in front, p1, k4 from cn, p6, slip the next st onto cn and hold in back, k4, p1 from cn.

Row 9: P1, slip the next 4 sts onto cn and hold in front, p1, k4 from cn, p4, slip the next st onto cn and hold in back, k4, p1 from cn, p1.

Row 11: P2, then, using an extra knitting needle, [k4, turn; p4, turn] 6 times. Place these 4 sts onto safety pin #1 and cut yarn, slip the next 4 sts onto safety pin #2 and hold in back, reattach yarn and [k4, turn; p4, turn] 6 times. Place these 4 sts onto safety pin #3 and cut yarn. With the right side of the stitches facing you and safety pin #2 in the back, twist the strip that is on safety pin #1 over and under the strip that is on safety pin #3 to form a knot. Slip the sts from safety pin #3 onto the left-hand needle and knit them, p4 from safety pin #2, k4 from safety pin #1, p2.

Row 13: P1, slip the next st onto cn and hold in back, k4, p1 from cn, p4, slip the next 4 sts onto cn and hold in front, p1, k4 from cn, p1.

Row 15: Slip the next st onto cn and hold in back, k4, p1 from cn, p6, slip the next 4 sts onto cn and hold in front, p1, k4 from cn.

Row 20: As Row 2.

Repeat Rows 1–20 for the pattern.

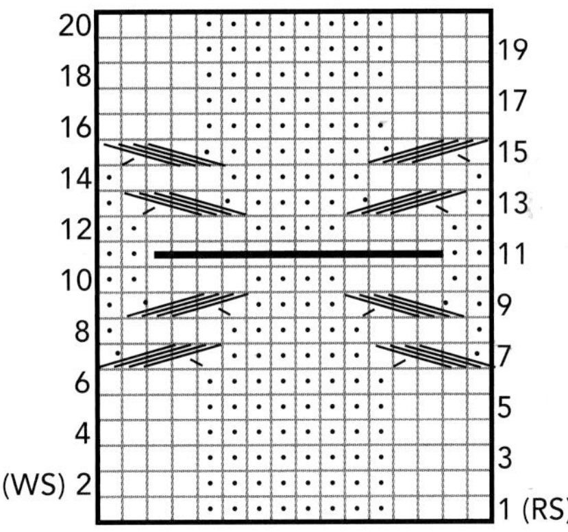

knotted lattice

(multiple of 26 stitches plus 22 stitches)

NOTE

- This pattern requires 3 safety pins or stitch holders and an extra knitting needle.

Rows 1 and 25 (RS): K4, p1, *p13, k4, p4, k4, p1; repeat from the * across, ending with p13, k4.

Row 2 and all WS rows: Knit the knit sts and purl the purl sts.

Rows 3 and 23: P1, k4, *p12, k4, p6, k4; repeat from the * across, ending with p12, k4, p1.

Rows 5 and 21: P2, k3, *k1, p10, k4, p8, k3; repeat from the * across, ending with k1, p10, k4, p2.

Rows 7 and 19: P3, k2, *k2, p8, k4, p10, k2; repeat from the * across, ending with k2, p8, k4, p3.

Rows 9 and 17: P4, k1,*k3, p6, k4, p12, k1; repeat from the * across, ending with k3, p6, k4, p4.

Rows 11 and 15: P5, *k4, p4, k4, p14; repeat from the * across, ending with k4, p4, k4, p5.

Row 13: P5, *using an extra knitting needle, [k4, turn; p4, turn] 6 times, then place these 4 sts onto safety pin #1 and cut the yarn, slip the next 4 sts onto safety pin #2 and hold in back, reattach the yarn and [k4, turn; p4, turn] 6 times, then place these 4 sts onto safety pin #3 and cut the yarn. With the right side of the stitches facing you and safety pin #2 in the back, twist the strip that is on safety pin #1 over and under the strip that is on safety pin #3 to form a knot, slip the sts from safety pin #3 onto the left-hand needle and knit them, p4 from safety pin #2, k4 from safety pin #1, p14; repeat from the * across, ending with using an extra knitting needle, [k4, turn; p4, turn] 6 times, then place these 4 sts onto safety pin #1 and cut the yarn, slip the next 4 sts onto safety pin #2 and hold in back, reattach the yarn and [k4, turn; p4, turn] 6 times, then place these 4 sts onto safety pin #3 and

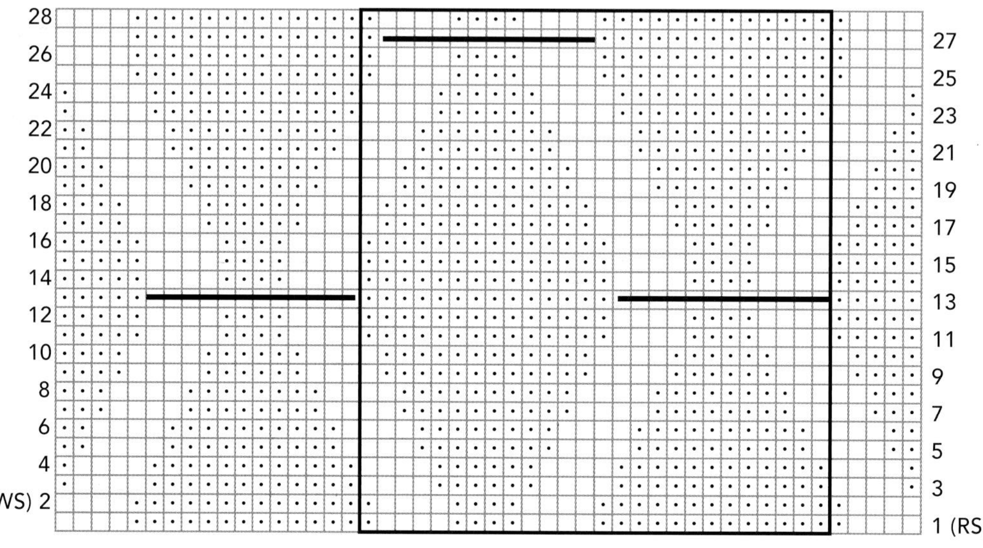

cut the yarn. With the right side of the stitches facing you and safety pin #2 in the back, twist the strip that is on safety pin #1 over and under the strip that is on safety pin #3 to form a knot, slip the sts from safety pin #3 onto the left-hand needle and knit them, p4 from safety pin #2, k4 from safety pin #1, p5.

Row 27: K4, p1,*p13, using an extra knitting needle, [k4, turn; p4, turn] 6 times, then place these 4 sts onto safety pin #1 and cut the yarn, slip the next 4 sts onto safety pin #2 and hold in back, reattach the yarn and [k4, turn; p4, turn] 6 times, then place these 4 sts onto safety pin #3 and cut the yarn. With the right side of the stitches facing you and safety pin #2 in the back, twist the strip that is on safety pin #1 over and under the strip that is on safety pin #3 to form a knot, slip the sts from safety pin #3 onto the left-hand needle and knit them, p4 from safety pin #2, k4 from safety pin #1, p1; repeat from the * across, ending with p13, k4.

Row 28: As Row 2.

Repeat Rows 1–28 for the pattern.

all tied up

(multiple of 13 stitches, increases to multiple of 15 stitches)

NOTE

- Stitch count varies from row to row.

Rows 1 and 3 (RS): *P3, k7, p3; repeat from the * across.

Rows 2 and 4: *K3, p7, k3; repeat from the * across.

Row 5: Knit across.

Rows 6 and 8: *P6, [yarn over] twice (page 284), p1, [yarn over] twice, p6; repeat from the * across.

Rows 7 and 9: *K6, drop the first set of yarn overs, k1, then drop the next set of yarn overs, k6; repeat from the * across. At the end of the row, insert the point of a knitting needle into each pair of loops and pull until taut, then use a square knot to tie the pair of loops together to form a tight bow.

Row 10: Purl across.

Repeat Rows 1–10 for the pattern.

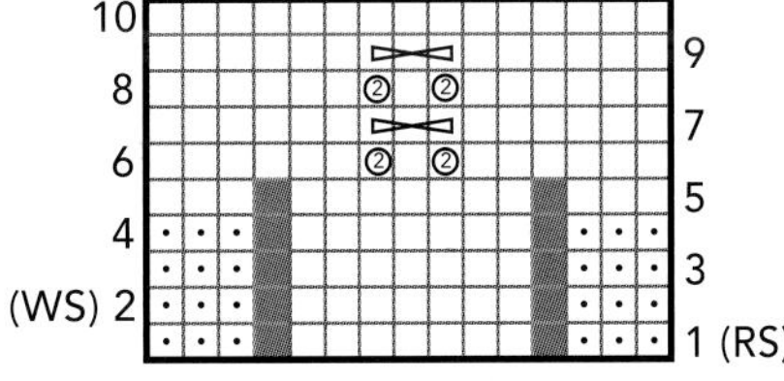

vineyard lattice 

(multiple of 40 stitches plus 4 stitches)

Row 1 (RS): P2, *p18, slip the next 2 sts onto cn and hold in back, k2, k2 from cn, p18; repeat from the * across, ending with p2.

Row 2 and all WS rows: Knit the knit sts and bobbles, and purl the purl sts.

Row 3: P2, *p16, slip the next 2 sts onto cn and hold in back, k2, p2 from cn, slip the next 2 sts onto cn and hold in front, p2, k2 from cn, p16; repeat from the * across, ending with p2.

Row 5: P2, *p14, slip the next 2 sts onto cn and hold in back, k2, p2 from cn, p4, slip the next 2 sts onto cn and hold in front, p2, k2 from cn, p14; repeat from the * across, ending with p2.

Row 7: P2, *p12, slip the next 2 sts onto cn and hold in back, k2, p2 from cn, p8, slip the next 2 sts onto cn and hold in front, p2, k2 from cn, p12; repeat from the * across, ending with p2.

Row 9: P2, *p10, slip the next 2 sts onto cn and hold in back, k2, p2 from cn, p11, make a bobble (page 270), slip the next 2 sts onto cn and hold in front, p2, k2 from cn, p10; repeat from the * across, ending with p2.

Row 11: P2, *p8, slip the next 2 sts onto cn and hold in back, k2, p2 from cn, p12, [make a bobble, p1] twice, slip the next 2 sts onto cn and hold in front, p2, k2 from cn, p8; repeat from the * across, ending with p2.

Row 13: P2, *p6, slip the next 2 sts onto cn and hold in back, k2, p2 from cn, p13, [make a bobble, p1] 3 times, p1, slip the next 2 sts onto cn and hold in front, p2, k2 from cn, p6; repeat from the * across, ending with p2.

Row 15: P2, *p4, slip the next 2 sts onto cn and hold in back, k2, p2 from cn, p14, [make a bobble, p1] 4 times, p2, slip the next 2 sts onto cn and hold in front, p2, k2 from cn, p4; repeat from the * across, ending with p2.

Row 17: P2, *p2, slip the next 2 sts onto cn and hold in back, k2, p2 from cn, p15, [make a bobble, p1] 5 times, p3, slip the next 2 sts onto cn and hold in front, p2, k2 from cn, p2; repeat from the * across, ending with p2.

Row 19: P2, *slip the next 2 sts onto cn and hold in back, k2, p2 from cn, p18, [make a bobble, p1] 4 times, p6, slip the next 2 sts onto cn and hold in front, p2, k2 from cn; repeat from the * across, ending with p2.

Row 21: *Slip the next 2 sts onto cn and hold in front, k2, k2 from cn, p36; repeat from the * across, ending with slip the next 2 sts onto cn and hold in front, k2, k2 from cn.

Row 23: P2, *slip the next 2 sts onto cn and hold in front, p2, k2 from cn, p32, slip the next 2 sts onto cn and hold in back, k2, p2 from cn; repeat from the * across, ending with p2.

Row 25: P2, *p2, slip the next 2 sts onto cn and hold in front, p2, k2 from cn, p28, slip the next 2 sts onto cn and hold in back, k2, p2 from cn, p2; repeat from the * across, ending with p2.

Row 27: P2, *p4, slip the next 2 sts onto cn and hold in front, p2, k2 from cn, p24, slip the next 2 sts onto cn and hold in back, k2, p2 from cn, p4; repeat from the * across, ending with p2.

Row 29: P2, *p5, make a bobble, slip the next 2 sts onto cn and hold in front, p2, k2 from cn, p20, slip

(continued on page 256)

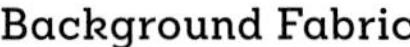

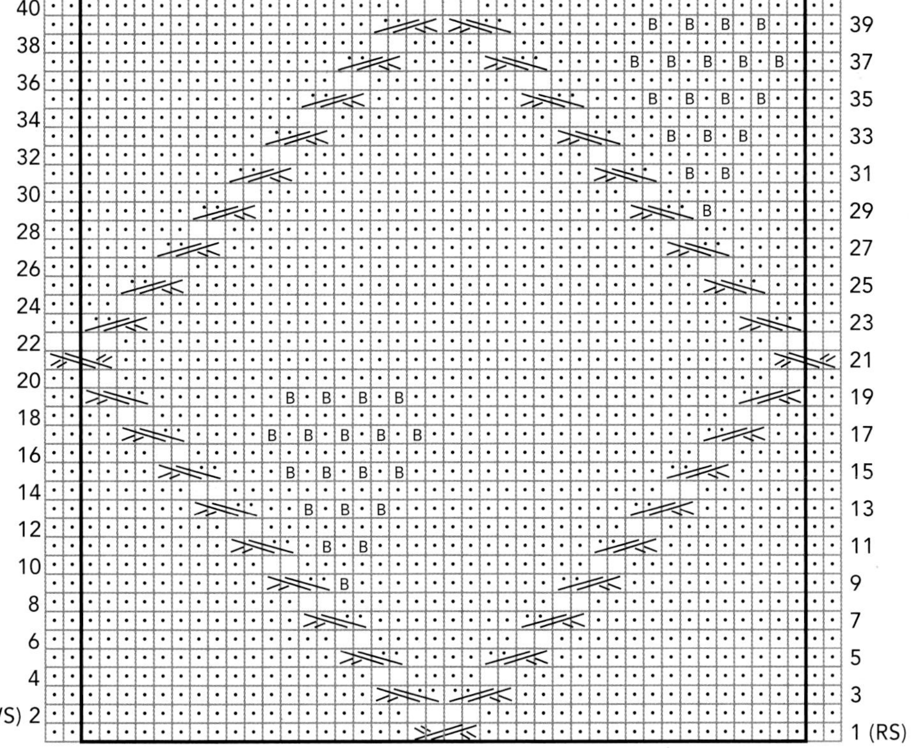

NOTES

- When working Row 5 of the Leaf Appliqué, work Rows 5–7 on the right-hand tip first, then break yarn; reattach the yarn to the next stitch on Row 5, and work Rows 5–11 on the middle tip, then break yarn; reattach the yarn to the next stitch on Row 5, and work Rows 5–7 on the left-hand tip.
- Finishing: See instructions on page 256.

the next 2 sts onto cn and hold in back, k2, p2 from cn, p6; repeat from the * across, ending with p2.

Row 31: P2, *p4, [make a bobble, p1] twice, slip the next 2 sts onto cn and hold in front, p2, k2 from cn, p16, slip the next 2 sts onto cn and hold in back, k2, p2 from cn, p8; repeat from the * across, ending with p2.

Row 33: P2, *p3, [make a bobble, p1] 3 times, p1, slip the next 2 sts onto cn and hold in front, p2, k2 from cn, p12, slip the next 2 sts onto cn and hold in back, k2, p2 from cn, p10; repeat from the * across, ending with p2.

Row 35: P2, *p2, [make a bobble, p1] 4 times, p2, slip the next 2 sts onto cn and hold in front, p2, k2 from cn, p8, slip the next 2 sts onto cn and hold in back, k2, p2 from cn, p12; repeat from the * across, ending with p2.

Row 37: P2, *p1, [make a bobble, p1] 5 times, p3, slip the next 2 sts onto cn and hold in front, p2, k2 from cn, p4, slip the next 2 sts onto cn and hold in back, k2, p2 from cn, p14; repeat from the * across, ending with p2.

Row 39: P2, *p2, [make a bobble, p1] 4 times, p6, slip the next 2 sts onto cn and hold in front, p2, k2 from cn, slip the next 2 sts onto cn and hold in back, k2, p2 from cn, p16; repeat from the * across, ending with p2.

Row 40: As Row 2.

Leaf Appliqué

NOTE

- See the note on the chart before working Row 5.

Cast on 5 sts.

Row 1 (RS): [K1, yarn over] 4 times, k1.

Row 2 and all WS rows: Purl across.

Row 3: [K1, yarn over] twice, k2, yarn over, k1, yarn over, k2, [yarn over, k1] twice.

Row 5: Ssk, k1, k2tog, turn, p3, turn, s2kp2 (page 272), fasten off this leaf tip; reattach the yarn to the next st of Row 5 and k2, yarn over, k1, yarn over, k2, turn, p7, turn, ssk, k3, k2tog, turn, p5, turn, ssk, k1, k2tog, turn, p3, turn, s2kp2, fasten off this leaf tip; reattach the yarn to the next st of Row 5 and ssk, k1, k2tog, turn, p3, turn, s2kp2, fasten off this leaf tip.

Leaf Appliqué

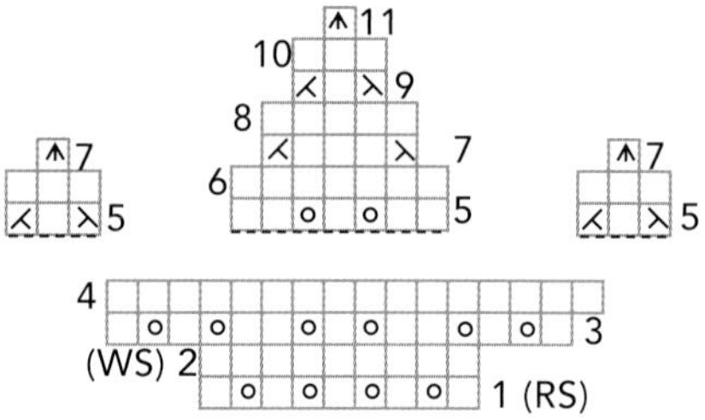

Finishing

Sew leaves as desired on the knitted lattice. Use the crocheted chain stitch (page 273) to add stems and vines as shown in photograph, tacking the vines in place. (Several chains were used in the sample swatch, each approximately 18"/[45.5cm] long.)

How to Read Instructions for Knitting Stitch Patterns

In this book, each pattern is offered in both text and chart form. Many knitters prefer using the graphics of the charts, but others like everything written out in text. Choose the format that makes your knitting easier and more fun.

The Foreign Language of Knitting Symbols and Charts: A Crash Course in Translation

To some knitters, charted patterns seem like a secret code of cryptic characters laid out mysteriously on a grid. Actually, like foreign languages, knitting charts and their symbols are simple to translate once you become familiar with the "grammar" and "vocabulary."

A Quick Lesson in Grammar

A knitting chart is a visual representation of the public side of knitted fabric.

Each square of the grid corresponds to one stitch and each row of squares corresponds to one row of stitches.

Charts are read in the same way that the fabric is knit—from the lower edge up, with the first row at the bottom of the chart and the last row at the top.

Right-side rows are read from right to left, in the same order that stitches present themselves to you on the left-hand knitting needle. The following illustration shows the order that stitches will be worked for Row 1, a right-side row (the side of the fabric which the public will see), in a chart:

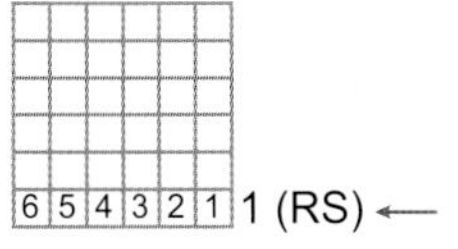

Of course, if you're knitting back and forth in rows, at the end of this first row, you flip your knitting before starting the next row, and the wrong side of the fabric faces you. Physically, the first stitch of this wrong-side row is the same stitch as the last stitch of the right-side row you just completed. Thus, wrong-side rows on charts are read in the opposite direction, from left to right, as shown below:

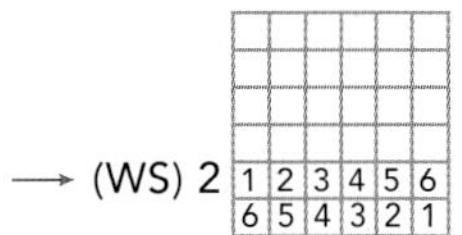

When working in the round rather than back and forth in rows, such as for a hat or sock, the right side of the fabric is always facing you so, in these cases, all rows of the chart are read from right to left.

Some patterns are reversible and have no real right or wrong sides. In most of those patterns, such as Embossed Flow (page 95), I have arbitrarily designated one of the sides as the right side. Other patterns, however, are heavily cabled on both sides to create fabrics that are equally beautiful on both sides, such as Reversible Kerry Braids (page 189). Here, for ease of knitting, two charts are given. You'll use Chart A when working on Side A and Chart B when working on Side B. Because these patterns truly have no right or wrong side, both charts and all the symbols on them are read as right-side rows, from right to left. Patterns that work this way are clearly indicated.

Knitting charts make it easy to see how many stitches are involved in a pattern. A bold rectangular frame is used in this book to indicate the stitch repeat. If extra stitches are required on each side to center the pattern on the fabric, they are shown to the left and/or right of the repeat. Cross Hatch (page 81), for example, has a multiple of 10 plus 2 stitches; it is a 10-stitch repeat with one "balancing" stitch on each side.

To read the chart below, for example, you'd start at the lower right-hand corner, read from right to left, work the four stitches inside the bold rectangle as many times as is necessary to get across your fabric, and end the row with the stitch represented in this sample chart by the star. This stitch sits outside the stitch repeat and so is worked once per row. It is the last stitch of every right-side row, and since wrong-side rows are read from left to right, it is the first stitch of every wrong-side row.

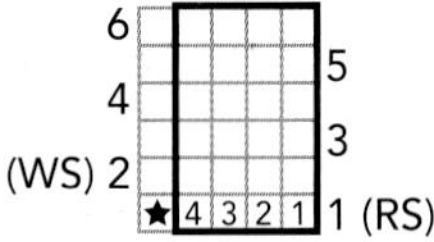

As you journey through this book, you will notice that some of the charts, like the leaf appliqué in Vineyard Lattice (page 254), for instance, have irregular shapes rather than being rectangular (as is usually the case). That's because the stitch count is not a constant for all rows in the pattern; stitches are being added or taken away to create pattern interest.

In other charts, changing stitch counts are dealt with in a different way. In cases such as Caedmon Celtic Knot (page 184), gray-filled squares "hold" the spot where stitches either were or will eventually be. Those gray squares are called "no stitch" in the Comprehensive Stitch Key (page 263) because you pay no attention to them when you see them in the chart. Don't slip a stitch on your needles, just skip over the gray square and move on to the next symbol and the next stitch on your needle.

Some patterns are worked as panels or motifs on simple backgrounds to make them "pop." For a stockinette background, knit on the right side and purl on the wrong side; for a reverse stockinette ground, purl on the right side and knit on the wrong side.

The Vocabulary List

Each symbol on a chart indicates the way a stitch or group of stitches will be worked, and the arrangement of symbols on the chart determines the stitch pattern.

Usually, the symbols visually resemble the way the resulting stitches will appear on the public side of the knitted fabric. The symbol for a knit stitch, for example, is a blank box, mimicking the flat appearance of the knit stitch itself; the dot symbol for a purl stitch depicts the bumpy appearance of a purled stitch.

A symbol that occupies several squares of the grid indicates the number of stitches that will be involved in that particular knitting maneuver. Cables, for instance, are worked over more than one stitch, so cable symbols occupy several adjacent squares. In most of the charts in this book, each line or dot within every cable symbol represents one of the stitches being crossed, so you can quickly tell at a glance the number of stitches involved. For instance, three lines crossing three other lines would symbolize a six-stitch cable.

Even cable symbols look like the knitting maneuvers they represent. In a Left Cross, the dominant lines in the symbol cross toward the left, with the right-hand stitches moving in front of the others. When knitting the symbol, this is your clue to place the cable needle holding those stitches in front of your work.

eft ross

On the other hand, Right Cross cable symbols show the left-hand stitches moving over the others toward the right. Since the right-hand stitches appear to be moving behind the left-hand ones, you will slip them onto your cable needle and hold them in back of your work.

ight ross

When knit stitches travel over other knit stitches in a cable, the symbol has diagonal lines representing the background stitches. However, if knit stitches travel over purl stitches instead, the cable symbol will have dots to represent the background stitches, as seen below.

When instructions say to hold yarn or stitches in front or in back, it means in front or in back of the piece of work as you see it on your needles. In front is the side you are looking at; in back is the side away from you at that time.

Needless to say, designers and editors may use different sets of symbols to represent the same knitting maneuvers, but they are usually variations on a theme; generally, all symbols resemble the resulting stitch. Just think about them as unique "dialects" of this "foreign language"! They're usually pretty easy to decipher, since every chart has a key somewhere near it. The Comprehensive Stitch Key used in this book is on pages 263–267.

Most of the time, all rows in charts are shown as they appear on the public side of the fabric. There are some exceptions, such as Reversible Kerry Braids (page 189) and Reversible Dungourney Cables (page 190). Consequently, the same symbol can mean different things on right-side and wrong-side rows. The blank box, for instance, represents a knit stitch on a right-side row, but if you're on a wrong-side row and want the stitch to appear as a knit stitch on the reverse side of the fabric, you must purl it.

If a symbol is used on both right- and wrong-side rows of the chart, the Comprehensive Stitch Key (pages 263–267) will tell you which knitting maneuver to use where.

Often, wrong-side rows are pretty simple: you just knit the knit stitches and purl the purl stitches as they present themselves to you on the knitting needle. Scan the entire chart before you begin knitting to confirm that this is the case, or just look for the handy easy icon used in this book. If so, you can zip along those wrong-side rows reading your knitting rather than the chart!

Some publications don't even include the wrong-side rows on the charts at all! Their rows are marked on the right-hand side with odd numbers only. This means that on wrong-side rows you'll just knit the knits and purl the purls when you get to them.

I'll bet that with some practice—and yes, a little bit of patience!—you'll find knitting from charts easy, fast, and maybe even fun!

tips

- Enlarge your charts on a copy machine to make reading them easier.
- If you're an exceptionally visual person, use a color key to simplify reading the symbols: choose a different color highlighting pen for each symbol in your key and throughout the chart (see illustration below). Instead of deciphering each symbol individually, you'll have your own, useful color code!

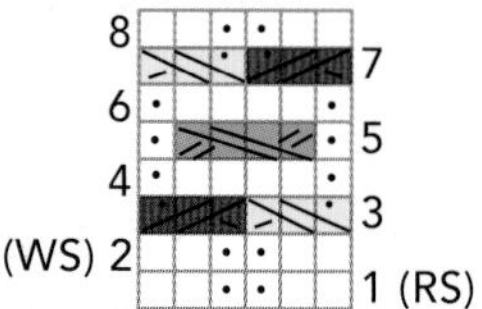

KEY
- □ = Knit on RS; purl on WS
- • = Purl on RS; knit on WS
- = Slip 2 sts onto cn and hold in front; p1; k2 from cn
- = Slip next st onto cn and hold in back; k2; p1 from cn
- = Slip 2 sts onto cn and hold in front; k2; k2 from cn

- If you're working more than one stitch pattern across your needles, place stitch markers on your knitting needles to separate each pattern repeat or panel.
- Use a row counter or a sticky note to keep track of where you are on the chart. Put the note above the row you're currently working on so you can see how it integrates with the existing fabric.

Knitting Patterns Written in Words

Since some knitters prefer word-for-word patterns, each stitch pattern in this book is written out in text form as well as chart format.

Row-by-row instructions are typed out in numerical order. If the pattern has a repeat heightwise, the rows to be repeated will be indicated at the end of the pattern.

As mentioned earlier, the "stitch multiple" indicates the number of stitches needed to repeat the pattern across the width of the fabric. In the text instructions, the stitch repeat is typed between the asterisk and semicolon. Any stitches outside the asterisk and semicolon are needed for symmetry.

Row 1 of Garter Rib (page 20), for example, reads like this:

Row 1 (RS): *K1, p1; repeat from the * across, ending with k1.

To knit this row, you would knit one stitch, then purl one stitch all the way across the row. At the end of the row, there would be one stitch left, and that stitch would be knitted.

Sometimes, the number of knit or purl stitches is broken up at the beginning and end of the stitch repeat, as in Brocade (page 30).

Row 1 of this pattern reads:

Row 1 (RS): *K5, p7, k4; repeat from the * across, ending with k1.

This row can also be written as:

Row 1 (RS): K5, p7, *k9, p7; repeat from the * across, ending with k5.

Although they may look different, they both say the same thing: To knit this right-side row, you would knit five stitches, purl seven stitches, then knit *nine* stitches (which is the four stitches from the end of the repeat plus the five stitches at the beginning of the repeat). This book uses both methods of writing out a row, trying to balance clarity with ease of use.

Some patterns have sections of text shown inside brackets like these [ ]. The brackets will be followed by instructions regarding the stitches contained within.

These brackets may indicate that a certain sequence of stitches is supposed to be worked all into a single stitch. Row 5 of String of Pearls (page 224), for example, reads:

Row 5: With B, k1, *[k1, yarn over, k1] all into the next st, slip the next st with the yarn in back; repeat from the * across, ending with k1.

The brackets mean that after knitting the first stitch with Color B, you would do the following all into the next stitch before removing the original stitch from the left-hand needle: Knit the stitch, then wrap the yarn around the right-hand needle to make a yarn over, then insert the right-hand needle into that same stitch again to knit it once more. Three stitches are made out of a single stitch.

Other times, brackets show a set of instructions that will be repeated a certain number of times. Row 9 of Ribbed Squares (page 26), for example, reads:

Row 9: *P8, [k2, p2] twice; repeat from the * across.

This row can also be written as:

Row 9: *P8, k2, p2, k2, p2; repeat from the * across.

To work this row, you would purl eight stitches, knit two stitches, purl two stitches, knit two stitches, purl two stitches, then repeat from the beginning, all the way across.

To save space in the pattern instructions, standard abbreviations are used. See page 262 for a list of the ones used in this book.

Abbreviations

Following is a list of abbreviations used in the patterns of this book. Many of the techniques are discussed in the Knitting Techniques section (pages 268–285).

cn cable needle

k knit

k1f&b knit into the front and then the back of a stitch; this increases 1 stitch

k1-tbl knit stitch through its back loop

k2tog knit 2 stitches together as one; this is a right-slanting decrease.

k3tog knit 3 stitches together as one; this is a right-slanting double decrease.

M1 make 1; this increases 1 stitch

p purl

p1-tbl purl next stitch through its back loop

p2tog purl the next 2 stitches together

p3tog purl the next 3 stitches together as one

RS right side (of work)

s2kp2 This is a central double decrease. On the knit side of the fabric: slip next 2 stitches together knitwise, knit the next stitch, pass the 2 slipped stitches over the knitted stitch. On the purl side of the fabric: insert the needle into the second and then the first stitch (in that order) as if to p2tog-tbl. Slip both stitches at once onto the right-hand needle from this position. Purl the next st, then pass the 2 slipped stitches over the purled stitch.

ssk slip the next 2 stitches knitwise, one at a time, from the left-hand needle to the right-hand one. Insert the left-hand needle tip into the fronts of both slipped stitches and knit them together from this position; this is a left-slanting decrease.

ssp slip the next 2 stitches knitwise, one at a time, from the left-hand needle to the right-hand one. Return both stitches to the left-hand needle and insert the right-hand needle into them from left to right and from back to front, then purl them together through their back loops; this is a left-slanting decrease.

sssk slip the next 3 stitches knitwise, one at a time, from the left-hand needle to the right-hand one. Insert the left-hand needle tip into the fronts of all slipped stitches then knit them together from this position; this is a left-slanting double decrease.

sssp slip the next 3 stitches knitwise, one at a time, from the left-hand needle to the right-hand one. Return all stitches to left-hand needle and insert the right-hand needle into them from left to right and from back to front, then purl them together through their back loops; this is a left-slanting double decrease.

st(s) stitch(es)

WS wrong side (of work)

***** repeat instructions after asterisk or between the asterisks across the row or for as many times as instructed.

****** the end of a stitch repeat

[ ] repeat the instructions within the brackets for as many times as instructed .

Comprehensive Stitch Key

One-Stitch Symbols

□ = On right-side rows: Knit
On wrong-side rows: Purl

• = On right-side rows: Purl
On wrong-side rows: Knit

■ = No stitch

B = Bobble = Knit into [front, back, front] of the next st, turn; p1 [p1, yarn over, p1] all into the next st, p1, turn; k5, turn; p2tog, p1, p2tog, turn; slip the next 2 sts at once knitwise, k1, p2sso

K = Knot = Knit into [front, back, front] of the next st, turn; p3, turn; slip 2 sts at once knitwise, k1, p2sso

= On right-side rows: k2tog
On wrong-side rows: p2tog

= On right-side rows: ssk
On wrong-side rows: ssp

= P2tog on RS; k2tog on WS

= On wrong-side rows: ssk

= s2kp2 = On right-side rows: Slip the next 2 sts at once knitwise; k1; p2sso
On wrong-side rows: Insert the needle into the second and then the first stitch (in that order) as if to p2tog-tbl; slip both stitches at once onto the right-hand needle from this position; purl the next st, then pass the 2 slipped stitches over the purled stitch; this is a central double decrease.

= On right-side rows: k3tog
On wrong-side rows: p3tog

= On right-side rows: sssk
On wrong-side rows: sssp

= On right-side rows: p3tog
On wrong-side rows: k3tog

= On wrong-side rows: k3tog-tbl

= (Decreases from 5 sts to 1 st) = Slip the next 2 sts with the yarn in back, drop the yarn, *pass the second st on the right-hand needle over the first st on the right-hand needle; slip the first st from the right-hand needle back to the left-hand needle; pass the second st on the left-hand needle over the first st on the left-hand needle, **slip the first st from the left-hand needle back to the right-hand needle and repeat from the * to the ** once more; pick up the yarn and knit the remaining st

= (Decreases from 7 sts to 1 st) = Slip the next 4 sts with the yarn in back, drop the yarn; *pass the second st on the right-hand needle over the first st on the right-hand needle; slip the first st from the right-hand needle back to the left-hand needle; pass the second st on the left-hand needle over the first st on the left-hand needle; **slip the first st from the left-hand needle back to the right-hand needle and repeat from the * to the ** twice more; pick up the yarn and knit the remaining slipped st

o = Yarn over

② = [Yarn over] twice

M = M1 Knitwise = Insert the left-hand needle *from front to back* under the horizontal strand between 2 sts and knit it *through its back loop*

M = M1 Purlwise = Insert the left-hand needle *from front to back* under the horizontal strand between two sts and purl it *through its back loop*

= Right Lifted Increase (page 276)

= Left Lifted Increase (page 276)

= k1f&b (Increases from 1 st to 2 sts) = [Knit into the front and then the back] of the next st

= Central Double Increase = (Increases from 1 st to 3 sts) = Knit into the back and then into the front of the indicated st and slip these 2 new sts onto the right-hand needle; insert the point of the left-hand needle behind the vertical strand that runs downward between the 2 sts just made and knit into the front of it

= (Increases from 1 st to 5 sts) = [[K1, yarn over] twice, k1] all into one st

= (Increases from 1 st to 3 sts) = [K1, p1, k1] all into one st

= (Increases from 1 st to 3 sts) = On right-side rows: [K1, yarn over, k1] into the next st
On wrong-side rows: [P1, yarn over, p1] into the next st

= On right-side rows: k1-tbl (page 275)
On wrong-side rows: p1-tbl (page 279)

= On right-side rows: p1-tbl (page 279)
On wrong-side rows: k1-tbl (page 275)

IIIII = On right-side rows: k5
On wrong-side rows: p5

III = On right-side rows: k3
On wrong-side rows: p3

V = On right-side rows: Slip the next st purlwise with the yarn in back
On wrong-side rows: Slip the next st purlwise with the yarn in front

∀ = On right-side rows: Slip the next st purlwise with the yarn in front
On wrong-side rows: Slip the next st purlwise with the yarn in back

∩ = On right-side rows: Knit the st in the row below
On wrong-side rows: Purl the st in the row below

∩ = On right-side rows: Purl the st in the row below
On wrong-side rows: Knit the st in the row below

↓ = Remove the next st from the left-hand needle and unravel it 10 rows

▼ = Purl the next st together with the st 7 rows directly below it

– = Use the cable cast-on technique (page 272) to cast on one st

L = Loop Stitch = Knit the next stitch, but do not remove it from the left-hand needle; yarn over; then pass the yarn around your thumb (or a piece of cardboard) to make a loop of your desired length; finally, take the yarn back in between the needle tips, and knit the original stitch again, allowing it to drop. To lock the loop, make another yarn over, this time from front to back, then pass the last 2 stitches on the right-hand needle over the second yarn over as if binding them off; to end, drop the elongated loop.

C = Crocheted Chain Loop = Insert a crochet hook into the next st on the left-hand needle, yarn over the hook and pull it through the st, leaving the original st on the left-hand needle; make 11 more chain sts in this way, then insert the hook into the same original st on the left-hand needle, yarn over hook, and draw it through the original st and the last chain on the hook; slip this chain st to the right-hand needle.

S = Shag Stitch = Use the cable cast-on technique (page 272) to cast on 4 sts, then bind off the same 4 sts.

ɤ = Long Stitch = Insert the right-hand needle into the indicated st 8 rows below and knit it, drawing up a long loop; transfer loop onto the left-hand needle and knit it together with the next st on the needle.

∧ = Picot bind off = Using the cable cast-on technique (page 272), cast on 1 st, bind off the next 3 sts as you purl them; repeat from the * across, ending with cast on 1 st, bind off the next 2 sts.

ℓℓ = 2X Elongated Knit St = Insert the right-hand needle knitwise into the indicated st and knit it, wrapping yarn twice as you make the stitch; on the next row, allow the extra loops to drop.

ℓℓ = 2X Elongated Purl St = Insert the right-hand needle purlwise into the indicated st and purl it, wrapping yarn twice as you make the stitch; on the next row, allow the extra loops to drop

ℓℓℓ = 3X Elongated Knit St = On right-side rows: Insert the right-hand needle knitwise into the indicated st and knit it, wrapping yarn 3 times as you make the stitch; on the next row, allow the extra loops to drop.
On wrong-side rows: Insert the right-hand needle purlwise into the indicated st and purl it, wrapping yarn 3 times as you make the stitch; on the next row, allow the extra loops to drop

▽ = Slip the st purlwise with the yarn in the front, allowing the extra loop to drop

↓ = P1, allowing the extra loop or yarn over to drop

↓ = Drop the yarn over

‡ = Insert the right-hand needle under the loose strand(s) several rows below, and knit the next stitch, catching the strand(s)

⋈ = Drop the first set of yarn overs, k1, then drop the next set of yarn overs; at the end of the row, insert the point of a knitting needle into each pair of loops and pull until taut, then use a square knot to tie the pair of loops together to form a tight bow

4 = Four-Row Tuck Stitch = Drop the next st off the left-hand needle and, using the tip of the right-hand needle, unravel the st 4 rows down; insert the right-hand needle into the live st and knit it, catching the 4 loose strands into the st as you knit

6 = Six-Row Tuck Stitch = Drop the next st off the left-hand needle and, using the tip of the right-hand needle, unravel the st 6 rows down; insert the right-hand needle into the live st and knit it, catching the 6 loose strands into the st as you knit

Two-Stitch Symbols

= Right Twist = K2tog, leaving the sts on the left-hand needle, then insert the point of the right-hand needle between these 2 sts and knit the first one again

= Left Twist = On right-side rows: Skip the first st and k1-tbl, then knit the skipped st and slip both sts off the left-hand needle together
On wrong-side rows: Skip the first st and p1-tbl, then purl the skipped st, and slip both sts off at once

= Slip the next st onto cn and hold in back, k1, p1 from cn

= Slip the next st onto cn and hold in front, p1, k1 from cn

= On right-side rows: Slip the next st onto cn and hold in back, k1-tbl, k1-tbl from cn
On wrong-side rows: Slip the next st onto cn and hold in back, p1-tbl, p1-tbl from cn

= On right-side rows: Slip the next st onto cn and hold in front, k1-tbl, k1-tbl from cn
On wrong-side rows: Slip the next st onto cn and hold in front, p1-tbl, p1-tbl from cn

= On right-side rows: Slip the next st onto cn and hold in back, k1-tbl, p1 from cn
On wrong-side rows: Slip the next st onto cn and hold in back, k1, p1-tbl from cn

= On right-side rows: Slip the next st onto cn and hold in front, p1, k1-tbl from cn
On wrong-side rows: Slip the next st onto cn and hold in front, p1-tbl, k1 from cn

Three-Stitch Symbols

= Slip the next 2 sts onto cn and hold in back, k1, k2 from cn

= Slip the next st onto cn and hold in front, k2, k1 from cn

= Slip the next 2 sts onto cn and hold in back; k1; p2 from cn

= Slip the next st onto cn and hold in front; p2; k1 from cn

= Slip the next st onto cn and hold in back, k2, p1 from cn

= Slip the next 2 sts onto cn and hold in front, p1, k2 from cn

= Slip the next st onto cn and hold in back, k2, k1 from cn

= Slip the next 2 sts onto cn and hold in front, k1, k2 from cn

= Slip the next st onto cn and hold in back, k2, k1-tbl from cn

= Slip the next 2 sts onto cn and hold in front, k1-tbl, k2 from cn

= Slip the next st onto cn #1 and hold in back, slip the next st onto cn #2 and hold in back, k1-tbl, p1 from cn #2, k1-tbl from cn #1

= Slip the next st onto cn #1 and hold in front, slip the next st onto cn #2 and hold in back, k1-tbl, p1 from cn #2, k1-tbl from cn #1

= Slip the next 3 sts onto cn and wrap the yarn counterclockwise 6 times around them just below cn, k3 from cn

= On right-side rows: Slip the next st onto cn and hold in back, [k1-tbl] twice, p1 from cn
On wrong-side rows: Slip the next 2 sts onto cn and hold in back, k1, [p1-tbl] twice from cn

= On right-side rows: Slip the next 2 sts onto cn and hold in front, p1; [k1-tbl] twice from cn
On wrong-side rows: Slip the next st onto cn and hold in front, [p1-tbl] twice, k1 from cn

= Yarn over, k3, pass the yarn over loop over the 3 sts just knit

= Slip next 3 sts onto the right-hand needle, pass the 3rd st on the right-hand needle over the first 2 sts as if you're binding it off, slip those 2 sts back onto the left-hand needle, k1, yarn over, k1

= K3tog but do not remove them from the left-hand needle, yarn over, then knit the 3 sts together again before removing them from the left-hand needle

Four-Stitch Symbols

= Slip the next st onto cn and hold in back, k3, p1 from cn

= Slip the next 3 sts onto cn and hold in front, p1, k3 from cn

= Slip the next 2 sts onto cn and hold in back, k2, k2 from cn

= On right-side rows: Slip the next 2 sts onto cn and hold in front, k2, k2 from cn
On wrong-side rows: Slip the next 2 sts onto cn and hold in front, p2, p2 from cn

= Slip the next st onto cn and hold in front [k1, p1] from left-hand needle, k st from cn

= Slip the next 2 sts onto cn and hold in back, k2, p2 from cn

= Slip the next 2 sts onto cn and hold in front, p2, k2 from cn

= Slip the next 3 sts onto cn and hold in back, k1, k3 from cn

= Slip the next st onto cn and hold in front, k3, k1 from cn

= Slip the next st onto cn and hold in back, [k1, p1, k1] from the left-hand needle, p1 from cn

= Slip the next 3 sts onto cn and hold in front, p1 from the left-hand needle, [k1, p1, k1] from cn

= Slip the next 3 sts onto cn and hold in front, k1 from the left-hand needle, [k1, p1, k1] from cn

= Slip the next st onto cn and hold in back, [k1, p1, k1] from the left-hand needle, k1 from cn

= Slip the next 2 sts onto cn and hold in front, [k1, p1] from the left-hand needle, k2 from cn

= Slip the next 2 sts onto cn and hold in back, k2 from the left-hand needle, [p1, k1] from cn

= Slip the next 2 sts onto cn and hold in front, p2, p2 from cn

= Slip the next 2 sts onto cn and hold in back, p2, p2 from cn

= Slip the next st onto cn and hold in back, k3, k1 from cn

= Slip the next 3 sts onto cn and hold in front, k1, k3 from cn

= Slip the next 4 sts onto cn and hold in front, p3, [ssk, k2tog] from cn, turn, p2, turn, ssk

= Slip the next 3 sts onto cn and hold in back, [ssk, k2tog] from the left-hand needle, turn, p2, turn, k2tog from the left-hand needle, p3 from cn

Five-Stitch Symbols

= Slip the next 2 sts onto cn and hold in back, k3, p2 from cn

= Slip the next 3 sts onto cn and hold in front, p2, k3 from cn

= Slip the next 4 sts onto cn and hold in back, k1, k4 from cn

= Slip the next st onto cn and hold in front, k4, k1 from cn

= Slip the next 2 sts onto cn #1 and hold in front, slip next st onto cn #2 and hold in back, k2 from the left-hand needle, p1 from cn #2, k2 from cn #1

= Slip the next 2 sts onto cn #1 and hold in back, slip next st onto cn #2 and hold in back, k2 from the left-hand needle, p1 from cn #2, k2 from cn #1

= Slip the next 3 sts onto cn and hold in front, k2, k3 from cn

= Slip the next 2 sts onto cn and hold in back, k3, k2 from cn

= Slip the next st onto cn and hold in back, k4, p1 from cn

= Slip the next 4 sts onto cn and hold in front, p1, k4 from cn

5 = Slip 5 sts purlwise, allowing the extra loops to drop. Return the 5 sts to the left-hand needle, insert the right-hand needle knitwise into all 5 of them at once, and [k1, p1, k1, p1, k1] into them.

Six-Stitch Symbols

= On right-side rows: Slip the next 3 sts onto cn and hold in back, k3, k3 from cn
On wrong-side rows: Slip the next 3 sts onto cn and hold in front, p3, p3 from cn

= Slip the next 3 sts onto cn and hold in front, k3, k3 from cn

= Slip the next 3 sts onto cn and hold in back, k3, p3 from cn

= Slip the next 3 sts onto cn and hold in front, p3, k3 from cn

= Slip the next 6 sts onto cn and wrap the yarn around them counterclockwise 4 times just below cn, k6 from cn

= Slip the next 2 sts onto cn #1 and hold in front, slip the next 2 sts onto cn #2 and hold in back, k2 from the left-hand needle, p2 from cn #2, k2 from cn #1

= Slip the next 4 sts onto cn and hold in back, k2 from the left-hand needle, slip the 2 purl sts back to the left-hand needle, and hold the 2 knit sts on cn in front, p2 from the left-hand needle, k2 from cn

= Slip the next 3 sts onto cn and hold in back, [k1, p1, k1] from the left-hand needle, [k1, p1, k1] from cn

= Slip the next 3 sts onto cn and hold in front; [k1, p1, k1] from the left-hand needle, [k1, p1, k1] from cn

= Slip the next 6 sts onto cn and wrap the yarn around them counterclockwise 4 times just below cn, [k2, p2, k2] the sts from cn

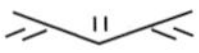

= Slip the next 2 sts onto cn #1 and hold in front, slip the next 2 sts onto cn #2 and hold in back, k2 from the left-hand needle, k2 from cn #2, k2 from cn #1

= Slip the next 2 sts onto cn #1 and hold in back, slip the next 2 sts onto cn #2 and hold in front, k2 from the left-hand needle, p2 from cn #2, k2 from cn #1

Seven-Stitch Symbols

= Slip the next 3 sts onto cn #1 and hold in back, slip the next st onto cn #2 and hold in back, k3 from the left-hand needle, p1 from cn #2, k3 from cn #1

= Slip the next 3 sts onto cn #1 and hold in front, slip the next st onto cn #2 and hold in back, k3 from the left-hand needle, p1 from cn #2, k3 from cn #1

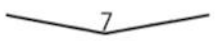

7 = 7 Stitches out of 1 st = [[K1, yarn over] 3 times, k1] all into one st

Eight-Stitch Symbols

= Slip the next 4 sts onto cn and hold in back, k4, k4 from cn

= Slip the next 4 sts onto cn and hold in front, k4, k4 from cn

2 6 = Slip the next 2 sts onto cn and hold in back *allowing the extra loops to drop*, k6, k2 from cn

= Slip the next 3 sts onto cn #1 and hold in back, slip the next 2 sts onto cn #2 and hold in back, k3 from the left-hand needle, p2 from cn #2, k3 from cn #1

= Slip the next 3 sts onto cn #1 and hold in front, slip the next 2 sts onto cn #2 and hold in back, k3 from the left-hand needle, p2 from cn #2; k3 from cn #1

= Slip the next 4 sts onto cn and hold in front, [k1, p2, k1] from the left-hand needle, [k1, p2, k1] from cn

= Slip the next 4 sts onto cn and hold in back, [k1, p2, k1] from the left-hand needle, [k1, p2, k1] from cn

= Slip the next 4 sts onto cn and hold in back, k4, p4 from cn

= Slip the next 4 sts onto cn and hold in front, p4, k4 from cn

Nine-Stitch Symbols

= Slip the next 3 sts onto cn #1 and hold in back, slip the next 3 sts onto cn #2 and hold in front, k3 from the left-hand needle, k3 from cn #2, k3 from cn #1

Ten-Stitch Symbols

6 4 = Slip the next 6 sts onto cn and hold in back, k4, k6 from cn

4 3 3 = Slip the next 4 sts onto cn #1 and hold in back, slip the next 3 sts onto cn #2 and hold in front, k3 from the left-hand needle, k3 from cn #2, k4 from cn #1

3 3 4 = Slip the next 3 sts onto cn #1 and hold in back, slip the next 3 sts onto cn #2 and hold in front, k4 from the left-hand needle, k3 from cn #2, k3 from cn #1

4 = Slip the next 4 sts onto cn and hold in front, [k2, p4] from the left-hand needle, k4 from cn

4 = Slip the next 6 sts onto cn and hold in back, k4 from the left-hand needle, [p4, k2] from cn

4 6 = Slip the next 4 sts onto cn and hold in front, k6, k4 from cn

Twelve-Stitch Symbols

= Slip the next 6 sts onto cn and hold in front, [k2, p2, k2] from the left-hand needle, [k2, p2, k2] from cn

= Slip the next 6 sts onto cn and hold in back, [k2, p2, k2] from the left-hand needle, [k2, p2, k2] from cn

= Using an extra knitting needle, [k4, turn, p4, turn] 6 times, then place these 4 sts onto safety pin #1 and cut the yarn. Slip the next 4 sts onto safety pin #2 and hold in back. Reattach the yarn and k4, turn, p4, turn] 6 times, then place these 4 sts onto safety pin #3 and cut the yarn. With the RS of sts facing you and safety pin #2 in the back, twist the strip that is on safety pin #1 over and under the strip that is on safety pin #3 to form a knot. Slip the sts from safety pin #3 onto the left-hand needle, and knit them, p4 from safety pin #2, k4 from safety pin #1.

Knitting Techniques

This section provides instructions for some of the techniques used in the stitch patterns.

1-to-3 st Knit Increases

Here's how to make three stitches out of a single stitch using a yarn over in between two knit stitches. Pattern instructions for this technique will read [k1, yarn over, k1] into one stitch:

With the yarn in back, insert the right-hand needle knitwise into the indicated stitch and make a knit stitch but don't remove the stitch from the left-hand needle.

Bring the yarn between the needle tips to the front and then take it all the way around the right-hand needle to the back to create a yarn over (illustration 1). *Do not remove the stitch from the left-hand needle yet.*

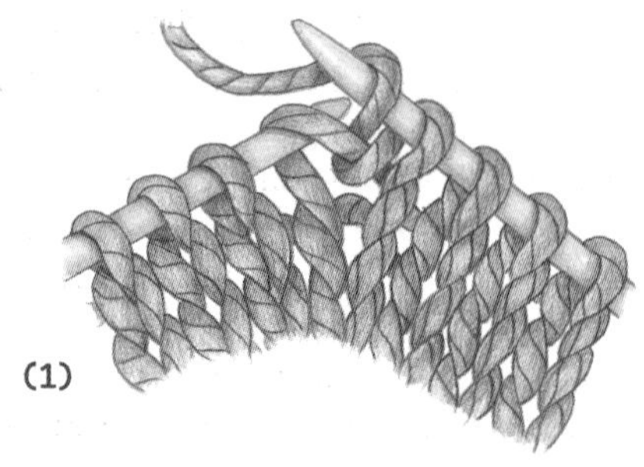
(1)

Next, to create the third stitch of this particular increase, reinsert the right-hand needle into that same stitch knitwise and knit the stitch once more (illustration 2).

Finally, slip the original stitch off the left-hand needle.

note: *To increase from one to five stitches, use the same technique but* **[***[k1, yarn over] twice, k1***]** *all into one st.*

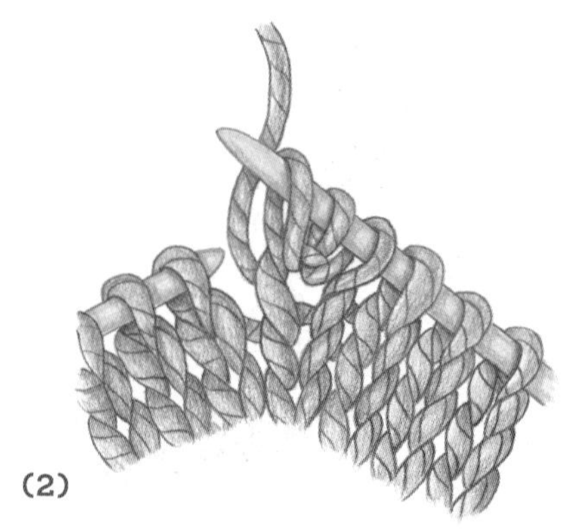
(2)

1-to-3 st Purl Increases

Here's how to make three stitches out of a single stitch using a yarn over in between two purl stitches. Pattern instructions for this technique will read [p1, yarn over, p1] into one stitch:

To begin, with the yarn in front, insert the right-hand needle purlwise into the indicated stitch and make a purl stitch but don't remove the stitch from the left-hand needle.

Now, wrap the yarn around the needle from front to back to front to create a yarn over (illustration 3). Do not remove the stitch from the left-hand needle yet.

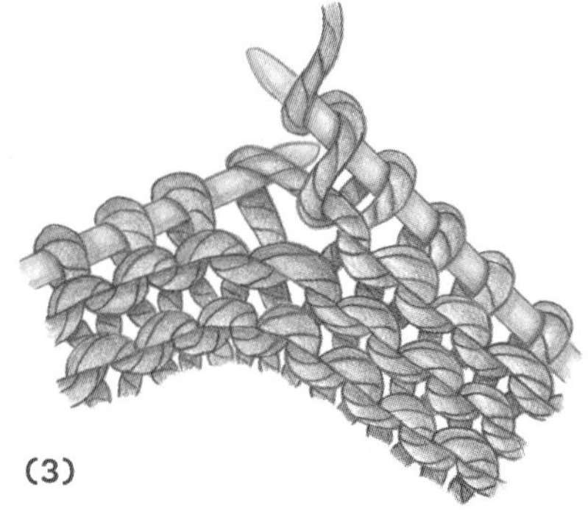
(3)

Next, to create the third stitch of this particular increase, reinsert the right-hand needle into that same stitch purlwise and purl the stitch once more (illustration 4).

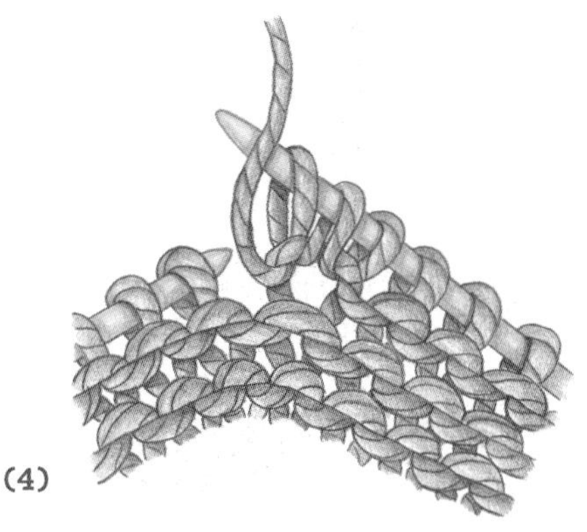

(4)

Finally, slip the original stitch off the left-hand needle.

5-to-1 st Decrease

This decrease technique involves manipulating stitches without knitting them, simply passing each stitch over a center stitch, one by one in alternate directions, until only the middle stitch remains. It is often used when knitting Celtic cables such as Enniskerry Cable (page 183). The first time you do it, you might find it helpful to have someone read the instructions to you aloud as you do it.

To do: Drop the working yarn to the back, and slip 3 stitches from the left-hand needle onto the right-hand needle.

*Pass the second stitch on the right-hand needle over the first stitch as if you're binding it off (illustration 5).

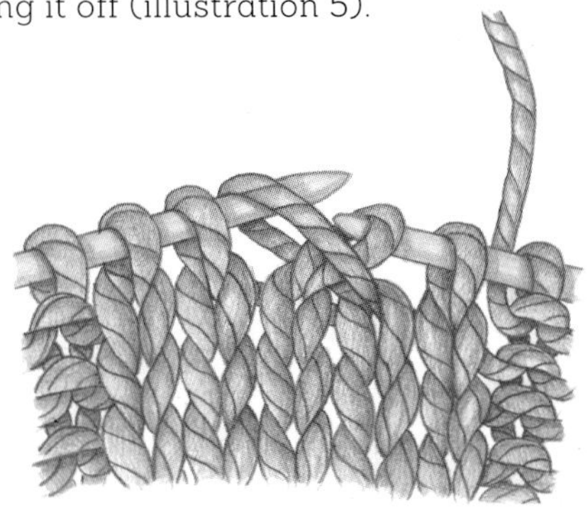

(5)

Slip this stitch from the right-hand needle back onto the left-hand needle, and pass the second stitch on the left-hand needle over the first stitch (as if you're binding it off, except it will be in the opposite direction)** (illustration 6).

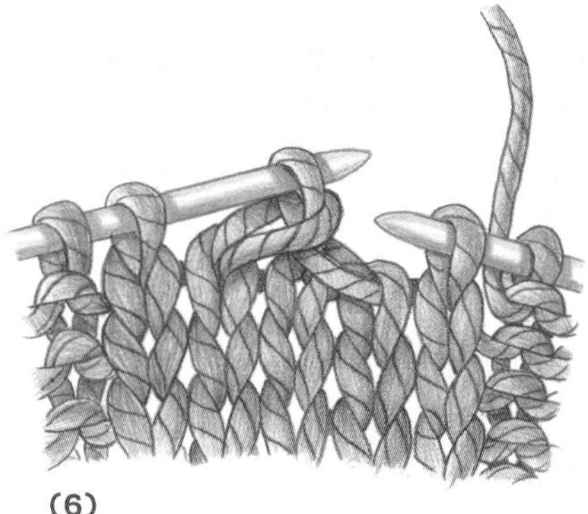

(6)

Now, slip this stitch from the left-hand needle back onto the right-hand needle, and repeat the steps between the * and the ** once more.

Finally, knit this remaining stitch. Five stitches have been combined into one stitch.

note: *If the stockinette sections of your cable are 3 stitches rather than 2 stitches across, as in Caedmon Celtic Knot (page 184), just use a 7-to-1 st decrease instead of the 5-to-1 st decrease. It is worked the same way, except 4 stitches are slipped to begin with, and the steps between the asterisks above are repeated twice more, instead of just once.*

Attaching New Yarn

Whenever possible, try to attach a new ball of yarn at the beginning of a row.

To start a new strand of yarn at the beginning of a knit row: Drop the old yarn, insert your right-hand needle into the first stitch of the row as if you are about to knit, grasp the new yarn and use it to knit the first stitch (illustration 7). Always begin and

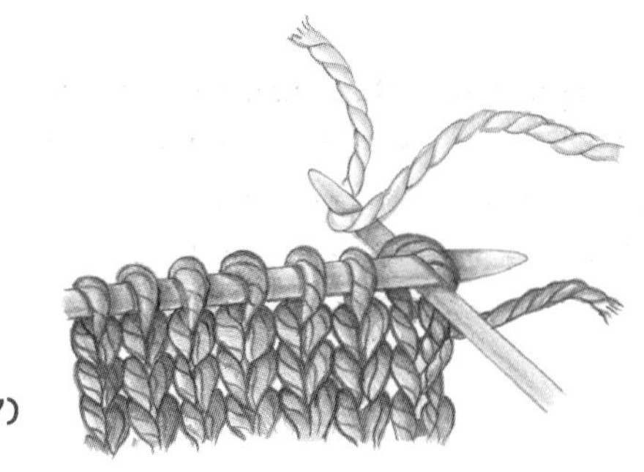

(7)

end every yarn with at least a 6"/[15cm] tail. Otherwise, you won't have enough length to weave it in sufficiently.

To start a new yarn at the beginning of a purl row: Drop the old yarn, insert your right-hand needle into that first stitch of the row as if you're about to purl rather than knit, and purl it.

Bobbles

Bobbles introduce wonderful surface texture (not to mention, playful whimsy) to fabrics. While some knitters find them time-consuming to knit, they are not difficult to do. To make a bobble, multiple increases are worked into a single stitch, a few rows are worked, and then multiple decreases are worked in order to return to the original stitch count. There are several ways to knit a bobble, but here's my favorite. It is used in Tuxedo Cable (page 153).

First, knit into the [front, back, front] of a single stitch, turn.

(8)

Next, working into these same three stitches, purl into the first one, [p1, yarn over, p1] *all into the next stitch* (page 268), then purl the third stitch, turn.

Knit the five sts, then turn.

Decrease from five stitches down to three stitches as follows: p2tog, p1, p2tog, turn.

Finally, decrease from three stitches down to one stitch using a central double decrease (s2kp2) (page 272).

Avoiding Gaps Between Purl and Knit Stitches

For some knitters, whenever a purl stitch is to the left of a knit stitch, such as in ribbings and in many cables, a gap occurs that makes the knit stitch appear oversized and wonky looking. It's easy to prevent this unevenness from occurring. In fact, the hardest part is remembering to do it! The trick involves the purl stitch to the left of the offending knit stitch. Here's how to do it: on right-side rows, work the offending knit stitch the way you normally would. Then, when working the purl stitch immediately to its left, insert your right-hand needle into the stitch purlwise as you normally would, *but wrap the yarn around the needle in the opposite direction*—clockwise rather than counterclockwise —as you purl the stitch. On the next row, this stitch will present itself to you as a twisted knit stitch. Knit it *through the back loop* to untwist it.

Cables

Cables are created when stitches exchange places with other stitches within a knitted row. One set of stitches is placed on a cable needle to keep them out of the way while another set of stitches is worked. Depending on whether those stitches are held to the front or to the back of the work, whether the cable uses two, three, or even seventeen stitches, and whether the stitches are ultimately knitted or purled or any combination of the two, creates the beautiful patterns.

Front Cross Cable (also known as Left Cross)

Slip the first set of stitches purlwise onto a cable needle and hold them in front (illustration 9).

Keeping the cable needle in front of the work, knit the next set of stitches on the left-hand needle (illustration 10).

Knit the set of stitches that is waiting on the cable needle (illustration 11).

Back Cross Cable (also known as Right Cross)

Slip the first set of stitches purlwise onto a cable needle and hold them in back (illustration 12).

Keeping the cable needle in back of the work, knit the next set of stitches on the left-hand needle (illustration 13).

Knit the 2 stitches that are waiting on the cable needle (illustration 14).

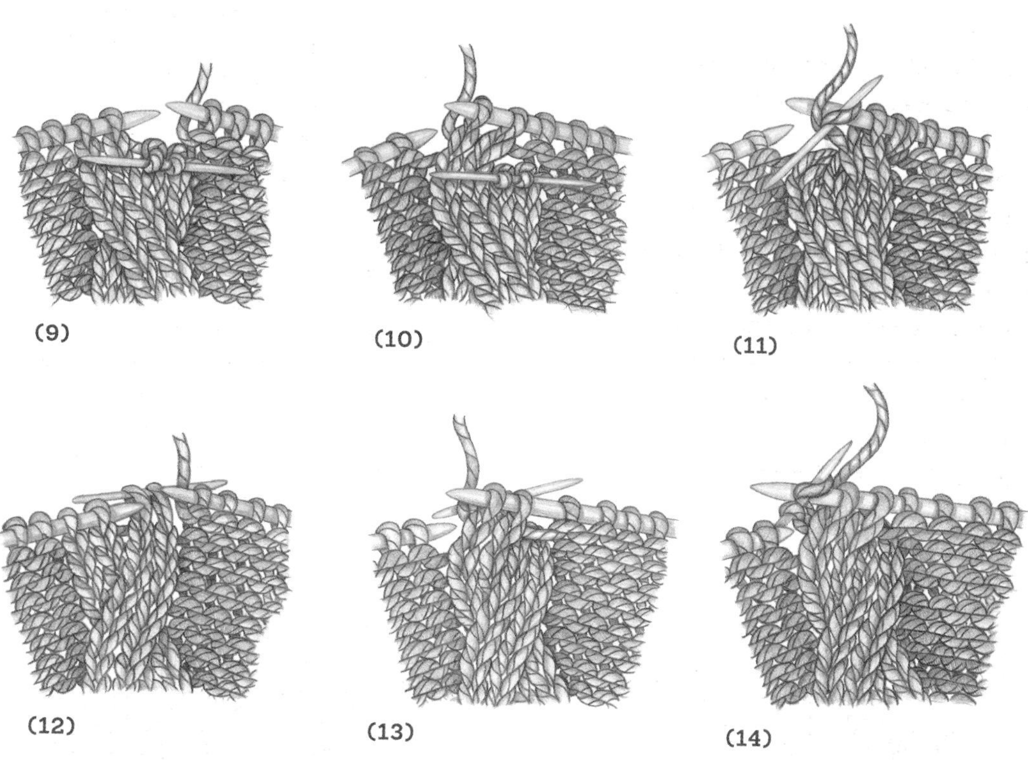

Cable Cast-On

Here's my favorite cast-on technique: It's beautiful, easy, and quick to do. Plus, it's perfect when the first row worked is a right-side row.

Start by making a slipknot on your knitting needle, then insert the tip of the right-hand needle knitwise into the loop that's sitting on the left-hand needle and knit up a stitch (illustration 15) *but don't remove the original stitch from the left-hand needle*; instead, transfer the new stitch from the right-hand needle back to the left-hand one. One new stitch has been cast on.

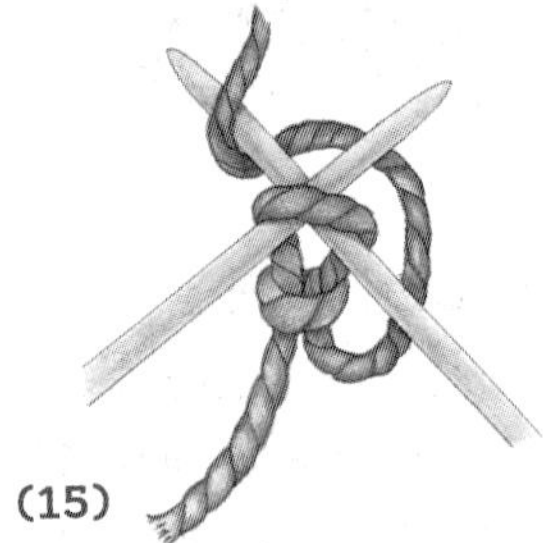
(15)

For each successive stitch to be cast on, insert the tip of the right-hand needle *between* the first 2 stitches on the left-hand needle to knit up a stitch (illustration 16).

(16)

As before, do not remove the old stitch, rather slip the new one back onto the left-hand needle; repeat until you have cast on the required number of stitches.

Central Double Decrease (abbreviated s2kp2)

A central double decrease takes 3 stitches down to 1 stitch, leaving the center stitch on top.

On the right (knit) side of the fabric, slip 2 stitches at once *knitwise* (illustration 17), knit the next stitch (illustration 18), then pass the 2 slipped stitches over the stitch you just knit (illustration 19).On the purl side of the fabric: insert the needle into the second and then the first stitch (in that order) as if to p2tog-tbl. Slip both stitches at once onto the right-hand needle from this position. Purl the next st, then pass the 2 slipped stitches over the purled stitch.

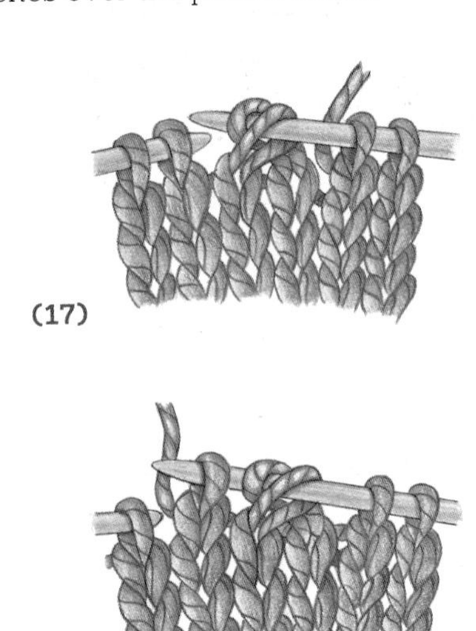
(17)

(18)

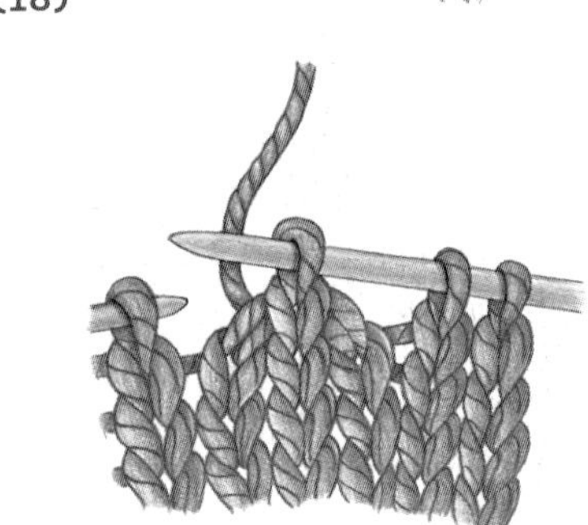
(19)

Central Double Increase

Use this type of increase to create three stitches out of a single stitch without a hole or bump. It is especially perfect for the dramatic increasing that is necessary in cabled Celtic knots such as Caedmon Celtic Knot (page 184).

Knit into the back and then into the front of the indicated stitch, in that order, and then slip the original stitch off the left-hand needle (illustration 20). So far, 2 stitches have been made out of one stitch.

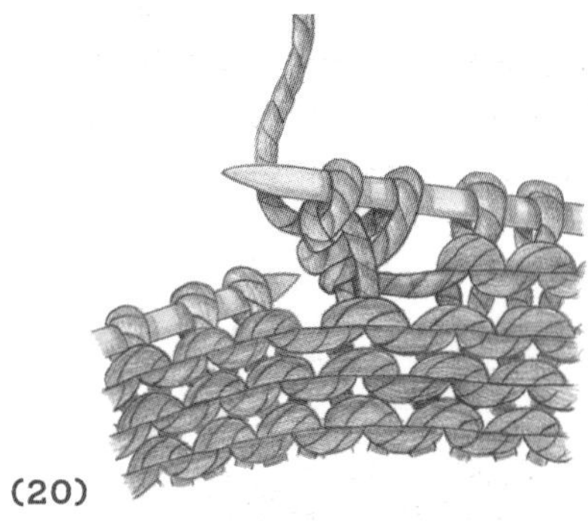

(20)

For the third stitch of this special increase, insert the left-hand needle from back to front into the little vertical strand that's beneath the two stitches just made (illustration 21). Just pull up on it a little to create enough space for your needle to fit.

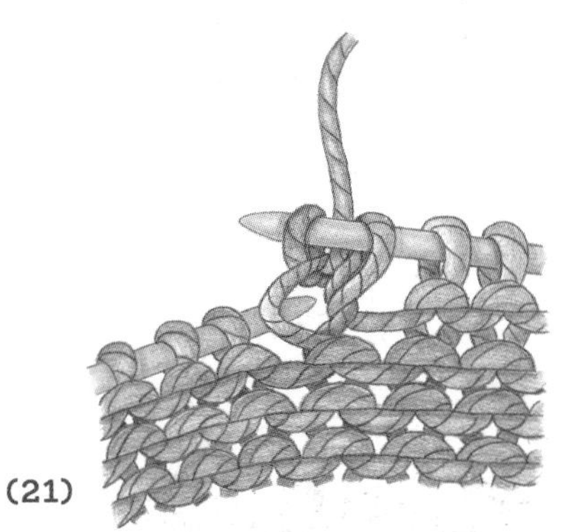

(21)

Now, swing your right-hand needle around and knit into this vertical strand through its front loop (illustration 22). This maneuver might seem awkward at first because of how tight it feels, but that's normal. After all, the main goal here is to add new stitches without creating holes below them!

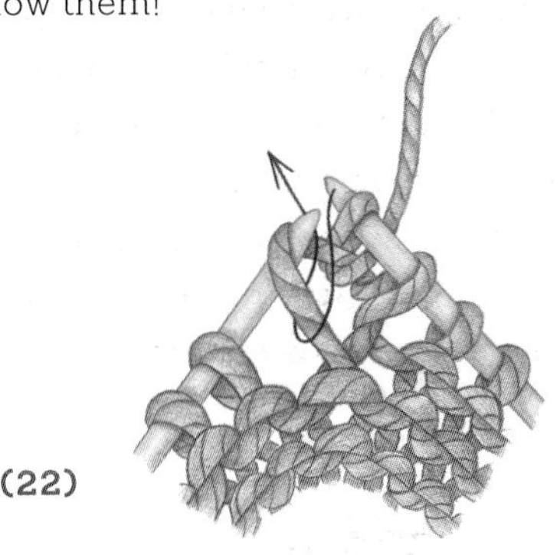

(22)

Crocheted Chain Stitch

Sometimes, a little crochet makes knitting even better! For example, a loop of basic crocheted chain stitches adds a unique texture to Lamb's Tails (page 248). It's easy. Here's how:

Place a slipknot on a crochet hook.

Yarn over the hook, and draw the loop through the loop on the hook to form the first chain. Repeat this step as many times as required.

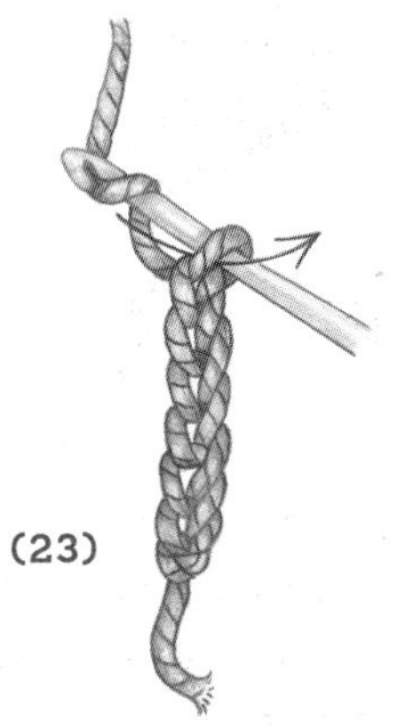

(23)

Elongated Stitches

Knitters can create quite interesting effects using elongated stitches. Best of all, they're easy to knit!

To make an elongated stitch, as you knit or purl the stitch, just wrap the yarn around the needle two or more times as indicated in the pattern (illustration 24).

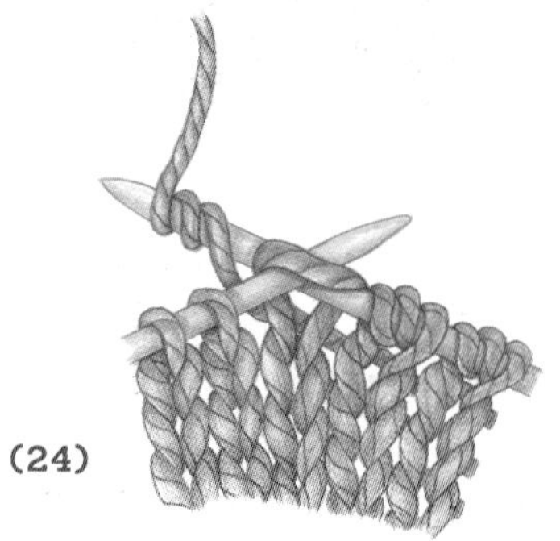

(24)

On the next row, simply drop those extra loops.

Knit into the Front and Back of a Stitch (abbreviated k1f&b)

This type of increase adds a bit of horizontal texture that looks very much like a purl bump. It is easy to work and is often used when knitting ribbings, since it serves to incorporate new stitches into the pattern quickly.

To do in a knit stitch: First, insert the right-hand needle into the indicated stitch knitwise, wrap the working yarn around the needle the regular way to knit up a stitch *but don't remove the original stitch from the left-hand needle* (illustration 25).

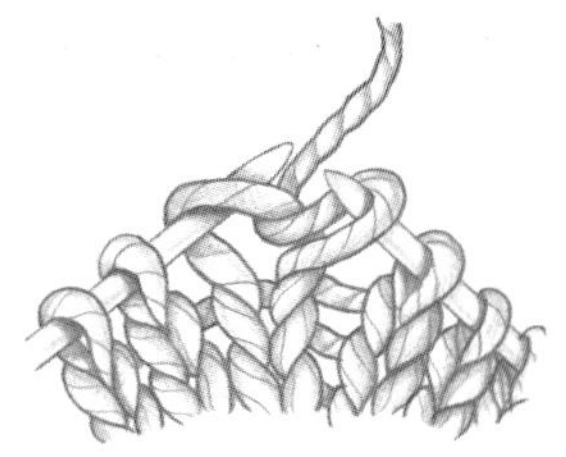

(25)

Then, reinsert your right-hand needle knitwise into the back of the same stitch, wrap the yarn around the needle to knit up a stitch (illustration 26), then slip the original stitch off. Two stitches are made out of one stitch.

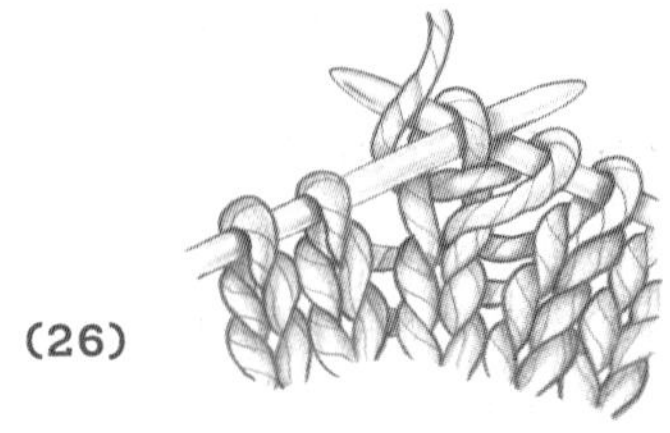

(26)

To do in a purl stitch: Insert the right-hand needle into the indicated stitch purlwise, wrap the working yarn around the regular way to purl a stitch *but don't remove the original stitch from the left-hand needle*; then *purl through the back* loop of the same stitch; finally, slip the original stitch off the left-hand needle. Two stitches are made out of one stitch.

Knit Two Together Decrease (abbreviated k2tog) (right-leaning decrease)

To do: With the working yarn toward the back, insert the right-hand needle, knitwise (page 275), into the first two stitches on the left-hand needle as if they were a single stitch, and wrap the yarn around the right-hand needle as you would for a knit stitch (illustration 27). Pull the yarn through both stitches, and slip both stitches off the left-hand needle at once. One stitch has been decreased, and the resulting stitch slants to the right.

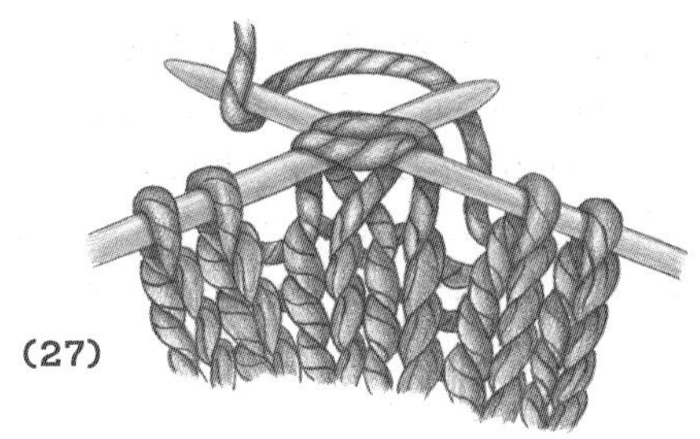

(27)

Knit a Stitch Through Its Back Loop (abbreviated k1-tbl)

This technique twists a stitch. It is often used to make stitches appear embossed on top of fabric, such as in Alpine Tulips (page 175).

To work this technique, just insert your right-hand needle into the indicated stitch from right to left and from front to back, and wrap the working yarn around the needle the regular way to knit the stitch (illustration 28).

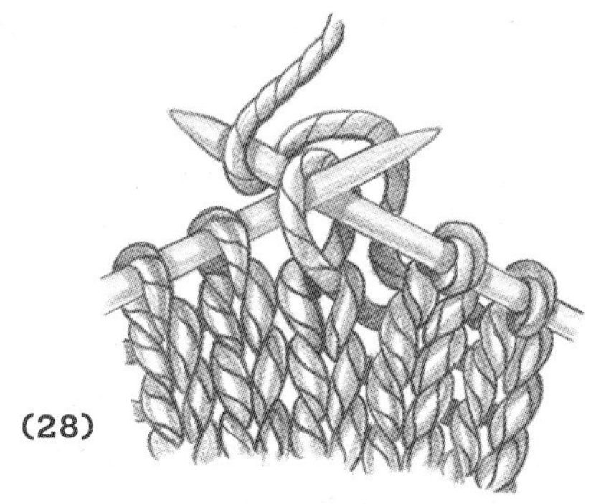

(28)

Knit in the Row Below

This technique is used to create novelty stitch patterns, such as the Bee Stitch (page 236).

To do: Simply insert the tip of the right-hand needle into the stitch that's directly below the first stitch on the left-hand needle and knit it. Slip the original stitch off the left-hand needle.

note: *To purl a stitch into the row below, insert the right-hand needle purlwise into the stitch in the row below and purl it.*

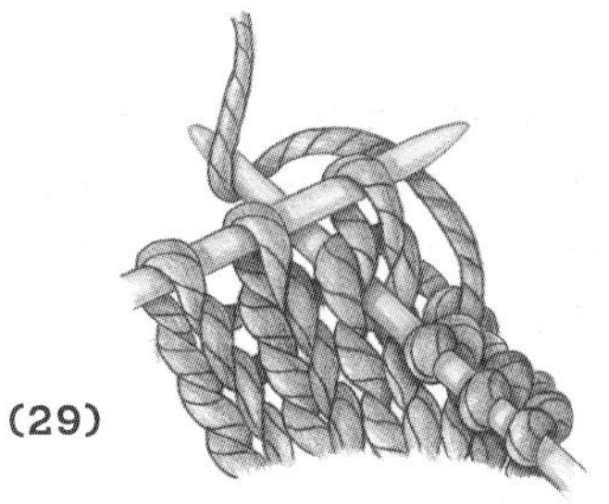

(29)

Knitwise

Instructions will sometimes tell you to insert your knitting needle into a stitch knitwise. To do this, simply insert the tip of your right-hand needle into the indicated stitch as if you were about to knit that stitch—in other words, from left to right and *from front to back* (illustration 30).

(30)

If you're told to *slip a stitch knitwise*, insert the tip of your right-hand needle into the front of the stitch as if you're about to knit it and slide that stitch off of the left-hand needle and onto the right-hand one, allowing the stitch to sit on the right-hand needle with its left "leg" in the front. Usually, stitches are slipped knitwise during a decrease.

Knot

A knot is a miniature bobble. It is used as the tip of the antennae in the Butterfly Motif (page 244).

To make a knitted knot: Knit into [front, back, front] of the next stitch, then turn; purl those same three stitches, then turn; then slip 2 stitches at once knitwise, knit the next stitch, then pass those two slipped stitches over the stitch just knitted.

Left Twist

The left twist is a mini cable that is worked over two stitches without the use of a cable needle. It is quick and easy to do.

First, skip the first stitch on the left-hand needle, and with the right-hand needle behind the left one, knit next stitch *in its back loop* (illustration 31).

(31)

Then, knit the first stitch in its front loop the regular way, and then slip both stitches off the left-hand needle together (illustration 32).

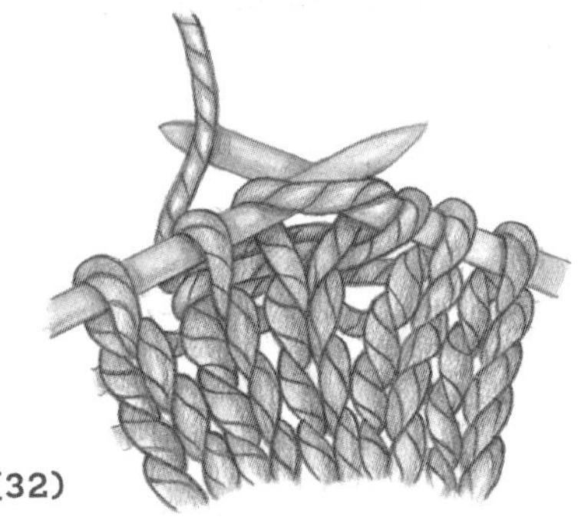

(32)

Lifted Increases

This type of increase is made by working into a stitch in the row below the stitch that is currently on the needle, and also working into the stitch on the needle in the regular way. It is handy to be able to perform the lifted increase slanting to either the left or to the right, depending on the desired effect.

To do a lifted increase slanting to the left: Insert the left-hand needle into the back of the first stitch on the right-hand needle, just below the stitch just knit (illustration 33), and knit it (illustration 34).

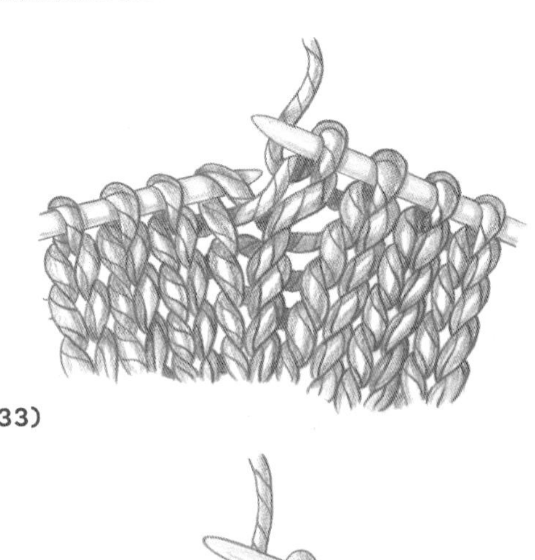

(33)

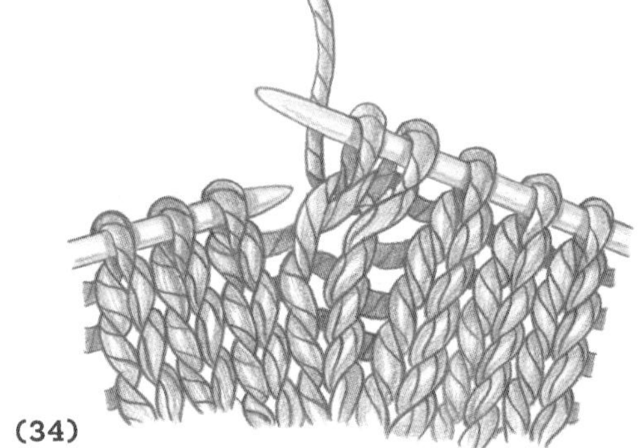

(34)

For a lifted increase slanting to the right: Knit into the back of the stitch in the row directly below the first stitch on the left-hand needle (into its purl "bump") (illustration 35).

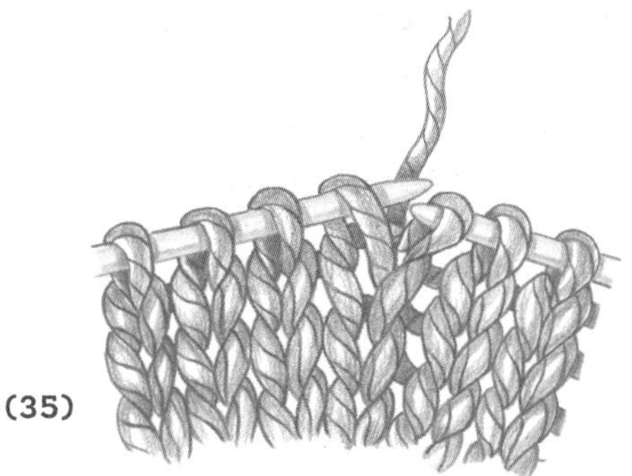
(35)

For a lifted purl increase, work the same as the knitted version, except purl instead of knit.

Loop Stitch (also known as Fur Stitch)

This technique creates a super warm fabric with lots of texture. It's easy to change the pile depth by just making the loops longer or shorter.

To do: First, insert the right needle into the stitch on the left needle as if to knit.

Then, wrap the yarn around the tip of the right needle, then clockwise around your left thumb, bring the yarn to the back between the needles (illustration 36).

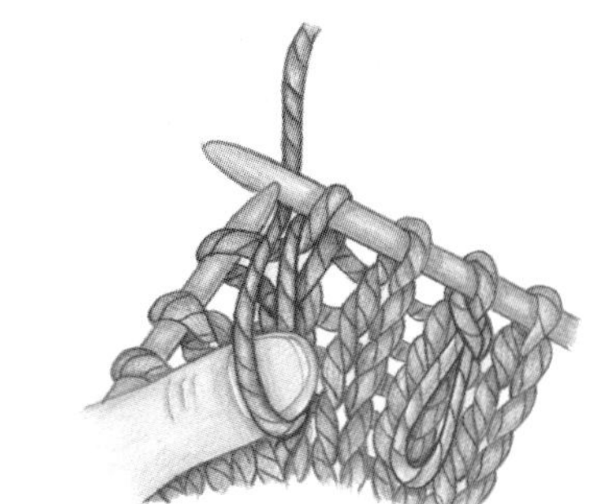
(36)

Adjust the length of the loop.

Then, knit the stitch on the left needle (illustration 37). This step gives you two loops on the right-hand needle.

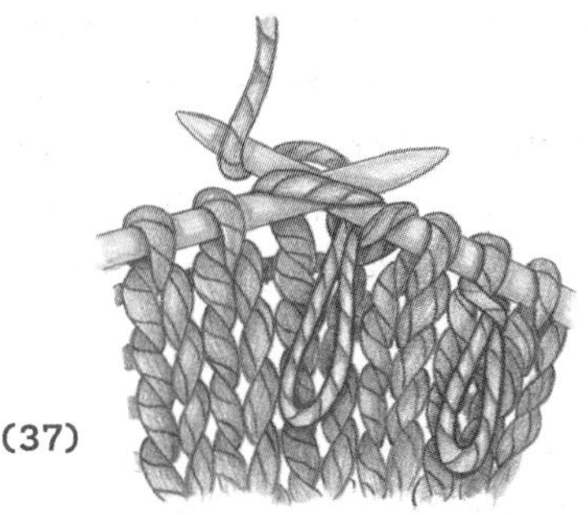
(37)

Finally, pass the second stitch on the right needle over the first stitch.

Raised Make One Increases (abbreviated M1)

This method of adding stitches uses the horizontal strand of yarn that hangs between the knitting needles. The knitter works into the strand, carefully twisting it to prevent a hole. As with the lifted increases above, raised increases can slant to the right or to the left.

For raised knit increases slanting to the left *(abbreviated M1-L)*

Use the left-hand needle to lift up the horizontal strand that's hanging between the needles, *from front to back*, and knit the strand *through its back loop*, twisting it to prevent a hole in your fabric (illustration 38).

(38)

For raised knit increases slanting to the right *(abbreviated M1-R)*
Use the left-hand needle to lift up the horizontal strand that is hanging between the needles *from back to front*, and knit the strand *through its front loop*, twisting it to prevent a hole in the work (illustration 39).

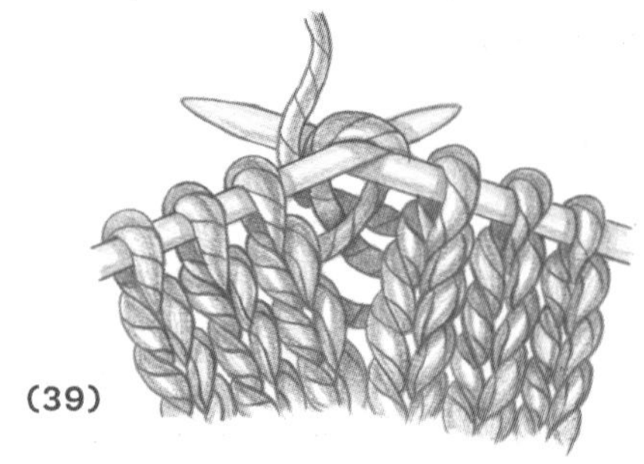
(39)

note: *If no direction is specified, use the M1-L increase.*

Sometimes raised increases are worked as purl stitches:

For a raised purl increase that slants to the right on the right side of the fabric:
Use the left-hand needle to lift up the horizontal strand between the needles *from back to front*, then purl the strand *through its front loop*, twisting it to prevent a hole in your fabric (illustration 40).

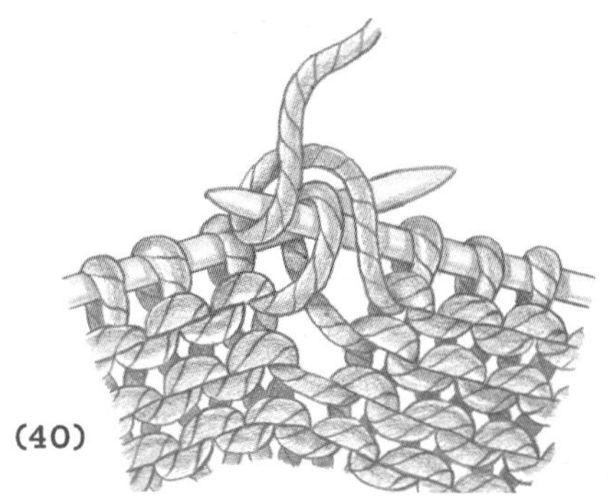
(40)

For a raised purl increase that slants to the left on the right side of the fabric
Use the left-hand needle to lift up the horizontal strand between the needles *from front to back*, then purl the strand *through its back loop*, twisting it to prevent a hole in your fabric.

M1 purlwise increases are usually worked on right-side rows whenever a purl stitch is needed and in these cases, the difference between left- and right-slanting stitches is hardly visible; no directional raised purl increases are necessary. Just use whichever version is easier for you.

P2tog Decrease (abbreviated p2tog)

To do: With the working yarn toward the front, insert the tip of the right-hand needle into the first two stitches on the left-hand needle, purlwise (page 279), as if they were a single stitch, and wrap the yarn around the right-hand needle as you would for a purl stitch (illustration 41). Pull the yarn through both stitches, and then slip both stitches off the left-hand needle at once. One stitch has been decreased, and the resulting stitch slants to the right on the knit side of the fabric.

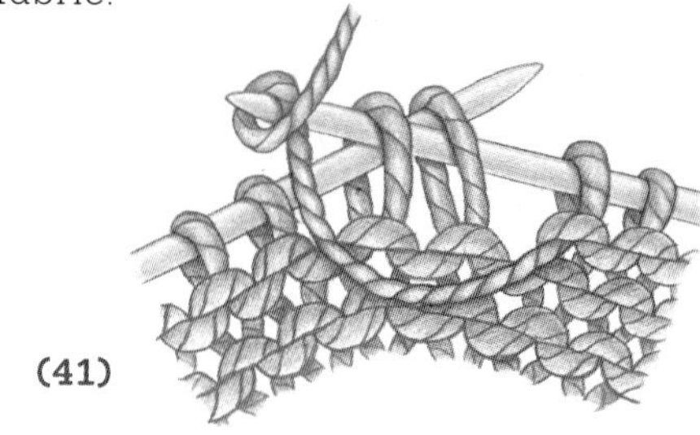
(41)

Purl a Stitch Through Its Back Loop (abbreviated p1-tbl)

Like knitting a stitch through the back loop, this technique twists a stitch.

To work this technique, just insert your right-hand needle into the indicated stitch from left to right and from back to front, and wrap the working yarn around the needle the regular way to purl the stitch.

(42)

Purlwise

When instructed to insert your knitting needle into a stitch purlwise, simply insert the tip of your right-hand needle into the indicated stitch as if you were about to purl that stitch—in other words, from right to left and *from back to front* (illustration 43).

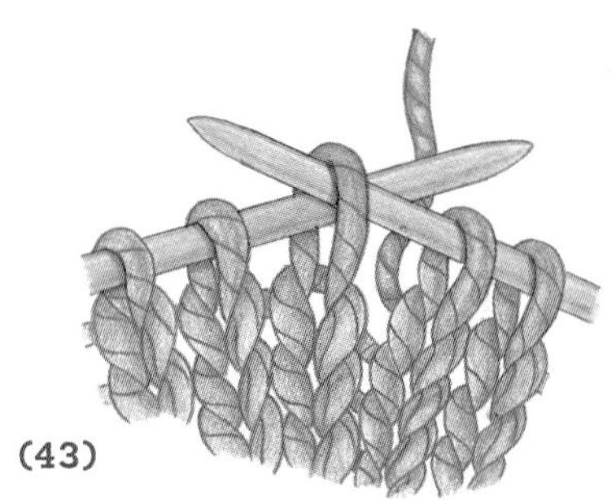

(43)

The convention in knitting is to always slip stitches purlwise unless told otherwise. When told to *slip a stitch purlwise*, insert the tip of your right-hand needle into the indicated stitch as if you're about to purl it and slide that stitch off of the left-hand needle and onto the right-hand one, allowing the stitch to sit on the right-hand needle with its right "leg" in the front.

Right Twist

The right twist is a mini cable that is worked over two stitches without the use of a cable needle for speed.

Here's how: Knit two stitches together the regular way, but do not remove them from the left-hand needle (illustration 44).

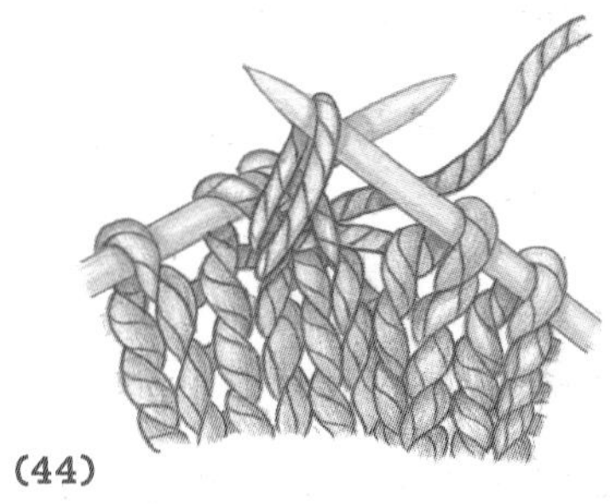

(44)

Next, insert the point of right-hand needle between these two stitches, and knit the first stitch again *through its front loop* (illustration 45), and slip both stitches off the left-hand needle together.

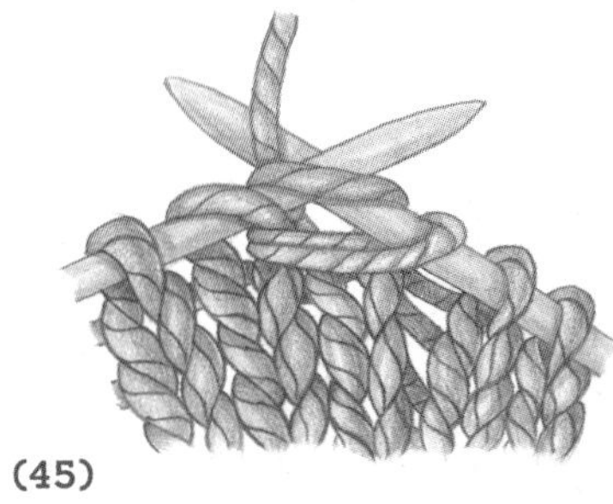

(45)

Slipping Stitches

Interesting texture and colorwork can be created simply by slipping stitches from the left-hand needle to the right-hand one intermittently in a pattern. Sometimes the stitches are moved with the yarn toward the front of the stitch and other times toward the back. Here's the difference:

Slipping Stitches with Yarn in Back

When instructed to hold the yarn in back, slip the stitch onto the right-hand needle purlwise (see page 279), keeping the working yarn behind the fabric *as it faces you* (illustration 46). The yarn will be toward the wrong side of the fabric if you are on a right-side row and toward the public side of the fabric if you're on a wrong-side row.

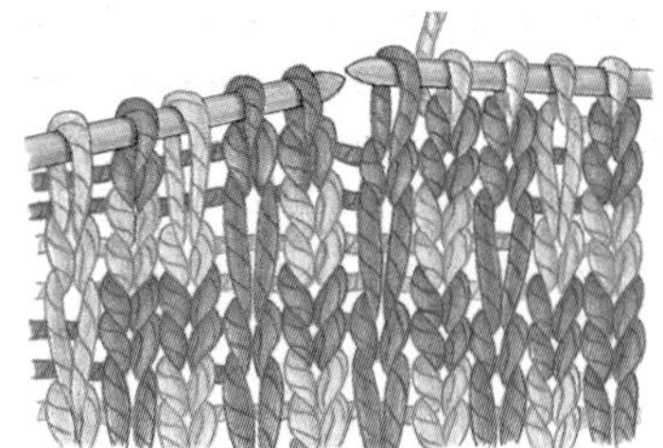

(46)

Slipping Stitches with Yarn in Front

To slip a stitch with the yarn in front, if the working yarn is not already in front of the fabric (toward you) (such as when purling), bring it forward and slip the stitch (see illustration 47). The yarn will be toward the public side of the fabric if you are on a right-side row and toward the wrong side of the fabric if you're on a wrong-side row.

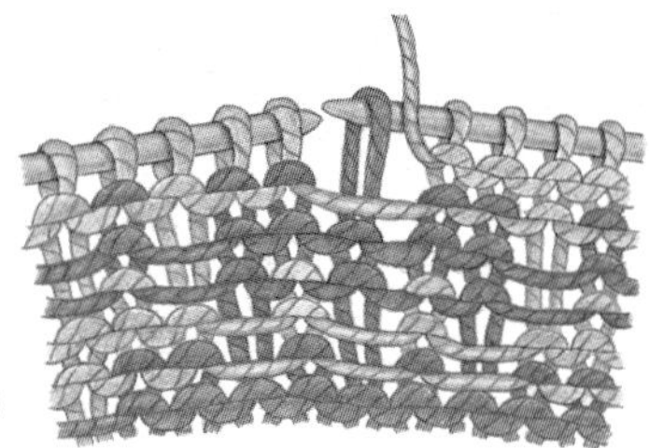

(47)

note: *When moving the yarn from front to back or from back to front, be careful to always bring it* between the points *of the knitting needles and not over the right-hand needle. Otherwise, a yarn over will be created, increasing your stitch count and making an unexpected hole in your fabric.*

Manipulating Floats

Sometimes you need a float to create a decorative effect. Insert the right-hand needle under the floating strands, being sure to catch all of them at once without piercing the fabric behind, then work the next stitch, catching the extra strands inside (illustration 48).

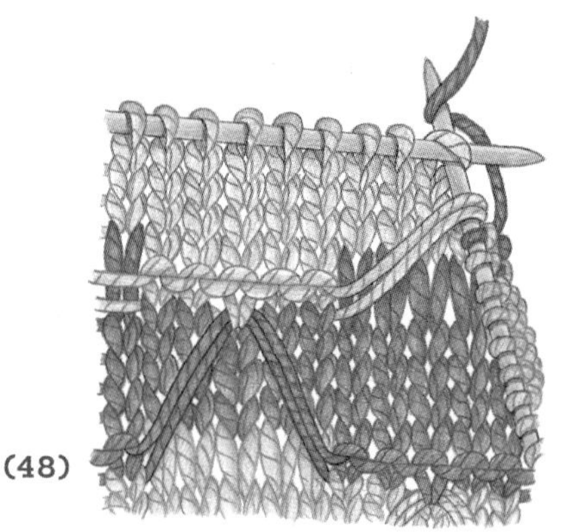

(48)

Slip, Slip, Knit Decrease (abbreviated ssk) (left-leaning decrease)

This knit decrease requires an extra step, but it creates a mirror image of the k2tog decrease described above.

To do: With the working yarn toward the back, slip the next two stitches, *knitwise*, and *one at a time*, onto the right-hand needle (illustration 49).

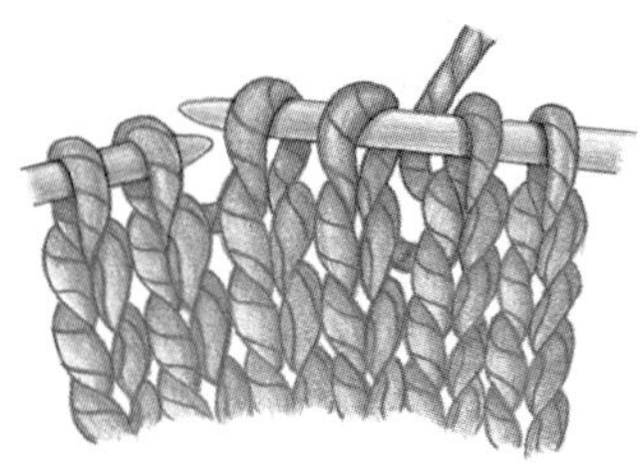

(49)

Then, insert the tip of the left-hand needle into the fronts of both slipped stitches (illustration 50) and knit them together from this position, through their back loops. One stitch has been decreased, and the resulting stitch slants to the left.

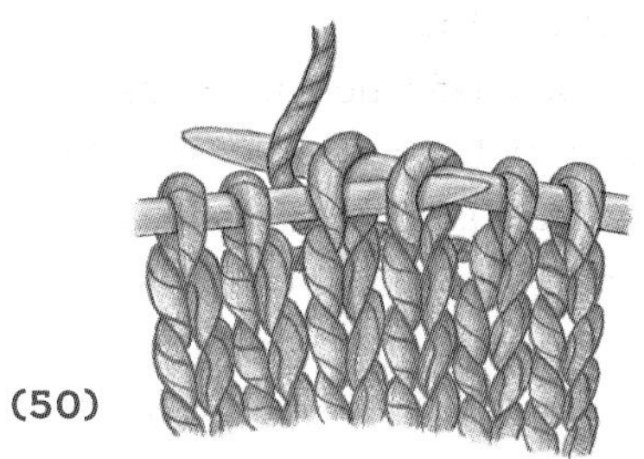

(50)

Slip, Slip, Slip, Knit Decrease (abbreviated sssk) (left-leaning double decrease)

Same as the ssk decrease (page 280), except *three* stitches are slipped knitwise, one at a time, and then are knitted together from their new positions.

Slip, Slip, Purl Decrease (abbreviated ssp)

This technique is often used on wrong-side rows to mimic the left-slanting look of the ssk decrease on the knit side of the fabric.

To do: With the working yarn toward the front, slip the first two stitches knitwise, one at a time, from the left-hand needle to the right-hand needle. Then, slip these two stitches back to the left-hand needle in their twisted position. Finally, insert the tip of the right-hand needle into the back loops of these two stitches, going into the second stitch first, and then the first stitch, and purl them together through their back loops as if they were a single stitch (illustration 51). One stitch has been decreased, and the resulting stitch leans toward the left on the knit side of the fabric.

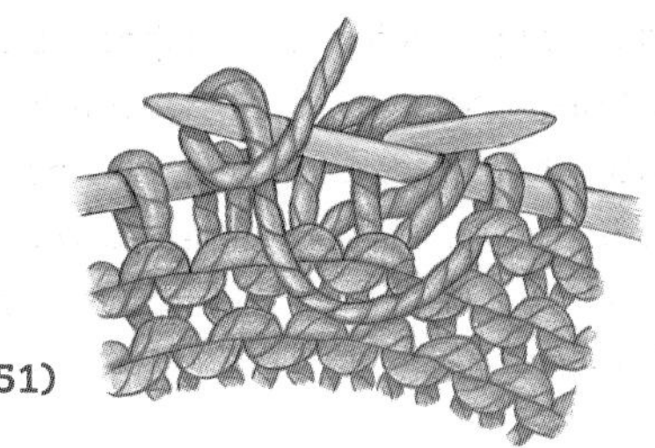

(51)

A More Refined Ssk Decrease

For some knitters, the ssk decrease worked the typical way does not mirror the k2tog decrease perfectly. If you are among them and would like to make your left-leaning decrease look smoother and less like stair steps, try this method:

Slip the first stitch *knitwise* and the second stitch *purlwise* (page 279) from the left-hand needle to the right-hand needle (illustration 52). Slipping the first stitch knitwise keeps it from twisting at the bottom, producing a smoother and neater stitch.

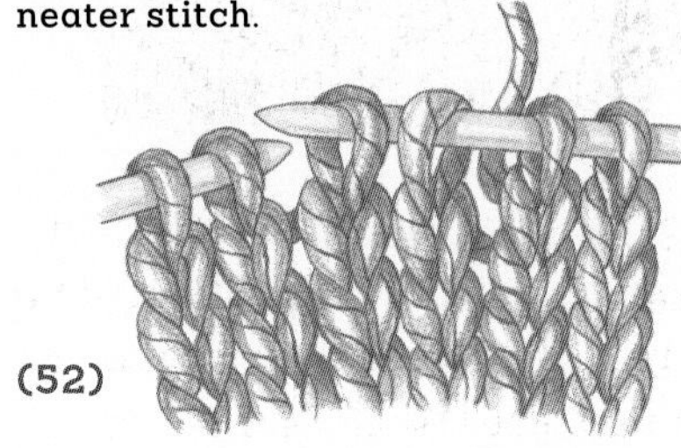

(52)

Then insert the left-hand needle into the fronts of both slipped stitches (illustration 53) and knit them together from this position, through their back loops.

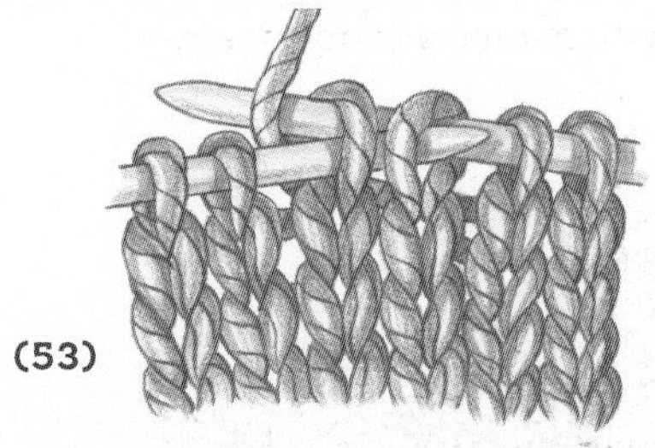

(53)

Slip, Slip, Slip, Purl Decrease (abbreviated sssp)

Same as the ssp decrease (page 281), except *three* stitches are slipped knitwise, one at a time, and then are purled together from their new positions.

Smocking

Sometimes a cable needle is used to wrap the yarn around stitches to create a decorative look, as in Smocked Ribbing (page 245).

To do: Slip the group of stitches purlwise onto a cable needle, and wrap the yarn counterclockwise around the stitches (just below the cable needle) the indicated number of times. Then work the stitches off the cable needle as instructed.

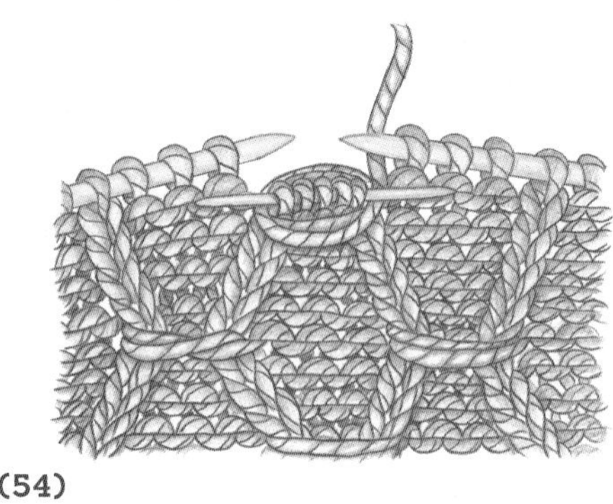

(54)

Stranded Technique

In this color knitting technique, used in Two-Color Hanover Cables (page 181), two colors are worked across each row and, when a color is not in use, it is carried loosely across the wrong side of the fabric, creating horizontal floats. Knitters can choose between three possible methods for holding the yarn:

Holding One Color in Each Hand:

Here's the most efficient way to work stranded knitting: Hold one yarn in each hand, wrapping them around your fingers to control the tension the way you normally do (illustration 55). To work a stitch with the color from the right-hand yarn, insert the needle into the next stitch knitwise or purlwise according to your pattern, wrap the right-hand yarn around the needle to make either a knit or purl stitch; to make a stitch with the color of the yarn you're holding in your left hand, insert the needle into the next stitch knitwise or purlwise depending on your pattern, and wrap the left-hand yarn around the needle to complete the stitch.

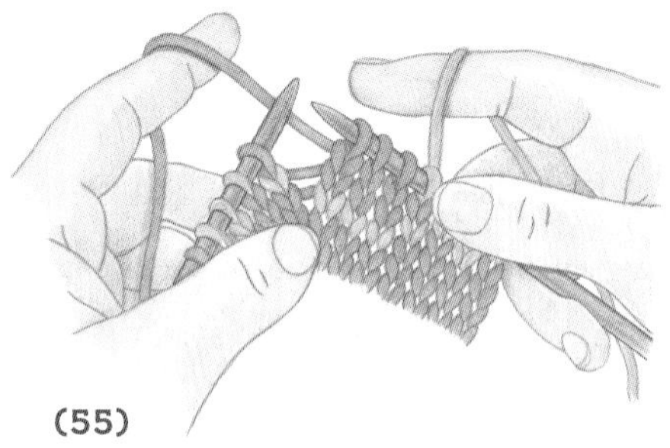

(55)

Holding Both Colors in the Right Hand:

If you're normally a "thrower," sometimes called an English-style knitter, you can put both yarns in your right hand and use the appropriate color to knit or purl each stitch. Knitters have two possible methods to choose from.

Method 1: Loop both yarns around the right index finger (illustration 56). Use the bend of the top joint of your finger to keep the 2 yarns apart.

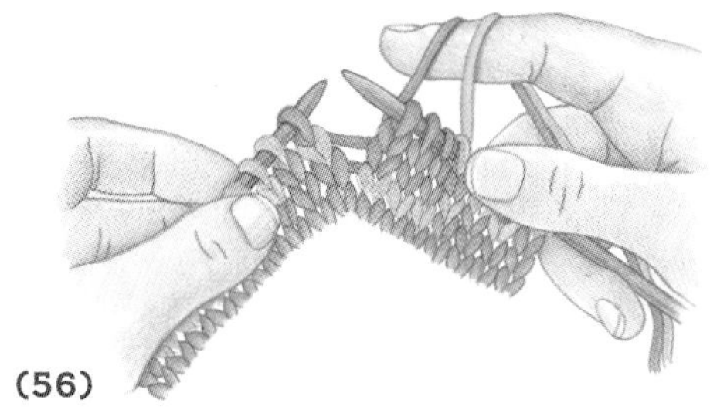

(56)

Method 2: Hold one color yarn over the index finger and the other color yarn over the middle finger (illustration 57).

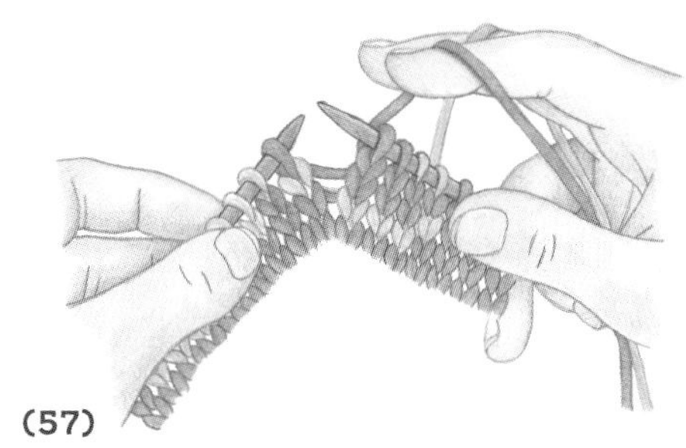

(57)

Holding Both Colors in the Left Hand:

If you typically knit Continental-style, you can work with both yarns in your left hand. Again, knitters have two possible methods to choose from. With either method, the right-hand needle can easily "pick" the yarn called for in the color pattern.

Method 1: Place both color yarns over the left index finger (illustration 58). Use the bend of the top joint of your finger to keep the two yarns apart.

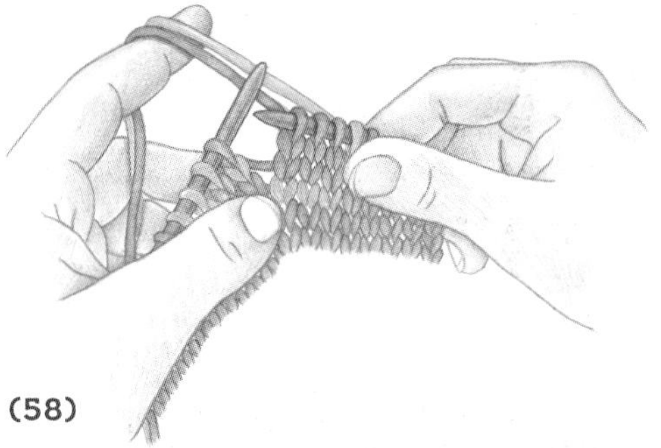

(58)

Method 2: Put one color yarn over the left index finger and the other color yarn over the middle finger (illustration 59).

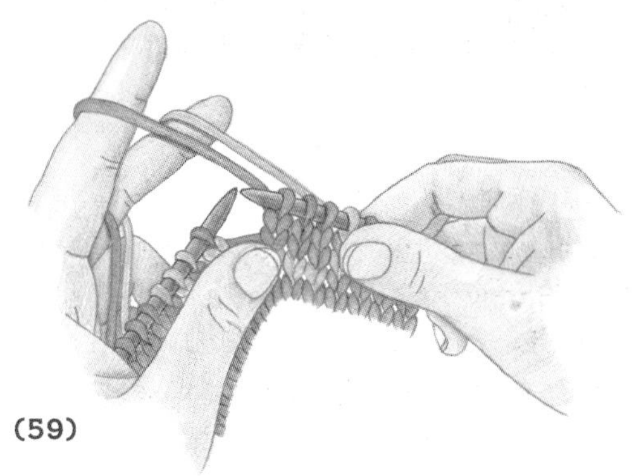

(59)

Tuck Stitch

With this technique, a stitch is unraveled for a number of rows. Then the stitch and all the horizontal ladders created from the unraveling are knitted together. It is used in Two-Color Garter Tuck Stitch (page 239), for example.

To do: Drop the first stitch off the left-hand needle (see illustration 60) and use the tip of the right-hand needle to unravel the specified number of rows (see illustration 61). Then insert the right-hand needle into the live stitch, catching the horizontal strands on top of the needle (see illustration 62). Finally, knit into the live stitch, working all those strands into the new stitch (see illustration 63).

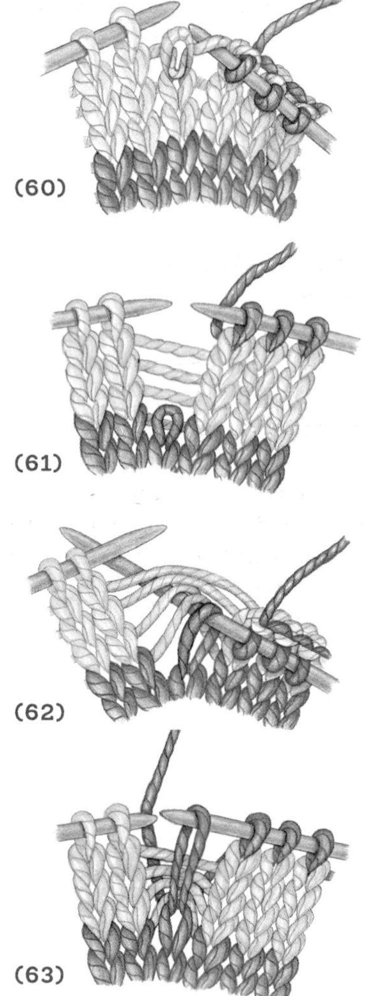
(60)
(61)
(62)
(63)

Yarn Over Increase

This method of increasing places an eyelet hole in the fabric just below the new stitch. The technique is different depending on whether the stitch following the yarn over is a knit or a purl stitch.

To make a yarn over before a knit stitch: Bring the working yarn to the front, between the tips of the two knitting needles (illustration 64). As you knit the next stitch, the yarn will go over the right-hand needle to create the extra stitch.

To make a yarn over before a purl stitch: Bring the working yarn to the front, between the tips of the knitting needles, and then wrap it *completely around* the right-hand needle and back to the front (illustration 65). Simply bringing the yarn to the front does not add a new stitch; the yarn must go all the way around the right-hand needle to make the increase before a purl stitch.

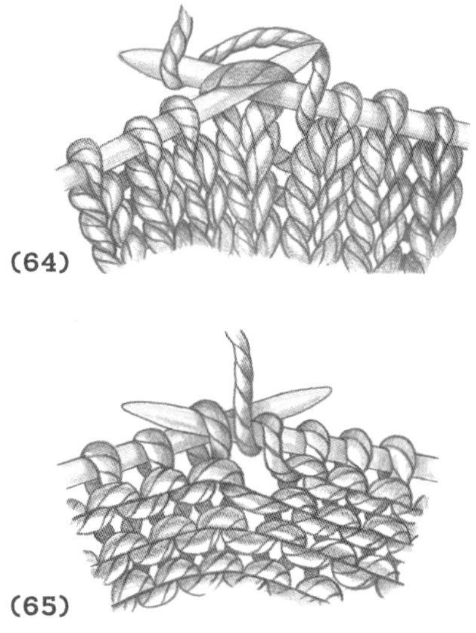
(64)
(65)

Sometimes multiple yarn overs are used to make an extra large eyelet hole, as in the Diamond Openwork Panel (page 99).

To do: Simply wrap the yarn around the right-hand needle the required number of times (illustration 66).

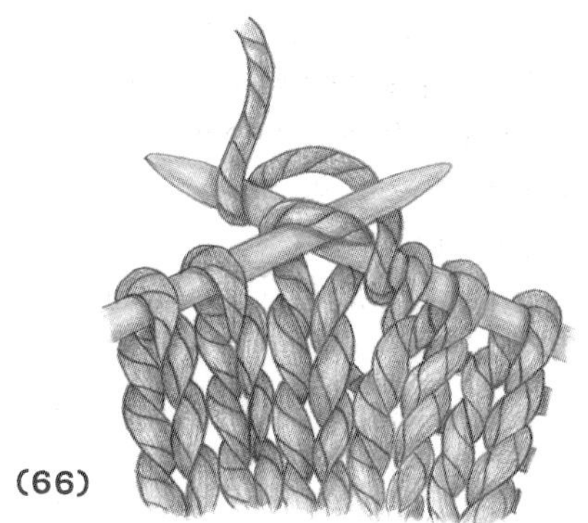

(66)

On the next row, more than one stitch (e.g., knit and then purl, for example) is usually worked into the multiple yarn over to ensure a steady stitch count.

Resources

Material Resources

Cascade 220 yarn was used for all the swatches in this book. I highly recommend this beautiful yarn.

Cascade Yarns
1224 Andover Park E
Tukwila, WA 98188
www.cascadeyarns.com

The Knitting Community

To meet other knitters and to learn more about the craft, contact the following. I currently sit on their Advisory Board and can attest to the educational value—and the pure, knitterly fun—of this great group:

The Knitting Guild Association
1100-H Brandywine Boulevard
Zanesville, OH 43701-7303
(740) 452-4541
E-mail: TKGA@TKGA.com
www.tkga.com

To meet other knitters online, visit:

* www.ravelry.com
* www.knittersreview.com

Join my fan group on Ravelry to share photos of your projects and to keep up with my work. Go to www.ravelry.com/groups/melissa-leapman-rocks to be part of the fun!

Index